A Journey Through the Bible

Through the

Dorothy Dobson

A JOURNEY THROUGH THE BIBLE
Copyright © 2013 by Dorothy Dobson

Printed in Canada

ISBN: 978-1-77069-708-9

Word Alive Press
131 Cordite Road, Winnipeg, MB R3W 1S1
www.wordalivepress.ca

Library and Archives Canada Cataloguing in Publication

Dobson, Dorothy, 1919-
      A journey through the Bible / Dorothy Dobson.

ISBN 978-1-77069-708-9

      1. Bible--Study and teaching. I. Title.

BS600.3.J68 2012   220.071   C2012-904876-3

DEDICATION

To my husband, Bob.
Without his encouragement, I would never have got this started.

Acknowledgements

My grateful thanks go to the following:
My daughter, Marnie Spencelayh, who has guided me through the publishing
steps that I could not have done on my own. Her constant encouragement and
leading have kept me going on this project.
Rev. Gordon Patterson, a valued friend who has spent many hours helping
me edit the original manuscript and has offered me valuable advice. He has
prepared questions to go along with this book, as part of an invaluable study
guide which can be purchased separately.

TABLE OF CONTENTS

INTRODUCTION

There are two very important truths that are often neglected. The first is that God can and will speak to us. Although I've read about Him speaking to Moses, Samuel, Mary, and a host of others in the Bible, I have often wondered why He doesn't speak to us today. Then I was challenged to spend the first hour of every day in silence, listening for Him to speak to me. It was suggested that I write down my thoughts, beginning with the places I thought He would like me to change. To my surprise, I wrote pages of attitudes and practices in my life that didn't measure up to what I knew about Jesus' teaching. Somehow, though, I still felt a block.

Finally, in despair I cried, "God, I know there's a barrier between You and me and I don't know what it is!"

As clear as could be, He dropped a thought into my mind: "It's the fear of losing other people's approval, especially those closest to you."

That convinced me that God speaks today, just as He always has, if we're willing to listen. This thought changed my whole direction, because I had never considered that trying to please others in order to get approval for myself was a sin. But when I recognized it, confessed it, and accepted God's forgiveness, I was able to put Jesus on the throne of my life and experience a whole new freedom I had never known before!

The second important truth is that since the Bible is the Word of God, it's the most important book ever published. I've believed this for many years, but for most of those years I had never read it all the way through. I read straight through any other book I appreciate, so why didn't I do the same with the Bible?

I accepted the fact that God can speak to me directly and that the Bible is His inspired Word. I was now convinced that it was worth reading from beginning to end.

Thus, I embarked on the exciting adventure of reading through the Bible every year. With the expectation that God would teach me through His Holy Spirit, as Jesus promised, my morning quiet times have become the part of my day I look forward to the most. The exact hour has varied through the years, but somewhere before 7:30 a.m. seems to be the best, since that's likely to be when the activity of the day begins.

I've found it helpful to pick out one or more verses each morning to write in my quiet-time book. This forces me to focus on what I'm reading. The message that comes across in the Old Testament is that the most important goal in life is obedience to God. To this is added (especially in the Psalms) the need for praising and giving thanks to God in order to come into His presence.

Enter his gates with thanksgiving and his courts with praise. (Psalm 100:4)

In the New Testament, we find God's plan of redemption for mankind through the life, death, and resurrection of Jesus. Added to that is how we may experience the power of the Holy Spirit. Running throughout the whole of the New Testament is a pattern of how we are to live as followers of Jesus.

With great pleasure and anticipation, I want to share with you some of the things I've learned through my morning quiet times with God. I never cease to marvel at the fact that the great Creator, the omnipotent God, loves me so much that He sends His Holy Spirit to spend an hour with me every morning! He'll do the same for you! How could we ever say no to such an amazing opportunity?

Note: Instead of going through the books of the Bible in their published order, I have decided to intermix the two Testaments. Therefore, after every two books of the Old Testament, I include one from the New Testament.

THE BOOK OF

Genesis

READ: Genesis 1–3

In the beginning God created the heavens and the earth. (Genesis 1:1)

Then He made light and separated it from darkness so there was day and night.
He created water and land, plants to grow that could produce seed, and trees that
would produce fruit. He went on to create the sun and the moon, fish to live in
the water, birds to fly in the air, and animals to live on the land. And God saw
that it was good.

Then, as the climax to the whole thing—

So God created man in his own image, in the image of God he created him;
male and female he created them. (Genesis 1:27)

This is an amazing thought, that we were created in God's image. We have
the ability and opportunity to make choices—to understand good and evil. We
must have great potential that we've never really tapped into. It means that each
of us is special, of unique value in His sight.

By the seventh day God had finished the work he had been doing; so on the
seventh day he rested from all his work. And God blessed the seventh day and
made it holy, because on it he rested from all the work of creating that he had
done. (Genesis 2:2–3)

Setting aside one day a week for rest is such an important feature that He
later made it a commandment for us—to keep the sabbath holy.

God put the first man and woman in a beautiful garden where all their needs
were provided, but they blew it! Eve fell for the lie that God didn't mean what

He said and figured she would become wise if she ate the fruit from the beautiful tree of knowledge of good and evil, the one tree in the garden God had told them not to eat from. Adam followed her example without question and they suddenly knew they had committed a sin! Their reaction, when caught, has been typical of mankind ever since: "It isn't my fault; it's someone else's."

However, God held them accountable for their own choice (as He still holds us) and they were sent out of the garden. Once out in the world, they had to work for their food and life wasn't as easy.

It's interesting that when they knew they had done wrong, they hid from God. Before that, they had walked with Him in the garden in perfect fellowship. That's what sin does; it separates us from true fellowship with Him.

These first three chapters set the stage for the whole Bible. They show God to be the Creator of all things with a perfect plan in mind for all. However, He gave man the power of choice. Self-centeredness stepped in almost immediately, so the struggle between obedience and disobedience began.

READ: Genesis 4–6

Noah did everything just as God commanded him. (Genesis 6:22)

In these early chapters of Genesis, we see a contrast between three attitudes:
• Eve, who listened to the wrong voice—the voice of temptation;
• Cain, who didn't pay attention to God's voice, but allowed his anger to dictate his actions; and
• Noah, who walked with God and was obedient, even when the directions seemed strange and brought upon him ridicule from his neighbours.

I've often wished God would give me directions as specific as those He gave Noah. That way, even if they were difficult, I'd be able to carry them out because they were so clear. Well, sometimes His directions are pretty clear; other times I'm really not sure what I'm meant to do. Still other times, I don't like what He seems to be saying! In such moments, I'm just like the man who said God didn't speak to him; all he could think of was his brother. When asked about his relationship with his brother, he replied, "We don't get along at all—we never have." God was speaking to him all right, but he didn't like what he was hearing. In my experience, I can't seem to feel His presence at all if I have any anger, unforgiveness, or even unfinished business that I refuse to deal with. The broken relationships in our lives need to be repaired if we want to hear from God.

If I want to keep moving forward in my walk with God, I must clear out the debris that's blocking His way. Fortunately, He's willing to show me what it is and help me get rid of it—if I ask Him for help.

Like Noah, I must walk with Him daily if I am to recognize His voice in the crises of life.

READ: Genesis 7–9

I have set my rainbow in the clouds, and it will be the sign of the covenant between me and the earth. (Genesis 9:13)

No wonder we all love to see a rainbow!

His covenant is found in Genesis 8:21, where the Lord says that He will never again destroy every living creature. The following verse says,

As long as the earth endures, seedtime and harvest, cold and heat, summer and winter, day and night will never cease. (Genesis 8:22)

When I crawl into bed at night and think about how I've been doing this over and over again all my life, I'm amazed at how quickly the days pass and soon add up to years. Really, life is very short when I consider all of history. What a shame it is to waste time with useless attitudes like self-pity or complaining!

As a little girl, I used to look forward to when I was grown up. I wanted to be a teacher. Someday I would be married, and I thought four children would be a good number to have (I was the youngest of four girls). Well, the years went by, and I did teach for six years. Then I got married, and over a period of ten years I had four children! After twenty years of being a housewife and mother (often complaining about my lot in life), I went back to teaching.

My children became adults, and then the grandchildren started to arrive. It seemed a short time before they were adults and I began to have great-grandchildren. I can hardly believe how rapidly these many years have gone by. I don't feel like a different person, though my grey hair and wrinkles have somewhat altered my appearance! I know God has brought changes in my attitude towards Him, towards others, and towards life itself. I am grateful for that.

Because of my daily quiet times, my love and appreciation for Him is the biggest thing in my life. He has taught me some important principles:

- to forgive and not hold resentments.
- to accept His forgiveness and not carry guilt.

- to look for good in others and not be critical.
- to be thankful for things I have and not to long for things I don't have.
- to love unconditionally, for that is the way He loves me.

I don't always get the message the first time, and I don't always obey immediately, but He keeps drawing my attention back to the subject. Many of His lessons have been uncomfortable, but when I put them into practice, the joy is worth the struggle. He is still teaching me and I expect that to continue until my time comes to leave this life.

READ: Genesis 10–12

Through the generations, Noah's descendants increased in number. In Babel, they devised a plan to build a high tower to demonstrate how great they were. This wasn't pleasing to God, so He confused their language to prevent them from understanding each other. Then He scattered them abroad. Their idea can be a modern pitfall as well—to establish what seems to be a good plan without consulting God to see what He thinks about it. That is why it's so important to spend time with Him daily listening for His direction.

Following the family line from Noah's son Shem, God chose Terah's son Abram to be the beginning of the nation through whom God would reveal Himself to the world.

> *I will make you into a great nation and I will bless you; I will make your name great, and you will be a blessing. I will bless those who bless you, and whoever curses you I will curse; and all peoples on earth will be blessed through you.* (Genesis 12:2–3)

God never changes. We can depend upon His word. We know that Jesus was born into this "great nation," and through Him we may now truly receive a blessing, if we choose! But it's easy for Christians to ignore the part of the promise that says, *"I will bless those who bless you, and whoever curses you I will curse."*

Jesus must grieve as He watches how the world, and sometimes even the church, has rejected the Jews, His people, throughout history!

As we continue to read the Old Testament, we will see how the people of Israel constantly turned away from God. Even after He drew them back to Himself, they disobeyed again. But He never gave up on them, and He still hasn't! This is a great source of hope for me, assuring me that God never gives up on me, either. When I get off-track, He patiently waits for me to recognize my sin. He then forgives and receives me back into His fellowship.

This promise to Abram is the beginning of God's plan of redemption, and if we ignore it we can't get a true picture of what He's doing in the world today. The blessing was for Abram himself, for his family (*"I will make your name great"*), for his nation, and for the world. God's hand on the Jewish people has never been more evident than in the twentieth century when Israel became a modern nation, a homeland for the Jewish people.

READ: Genesis 13–15

The Lord said to Abram after Lot had parted from him, "Lift up your eyes from where you are and look north and south, east and west. All the land that you see I will give to you and your offspring forever." (Genesis 13:14–15)

Two important things are pointed out in this verse:
  1. The disagreements between Lot's men and Abram's men had forced them to part company.
  2. God gave Abram and his descendants all the land he could see in every direction, and it was to be forever.

In regard to the first point, relationships with others are central to our relationship with God, and Abram accepted the solution that seemed best at the time. The Bible is full of teaching about our relationships with each other.

The second point still influences the world today. God gave the land to His chosen people. This is the only time in history I know of when God joined a people and a land together and said, "This will be yours forever." The geographical setting for most of the Bible is modern-day Israel, and historically its theme is the people of Israel and how God revealed Himself to the world through them.

Throughout the centuries, even when they were scattered around the world, the Jews have felt a bond with Israel, and especially with the city of Jerusalem. Each year, as the Jews celebrated the Feast of Passover, they ended it with the words "next year in Jerusalem." Even though there was little chance of this happening, the hope was still there.

In the early part of the twentieth century, God began to call His people back to their land. Those who left their homes and answered that call escaped the dark blot in history known as the Holocaust, when Hitler determined to obliterate the Jewish race. In the aftermath, many of the survivors, in desperate circumstances, made their way to the Promised Land. In 1948, with the approval of the United Nations, the state of Israel was formed to be a homeland for the Jewish people.

I believe that those of us who desire to be totally committed to Jesus are today also being drawn by God towards Israel and the Jewish people. It seems that Jesus is reaching out to His natural brothers and sisters (the Israelites) and to the engrafted ones (the Gentiles). And so, we are coming closer together. My husband and I were excited when we landed in Tel Aviv some years ago. As we stepped onto the tarmac, someone remarked, "It's like coming home. This is where our roots are!"

I wonder if Abram felt the same sense of coming home when he arrived here?

READ: Genesis 16–18

Then God said… "[Y]our wife Sarah will bear you a son, and you will call him Isaac. I will establish my covenant with him as an everlasting covenant for his descendants after him." (Genesis 17:19)

God changed Abram's name to Abraham and Sarai's name to Sarah. He repeated His covenant with Abraham, that he would be the father of a powerful nation and that all other nations would be blessed through him and his wife.

However, Abraham was approaching eighty-six years of age. Sarah was ten years younger, but since they had no children, they couldn't see how God could bring it about! They took matters into their own hands and Abraham had a son by Hagar, Sarah's maid. Almost immediately, the cost of that act was felt in the enmity that grew between Sarah and Hagar. That was not the end of it, for the descendants of Ishmael (the Arabs) and of Isaac (the Jews) are still in conflict today.

When we feel God calling us to a particular ministry, it's hard to be patient and wait for God's timing. We want to do it right now! Jesus proclaimed His calling when He was twelve years old, when He said to Mary and Joseph, "Didn't you know I have to be about My Father's business?" But eighteen years passed before He went forth to proclaim God's love to the world!

While I chafed for twenty years or so at the seemingly unimportant business of preparing meals, cleaning house, and doing laundry, God was constantly training me, helping me to be aware of my negative attitudes and showing me where He wanted me to change. Throughout this time, my husband Bob was a chaplain in the Canadian Army and was out every day doing interesting things. How I struggled with envy and self-pity! I learned that my attitude at the present moment is what God is interested in, and if I don't deal with that, I can be of no use to Him now or in the future.

Abraham paid heavily for his mistake of running ahead of God, and I'm sure he had no idea how future generations were also going to pay. It's important to wait on God's directions!

READ: Genesis 19–21

Now the Lord was gracious to Sarah as he had said, and the Lord did for Sarah what he had promised. Sarah became pregnant and bore a son to Abraham in his old age, at the very time God had promised him. (Genesis 21:1–2)

God kept His promise, and it happened at the appointed time. God always keeps His promises; He never makes mistakes and His timing is perfect. He is the source of all that is good—all wisdom, all power, all love, all joy, all peace, and much, much more than we can even imagine. He says that He'll pour out these blessings upon us to the extent that we're willing to come into His presence, be cleansed, and trust and obey His word.

He showed me a picture one day of His storehouse and the steps leading up to it. There were people at every level. Blessings flowed out from the storehouse and those closest received the most. As the stream went down the steps, the blessings diminished.

Then God explained, "Even if you just take the first step into My kingdom and stay at that level, you will be blessed. But if you want to receive all that I have for you, keep moving closer. Some of the steps will be difficult and you must be willing to change, but your obedience to Me puts you into the flow of My perfect plan for the world. Each person chooses his own position."

Just as it takes daily practice to learn the piano, be a runner, or speak another language, it takes a daily discipline of Bible-reading, prayer, and listening to God to attune our minds to His plan.

READ: Genesis 22–24

Each of these chapters has a particular story. In Genesis 22, God tested Abraham in a way that would cause most of us to fail! I wonder what Abraham was thinking as he climbed that mountain? *Is this really from God? Why me, Lord? Is it possible Sarah will have another baby? There must be some mistake!*

Whether or not he had doubts, he carried on in full and total obedience to what he believed God had told him to do. He passed the test and God reiterated His promise:

And through your offspring all nations on earth will be blessed, because you have obeyed me. (Genesis 22:18)

The next chapter tells of Abraham making arrangements for the burial of Sarah, his partner for so many years and the mother of Isaac, on whom God's promise would fall.

Genesis 24 contains the beautiful story of the choosing of Rebekah to be Isaac's wife. Abraham's trusted servant was a strong believer in God's desire to guide us in everything we do. Not wanting to miss God's perfect choice for Isaac, he asked Him to point out the right girl in a very specific way. When God answered his prayer so clearly, the man bowed down and worshipped the Lord.

When he told the story to Rebekah's brother and father, they recognized it as God's will.

Laban and Bethuel answered, "This is from the Lord; we can say nothing to you one way or the other. Here is Rebekah; take her and go, and let her become the wife of your master's son, as the Lord has directed." (Genesis 24:50)

This reminds me of a time when Bob and I were driving in Ireland. We wanted to visit a couple whose daughter had been to our home in Victoria, British Columbia. We had lost their address and knew they had no phone. (I had accidentally left an envelope of addresses in a hotel in England!) We were just learning to praise God in every situation and were reading *Let Us Praise*, by Judson Cornwall, as we travelled.

We prayed, "You know where they are, Lord. Please give us the clues we need to find them." We knew they lived on a farm. Then we remembered that it was in the county of Donegal. The next clue God gave us was that the name of the town started with "Bally." There were six of those on our map, though! We soon came to Ballybofey, stopped on the main street, and prayed for guidance.

I pointed to a man standing nearby. "Go and ask that man with the cap if he knows our friend," I said to Bob.

Rather reluctantly, Bob did go.

"Oh, aye, I know him well," the man said. "I'll draw you a map of how to get to his farm. It's about four miles from here."

Sure enough, we found the farm and were greeted by our friends.

"We knew you were coming," they said. "A letter came for you this morning. We have your bed all ready for you!"

The letter had come from our son back in Victoria, and within it was enclosed the lost envelope of addresses. Someone from the English hotel had mailed it to our home. God's timing is perfect!

READ: Genesis 25–28

That night the Lord appeared to him [Isaac] and said, "I am the God of your father Abraham. Do not be afraid, for I am with you; I will bless you and will increase the number of your descendants for the sake of my servant Abraham." (Genesis 26:24)

In spite of the fact that Ishmael was the firstborn son and Abraham also had a number of children in his next marriage (despite his age), God had chosen Isaac, even before he was born, to be in the lineage that would eventually lead to Jesus. These people whom God chose weren't perfect! While in Egypt, Isaac tried to make out that Rebekah was his sister for his own safety, just as his father had done with his own wife (Genesis 20). Then Esau, the firstborn of the twins, sold his birthright to his younger brother for something to eat. And finally, Rebekah helped Jacob deceive his father into giving him the blessing which Isaac had intended to give Esau.

I can't help wondering if Rebekah, like Sarah before her, couldn't see how God could work out the promise He had given her. So she schemed to make it happen. I wonder how He would have done it and what blessings they may have missed because they didn't wait for His perfect timing.

I don't know about that, but I do know that if I become anxious and impatient, I need to ask the Lord to reveal to me the root of these negative reactions. Perhaps my uneasiness comes from refusing to take a step He has shown me. Or it could be that I've been cutting down on my time with Him. It's important that I spend quiet time acknowledging God's presence, praising Him for who He is and thanking Him for the many good things in my life. That's the best cure for negative reactions.

As Jacob fled from Esau's wrath, in a dream God gave him the same promise He had given his father Isaac and his grandfather Abraham, confirming that his descendants were to be the ones through whom God would reveal Himself to the world.

READ: Genesis 29–31

This portion starts out with a lovely story about Jacob finding Rachel much the same way Abraham's servant found a wife for Isaac, but from there on we see some of the problems that arise from living in an extended family situation.

Laban tricked Jacob into marrying Leah first. Even after both were married to him, Leah began bearing children while Rachel didn't. This was a disgrace for women in those days. Since Jacob showed favouritism for Rachel, jealousy soon grew between the two sisters. In the hopes of gaining favour, both women offered their maids to Jacob and they also bore him sons. In the meantime, Jacob and Laban proved to be a real match for each other; they both strove to be on top and to gain wealth for themselves. Eventually, Laban recognized that God was with Jacob and that it was to his benefit for them to work together.

I've come to recognize that the real you is what you're like at home. It's reasonably easy to put on a good front when you're out among others, but what are you like at home?

When I first went back to teaching and our children were still in school, it wasn't long before I ended my days tired, crabby, and hard to live with! One day, in my quiet time, the Lord said to me, "Why do you give your best to the children at school, but sink into self-concern when you come home to those you love the most?" Our homes are the training ground for Christian living, for that's where our seamier side shows up. But God can help us achieve victory over our self-centredness.

God certainly didn't choose Jacob to carry Abraham's blessing because he was a perfect man! Jacob deceived his brother Esau and wasn't always honest with his cousin Laban. God doesn't wait for us to become perfect before He blesses and uses us. It's a good thing, because if He did, none of us would qualify!

The following passage has meaning for me because it brings back memories from my childhood:

> *May the Lord keep watch between you and me when we are away from each other.* (Genesis 31:49)

Our church had a mid-week group for young children, and we always ended our meetings by joining hands in a circle and repeating this verse. I remember getting a picture of God walking with each one of us as we headed home. It was a real comfort to me.

READ: Genesis 32–35

I have underlined several verses in these chapters that bear a message for me. Jacob was returning home after twenty years of working for Laban, but as he ventured closer, he became fearful of meeting his brother Esau. Would Esau still be angry enough to kill him after all these years? Then one of his men, who had gone ahead, came back with word that Esau was coming out to meet him with a company of four hundred men!

Jacob began to pray, reminding God that He had directed him to return to his own country. Perhaps it was his fear that made him aware of his own weakness, but Jacob seemed to have experienced a change after speaking so boldly to Laban. Jacob prayed,

I am unworthy of all the kindness and faithfulness you have shown your servant. I had only my staff when I crossed this Jordan, but now I have become two groups. (Genesis 32:10)

It's no use trying to build ourselves up before God. He knows us better than we know ourselves and we are never worthy of His blessings! But isn't it a great freedom to be able to come to Him without pretence, just as we are? When I allow Him to reach into my heart and mind, He helps me gain a clear picture of my motives and attitudes. It's wonderful! I feel so clean when I agree with Him and accept His forgiveness.

The two brothers met.

But Esau ran to meet Jacob and embraced him; he threw his arms around his neck and kissed him. And they wept. (Genesis 33:4)

It would be nice to be able to say that this kind of friendship existed between their descendants, but history shows that it wasn't so. The reason seems obvious: Esau's wives and their families didn't worship God, and although the people of Israel (Jacob's new name) often went astray, God had chosen them to be the ones through whom He would bless the world.

And God said to him, "I am God Almighty; be fruitful and increase in number. A nation and a community of nations will come from you, and kings will come from your body. The land I gave to Abraham and Isaac I

also give to you, and I will give this land to your descendants after you."
(Genesis 35:11–12)

READ: Genesis 36–39

Esau's family became the Edomites, but recorded in the Bible is the history of Jacob's family, whose twelve sons originated the twelve tribes of Israel. They were born of four different mothers, and since Rachel was the one Jacob loved the most, her son Joseph was his favourite.

Jealousy towards Joseph grew up among the other brothers, especially when Joseph shared with his family two dreams he'd had. In order to keep them from coming true, the brothers decided to get rid of Joseph. They sold him, and Joseph became a slave in the home of an Egyptian captain.

A few times in my life, I've had vivid dreams which woke me with a strong sense that I'd been given a message from God. On one particular occasion, following an especially gratifying meeting at our church, I had two dreams. In the first one, I was living in a house with a number of others, all of whom I seemed to know really well. I had no recollection of who these friends were when I woke up. The house had been on an island facing the water.

During the dream, someone commented that we were fortunate to be on an island where there were no tigers, for they were common on the mainland. Someone else pointed out the window and said, "Don't be too sure about that! Look!" There, coming out of the water, was a tiger!

Two tigers then seemed to appear on the floor in the house. While they watched us, we walked carefully around them in order not to arouse their anger.

"We must close our bedroom doors tonight," someone said.

Another added, "Check under your beds in case a tiger is already in your room."

In the second dream, my sister was dying of cancer. As I passed a cup of tea to her husband, my hand shook so badly that I could hardly hold it.

"This has made me a bundle of nerves," I said.

He replied, "I know. I'm not thinking clearly and I can't make decisions."

Then I woke up. I realized at once that this had nothing to do with my sister, but that the two dreams were messages from God to the church—and to me personally.

As I prayed, I was given a message from God: "We can be attacked by Satan from inside (like the cancer) or outside (like the tiger)." When I allow negatives to take over my thoughts and habits, I not only destroy myself but I cause those close to me to become ineffective. Negative ideas are quickly spread. How often have I repeated a criticism I've heard from someone else?

God had a special plan for Joseph. The training ground He chose for him was as a slave and prisoner. If Joseph could remain faithful in those circumstances, God could use him as a leader. Difficult circumstances are often God's chosen training ground for us—let's learn what we can from them.

READ: Genesis 40–41

Joseph made the most of his time in prison. He must have been listening to God regularly, because when the butler and baker were downcast due to vivid dreams they could not understand, he said, *"Do not interpretations belong to God? Tell me your dreams"* (Genesis 40:8). He must have been so familiar with God's thoughts that he was confident God would give him the interpretation. Obviously, he hadn't been wasting his time in self-pity!

It must have taken courage to tell the baker the meaning of his dream. This may have been God's way of testing Joseph's willingness to be absolutely true to God and not seek the approval of others.

Then another test came (either that or God knew Joseph wasn't yet ready for the kind of leadership he would soon be taking on): the chief butler forgot his promise to seek Joseph's release. As a result, Joseph was left in prison for another two years!

Talk about injustice. Joseph had been sold by his brothers, framed by his master's wife, imprisoned for something he hadn't done, and now forgotten by a man he had befriended! It sounds like the grounds for a heavy case of bitterness and resentment. Joseph passed the test with flying colours, though he may have had to struggle against the negatives in his quiet times with God; we all do, if we're really seeking to be what He wants us to be.

When I was teaching, June was always a busy month. The class went on special field trips, reports had to be prepared, decisions had to be made, etc. One year, I was even expecting visitors from England! I didn't always sleep well at night and, looking back in my quiet time book, here's what I wrote at 3:00 a.m.:

> Lord, I'm sorry for my comment about wondering if I would live through June! I've been seeing things to do, plans to make, and visitors coming as burdens rather than exciting opportunities You have put in my way to encourage, strengthen, and bless me. Help me to see each day and its activities as gifts from You—opportunities to bless others and to be blessed.

Then I thanked Him for each thing I expected to do that day. In the evening, I wrote, "All those things happened and it was a great day!"

I'm learning that my attitude is so very important—and my attitude is my own choice. I can complain and be in self-pity or be grateful and get ready for adventure. I'm never overburdened when I'm in God's will.

God used dreams again to bring Joseph into a place of great responsibility in Egypt. A confirmation of how close his relationship with God is found in Genesis 41:38—

> *So Pharaoh asked them [his officials], "Can we find anyone like this man, one in whom is the spirit of God?"*

No higher compliment can be paid to anyone! Joseph proved his openness to God's wisdom and leading as he stored the grain in the good years. He trusted the message of the dreams even though there was no visible sign that a famine was coming. Like Joseph, we need to trust the word of God.

READ: Genesis 42–46

> *And now, do not be distressed and do not be angry with yourselves for selling me here, because it was to save lives that God sent me ahead of you… So then, it was not you who sent me here, but God.* (Genesis 45:5, 8)

Here we read the very moving story of Joseph recognizing his brothers, even though they had no idea who he was. As he watched them bow before him, I'm sure he recalled his dream of many years before. Maybe he wanted to see if they had changed, or perhaps he needed some time to himself to appreciate God's plan for this family reunion. Anyway, he was pretty rough with them. Any resentment or bitterness he may have had vanished, however, when he was able to assure them it was God who had sent him to Egypt.

In order to reach that level of relationship with God, we must acknowledge His presence and watch for the way He moves in our lives and in those around us. We soon recognize that His ways are not our ways, that His perception of a situation is quite different from how we see it. Our reasoning and common sense can get in the way of hearing God speak to us.

I don't know what method Joseph used while in prison to align his thoughts with God's, but I've learned a pattern that helps me when times are tough.

1. I write down my problem, including all the wrong things others have done; my own negative thoughts, words, and feelings; and bad circumstances. Everything.
2. I praise God through reading praise psalms or singing praise songs, acknowledging how great He is.
3. Then I look at my problem again and allow God to show me where I need to change. I have to be conscious of His greatness before I'm willing to let Him change me!

This plan evolved from an experience I had some years ago. We were living in a centre with a number of other Christians and operating a school for children with learning difficulties. I loved my morning quiet times in the big room with lots of windows. From there, I could see the snow-capped Olympic Mountains; in the other direction, I could see Mount Douglas, a lovely park where you could enjoy a beautiful view if you walked to the top.

I felt burdened one morning. Everything seemed to be going wrong—in the family, in the centre, in the school. I said, "Lord, what do I do when things are going so badly?"

"Leave your burdens at the door," He said. "Then start praising Me, and praising Me and praising Me, until you can feel the presence of My Holy Spirit. Then we'll turn around together and you'll see your problems through My eyes. Instead of being overwhelming, like the Olympic Mountains, they'll be like Mount Douglas, a beautiful hill we can walk up together and see the glory on the other side."

Once I'm in tune with Him, I can accept my situation and ask Him to be in control. That's when peace and joy floods in.

I expect that Joseph's capability came from his close walk with God. No doubt he was fun to be with as well, because joy comes from total obedience.

READ: Genesis 47–50

You intended to harm me, but God intended it for good to accomplish what is now being done, the saving of many lives. (Genesis 50:20)

God never promised His followers an easy life, and it seems we all have to go through difficult times in order to learn the lessons He has for us. How can we learn to be loving unless we come up against someone who's hard to love? How can we learn to be absolutely honest unless there are times when the easier choice would be to tell a lie? How can we learn to forgive unless someone hurts us? A coach makes his players practice beyond what's comfortable and easy. We only learn by doing something hard.

I'm always amazed that God can take what seems like a hopeless situation and bring blessing to everyone from it. God used the famine in Canaan to unite Jacob and all his family with Joseph. How blessed Jacob must have been to see his beloved son again after having believed him dead. They had a number of years together before Jacob died, during which time he and his sons were under Joseph's rule, just as those early dreams had portrayed. Jacob's twelve sons were the beginning of the twelve tribes of Israel. They prospered in the land of Goshen and *"were fruitful and multiplied greatly"* (Exodus 1:7).

Before Joseph died, he prophesied to his brothers:

But God will surely come to your aid and take you up out of this land to the land he promised on oath to Abraham, Isaac and Jacob. (Genesis 50:24)

Some four hundred years and several generations later, this would happen. God's plan is perfect. Who can understand it? Imagine using the jealousy of Joseph's brothers to get Joseph to Egypt, then using slavery and imprisonment to remove any arrogance Joseph may have had left over. God's ways are not our ways!

THE BOOK OF
Exodus

READ: Exodus 1–3

Here are the twelve sons of Jacob, whose descendants became the twelve tribes of Israel—Reuben, Simeon, Levi, Judah, Issachar, Zebulun, Benjamin, Dan, Naphtali, Gad, Asher, and Joseph. The latter tribe was divided into the half-tribes of Manasseh and Ephraim, Joseph's two sons.

While visiting the Hadasseh Hospital in Jerusalem, I saw beautiful stained glass windows representing each of these tribes. I'm sure those brothers would have been astonished to see ahead several thousand years to a time when their names would be honoured in this way!

God's plan for His chosen people continues. He called them, through a famine, into Egypt, where, after Joseph was forgotten by the reigning Pharaoh, they were treated as slaves and life became more and more intolerable as their numbers grew. His long-term plan to return them to their own land began with a baby in a basket floating in the bulrushes. This reminds us of a baby born in a stable.

Moses' training for leadership began with a short span of time spent in the loving care of his family. His growing years, however, were spent with Pharaoh's daughter, where he no doubt became intimately acquainted with life in the royal family. Perhaps he became too aware of his position, or perhaps he merely succumbed to a fit of anger, but he eventually committed a murder! How could God ever use someone like that? In fear of Pharaoh, Moses fled to Midian and spent some years with a priest and his family, eventually marrying one of the priest's daughters. This simple shepherd's life was the final training ground for one of the greatest leaders in history.

Just as we assign our children small tasks to teach them how to later take responsibility in larger matters, God puts us into situations where we can learn to practice the attitudes we'll need if we are to be of any use in building His kingdom. I expect Moses learned about patience, caring for others, and hard work, but most of all he must have learned to listen to God and recognize His leading. He would need all of those skills, and more, for the monumental task ahead.

> *The Lord said, "I have indeed seen the misery of my people in Egypt... So I have come down to rescue them from the hand of the Egyptians..." (Exodus 3:7–8)*

He seems to deliver us from our problems once we have learned the lessons He prepares for us and are ready to listen to His guidance. However, the Israelites were not yet completely ready!

READ: Exodus 4–6

Moses was overwhelmed by God's call on him and began to argue:

> *What if they [the people of Israel] do not believe me or listen to me...? O Lord, I have never been eloquent... I am slow of speech and tongue... O Lord, please send someone else to do it. (Exodus 4:1, 10, 13)*

God answered the first argument with two miraculous signs Moses could show the people to convince them God had really sent him. He answered the second by saying, *"Who gave man his mouth? ...Is it not I, the Lord?"* (Exodus 4:11) But then He assured Moses that He would be his mouth and teach him to speak. Finally, He suggested that Aaron go with Moses to be the spokesman. With his brother as moral support, and the rod in his hand as evidence of the presence of God's power, Moses agreed to accept the call.

When our provincial government stopped the daily reading of the Bible in public schools, my daughter Marnie and I decided to start a Christian school where the Bible could be central to the curriculum. That was the beginning of Lighthouse Christian Academy. As we prayed together weekly for God's guidance, it became evident that I should be the first principal! I reacted just like Moses: "I'm too old. I've never wanted to be a principal. There must be someone else younger and more qualified."

God used Marnie and a series of young teachers to encourage me and offer support through various stages of planning—forming a society, finding a building, recruiting teachers, etc. My husband, too, helped with every decision along the way, assuring me I could do it. Feeling the job was too big for me, I couldn't take any step without prayer and guidance. In spite of these misgivings, I must admit that deep down I felt a sense of excitement about the adventure ahead.

God chose Moses because He could trust him to listen and obey—not because he was wise and a good organizer. Giving us a task that's too big for us to accomplish on our own is God's way of helping us develop certain skills, but we also need to learn to depend on Him for daily guidance.

READ: Exodus 7–10

When I read this section of Exodus, I'm appalled at the dreadful plagues that came upon the Egyptians when Pharaoh refused to let the people of Israel leave his land. Although the Pharaoh stood to lose cheap labour, how could he have been so stubborn? How could he take a chance on what might happen next?

Here's an interesting verse, from near the beginning of the story:

Then the Lord said to Moses, "See, I have made you like God to Pharaoh, and your brother Aaron will be your prophet." (Exodus 7:1)

Moses' call to Pharaoh is like God's call to the Israelites, who with one or two exceptions were the only believers in the Old Testament. He kept telling them to obey His word and receive His blessing. When they refused to obey, they experienced a disaster of some kind. God's purpose was the same as His dealings with Pharaoh—that they would come to know Him as God.

And the Egyptians will know that I am the Lord when I stretch out my hand against Egypt and bring the Israelites out of it. (Exodus 7:5)

Modern-day believers face similar natural consequences when they know God is calling them to give up something in their lives and they stubbornly refuse to obey. In my married life, I found it extremely difficult to give up my preconceived ideas of what a husband should be. If Bob didn't measure up to my expectations, I developed all kinds of attitudes to manipulate him—cold silence with resentment simmering just below the surface ready to erupt at any moment, angry and unkind words, or even tears! There were times when Bob used similar tactics on me! Fortunately, as the years went by and we kept taking these matters to God in our quiet times, writing down the solutions that seemed right, we both changed, allowing each other the freedom to be ourselves. We were even able to accept each other's weaknesses and mistakes, not reacting to them as we once did.

God revealed Himself more and more to us as we went before Him with our problems and obeyed His voice when He said, "Let these selfish attitudes go." As long as we're alive, He's never finished teaching us.

> *Then the Lord said to Moses, "Go to Pharaoh, for I have hardened his heart and the hearts of his officials so that I may perform these miraculous signs of mine among them that you may tell your children and grandchildren how I dealt harshly with the Egyptians and how I performed my signs among them, and that you may know that I am the Lord." (Exodus 10:1–2)*

Here we are, thousands of years later, telling our children all about what God did to the Egyptians because Pharaoh wouldn't obey God's command to let His people go! Through hearing this story, we hope our children will be aware of God's power and come to know Him as their Lord.

READ: Exodus 11–13

God turned up the pressure on the Egyptians with each plague, until the final one, the most devastating of all: the killing of every family's firstborn son! Sometimes it takes a tragedy for God to get our attention. It's a dangerous thing to knowingly and stubbornly refuse to let go of an attitude or a habit that separates us from God's will. Someone dear to us may have to suffer the consequences.

The Feast of Passover has been celebrated in Jewish homes for many centuries, and still is, in accordance with God's directions. It was to be a reminder of how God delivered them from slavery.

> *This is a day you are to commemorate; for the generations to come you shall celebrate it as a festival to the Lord—a lasting ordinance. (Exodus 12:14)*

In God's love, He wanted so much for His people to show the world what His plan for mankind really is—and how they have failed Him! Ever since we Gentiles have been accepted into His plan, through Jesus, He has been calling us to give Him all we are so He can shape and mould us into His image. Looking back in history, the church, too, has failed Him miserably; the divisions are so apparent in the endless number of denominations, the persecution of the Jewish people, the superior attitude towards unbelievers, and so on. As an individual believer, have I done any better?

The whole thing would be a hopeless mess without the love and forgiveness of God, and we have the added benefit of the redeeming life, death, and resurrection of Jesus. This means that no life is hopeless, no situation is beyond His saving grace, and no one has sunk so low that God cannot reach down, clean out the sin, and create a new person free of guilt and condemnation.

Even as I write these words, I have a sense of anticipation. God wants to fill me with order and purpose if I will let Him. How could anyone refuse?

READ: Exodus 14–15

This story in Exodus has become so familiar that we're inclined to miss the wonder of God's power. His plan was so detailed that He even arranged for the Egyptians to give the Israelites silver and gold before they left (Exodus 11). He created a pillar of cloud to guide them by day and a pillar of fire by night. He decided to bring an end once and for all to Pharaoh's determination to rule the Israelites, so the horses, chariots, and men were all lost in the sea. What rejoicing there was in the Israelite camp! They sang a song of praise to God and Miriam led the women in a dance as they celebrated the triumph over the enemy.

It took only three days for their trust in God to wear off. When they found themselves without water, did they continue to praise God? Not at all! They began to complain and blame Moses for bringing them out of Egypt.

When God first delivers us out of our own special brand of slavery, it's easy to rejoice and praise Him. But when the going gets tough, we still have two choices: praise Him and look for His solution to the problem, or complain and sink into self-pity.

At one time, Bob and I were invited to speak at a weekend retreat in Cranbrook. We flew there on Friday afternoon and had a great evening meeting all the people. On Saturday morning, I awoke with a sore throat, a heavy head, and a plugged nose. I was ready to catch the first plane home.

I called out to God. "What can I do?"

"You have two choices," He replied. "You can feel sorry for yourself, tell everyone how awful you feel, and get some sympathy, or you can begin to praise Me and keep on praising Me, giving thanks all through the day. You see, praise and thanksgiving create an atmosphere where healing can take place. Self-pity is a breeding ground for germs."

I chose praise and thanksgiving and we had a great day. When we arrived home on Sunday, I went to bed feeling tired, but the cold never did develop.

He said, "If you will listen carefully to the voice of the Lord your God and do what is right in his eyes, if you pay attention to his commands and keep all his decrees, I will not bring you any of the diseases I brought on the Egyptians, for I am the Lord, who heals you." (Exodus 15:26)

There's no doubt about it. Obedience to God—and that includes keeping our thoughts positive and wholesome—creates an atmosphere for healing and good health.

READ: Exodus 16–18

It's hard to imagine this huge company of people—probably more than a hundred thousand—setting out to walk through a wilderness of desert and mountains. There were no hotels or restaurants along the way. Not even grocery stores! Although we wonder how they could lose faith in God after the miracles He performed in Egypt, under these circumstances how long would our faith last? In fact, in our comfortable circumstances today, what do we do when things go wrong? Who hasn't said, "Why me, Lord?" or "What have I done to deserve this?"

God is faithful. When the Israelites began to wish they were back in Egypt where food was plentiful, He said,

I will rain down bread from heaven for you. The people are to go out each day and gather enough for that day. In this way I will test them and see whether they will follow my instructions. (Exodus 16:4)

Every difficult situation we go through is a testing ground. Do I believe God has the answer, or do I fret and stew and complain? God's provision of manna and quail were given with explicit directions which had to be obeyed, and for forty years that manna came every day. How He yearned for His people to totally commit to His will!

At twilight you will eat flesh, and in the morning you will be filled with bread. Then you will know that I am the Lord your God. (Exodus 16:12)

He provided water when they were thirsty. He gave them victory over the Amalekites with the condition that Moses' hands be raised to Him as an acknowledgement of His power.

In Exodus 18, Moses' father-in-law Jethro came up with some good advice: "Don't try to do it all yourself; choose others to carry some of the load of responsibility."

When my children were young, a fellow Christian challenged me about the various responsibilities I had taken on outside my home. I sang in the choir, helped lead the Girl Guides, and attended the Ladies' Guild, to name a few. This was in addition to the social activities connected with being a chaplain's wife. She suggested that I look at each activity in my quiet time and ask God if that's where He wanted me to be.

It sounded like an interesting idea, so I tried it. Before long, to my surprise, I knew He was telling me to give up the choir. It was a small group and I was an alto (and the only one who could easily read music). It didn't make sense! However, I did give it up and at the very next practice a new lady joined who happened to be an alto soloist!

That experience taught me:

1. that God cares about everything I do,
2. that I am not indispensable,
3. and that He sees the whole picture while I can only see a small part.

READ: Exodus 19–20

God, through Moses, reminded the people of how He had rescued them from slavery in Egypt and that His covenant still holds, *"if you obey me fully"* (Exodus 19:5). God frees us from the habits that have us in bondage, such as anger, jealousy, pride, and self-pity—or the more obvious ones like alcohol, drugs, and smoking—not so we will be more comfortable but so we'll be free to obey Him. He had to separate these people from the fleshpots of Egypt in order to get their attention.

Sometimes something really drastic has to happen to us before we turn to God. Bob used to tell how losing some of his fingers in an accident caused him to stop and look for some meaning in life.

Some years ago, one of my friends was diagnosed with multiple sclerosis and was confined to a wheelchair. She had three lovely children and a wonderful husband, but the most outstanding feature about her was her joyous spirit. When I commented on it one day, she said, "I don't like being in this condition, but I can be truly thankful for it. I was a very active person and if I hadn't been forced to slow down, I'm sure I would never have stopped long enough to hear from God."

Then Moses led the people out of the camp to meet with God, and they stood at the foot of the mountain. (Exodus 19:17)

What an awesome experience that must have been—thunder, lightning, clouds, smoke, and fire! Perhaps He wanted to be sure the people knew without a doubt that the commandments He was about to give Moses really came from Him. These commandments are basic to a moral, worthwhile life. God must come first in our lives, ahead of any other person or security; we must rest from labour one day in seven. The last six commandments deal with our relationships with other people—our parents first, and then others. Do not kill, commit adultery, steal, lie, or covet. When we look at society today, all those things He warned us about are happening!

The Israelites found this experience very unsettling and said to Moses,

Speak to us yourself and we will listen. But do not have God speak to us or we will die. (Exodus 20:19)

A lot of us try to get our direction from other people rather than go directly to God. It isn't always comfortable to come into His presence and see ourselves through His eyes.

READ: Exodus 21–23

We find it hard to relate to some of the directions God gave the Israelites through Moses, but if we read carefully, some parts speak to us directly. It may have been Mark Twain who once said, "It's not the parts of the Bible I don't understand that bother me; it's the parts I do understand!" But that's the point: don't worry about directions that don't apply to you now. Look at the ones that do.

God said,

See, I am sending an angel ahead of you to guard you along the way and to bring you to the place I have prepared. (Exodus 23:20)

He goes on to say that He will wipe out the people now in the land. He warns them:

Do not bow down before their gods or worship them or follow their practices... Worship the Lord your God. (Exodus 23:24–25)

If these conditions are met, blessings will follow:

...and his blessing will be on your food and water. I will take away sickness from you. (Exodus 23:25)

We often ask God to bless our food when we sit down to eat. We ask Him to take away our sickness, but we don't always keep our side of the covenant.

God knew the weakness of the people and how easily they could go astray. Unless He totally wiped out the people dwelling in the Promised Land, the Israelites were likely to turn to worshipping idols, even though they had witnessed so many miracles of God. Instead of keeping their eyes on Him with gratitude, they saw the lack of food and water and totally forgot who their provider was.

That sounds rather familiar. When a problem confronts us, it looks so big that we can't see through it to God. We need to change our position. Instead of looking through the problem to God, we need to look through God at the problem, which doesn't seem nearly so overwhelming. Doing so gives us an opportunity to see God at work.

How much better it would have been if the Israelites had said, "There's no water here and we're very thirsty, but God created all things, even the water, so I wonder how He will provide for us this time?"

READ: Exodus 24–27

When Moses went and told the people all the Lord's words and laws, they responded with one voice, "Everything the Lord has said we will do." (Exodus 24:3)

Of course, we know they didn't keep this pledge, but I wonder if the story of the Israelites in the Old Testament bears some resemblance to my own life. I want so much to really mean it when I say, "All the words the Lord has spoken, I will do." And then I blow it! I get impatient, critical, or sink into self-pity! Fortunately for me, if I recognize my sin and ask God's forgiveness with a real desire to change, I have the assurance found in the New Testament that Jesus' blood, shed on the cross, can cleanse me of my sin.

As we read on, we see how Moses used the blood of sacrificial animals to consecrate the altar and seal the covenant God made with His people. We are part of the new covenant, sealed by the death and resurrection of Jesus.

The rest of Exodus 24 gives us a glimpse of God's glory, as experienced by Moses and a few of the leaders. What the majority of the people saw is told here:

To the Israelites the glory of the Lord looked like a consuming fire on top of the mountain. (Exodus 24:17)

What an awesome sight that must have been! Moses was then called further up the mountain, where he spent forty days in the presence of the Lord.

Exodus 25–27 tells of the detailed instructions God gave Moses for the building of the tabernacle, which was to be a sanctuary where God would meet them. I suppose this was the first church to be built. In it was to be an ark to hold the commandments, and a mercy seat.

God said,

There, above the cover between the two cherubim that are over the ark of the Testimony, I will meet with you and give you all my commands for the Israelites. (Exodus 25:22)

The ark and the mercy seat were to be placed in the most holy place. A curtain of *"blue, purple and scarlet yarn and finely twisted linen, with cherubim worked into it by a skilled craftsman"* (Exodus 26:31) was to separate the tent of meeting from the holy place. Most of the people would never get beyond the curtain into the holy of holies, until at the death of Jesus *"the curtain of the temple was torn in two from top to bottom"* (Matthew 27:51). This opened the way for people to come directly into God's presence, because Jesus paid the price for their sin. This is hard to understand but wonderful to experience! We can take everything to God directly. Nothing can stop us.

READ: Exodus 28–31

Then I will dwell among the Israelites and be their God. (Exodus 29:45)

These were no super-spiritual people with whom God was promising to dwell. He had chosen them and was revealing Himself to them so the world would know that He is God. This plan has been extended to include all believers, so you and I can be assured of His presence with us at all times. Our responsibility is to be tuned in to Him.

We are given a detailed description of how Aaron (and his sons after him) were to be dressed in their capacity of priests. The furnishings of the tabernacle are also described. Much has been written of the significance of each item, of the materials and the colours used and where each article was to be placed. It makes for a fascinating study.

In my daily walk, it is comforting to know that God cares about every detail of my life. If I'm totally committed to His plan for me, He is willing to help me choose my clothes, furnish my home, and even plan my meals. He and I doing things together can make the most mundane task a joyous adventure.

A favourite old hymn, "What a Friend We Have in Jesus," says:

O what peace we often forfeit
O what needless pain we bear
All because we do not carry
Everything to God in prayer.

When we talk everything over with Him, we begin to experience life as it is meant to be.

Also I have given skill to all the craftsmen to make everything I have commanded you. (Exodus 31:6)

God never gives us a plan without providing people with the necessary talents to carry it out. When we started Lighthouse Christian Academy, we watched this happen. Whatever needed to be done, someone was always ready to take it on. A bus driver, a secretary, an accountant, someone to clean the classrooms, a computer technician, someone who could put up shelves and build storage areas, people to organize special events—all these and more were provided just when we needed them. And each teacher came along at just the right time to fill a particular position. At many times in my life, I was convinced that where God guides, He provides.

READ: Exodus 32–34

Exodus 32 gives us a clear picture of what it cost God to give us free will. I never read this story without an ache in my heart and feeling, "How could they do such a thing after all the miraculous ways God showed them He would look after them?"

Having been a teacher, I recall times when I've been out of the room for a short period of time and come back to find chaos. Anger boils up immediately! There has to be some form of punishment for disobedience in order to bring about a change in attitude, and the Israelites paid heavily for their blatant disregard of God's first commandment, *"Thou shalt have no other gods before me"* (Exodus 20:3, KJV).

As parents, we know children are naturally self-centred. A new baby is very demanding, as any mother can attest! Part of our responsibility in bringing up children is to train and encourage them to become obedient and choose what is right. We have no guarantee they'll always be that way, however, because God has given us free will. Besides, are we always obedient to God? Do we always choose to do what is right? No, we don't. I wish I did. It is painful to face my mistakes and try to put them right!

Exodus 33–34 is much more encouraging.

The Lord replied, "My Presence will go with you, and I will give you rest." (Exodus 33:14)

That's a comforting thought. Not only will God walk with us through difficult times, but He'll provide times of rest. Moses' answer, in essence, was, "If You don't go with us, I don't want to go." That's exactly how I feel—"If this isn't God's plan, I don't want to be part of it." That's the only security we have in this world.

Look how God describes Himself :

The Lord, the Lord, the compassionate and gracious God, slow to anger, abounding in love and faithfulness, maintaining love to thousands, and forgiving wickedness, rebellion and sin. (Exodus 34:6–7)

But there's a warning in the last part of verse seven that we must be accountable for our sin:

Yet he does not leave the guilty unpunished; he punishes the children and their children for the sin of the fathers to the third and fourth generation. (Exodus 34:7)

Fortunately for us, God provided a way to break the power of that sin from being passed on in the family, through the forgiveness Jesus provided on the cross. However, it doesn't just happen! It comes through commitment to Him and prayer. We never fall so low that God can't provide a way out, if we truly seek Him in every area of life.

READ: Exodus 35–37

From what you have, take an offering for the Lord. Everyone who is willing is to bring to the Lord an offering... and everyone who was willing and whose heart moved him came and brought an offering to the Lord... (Exodus 35:5, 21)

Giving isn't just an outward act. True giving begins in the heart, and that's where the reward is as well. When I look for some other reward, such as gratitude or recognition, I've missed the biblical view of giving.

When God calls us to do a certain task, He equips us for it, even if we don't feel adequate. Moses announced that God had called Bezalel to be the head craftsman:

And he has filled him with the Spirit of God, with skill, ability and knowledge in all kinds of crafts. (Exodus 35:31)

Not only that, but look at this:

And he has given both him and Oholiab... the ability to teach others. He has filled them with skill to do all kinds of work as craftsmen, designers, embroiderers... (Exodus 35:34–35)

So Bezalel, Oholiab and every skilled person to whom the Lord has given skill and ability to know how to carry out all the work of constructing the sanctuary are to do the work just as the Lord commanded. (Exodus 36:1)

Here we are given a great picture of how work gets accomplished when it's done under God's direction. When the people began bringing in the offering, it wasn't long before they had all they needed. In God's eyes, no gift is too small or of less value.

The people are bringing more than enough for doing the work the Lord commanded to be done. (Exodus 36:5)

The directions for making the tabernacle are amazingly detailed—the materials necessary, the colours, the size, and how it was to be put together. God then told Moses how the ark was to be made, including the table, the lampstand, and the altars.

READ: Exodus 38–40

There's nothing like a building project to draw people together. I wonder how many of our churches are built under God's direction, as the Tabernacle was. There were even detailed instructions concerning the pattern, material, and colours to be used for the clothes worn by the priests. Imagine hammering gold until it was as thin as thread to be woven into cloth!

You feel a great sense of satisfaction and pride when you've completed a long and difficult task and know you've done it well. This makes me realize that God cares about the details of my life—how I spend my time, in what order I do my household tasks, and which people I see.

Moses inspected the work and saw that they had done it just as the Lord had commanded. So Moses blessed them. (Exodus 39:43)

Moses' word of appreciation would have been a blessing to the workers. That's something I must constantly remind myself to do—to encourage those around me and show my appreciation. Bob was always good at encouraging me. Early in our marriage, when I was experimenting with cooking, he was quick to compliment me for baking a good pie or setting an attractive table. Needless to say, I worked even harder to produce interesting and attractive meals. There's nothing like encouragement to inspire a person to greater effort!

When everything was in place as God directed, the tabernacle and everything in it was consecrated and anointed with oil.

Then the cloud covered the Tent of Meeting, and the glory of the Lord filled the tabernacle. (Exodus 40:34)

Visible signs of the presence of the Lord aren't common today. Perhaps this is because He has been drawing people to Himself through the outpouring of the Holy Spirit. His presence in our church services depends on the openness of the people's hearts.

This reminds me of the old story of a church that was built without lights. It was decided that each person should bring a lit candle to service. If anyone stayed away or forgot their candle, the light was lessened. Only when my heart attitude is conducive to the presence of the Holy Spirit can my church be filled with the light of Jesus.

THE BOOK OF

Matthew

READ: Matthew 1–2

It's interesting to trace the genealogy from Abraham, Isaac, and Jacob through David, Solomon, and a number of men whose names appear in Chronicles and Kings. Some of them obeyed God while many others did not.

Then we come to Joseph, the carpenter, who, from the little bits we read, must have been a fine, gentle person who knew God and was able to recognize His voice in a dream.

If we accept God and Jesus as being One, then Jesus was the only person who ever chose His own parents… and what an amazing choice! It had to be an unmarried girl, a virgin, so there could be no doubt, in her mind at least, that she had been impregnated by the Holy Spirit. She would need a male covering, so He chose a young woman who was engaged to a responsible man. Both were believers in God and desirous of being obedient to Him. He didn't want her to be a single parent and endure all the trauma that entails.

Though Mary and Joseph were of humble means, the coming of Jesus was for the wealthy as well. God revealed His plan to three wise men from an eastern country and inspired them to follow a star. It seems that though Jesus was to be born into an Israelite family and God had been preparing them for many generations for this historical event, right from the start this message was for all people everywhere in every generation.

His life was so significant that the whole world dates history as happening either before it (B.C.) or after it (A.D.), whether they accept Jesus as the Son of God or not!

God spoke to Joseph in a dream, after which he took his wife and child to Egypt. This is reminiscent of a time many years earlier when Pharaoh killed all the baby boys, though God had an ingenious plan to save Moses. Now Herod tried to destroy Jesus through a similar order, but God had other plans and told His parents to move. Jesus' purity and goodness always brings forth opposition, as we will see as we follow His life.

We shouldn't be surprised when we experience opposition to our walk with Jesus. We can be certain that God has a perfect plan for us that will carry us through these times, as long as we keep in close touch with Him so we recognize His voice.

God's plan of redemption for the world takes place as people are obedient to Him. My obedience not only helps my life; it's part of God's overall plan. Joseph didn't know that what he was doing would benefit me!

READ: Matthew 3

Matthew was writing primarily to the Jews, and many times he quotes from the Old Testament to show that Jesus was the promised Messiah whose coming was foretold by the prophets several hundred years before.

Unfortunately, many did not make that connection and the Jewish people have lived for centuries missing the redemption God planned for the world. The Christian church has failed to live in accordance with their belief in Jesus, so the Jews have been repelled rather than attracted to Him. Now, since the early 1900s, they are back in the land God designated as theirs and it seems they are beginning to look at Jesus directly rather than through the clouded image shown by the church.

As our tour guide in Israel told us, "We are waiting for the Messiah to come and you are waiting for Him to come back. Maybe that is where we come together."

Repent, for the kingdom of heaven is near. (Matthew 3:2)

Repentance is the key to experiencing God's presence—so simple and so difficult. How I hate to admit my selfishness, pride, resentment, and inadequacy! It's so much easier to cover it up, pretend it isn't there, or blame someone else.

Jesus spoke roughly to the Pharisees and Sadducees, leaders of the religious community:

Produce fruit in keeping with repentance. And do not think you can say to yourselves, "We have Abraham as our father." (Matthew 3:8–9)

Coming from a good Christian family doesn't guarantee a place in God's kingdom. It is a decision each person has to make, and it always begins with repentance—a willingness to admit our failures and be changed. Then follows water baptism, as a sign of the cleansing God provides when we confess our sins and ask for forgiveness. The next step is the baptism of the Holy Spirit, which Jesus provides.

Just as John the Baptist explained all this, Jesus arrived and asked to be baptized with water. What a surprise for John! Why would Jesus need to be baptised? Perhaps to identify with us as human beings. Perhaps to encourage us to take the next step. Perhaps to set the stage for God to proclaim His identity.

This is my Son, whom I love; with him I am well pleased. (Matthew 3:17)

I really don't know why Jesus chose to be baptized, but He doesn't have to be accountable to me; I'm the one who needs to be accountable to Him!

READ: Matthew 4

The Holy Spirit led Jesus off into the wilderness in order to meet Satan's temptations. What a strange thing to happen to the perfect life, for Jesus is the only one who has achieved that perfection here on earth. This says certain things to me:

1. No matter how close I'm walking to God's plan for me, temptations will come.
2. Temptations aren't a sign of failure.
3. Satan will try to catch anyone—even Jesus, the Son of God.

I need to look at how Jesus dealt with temptation. Obviously, He didn't succumb to it, even though He was in a weakened state after forty days of fasting. The first temptation presented an easy way to satisfy His physical hunger—turn stones into bread. Satan was saying, "I know what you want most right now. Here's how you can get it."

Some years ago, shortly after my daughter Marnie started a school called Discovery School, one family owed fees for six months of education. Despite repeated reminders, we received nothing. At a board meeting, it was suggested that we take them to court, and several people were strongly in favour of this course of action. We struggled for some time before eventually defeating that plan by a very slim margin. Those of us who were the last to leave the meeting noticed a very oppressive atmosphere, and we realized that we had been in spiritual warfare with Satan, who was saying, "I know you need the money. Here's how you can get it." Fortunately, we chose to trust God, and as always, He came through.

It is written: "Man does not live on bread alone, but on every word that comes from the mouth of God." (Matthew 4:4)

The second temptation seemed to say, "It doesn't matter what you do; you are in God's hands. He will protect you." But if we choose to take matters into our own hands and embark on some foolhardy course, God won't necessarily protect us from the natural consequences of our actions. Sometimes a child has to fall before he learns that it's dangerous to climb a ladder.

Jesus' answer was:

It is also written: "Do not put the Lord your God to the test." (Matthew 4:7)

The third temptation was for power. "You can rule over all these kingdoms," Satan said. But this would only come at a terrible price: "If you fall down and worship me." This was too much and Jesus said,

Away from me, Satan! For it is written: "Worship the Lord your God, and serve him only." (Matthew 4:10)

How did Jesus face temptation?
1. Head on. He didn't discuss it or consider it. He saw it for what it was—temptation from Satan.
2. He used the word of God to refute each suggestion and prove it wrong.
3. He sent Satan on his way. Be gone!

We can do the same.

READ: Matthew 5

Matthew 5–7 is known as the Sermon on the Mount, a summation of the major teachings of Jesus.

Here, the disciples sat on the hillside with Jesus and listened to His teaching. It must have sounded very strange to them—Blessed are the poor in spirit, those who mourn, the meek, those who hunger and thirst after righteousness, the merciful, the pure in heart, the peacemakers. But then it got really hard:

Blessed are those who are persecuted because of righteousness, for theirs is the kingdom of heaven. Blessed are you when people insult you, persecute

you and falsely say all kinds of evil against you because of me. (Matthew 5:10–11)

He goes on to say,

Rejoice and be glad, because great is your reward in heaven. (Matthew 5:12)

In these verses, Jesus lists the qualities He looks for in His followers. It's quite a different picture from the one we usually have of a successful person!

These are called the Beatitudes, which the dictionary defines as a supreme blessing, or exalted happiness.

The Beatitudes only took on meaning for me when I realized Jesus' teaching isn't concerned about our actions so much as our attitudes. In my inner being, I can control my attitudes. As I choose an attitude that's in line with His way, I experience supreme blessing and exalted happiness. It has nothing to do with the circumstances around me, only with my inner attitude. Reading Corrie ten Boom's books helped me see this truth in action, though there are many other books that illustrate the same reality.

Jesus said you could choose to rejoice and be glad in the midst of unjust persecution, so if I've invited Him into my life, I have that choice. I was startled to realize that I could choose to have joy in my heart no matter what was going on around me. Conversely, if I don't have joy, it's because I've chosen not to have it!

That's a generalized statement and some of you may argue its validity. All I can suggest is that you try it. Negative attitudes, no matter how small, have to be changed to positive ones. I can't harbour resentment, fear, criticism, self-pity, or pride and expect joy!

Look at these verses:

Let your light shine before men, that they may see your good deeds and praise your Father in heaven. (Matthew 5:16)

How I long to live a quality of life that makes people want to praise my Father in heaven!

You have heard that it was said, "Do not commit adultery." But I tell you that anyone who looks at a woman lustfully has already committed adultery with her in his heart. (Matthew 5:27–28)

The thought or attitude is as bad as the action.

> *But I tell you: Love your enemies and pray for those who persecute you, that you may be sons of your Father in heaven.* (Matthew 5:44–45)

That sounds tough, but Jesus gives us no excuse for not living up to these standards. If my love for people is to be like God's, it cannot fluctuate with peoples' behaviour.

> *Be perfect, therefore, as your heavenly Father is perfect.* (Matthew 5:48)

We must strive for absolute perfection—in His eyes, not ours. It boils down to this: live to please Jesus, every moment of every day—an exciting lifetime challenge.

READ: Matthew 6

As I read this chapter, I was struck by the fact that Jesus is saying, "Get your relationship with your Heavenly Father straight and don't let your concern for this earthly life and what people think get in your way." This is probably one of the most common traps to fall into, and it will cut down your effectiveness in the Kingdom of God. Look at the various facts.

> *Be careful not to do your "acts of righteousness" before men, to be seen by them. If you do, you will have no reward from your Father in heaven.* (Matthew 6:1)

It's such a temptation to tell others that you've helped someone or given some money to a needy cause, but Jesus says that if we do that to get their approval, we forfeit any reward God has for us!

> *But when you pray, go into your room, close the door and pray to your Father, who is unseen. Then your Father, who sees what is done in secret, will reward you.* (Matthew 6:6)

No amount of going to church will make up for the time we need to spend in secret with our Father.

> *For if you forgive men when they sin against you, your heavenly Father will forgive you. But if you do not forgive men their sins, your Father will not forgive your sins.* (Matthew 6:14–15)

That's very clear. In fact, uncomfortably so. I don't dare harbour resentment—it cuts off my path to eternal life. Without God's forgiveness, I would bear an intolerable burden of guilt, so I must forgive anyone who wrongs me at all.

Here are a few truths Jesus states clearly:

1. Fasting, for spiritual reasons, should be done in private (Matthew 6:16–18).
2. Building up wealth and possessions in order to have comforts here on earth can distract us from building our relationship with God (Matthew 6:19–21).
3. Whatever is in our minds colours our view of everything (Matthew 6:22–23).
4. It's impossible to seek God's approval and the world's approval at the same time (Matthew 6:24).
5. Finally, Matthew 6:33 says, *"But seek first his kingdom and his righteousness, and all these things will be given to you as well."*

If we get our priorities straight and put God first in all we think, say, or do, He will supply all our needs. What a promise! That takes away the strain. The final verse adds this idea: live one day at a time.

READ: Matthew 7

In my Bible, I have underlined several verses that have special meaning for me.

Do not judge, or you too will be judged. For in the same way you judge others, you will be judged, and with the measure you use, it will be measured to you. (Matthew 7:1–2)

Every now and then, I become aware that I'm getting very critical of somebody and realize that I've been voicing that criticism to others. Jesus makes no allowance for that. He doesn't say, "Yes, I know how you feel. That person certainly isn't acting properly and I can see why you are critical." No. He says, "Do not judge."

When He speaks of the speck and the plank, in essence He's saying, "If you think that person's attitude is bad, take a good look at your own."

When I'm critical, I'm putting myself in God's place, for He is the one and only Judge. From my limited point of view, I make the other person's sins bigger and my own smaller!

Matthew 7:7–11 is often taken out of context, but when we consider these verses as part of the Sermon on the Mount, it becomes clear that when we are in tune with God's will, we can ask for more and receive. As I become more familiar with God's plan, I'm more aware of how to ask for things that would be in keeping with it. A child soon learns that it's useless to ask for something of which his parents would not approve. I can always trust my Heavenly Father to give me what is best for me—even when it doesn't fit with my desires.

Thus, by their fruit you will recognize them. (Matthew 7:20)

People close to me can tell by my attitude how close I am to God. If I'm radiating love, joy, and peace, my spiritual walk is in good health, but if self-pity, anxiety, fear, or criticism are emanating from me, others can see that I'm off-track. Try as we might, we cannot hide our spiritual temperature from others. The masks we put on are easily spotted.

Therefore everyone who hears these words of mine and puts them into practice is like a wise man who built his house on the rock. (Matthew 7:24)

We are often careful in planning where we build our houses and how to make the structure sturdy for a future of fifty to a hundred years, yet we often neglect the more vital question of building our lives to withstand eternity.

One day when Bob and I were in Israel, we looked down from the Mount of Beatitudes towards the Sea of Galilee. I wrote in my quiet time book,

I could just imagine Jesus endeavouring to help the people see that the spiritual battle is in the mind. If our thinking is in line with God's thoughts, our actions will fall in line. I could feel Him there in our midst and I experienced something of His timelessness. Somehow, in my mind's eye, I was with Him the day He stood there, one of the crowd, eagerly listening to His message.

Later, a lady from England told me of her experience and the wonder of walking where He walked. The Lord then cautioned her in her prayer time, "Don't worship the ground I walked on. Worship Me."

READ: Matthew 8–9

What a picture these two chapters provide of the power of God working through Jesus to bring wholeness into people's lives! Each case is treated in a unique way, so we cannot create a set of rules on how to go about doing the work of the Kingdom of God.

A leper was healed when he knelt before Jesus (an acknowledgement that He was God, for no one knelt before a man) and said, "I know You can heal me if You want to." Jesus touched him with His hand and said, "I want to."

1. He found Peter's mother-in-law with a fever; He touched her hand and the fever left.

2. A Roman soldier wanted his servant healed and impressed Jesus with his faith that it could be done by Jesus just saying the word, rather than going to the patient. The healing did take place when Jesus said, "Go, be it done as you have believed."

3. A paralytic was healed when Jesus said, "Your sins are forgiven." To satisfy the scribes, He added, "Rise, take up your bed and walk."

4. A woman was healed when she touched the hem of His garment and Jesus said, "Your faith has made you well."

5. A little girl who had died was brought to life when He took her by the hand and the girl arose.

6. Two blind men came to Him. Jesus asked, "Do you believe that I'm able to do this?" When they said, "Yes, Lord," He touched their eyes, saying, "According to your faith be it done to you."

In some cases, He touched them. In others, He commented on their faith. In one case, He didn't even see the man. If we are to enter into the ministry of seeking His healing power for others, we must seek the wisdom and guidance of God in every situation.

Besides that, He cast out demons, calmed the storm, called Matthew to be a disciple, and did some teaching. This man was not like anyone the people had seen before!

> *When the crowd saw this, they were filled with awe; and they praised God, who had given such authority to men... The crowd was amazed and said, "Nothing like this has ever been seen in Israel." (Matthew 9:8, 33)*

READ: Matthew 10–11

I don't understand certain parts of these two chapters. I'm not sure what message is being given. But there are some verses that have spoken to me, and those I want to share.

The twelve disciples are listed here, and what a strange combination they were! Though they received only a short training, as far as we know, Jesus sent them out to the people of Israel, who should have known God but had lost their way. It's like a travelling evangelist coming into a church to awaken and inspire the congregation. The disciples were instructed to *"heal the sick, raise the dead, cleanse those who have leprosy, [and] drive out demons"* (Matthew 10:8). Quite a tall order!

For several years, Bob and I were B.C. representatives for the Renewal Fellowship of the United Church. We travelled across Canada and throughout our own province, meeting with groups of people, sharing with them, encouraging them, and praying with them. We prayed for healing and were aware of some results, but I must say we saw no raising of the dead, cleansing of lepers, or casting out of demons. The disciples were to preach that the Kingdom of Heaven was near. Our theme was similar: strengthen your relationship with Jesus.

We stayed at many homes, parking our Volkswagen van in driveways and often sleeping in it. As we asked for God's peace on each home, we found that we, too, received His peace. I can't remember any time the blessing was refused or we weren't welcomed.

When I read Matthew 10:16–23, I see a totally different picture. Jesus said there would be times when the disciples would be persecuted and brought before governors and kings. Then He explains why God allows this to happen. These would make for opportunities for those Gentiles (governors and kings) to hear the gospel. The Spirit of God would speak through the disciples! Jesus must have had tremendous faith in those twelve men, that in the midst of physical suffering (flogging) and the fearful experience of being dragged into court, they would be selfless enough to be open channels through whom the Holy Spirit could speak.

He encourages them!

> *So don't be afraid; you are worth more than many sparrows. Whoever acknowledges me before men, I will also acknowledge him before my Father in heaven.* (Matthew 10:31–32)

Jesus then went off teaching and preaching on His own. His message to John the Baptist was this: "If you're wondering who I am, look what's happening around Me."

What do people see when they look at what's happening around me? Once, when I was battling the hours I had to spend on housework, God said to me, "Look at it as creating an atmosphere where others can meet Me." I've since realized that my purpose in life should be to create an atmosphere where others can feel the presence of God! How? Jesus said it best:

> *Take my yoke upon you and learn from me, for I am gentle and humble in heart, and you will find rest for your souls. For my yoke is easy and my burden is light.* (Matthew 11:29–30)

READ: Matthew 12

The Pharisees decided that Jesus was causing trouble. He had upset their lives, undermining their authority in religious matters by saying that a relationship with God must come ahead of the laws that had built up around the Ten Commandments. They followed Him to see what He did and hear what He said, not to become His followers but to broadcast criticism of Him and His teaching.

This is a familiar tactic in today's society. If your leanings are towards free enterprise, you're likely to pounce on anything socialist leaders say or do. If you think socialism is the answer, you can always find places to point out the error in the causes the leaders of opposing parties espouse.

It happens in churches as well, when one denomination doesn't agree with another. And it happens in individuals—if I don't like or don't agree with another person, I see all the weaknesses in that person and totally overlook his strengths. The worst of it is that I'm likely to pass my opinions on to others! It is so easy to slip into the pharisaic pattern.

But the Pharisees went out and plotted how they might kill Jesus. (Matthew 12:14)

This is the strategy of Satan: to attack, look for flaws in behaviour, then twist the truth. Use it, but twist it.

For out of the overflow of the heart the mouth speaks. (Matthew 12:34)

Whatever I've stored in my mind and heart is going to come out in my words. We cannot hide our feelings, try as we might.

I remember one time making a very snappy comment to my daughter. Afterward, I thought, "Why did I do that? I had no reason to. I didn't even feel critical." As I thought about it, I remembered a resentment I had felt towards her the day before. Rather than face it, I had stored it away. In an unguarded moment, it came out in unkind words that were totally unrelated to the present event. I needed to listen to my own words, because they indicated what was in my heart.

For whoever does the will of my Father in heaven is my brother and sister and mother. (Matthew 12:50)

Jesus wasn't rejecting His family; He was including others in it. By being obedient to God, we can enter into a close family relationship with Jesus that lasts forever.

READ: Matthew 13

Whoever has will be given more, and he will have an abundance. Whoever does not have, even what he has will be taken from him. (Matthew 13:12)

That always seemed unfair to me in my early years. At that time, I saw it in a material way, as referring to wealth of some kind—and why should what little the poor have be taken away from them?

The mystery of the Kingdom of God seems to be just that—a mystery—until a person takes a step in faith and invites Jesus to be the Saviour and Lord of his life. The Bible has a spiritual message, and with the Holy Spirit within us we can begin to understand it. It needs to be read again and again, for new truths can come from old, familiar passages. I can now see that unless we make sure we're practicing the truths we've learned, we will lose them, as it says in Matthew 13:12. Life continues to be an exciting adventure if we constantly seek the abundance Jesus offers—and that doesn't necessarily mean material things, although He might give that as well.

The Kingdom of Heaven comes through having a close relationship with Jesus, and though it may have a small beginning without much sign of life, this relationship can grow into a tree that will bless others. It's worth letting go of everything else in order to attain it. It's a choice to be made.

At any point in my life, I can be open to hear and receive, or be closed to the message of the gospel. As we open ourselves to the word of God and let it take root in our hearts, our words and actions are affected and we show forth the fruit of the Holy Spirit. However, if I'm not showing the fruit, I've allowed negative thoughts to get in the way.

Here are the things that prevent a crop, or fruit:

1. Listening to Satan (Matthew 13:19).
2. Not developing strong roots (Matthew 13:21).
3. Worries, dwelling on material things (Matthew 13:22).

My constant prayer is, "Lord, I don't want to just know about You. I want to drop all shame and preconceived ideas, so I can venture closer into Your presence, experience the wonder of Your love, and become a channel through which that love can flow to others."

And they [Jesus' neighbours] took offense at him. And Jesus said to them, "Only in his hometown and in his own house is a prophet without honor." (Matthew 13:57)

Bob and I found the truth of this statement as we travelled across Canada from Victoria, B.C. to the Maritime provinces. The further we got from home, the more important we seemed to be considered. When we travelled overseas to Australia, even our accent added to our reputation!

READ: Matthew 14

John the Baptist's life had a terrible ending, but he fulfilled the important role of preparing the way for Jesus.

The crowds had followed Jesus and, when evening came, He fed them all from five loaves and two fish. When we give Him what we have, He can multiply it. Then He sent the disciples off, dismissed the crowd, and instead of lying down to rest (as I probably would have done), He went up into the hills to pray!

One evening, some time ago, I was with a group of people and the leader had us read the next section and meditate on it for half an hour. He suggested we picture ourselves there or look for a new meaning in the verses—in other words, we were to let the Holy Spirit speak to us in any way He chose.

I pictured myself in the boat and knew that if I saw someone coming across the water, I certainly wouldn't offer to go out and meet him as Peter did! But supposing Jesus called me to come, would I go? I might, but I'd probably look for some encouragement from the others in the boat. If my friends said, "Go ahead, Dorothy, you can do it," I might have tried. But if they said, "Don't be ridiculous, you can't walk on water," I would probably have said, "You're right," and waited to see what happened next. But supposing I did step out, my faith would be inclined to waver with the wind and waves and I would wonder if Jesus was aware that I was sinking! I realized how much I long to have total faith in Jesus' call and not depend on others.

Starting Lighthouse Christian Academy was a bit like that. I personally would never have had the courage to embark on an adventure that big, but others kept encouraging us and Jesus reached out and gave us two young teachers; He reached out again and gave us a bit of money and ten children. With that, we opened the school in September 1987.

I know He's the Son of God. I know He loves me and has a perfect plan for my life. When I face a storm, if I move towards Him, He calms the storm—especially the one in my heart.

READ: Matthew 15–16

[Speaking to the Pharisees,] Jesus replied, "And why do you break the commandment of God for the sake of your tradition?" (Matthew 15:3)

That looks to me like a warning to the church. Every denomination seems to have had this problem at some time or another, when the method has become a habit and the guidance of the Holy Spirit seems to have disappeared. It takes real self-discipline and a daily confession of sins in the members of the congregation to keep the channel open to hear God's voice. Negative attitudes block the way.

But the things that come out of the mouth come from the heart... (Matthew 15:18)

Here again, Jesus proclaims the importance of storing up in the heart (or the mind) thoughts and ideas that are good, positive, helpful, and true, so that the words we speak build up our own lives and those around us. Pornography, violence, and other negative, destructive material that's stored up through reading, TV, movies, or our own thoughts and fantasies will soon come out in conversations and then in actions. The immorality and crime infesting North America is the inevitable result of what's being stored in the hearts and minds of its people.

I long to see the tide of evil turned around; to see positive, faith-building stories on TV, on the internet, and in the movies; to see wholesome books written with a beautiful choice of vocabulary; and to hear music that inspires our youth to work, to respect others, and to give their lives to building a better world. I pray God will show me day by day what part I can play in helping to bring this about.

"But what about you?" [Jesus] asked. "Who do you say I am?"
Simon Peter answered, "You are Christ, the Son of the living God."
Jesus replied, "...and on this rock I will build my church, and the gates of Hades will not overcome it." (Matthew 16:15–18)

I believe the rock Jesus was referring to was Peter's declaration. If I really believe Jesus is the Christ, the Son of the living God, and live each day with that as the guiding force in my life, I will be helping to build His church. If I say I believe but my attitudes don't reflect His love, I'm like the hypocrites He spoke of.

These people honor me with their lips, but their hearts are far from me. (Matthew 15:8)

There are no halfway measures, or even three-quarter measures, in the Christian life. Jesus asks for one hundred percent commitment: our goal must be to be like Jesus Himself!

READ: Matthew 17–18

There he was transfigured before them. His face shone like the sun, and his clothes became as white as the light. (Matthew 17:2)

Peter, James, and John were given a foretaste of eternal life. They saw Jesus as He will one day appear as the glorified Lord, filled with light and love. Then they heard the voice of God proclaim, *"This is my Son, whom I love; with him I am well pleased"* (Matthew 17:5).

What an experience that must have been! No wonder they *"fell facedown to the ground, terrified"* (Matthew 17:6). But Jesus touched them and said, "Get up. Don't be afraid." A friend once pointed out to me that this phrase is repeated often in the Bible. When the angel appeared to Mary, he said, "Fear not." Again the angels said to the shepherds, "Fear Not." And when the disciples were terrified as Jesus came walking to them on the water, He said, "Have no fear."

Fear must be a tool of the devil to rob believers of power and reduce the influence of God's church on earth. Fear becomes a barrier to our relationship with Him. Reaching out to take the hand of Jesus can relieve fear and allow us to hear His voice.

Peter's reaction is so typical. Instead of basking in the glory of the Eternal Presence, he began to think of things he might do to help. I've done that! When I see God working in a situation, I jump in with some idea I think might help out, but all it does is detract from God's perfect plan.

Another example of the limitation of human thinking is found when Jesus told His disciples that He would be killed and rise again on the third day. Peter's response was "Never, Lord!" It seems they heard the first part but missed the glorious fact of the resurrection. Perhaps because they couldn't understand it. Those words went right by them.

And [Jesus] said: "I tell you the truth, unless you change and become like little children, you will never enter the kingdom of heaven." (Matthew 18:3)

As a Christian, there are some childlike qualities I need to emulate. Children know they're small (there's a freedom in admitting our inadequacies). When they trust an adult, they reach out to be held and our Heavenly Father welcomes us when we do that. They are eager to learn. Sometimes we adults are afraid of something new. For instance, all the new technology that's coming out these days can be scary, but what an exciting world it has opened for us!

Finally, towards the end of Matthew 18, Jesus tells a parable to emphasize again the importance of forgiving others if we want to be forgiven of our own mistakes and sins. Our door to heaven is the forgiveness of God that Jesus made available for us. But the key to that door is our willingness to forgive others!

READ: Matthew 19–20

Now a man came up to Jesus and asked, "Teacher, what good thing must I do to get eternal life?" (Matthew 19:16)

This question and Jesus' answer typifies the difference between human thinking and God's perspective. It's so like us to want an easy route to the Kingdom of Heaven or any other goal we might have—such as a sweepstake ticket, an easy way to win a million dollars. The young man wanted to know some good deed he could do to guarantee eternal life. Jesus gave him two suggestions:

1. Live a moral life according to the Ten Commandments. Our society today certainly needs to hear that one, because the general trend seems to be "Do as you please."
2. Give away your money. That really astounded the disciples, as well as the young man. In every generation, a sign of success in the world is the accumulation of wealth, and here Jesus says that it's a hindrance to entering the Kingdom of Heaven.

The first of the Ten Commandments says, *"You shall have no other gods before me"* (Exodus 20:3). The young man went sorrowfully away because his possessions meant more to him than following Jesus. How very sad that we can let material wealth, success, or popularity, all of which are taken from us when we die, become more important than where we will spend eternity!

In Matthew 20, Jesus shakes up another of our worldly value systems. Looking at the story of the householder who hired people to work in his vineyard, we are immediately struck with the injustice that all the workers were paid the same wage. Nowadays, we form unions to get a fair deal. When we try to treat everyone the same, other injustices arise. As I look back to when my children were coming into adulthood, I tried to treat them all the same by spending the same amount on each one. I was wrong. Sometimes one had more need than another. The worldly view of justice doesn't work!

God looks at the heart and pours out His riches and blessings as He sees fit. If I compare my lot with others, I can become dissatisfied and full of self-pity. If I constantly thank God for His goodness to me, I experience an inner joy and excitement about life, no matter what my circumstances are. There's an old song my generation used to sing: "You gotta get a glory in the work you do." We never experience the glory if we're constantly complaining about the pay we receive and compare it with those around us.

Ambition for lofty positions of honour has no place in the Kingdom of God. To be a follower of Jesus, I must be willing to serve others—and I don't always want to do that. The Bible keeps reminding me to want nothing for myself:

Jesus stopped and called them. "What do you want me to do for you?" he asked.
"Lord," they answered, "we want our sight." (Matthew 20:32–33)

The men knew they were physically blind and wanted to be able to see. Since the Bible is basically a spiritual book to reveal God's plan for us, we need to look at all its teaching from that point of view. Do we really want to be able to see where we are spiritually? Maybe our most important request should be, "Lord, let our eyes be opened to see this person or situation as You see it. Help us to see ourselves as You see us."

READ: Matthew 21–22

Zechariah 9:9 foretold the event that takes place in Matthew 21:5. Over and over again, I'm amazed at the Bible. Matthew quotes from something written several hundred years before, and there were no printing presses in those days to make books easily obtainable. As I read this unique book, I see the thread of God's plan for the world, and yet it was written by many different people over a period of hundreds of years. How did they gather all these writings and compile a volume that has been the best seller for probably a thousand years? No other writing even comes close to a record like that!

In these chapters, we get a few glimpses into what is important in the eyes of Jesus:

1. He willingly accepted the praise of people, especially the children, who proclaimed to the world that He was the Messiah.

2. The church is meant to be a place of prayer, and anything that detracts from that should be eliminated. Actually, I think that goes for my life as well. If anything detracts from my central purpose of listening to and obeying God, it must be cast out.

3. The fig tree was sometimes used in reference to Israel. Maybe this was a warning that if something doesn't produce fruit, it should be destroyed. Certainly, Israel as a nation was non-existent for almost two thousand years!

4. He speaks of faith that can move mountains. To me, that means being in tune with God's purpose, not just meaning that God can do it. There was nothing in Jesus' life that wasn't in perfect harmony with God—He was without sin. That's the channel through which God's power can flow.

5. Jesus' wisdom in answering those questioning Him astounded everyone. We can all draw on that wisdom when our lives are in line with Him.

6. And finally, in very simple words He gives us the keys to being in perfect harmony with God's purpose:

"Love the Lord your God with all your heart and with all your soul and with all your mind." This is the first and greatest commandment. And the second is like it: "Love your neighbor as yourself." (Matthew 22:37–39)

There it is—so easy to understand and so difficult to carry out! Love God with your whole being (which leaves no room for secondary motives). Love your neighbour (every person) as yourself (meaning to have a good self-concept, without false pride or humility).

It's important for me to start each morning by acknowledging God for who He is and letting my mind and heart be lifted through praise and thanksgiving. The next step is to hold up each person who comes to mind (especially the difficult ones), seeing each as a beloved child of God, no matter how I feel about them. That makes a great start for the day!

READ: Matthew 23–25

Woe to you, teachers of the law and Pharisees, you hypocrites! You clean the outside of the cup and dish, but inside they are full of greed and self-indulgence. Blind Pharisee! First clean the inside of the cup and dish, and then the outside also will be clean. (Matthew 23:25–26)

Jesus is strong in His condemnation of the religious leaders. They were so concerned about looking good to others that they neglected their inner souls.

This brings us back to the old pitfall of wanting other peoples' approval. One morning, I wrote in my quiet-time book:

What need in me do You want to cleanse this morning?

His answer came quite clearly: "You are still buffeted by peoples' opinion of you and your desire to please others and have their approval. This distorts your love for them, and it also distorts My guidance for you. Pray especially for your relationship with your family and close friends."

If I'm not daily monitoring my attitudes, that's where I am likely to end up. While we, as people, look at the outer appearance, God is interested in what's inside. He knows our thoughts and motives.

Somewhere I heard the story of an artist who was doing some ornamental painting on the inside of a new church. He was working in a rather dark corner, but still taking care with every detail. His friend said, "Why do you spend so much time in that dark corner where no one will ever see it?" The artist answered, "Because God will see it."

Every corner in my life is important, because God can see it. I believe Jesus is coming again to the earth. What an incredible experience that will be! It won't be like the last time—a baby born in a stable with only a few people realizing who He was. No, He says,

They will see the Son of Man coming on the clouds of the sky, with power and great glory. (Matthew 24:30)

I wonder what the television reporters will do with that? It would be exciting if it were to happen in my lifetime, but on the other hand, if God calls me home, I'll be spending eternity with Him. Either way, I can't lose!

However, Jesus warns us not to become complacent, like the five maidens who didn't have enough oil for their lamps and therefore missed the marriage feast!

So you also must be ready, because the Son of Man will come at an hour when you do not expect him. (Matthew 24:44)

How can we be ready? By doing whatever task God has given us, and doing it to the best of our ability, whether others commend us for it or not. The daily task is of prime importance, whatever it may be, and He expects us to be faithful. I can only know what He wants me to do if I report to Him every day and receive His orders. Like the manna, He only provides enough guidance and wisdom for the present; we need to replenish the supply daily. There will be a time of judgment when we stand before the throne. As an Irish pastor once said, "He may ask us, 'What did you think of My world? What did you think of My book? What did you think of My Son?'"

READ: Matthew 26–28

We are inclined to look at the various events in these chapters as separate entities, but it's important now and then to read about the Last Supper, the arrest and trial, the crucifixion, and the resurrection as one continuous story.

The incident with the woman and the ointment points out that even though the disciples had been with Jesus three years, they missed the love in the woman's heart and saw only the monetary value of the perfume. When will we learn to look beyond the outward appearance and see the spiritual value of the happenings around us?

The Last Supper could have been a disappointing experience for Jesus. He was aware of Judas' plan and gave him an opportunity to confess, but Judas passed it by. Then He proclaimed the gift His death would be to us all.

This is my blood of the covenant, which is poured out for many for the forgiveness of sins. (Matthew 26:28)

He knew all the disciples would desert Him, despite Peter's protestations. He went forth and chose Gethsemane as a place to pray, taking along Peter, James, and John. Again, they failed to realize what was happening. While He prayed, they slept! How often have you and I slept when we should have been praying? I know I've failed to recognize the significance of a situation and neglected to pray, but I'm learning that every day is significant; I cannot afford to miss spending time in prayer. Jesus pointed this out to His followers:

"Watch and pray so that you will not enter into temptation." (Matthew 26:41)

That's the key to life!

Jesus showed His humanity when He asked God to remove this ordeal from Him, but He showed His total commitment by saying, *"Yet not as I will, but as you will"* (Matthew 26:39)

The taking of Jesus and the so-called trials, first before the High Priest and then before Pilate, dramatize the spiritual battle of evil vs. good. In this case, evil appears to win—God could have intervened, but then Jesus' sacrifice for us would never have been accomplished. It's easy to blame the Jews (as the church has so often done) or the Roman rulers, but really, all rebellious humanity must take responsibility. In fact, if we don't take responsibility for the crucifixion, we can't claim the gift of the resurrection. If my sins weren't nailed to the cross, how could I be forgiven?

Satan seemed to have done his worst—dispatching Jesus with the most horrible, cruel, and hideous death—but out of it came triumph! If God could turn that ultimate evil into ultimate good (forgiveness and eternal life), why can't I trust Him with the problems of my life?

As the old hymn declares, "He lives, He lives, Christ Jesus lives today."

I believe that, and I hope you do, too.

THE BOOK OF
Leviticus

READ: Leviticus 1–7

God gave Moses detailed instructions for the burnt offerings and sacrifices people were to make to Him. The animal was to be a male without blemish; it was to be an atonement for sin, and the blood was to be poured out on the altar.

When Jesus offered Himself as God's plan for the redemption of mankind, He fulfilled the requirements of a male without blemish whose blood was poured out as an atonement for the sins of the world. The years during which the Israelites carried out God's instructions were a preparation for mankind to accept Jesus' gift to us. But how misunderstood He has been, both among His own people (the Jews) and the church today, where we have failed to see God's ongoing plan.

It seems that with the outpouring of God's Holy Spirit in the last century, we're beginning to catch a glimpse of what He is doing, but oh how much we still have to learn! Seeking to know God through His Son Jesus is a lifetime commitment, and He constantly surprises us with new revelation.

Reading Leviticus can be a bit tedious, but there are verses here and there that reveal truth, helping us to gain a more complete picture of the faith in which Jesus was brought up. It was important that common people, rulers, and even the whole nation of Israel face their own sin, often committed unintentionally, and make atonement for it.

Jesus said, *"Repent, for the kingdom of heaven is near"* (Matthew 4:17). Facing our sin, being honest about it, and repenting are the first steps towards living lives of faith, but these steps also keep us in right relationship with God.

I remember once attending a women's conference at which the speaker urged us, as members of the Body of Christ, to face our sin and repent, for hidden sin is a block to our spiritual growth, as well as the growth of the church. Things were getting a bit heavy and I quietly asked God how we could find the hidden sin if we weren't aware of it. He gave me these words to share with the group: "You do not have to strain to see your sin, but you must listen to Me. I won't shout at you; I'll drop a thought into your mind, and it's your choice whether you heed it or not. Do not discard the tiniest hint—a name, a memory, a circumstance, or a relationship. Let Me walk through your mind, touching gently on the spots that need to be healed."

Facing my sins is painful, but the freedom that comes with forgiveness is glorious!

READ: Leviticus 8–12

Then Moses took the anointing oil and anointed the tabernacle and everything in it, and so consecrated them… Then Moses took some of the anointing oil and some of the blood from the altar and sprinkled them on Aaron and his garments and on his sons and their garments. So he consecrated Aaron and his garments and his sons and their garments. (Leviticus 8:10, 30)

Anointing oil has been used throughout the centuries, and people see it as representing the Holy Spirit. The blood represents Jesus, who shed His blood for us. These commands come from God, and so we see the beginning of the awareness of the Trinity—the Father, Son, and Holy Spirit. It would be many years before the people of the world saw the fulfillment of the atoning blood of Jesus.

After the people brought the sacrifice to the tent of meeting, as they had been commanded,

…Moses said, "This is what the Lord has commanded you to do, so that the glory of the Lord may appear to you." (Leviticus 9:6)

When the sacrifices had been presented, Moses and Aaron came out of the tent of meeting and blessed the people. Then *"the glory of the Lord appeared to all the people"* (Leviticus 9:23) and fire came forth, consuming the burnt offering.

And when all the people saw it, they shouted for joy and fell facedown. (Leviticus 9:24)

What an awesome experience! In the presence of the mighty God, the people couldn't stand!

When Bob and I were preparing for our first trip across Canada, for the Renewal Fellowship of the United Church, I prayed that God would give us the experiences we needed to take His message to the people. One evening, we attended a meeting where the speaker explained the experience of "being slain in the spirit" or "falling under the power of the Spirit." I had heard of it but had never seen it happen. As he spoke, I somehow knew that it was going to happen to me that night. Sure enough, I felt compelled to go forward for prayer. Though the speaker didn't touch me, I fell to the floor as soon as he began to pray. I was conscious of a wonderful feeling of peace flowing through me. Then I realized I couldn't move my hands. As I lay there, perfectly contented, I knew without a doubt that God was in control. Before long, my hands were normal again and I got up.

When we returned home, I asked God about my hands. He said, "I want you to use your hands for Me. I want you to know that only as I give you power are you able to do anything. I can use you as much as you relinquish yourself to Me." God has His own unique way of teaching us, if we are willing to listen. He wants complete obedience.

Leviticus 10 is startling in its depiction of the consequences of Aaron's two sons' disobedience.

> *Moses then said to Aaron, "This is what the Lord spoke of when he said, 'Among those who approach me I will show myself holy; in the sight of all the people I will be honored.'"* (Leviticus 10:3)

God is not mocked. We may be able to fool others, but God knows us better than we know ourselves. There is a great freedom in that truth; I don't have to try to explain myself to Him. I can even ask Him to explain to me why I react the way I do! He wants the highest for each of His followers.

READ: Leviticus 13–17

If you gave up reading these chapters, or skipped parts of them, remember this is God speaking to Moses, and if God said it, it must be important enough for us to read. Otherwise, why is it still being printed? As I read this again, my heart aches for those people who went to the priest and were pronounced unclean:

> *The person with such an infectious disease must wear torn clothes, let his hair be unkempt, cover the lower part of his face and cry out, "Unclean!*

Unclean!" As long as he has the infection he remains unclean. He must live alone; he must live outside the camp. (Leviticus 13:45–46)

What a terrible fate! I suppose they moved with the rest of the people as they travelled through the wilderness, and I expect they were able to collect manna each day. But imagine that members of your family were stricken with leprosy; they would be so near, but in all probability you would never be able to see them again, since leprosy had no cure, although apparently a mild case could heal of its own accord.

We are fortunate to live in a time when many diseases can be cured, and even for those that remain elusive, trained people are working to find a cure.

Leviticus 16 tells the story of a scapegoat. Once a year, a live goat was taken and Aaron the priest would lay his hands upon its head

…and confess over it all the wickedness and rebellion of the Israelites—all their sins—and put them on the goat's head. He [the priest] shall send the goat away into the desert in the care of a man appointed for the task. The goat will carry on itself all their sins to a solitary place; and the man shall release it in the desert. (Leviticus 16:21–22)

This was God's provision for people to receive forgiveness for their sins until it was time for Jesus to come. There were other sin offerings as well, but this appears to have been an annual cleansing. When someone takes the blame for the wrongs of another, we may hear him called a scapegoat. This is where the expression originated.

"This is to be a lasting ordinance for you: Atonement is to be made once a year for all the sins of the Israelites." And it was done, as the Lord commanded Moses. (Leviticus 16:34)

There are two necessary ingredients to living a Christian life:
1. We must confess our sins and accept God's gift of atonement. In our case, the atonement comes through Jesus, who has taken the burden of our sin upon Himself.
2. We must seek God's will in every detail of our lives.

READ: Leviticus 18–22

These chapters aren't easy reading, but there are gems of wisdom to be found and certain truths are emphasized through repetition. The first and most important truth which God repeats is this: "I am the Lord your God." I'm sure He longs for us to accept this, but even more, He longs for us to live as though we believed it. Another emphasized truth tells us how it can be done:

Be holy because I, the Lord your God, am holy. (Leviticus 19:2)

Yet another direction comes through loud and clear. Do not accept the standards of other people. For the Israelites, that meant the standards of the Egyptians or the people presently living in the Promised Land. God is well aware of our tendency to follow the crowd, so He gave His people explicit directions about their practices and relationships.

Because God is perfect and made us in His image, He gave us a high goal at which to aim. No other goal is worth aiming for. If our standard is anything less than absolute perfection, how far down the line should we set it? How honest should I be if I don't think absolute honesty is my goal?

One day, I read a newspaper article about honesty in children. It spoke of how upset parents get when they catch their child in a lie. One mother reported that after she caught her son lying, she monitored herself for a week and found that eight times she caught herself saying something that wasn't quite true. How often do we colour our statements to get a point across?

Some years ago, our family was challenged not only to have an hour of quiet time with God each morning, but to measure everything in our lives by absolute honesty, purity, unselfishness, and love. (As I think about it, those standards more or less sum up the five chapters we've just read.) Even though I've been working on this for many years, I still catch myself colouring stories to make myself look better. That's not absolute honesty; it's only "almost." I constantly battle my tendency to repeat an unkind story about others, because that's certainly not absolute love!

A personal challenge should be to undergo a check of our actions, words, thoughts, and motives in our daily quiet time, asking God where He wants us to change. One morning when I was teaching a class of first-grade children, I wrote in my quiet time notebook:

Reach out as a personal friend to each child (absolute love). Let him feel your love personally and individually. Little troublemakers need this most.

On another day, I wrote:

I'm tired and I want to go back to bed. There are two choices: 1) feel sorry for myself, or 2) put others first. The first makes me feel more tired and the other adds strength and joy to my well-being. So what choice is there, really? Only a wallowing sort of pleasure comes from self-pity!

There is no holiness in me. I can only obey God's commandments by accepting His forgiveness and opening my life to His holiness.

READ: Leviticus 23–25

Several of the Jewish festivals are mentioned in this section, beginning with the Sabbath. From the beginning of time, it was God's ordinance to work six days and rest on the seventh. In our society, where Sunday is a workday in most places, we're inclined to forget that the body needs a day of rest. Perhaps we wouldn't need to use the word "burnout" if everyone observed a Sabbath day of rest after six days of work.

The Passover reminds the people that God brought them out of slavery in Egypt. Each year, the Jews were to bring an offering of the First Fruits—the beginning of the harvest, in gratitude to the Lord who provided for it. Later came the Day of Atonement—a time of confession of sin. And finally there was the Feast of Booths, held at the end of the harvest.

On our first trip to Israel, we landed in Tel Aviv. What excitement my husband and I felt as we stepped out of the airplane and found ourselves in the "Promised Land." We spent our first two nights in a hotel that was owned and operated by Arabs. The day after we arrived was Yom Kippur, the day of atonement when the Jewish people fast for twenty-four hours and make confession of their sin. Although regular meals were served at the hotel, we decided to join those who chose to fast. Therefore, our dinner was served at 3:00 p.m. and we didn't eat again until breaking our fast at 7:00 p.m. the next day (spice cake and juice), followed by dinner an hour later.

On the first evening in Israel, we attended a synagogue service. It was a privilege to participate in this Jewish observance and we felt refreshed, just as we always do when we make confession of our sin and receive forgiveness.

When our tour proceeded to Jerusalem, we spent several days at the Christian celebration of the Feast of Tabernacles (or Feast of Booths). Back in 1967, when Israel gained control of Jerusalem and moved their capital there, many nations, including Canada, withdrew their embassies in protest. Some Christians living there, however, realized it was part of God's plan for Jerusalem to be the capital of Israel, as foretold in the Bible, so to show their support they established the International Christian Embassy in Jerusalem (ICEJ). They sponsored this celebration, which was attended by about four thousand Christians from around the world. And what a gala it was! We were so blessed by it that we went back again two years later with thirty-five others.

You might wonder why the modern-day Christian church doesn't celebrate these four festivals. Jesus certainly did!

1. Passover—a time to acknowledge the sovereignty and power of God.
2. First Fruits—a time to recognize that He has made provision for our food.
3. Atonement—a time of confession.
4. Feast of Tabernacles—eight days of rejoicing and gratitude for the full harvest.

It seems that when the church became predominantly Gentile, all Jewish observances were thrown out and a different form of worship was instituted.

For many years, I was bothered that if a Jewish person accepted Jesus as the Messiah, he had to leave his familiar pattern of worship and enter into something quite different in the Christian church. As more Jews recognize Jesus, especially in Israel, Messianic congregations appear. These believers carry on their traditional forms of worship with the added dimension of worshipping Jesus and experiencing the power of the Holy Spirit. It appears that the natural branch (Jews) and ingrafted branch (Christians) of God's people are beginning to come together.

READ: Leviticus 26–27

In Leviticus 25, the Lord told Moses that even the land must have a Sabbath year of rest. Any farmer knows that land can become depleted of its goodness if there's no plan for crop rotation or leaving the field for a season with no crop at all. Therefore, we really need to pay attention to Leviticus 26, where God proclaims that His people must put Him first in their lives.

> I am the Lord your God... If you follow my decrees and are careful to obey my commands, I will send you rain in its season, and the ground will yield its crops and the trees of the field their fruit... I will grant peace in the land... I will look on you with favor and make you fruitful and increase your numbers... (Leviticus 26:1, 3–4, 6, 9)

That is what would happen if the Israelites walked in obedience to God. If they didn't, the rest of the chapter tells of the dreadful things that would happen:

I will scatter you among the nations and will draw out my sword and pursue you. Your land will be laid waste, and your cities will lie in ruins. (Leviticus 26:33)

As we look back at history, the Israelites stayed in their own land for many years, sometimes following God's commandments and at other times straying far from Him. When Jesus came, many of them rejected Him as the Messiah. After the Temple was destroyed around 70 A.D., all but a remnant of the Jews were banished from their land and were scattered throughout the world, where they remained for some 1,800 years! Not until the twentieth century did they begin to return to the Promised Land.

Sometimes they were reasonably free to plan their own lives, and at other times they suffered great persecution. The amazing part is that, even though they adopted the language and customs of the countries in which they lived, they remained Jews! No other people group has been able to do that. The Jewish phenomenon is unique in world history. But God never took His hand from them, even though they didn't always acknowledge Him. At the appointed time, He began to draw them back to the Promised Land. They came from every direction and from many different countries, and in 1948 the country of Israel was formed.

We dare not ignore this chapter today. If we're going to accept the first part, where God gives His promises for those who accept Him as Lord and King, and obey His commandments, we must also accept the second part, where He tells what will happen to a nation that falls away from Him. As we look at what's happening in western culture today, we must ask ourselves: is this the natural result of putting material gain, personal comfort, and selfish goals ahead of the worship of God?

I lived through World War II, when many young men and women died for our country to prevent the Nazis from taking over the world. Now it's up to us to live for our country. The only worthwhile thing I can do is live daily under God's guidance and encourage others to do the same. I cannot expect my nation to do any better than I do personally.

THE BOOK OF
Numbers

READ: Numbers 1–4

God wasn't interested in Israel only as a nation, but as individuals and families. He instructed Moses, with the help of a chosen leader from each tribe, to take a census of all the men who were able to go to war—those who were twenty years or older. The numbers were calculated not just by individuals but by families within each tribe. The total number was astonishing: 550,603 men. That wasn't counting the women and children, who would have numbered at least four or five to each man. No wonder Moses had difficulty keeping them in line!

In our country, where there has been such a breakdown of the family unit, counting the adult men would no longer provide an indication of the number of families. Many children today have trouble figuring out their family tree. It's a sorry state of affairs.

The Lord gave the Israelites a plan for arranging their tents when they camped. The tabernacle was to be placed in the centre, facing east, with the Levites camping next to it on the north, west, and south sides. Moses, Aaron, and his sons were to encamp in front of it. All these people were responsible for the moving and setting up of the tabernacle and its contents, each group bearing its own special responsibilities.

Each tribe had its own place to set up camp, and they were to have their own ensign raised. Out in front, on the eastern flank, was to be the tribe of Judah, then Issachar and Zebulun. Led by Judah, they were to set out first on the march. That's rather significant, because Judah means "praise." If we start a journey with praise, we are sure to have the presence of God with us.

On the south side was to be the standard of Reuben (Numbers 3:10), and with them Simeon and Gad. They were to be the second group to march out. The tent of meeting would be the next in line, carried by the Levites, who were to be at the centre of the procession. Camped to the west side of the tabernacle was the tribe of Ephraim and Manasseh, followed by Benjamin. They followed the Levites. On the north was the camp of Dan, with Asher and Naphtali, who were to set out last.

You can imagine what an impressive crowd that must have been! God is a God of order, not chaos. When we're in His will, He shows us how to be organized in our planning. In fact, if I am in confusion, or if my house, work, or plans are in confusion, I can be sure that I'm not totally in His will. He isn't a God of confusion!

READ: Numbers 5–9

In Numbers 6, we find a familiar blessing which I've heard used many times as a benediction at the end of a worship service. These words were given by God through Moses to Aaron and his sons to bless the people of Israel. Think of the host of believers down through the ages, including all of us today, who have been blessed by the presence of God as they received these words:

The Lord bless you and keep you; the Lord make his face shine upon you and be gracious to you; the Lord turn his face toward you and give you peace. (Numbers 6:24–26)

If you read those words several times, you'll probably feel His peace, just as I do when I read them.

I'm amazed at the number of animals given as offerings by each of the tribes! It really is beyond my imagination.

The dedication of the Levites must have been quite a sight. There were 8,580 of them (Numbers 4:48), and the people gathered around and laid hands on them.

From the time of the first Passover, when the firstborn in each Egyptian household died, God consecrated the firstborn for Himself. Now, He says:

Of all the Israelites, I have given the Levites as gifts to Aaron and his sons to do the work at the Tent of Meeting on behalf of the Israelites and to make atonement for them so that no plague will strike the Israelites when they go near the sanctuary. (Numbers 8:19)

The Passover was to be celebrated at the proper time. This was an order and the people obeyed.

I've always thought it must have been exciting to see the cloud come down on the tabernacle when it was properly set up. Thousands of people must have watched from their tent doors. As night came along and darkness settled in, what a sight it must have been to see the cloud change to a glowing fire, which remained until dawn the next morning! This was a visible sign of God's presence, no doubt a reassuring sight when they were out in the wilderness without knowing what lay ahead of them. Each morning, they must have watched anxiously to see if the cloud stayed upon the tabernacle, for that would be the sign that they were to remain in place. If the cloud had been taken up, they were to pack and move on.

Basically, these people wanted to obey God's will. They moved or stayed put as He directed them. We, too, can get direction from Him. Perhaps it's not always as clear as a pillar of cloud or fire, but He does desire to direct our ways and will find a way of letting us know. It's important to be open to receive His direction.

READ: Numbers 10–12

Numbers 10 tells us that two silver trumpets were used as signals for the entire company. When they were both blown, the people were to assemble; just one being sounded meant the leaders were to meet. The trumpet blasts were also signals indicating that it was time for everyone to get ready to move on.

> *Whenever the ark set out, Moses said, "Rise up, O Lord! May your enemies be scattered; may your foes flee before you." Whenever it came to rest, he said, "Return, O Lord, to the countless thousands of Israel."* (Numbers 10:35–36)

Numbers 11 tells how the multitude tried Moses' patience with their complaints about the lack of variety in their food—and Moses complained to God about his heavy responsibility in leading these people.

> *The Lord answered Moses, "Is the Lord's arm too short? You will now see whether or not what I say will come true for you."* (Numbers 11:23)

God's answer was to provide meat for all the people. He then designated seventy leaders to help Moses make decisions.

In Numbers 12, Miriam and Aaron rebelled against Moses' leadership. But God didn't leave rebellious behaviour unpunished; Miriam developed leprosy!

God answered Moses' prayer and she was healed, but not without having to pay the price of spending seven days outside the camp.

There are lessons to learn from this reading:

1. Negative complaints do not bring good results.
2. God's plan for us isn't always easy.
3. Gratitude is the answer to complaining.

READ: Numbers 13–17

The people of Israel finally came close to Canaan: the Promised Land. God told Moses to send twelve men—one from each tribe—to spy out the area. They were to check how fertile the land was, determine the military strength of the people living there, and bring back some fruit of the land.

They came back with some pomegranates and figs, as well as huge bunches of grapes that they carried on a pole between two men. They saw the wealth of this land *"flowing with milk and honey"* (Numbers 14:8). There was, however, a formidable enemy and so they forgot that with God on their side they could conquer any foe! Of the twelve, Joshua and Caleb said,

> *Only do not rebel against the Lord. And do not be afraid of the people of the land, because we will swallow them up. Their protection is gone, but the Lord is with us. Do not be afraid of them.* (Numbers 14:9)

While looking for a building to house our new school, my daughter and I came across a small, rundown church hall that wasn't being used. The roof leaked, the walls badly needed paint, and a number of repairs were needed. It didn't seem possible to even consider this building. However, after exhausting all alternatives, we returned to the hall, this time with a contractor who knew what could be done. Miraculously, our attitude was completely different. This time we saw the possibilities instead of the problems! Some weeks later, we moved into that little hall, which was clean and sparkling with fresh paint. Lighthouse Christian Academy was launched!

> *The Lord said to Moses, "How long will these people treat me with contempt? How long will they refuse to believe in me, in spite of the miraculous signs I have performed among them?"* (Numbers 14:11)

God must weary of us always focusing on problems. He was ready to give up on the Israelites, but Moses and Aaron prayed for forgiveness for them. Their punishment was another forty years in the wilderness! Is it possible that we bring some of our problems on ourselves by not trusting God the first time around? He wants to teach us obedience, but how can He do it without giving us some difficult situations through which He can demonstrate His love and provision for us?

To train a child to be obedient, a parent must punish him when he is disobedient. The severity of God's punishment against the man carrying sticks on the Sabbath—and of Korah, his family, and his followers—is shocking. It is a serious business to question the wisdom and sovereignty of God! The more we get to know Him, and the closer we come to Him, the more serious it becomes to turn away from Him.

Korah questioned the right of Moses and Aaron to be in authority. In other words, he questioned God's choice of leaders, as well as the wisdom of His plan. We take a chance when we become critical of the men and women God has raised up in the world today. Though some get off-track and start building their own empires, many have had God's hand laid upon them, and if we criticize and speak out against them, we may find ourselves against God!

Numbers 17 includes a lovely story of how God showed His people that Aaron, representing the tribe of Levi, was chosen by Him.

READ: Numbers 18–21

In Numbers 18, God spoke to Aaron and told him of the provision made for the Levites and priests through the tithes given by the people. One sentence seems significant to me:

I am giving you the service of the priesthood as a gift. (Numbers 18:7)

I wonder if Aaron always saw his position as a gift from God. I expect there were times when he found his tasks onerous and wished he could be rid of them. We all struggle at times with facing difficult tasks.

The position of housewife and mother seems to be one of the hardest gifts to accept from God. Yes, we love our husbands, and yes, we take great pleasure in watching our children grow, but what about the drudgery of a job that forces us to repeat the same mundane tasks over and over again, twenty-four hours a day, 365 days a year?

There is another side to this coin—the compliment for a well-planned meal; the satisfaction of seeing people enjoy the food; the accomplishment of a child when he learns to walk; or the joy of a family time together, whether it be at church, an evening at home, or a camping trip. When we start thanking God for the good things He has provided for us, we can truly say, "Yes, this responsibility He has given me is indeed a gift!"

Miriam died. Then another crisis arose! There was no water to drink. Again, the people assembled against Moses and Aaron, saying, "Why did you bring us out of Egypt?" Again, Moses and Aaron prayed. The glory of the Lord appeared to them and He said to Moses:

> *Take the staff, and you and your brother Aaron gather the assembly together. Speak to that rock before their eyes and it will pour out its water. You will bring water out of the rock for the community so they and their livestock can drink.* (Numbers 20:8)

That sounds very gentle, but it's not what Moses actually did. Instead his attitude was one of impatience and frustration. He said,

> *Listen, you rebels, must we bring you water out of this rock?* (Numbers 20:10)

Moses struck the rock twice and water gushed forth. Was it this attitude that led God to ban him and Aaron from entering the Promised Land? Shortly after, Aaron died.

The multitude travelled on, and with God's help they wiped out the Canaanites. Then came another round of complaints and nostalgic memories of Egypt, which brought upon them a plague of serpents.

The more I read the story of the Israelites, the more I see parallels in our modern-day Christian walk. When things go well, we're happy, but as soon as the going gets tough (or monotonous), we complain! Like the Israelites, we complain about the same things over and over again. In my experience, complaining has its own negative consequences—or are they punishments from God? Only a change in attitude—such as looking for creative answers—can bring positive results.

READ: Numbers 22–24

Here is the story of Balak, king of Moab; Balaam, a man who listens to God; and Balaam's donkey, who has a conversation with his master. Balak is afraid of the huge crowd of Israelites approaching his country and figures he can get Balaam to put a curse on them.

> *But God said to Balaam, "Do not go with them. You must not put a curse on those people, because they are blessed."* (Numbers 22:12)

Even when offered honour and riches by the king, Balaam replied,

Even if Balak gave me his palace filled with silver and gold, I could not do anything great or small to go beyond the command of the Lord my God. (Numbers 22:18)

The rest of Numbers 22 tells of the part the donkey played in this story. Balaam showed his human nature in an outburst of anger.

Carrying on in the next two chapters, we find that instead of cursing the Israelites, as Balak asked him to do, Balaam following God's direction and gave them a blessing.

Balaam saw that it pleased the Lord to bless Israel. (Numbers 24:1)

Balaam's second blessing ended with these words:

May those who bless you be blessed and those who curse you be cursed! (Numbers 24:9)

This same promise was given to Abram (Genesis 12:3), and then Isaac passed it on to Jacob (Genesis 27:29). Repetition in the Bible seems to be for emphasis—a message God really wants us to receive. We need to watch Israel today, praying for her and asking God to guide her leaders. Moab's desire to curse the Israelites meant the downfall of his nation. God's plan cannot be thwarted. Nations against Israel today may have to face God's judgment.

Balaam's commitment to being obedient to God's word rather than accepting wealth and position is an outstanding example for us today.

At one time, I attended a dinner where a well-known evangelist spoke. He said that it was a great temptation for any pastor or Christian leader to stray from the track by thinking too highly of himself and not highly enough of God. Self-centredness is one of the common tools Satan uses to lure us away from a God-centred life. As a pastor's wife, I am aware that many people expect their pastor not to have any problems or sins. This can have two unfortunate results:

1. They become critical when the pastor's behaviour doesn't measure up to their expectations.
2. The pastor pretends he doesn't have any problems.

It's just as important for a pastor to confess his faults to God and receive forgiveness as it is for the rest of us. For God to use us, He must be number one in our lives: *"You shall have no other gods before me"* (Exodus 20:3).

READ: Numbers 25–29

This section starts with a sad commentary on the people of Israel.

> *[The Moabites] invited them [the Israelites] to the sacrifices to their gods. The people ate and bowed down before these gods. So Israel joined in worshipping Baal of Peor. And the Lord's anger burned against them.* (Numbers 25:2–3)

When we associate with people who don't put God first in their lives, we either influence them or get drawn into their priorities. Concerns like popularity, worldly pleasures, and making money could become so important that the days slip by and we find no time for God. Disobedience is a serious business to God. He cannot fulfill His purposes without willing followers, so He got rid of those who turned away.

Years passed before God called for another census, taken according to the families within the tribes. Altogether, there were 601,730 families.

> *Not one of them was among those counted by Moses and Aaron the priest when they counted the Israelites in the Desert of Sinai. For the Lord had told those Israelites they would surely die in the desert, and not one of them was left except Caleb son of Jephunneh and Joshua son of Nun.* (Numbers 26:64–65)

The men who entered the Promised Land and returned filled with fear, telling the people of the dangers of moving into it, weren't allowed to enter. God has a promised land for each of us in this life, a place He has chosen. If we face the future with fear, certain of defeat, we'll miss the opportunity He has prepared for us. If we say, like Caleb and Joshua, "Yes, the people are big, but God is with us and we have nothing to fear," we can move ahead and experience the power of God to protect, guide, and bless us.

Fear paralyses us! I remember once praying to God and asking Him what to do about fear. He encouraged me to come close to Him through praise and thanksgiving, looking at the fear through His eyes. Picture a child being afraid of a dog and running to his mother. Then, with her assurances and his hand in hers, he is able to approach the dog and the fear diminishes. With the comforting presence of the Heavenly Father, I can approach my fear. With my hand in His, I can face it and carry on.

Moses continued to be faithful in being God's spokesman to his people. What a calling! When some sisters came to him regarding their father's property,

Moses brought their case before the Lord... (Numbers 27:5)

If you face a problem, take it to the Lord and get His answer.

God told Moses that both he and Aaron would die before entering the Promised Land, but He had Moses go up on a mountain where he could see it. Moses then asked the Lord to appoint someone else to be the leader. This was God's answer:

Take Joshua son of Nun, a man in whom is the spirit, and lay your hand on him. (Numbers 27:18)

And so Moses' successor was appointed.

READ: Numbers 30–36

When a man makes a vow to the Lord or takes an oath to obligate himself by a pledge, he must not break his word but must do everything he said. (Numbers 30:2)

This is an important injunction to us all. Can our word really be trusted? Do we always keep our promises? It's wonderful to work with someone who always carries through on the commitments he or she makes.

I remember the true story of a farmer who sat on the council of his town. Each year, the town had to send in an assessment of its expenditures in order to receive a grant from the provincial government. It had been their practice to overestimate their expenses, figuring their request would be cut down anyway. One year, this farmer persuaded the council to be absolutely honest in their estimate and write a letter to the government stating this to be the case. For the first time, they received the full amount requested, with a note of gratitude for their honesty!

Have we become a nation whose word cannot be trusted? Do we pad our expense accounts? Are we less than honest on the forms we fill out? Do we fulfill the promises we make to our children? That's where the training starts.

The tribes of Reuben, Gad, and Manasseh (a half-tribe) wanted to stay where there was good pasture land for their cattle. Moses told them they could have the land as long as the men of military age travelled with the rest of the people to take the areas God had promised them. Afterward, they could return to their families.

But if you fail to do this, you will be sinning against the Lord; and you may be sure that your sin will find you out. (Numbers 32:23)

We cannot sin against the Lord and hide it. He knows all, and at some point that sin must come to the surface, be confessed, and ultimately be forgiven if we are to experience freedom.

Aaron died at the age of 123 at Mount Hor. The people travelled on and finally came to Jericho, by the River Jordan. On the other side of the river was Canaan, the Promised Land! The Lord then gave Moses directions. First, they were to drive out all the inhabitants of the land and destroy their idols.

But if you do not drive out the inhabitants of the land, those you allow to remain will become barbs in your eyes and thorns in your sides. They will give you trouble in the land where you will live. (Numbers 33:55)

Sometimes God's ways seem harsh to us, but He knows us better than we know ourselves. He's aware of how easily we can be led astray. An evil influence can poison the whole group. Many times in my life, I've seen one negative person spoil the atmosphere in a home, business, or classroom. We need to seek God's wisdom to deal with these situations. To the Israelites, He said, "Get rid of those people."

God showed Moses the boundaries of the new land. Eleazer (the priest), Joshua, and one leader from each of the nine and a half tribes, were to divide the land for their inheritance. But He cautioned them:

Do not defile the land where you live and where I dwell, for I, the Lord, dwell among the Israelites. (Numbers 35:34)

We often wonder if we're misusing our environment. This is God's land, so we can ask Him how we should use it.

THE BOOK OF

Mark

READ: Mark 1

In this chapter, Mark introduces Jesus in a powerful way. He starts by calling Him the Son of God and, like Matthew, he quotes from Isaiah to identify Him with the Messiah who was foretold five hundred years earlier to the people of Israel. He sees the fulfillment of the messenger in John the Baptist, who preached repentance followed by water baptism in preparation for a deeper spiritual experience.

> *And this was his message: "After me will come one more powerful than I, the thongs of whose sandals I am not worthy to stoop down and untie. I baptize you with water, but he will baptize you with the Holy Spirit. (Mark 1:7–8)*

These are the same steps Matthew clearly laid down: repent, be baptized in water (by a church leader), then be baptized in the Holy Spirit by Jesus Himself. Jesus came to John for water baptism, where He received the Holy Spirit in power and was proclaimed the Son of God. To prepare Him for ministry, Jesus experienced the worldly temptations of Satan we all face—and then He was ready to begin.

He gathered a team of four fishermen to go with Him and start teaching. People marvelled at His authority as He cast out unclean spirits and healed the sick. But He didn't just depend on His own wisdom and strength:

> *Very early in the morning, while it was still dark, Jesus got up, left the house and went off to a solitary place, where he prayed. (Mark 1:35)*

Notice that it says *"very early in the morning."* When I began to set aside morning quiet times many years ago, my children were quite young. I soon realized that I was doing it not just for myself, but to be an example for the rest of the family. I knew that those around me would be more influenced by my actions than my words. If I wanted to teach my children that prayer was important, I had to show them that it was important to me. If I wanted them to keep their room tidy, I had to keep the rest of the house tidy. Jesus knew the importance of being an example and the importance of prayer. He let His disciples see His need of spending time with His Father. Fortunately for us, it was written down as an example that we, too, may follow.

After healing the leper, He cautioned him, saying,

See that you don't tell this to anyone. (Mark 1:44)

The leper, no doubt overjoyed to be freed from being an outcast, couldn't keep it to himself, and went around telling everyone! The result was that Jesus couldn't even enter the towns because the crowds looking for Him grew too large. At times in my life, I should have kept quiet and didn't—and it has been costly to someone. Once when I made an unkind remark about a neighbour, it got back to her through our daughters. Apologizing to her was a painful experience. It is a hard thing to control our tongues!

READ: Mark 2–3

Both incidents in these chapters demonstrate that it's worth spending time in prayer, asking God to reveal the truth we need to learn.

The first incident takes place at the beginning of Mark 2. Crowds gathered wherever Jesus went, because He was healing the sick. Families and friends brought their loved ones so He would touch them and make them well again. In this story, four friends brought a paralyzed man to a house where Jesus was staying, but they could find no way in. Imagine the astonishment of the crowd when they saw the roof being removed and the crippled man being let down on a pallet!

If I were watching, my attitude would depend on my opinion of Jesus. If I found Him exciting and wanted to learn more, I would probably think, *Look at that! I wonder what He'll do. Will He scold them for destroying the roof and interrupting the meeting? Or will He welcome the opportunity to heal a man so disabled?*

Amazingly, Jesus looked at him, saw what love his friends had for him, and said,

Son, your sins are forgiven. (Mark 2:5)

At this point, if I was already critical of Jesus and His unorthodox behaviour, like the Pharisees, I would probably think:

Why does this fellow talk like that? He's blaspheming! Who can forgive sins but God alone? (Mark 2:7)

Jesus took this opportunity to tell the people He was the Son of God. Those who were open and wanted to hear this accepted it when they saw the cripple healed.

He got up, took his mat and walked out in full view of them all. This amazed everyone and they praised God, saying, "We have never seen anything like this!" (Mark 2:12)

The scribes, and others who already had a negative attitude, missed it.

I wonder how often I've missed a message from God because I was negative about the speaker and therefore heard only what I thought could fuel my criticism.

The second incident is found in Mark 3:31–35. While preaching one day, Jesus was given a message that his family was waiting for him outside the house. His family may have been as mystified as everyone else about what Jesus was doing, or maybe they had some family news they wanted to share with Him. The truth is, we don't know.

Many people jump to the conclusion that by accepting all believers as His brothers and sisters, Jesus excluded His earthly family. Somehow, having experienced His great love for me, I can't imagine Him rejecting His mother and brothers. Rather, I can imagine the kindly look in His eyes.

Then he looked at those seated in a circle around him and said, "Here are my mother and my brothers! Whoever does God's will is my brother and sister and mother." (Mark 3:34–35)

He was adding to His natural family. Obedience to God puts me in direct family relationship with Him! At my church, we used to sing a chorus that meant just that to me: "I'm so glad I'm a part of the family of God."

READ: Mark 4–5

In the parable of the sower and the seed, we usually think of the soil as representing those who hear word for the first time. Here is the interpretation for the parable:

- Some don't even hear the word, and Satan causes them to be unaware of the message.
- Some hear it, are impressed, and then forget it when things go wrong.
- Some are so full of problems and bitterness that they cannot accept the good news.
- Some are ready and waiting, and it immediately becomes their way of life.

Now let's look at it from the point of view of long-time Christians who dutifully read the Bible every day.

- The story is so familiar they skip over it and finish reading the allotted chapter. They then go about the business of the day, totally forgetting what they read.
- The second group read it and think, "Yes, I know that story." But when they disapprove of someone's behaviour, they still get angry and critical.
- The third group is made up of those whose days are so filled with activities (perhaps good ones, like church meetings, visiting the sick, and running here and there) that although they took ten minutes in the morning to read the scripture, their minds were on the activities ahead of them and they skipped the last few verses in order to get on their way.

Do any of these look familiar to you? If I hadn't experienced each of them, I wouldn't have been able to write about them. But I'm grateful to say that I also understand the fourth group:

- Those times when I dressed in the morning, reached for my Bible with a sense of expectancy, and received some inspiration from the throne of God!

Those are the days when I feel an inner joy that bears fruit in my love for those around me, making me thankful to be alive!

I can relate to the disciples' concern about the storm. My husband and I owned a sailboat for a number of years and Bob was an enthusiastic sailor. I went along to "crew," and if the conditions were just right (warm with a slight breeze) I really enjoyed myself. But if the weather was cold or the wind a bit strong, I wanted no part of it. A storm strong enough to send waves beating into the boat "so that it was nearly swamped" would have totally unnerved me!

It must have been quite a sight to witness a demon-possessed man be released; afterward, he was able to sit and listen to Jesus *"dressed and in his right mind"* (Mark 5:15). He wanted to follow Jesus right then, but He told the man to stay and share his story with others. They needed to hear it because, although they saw the power of God at work, they were rejecting it.

> *Then the people began to plead with Jesus to leave their region.* (Mark 5:17)

The power of God manifested in Jesus is awesome! We can withdraw from it (as the Gerasenes in Mark 5 did), find fault with it (as the Pharisees did), try to ignore it (as many people do), or recognize it as the way life is meant to be and embrace it with total commitment! This last choice is what Jesus calls us to do.

READ: Mark 6–7

People who had known Jesus as He was growing up were perplexed by Him. He and the disciples travelled to His home area and He spoke in the synagogue on the sabbath.

> *"Where did this man get these things?" they asked. "What's this wisdom that has been given him, that he even does miracles? Isn't this the carpenter? Isn't this Mary's son and the brother of James, Joseph, Judas and Simon? Aren't his sisters here with us?" And they took offense at him.* (Mark 6:2–3)

Most new Christians probably find that those closest to them aren't necessarily the ones who want to hear about their new experience. I remember once coming home from a conference filled with excitement about how good life could be if I listened to God for guidance every day. I was sure everyone would be just as keen as I was. Not so! In my enthusiasm, I turned a number of people off, and it was years before I regained their trust.

Jesus didn't make the mistake I made, but neither did He water down His message to make people comfortable. He healed a few, marvelled at the unbelief of those He knew so well, and went on His way to other villages.

Jesus didn't allow His disciples to just have a cosy, warm relationship with Him. He sent them out two-by-two to spread the gospel:

> *They went out and preached that people should repent. They drove out many demons and anointed many sick people with oil and healed them.* (Mark 6:12–13)

To preach repentance, cast out demons, and anoint the sick for healing—that was quite a responsibility!

The death of John the Baptist seems like a tragic waste of a man dedicated to God's service. God could have intervened, but maybe John's work was finished. He had certainly awakened the people to their need of a new relationship with God, and having done so prepared the way (as Isaiah foretold) for Jesus to proclaim the Kingdom of Heaven.

Really, Herod was the loser! He had been puzzled by John but was also impressed by him.

> *When Herod heard John, he was greatly puzzled; yet he liked to listen to him.* (Mark 6:20)

However, pleasing his wife and her daughter, as well as saving face before his guests, took precedence over his better judgment and he ordered John to be put to death.

In Mark 7, Jesus warned the Pharisees about wrong priorities:

> *You have let go of the commandments of God and are holding on to the traditions of men.* (Mark 7:8)

That can still be a danger in the church today.

READ: Mark 8–9

Several times in the gospels, Jesus fed thousands of people with very little food. In this case, Jesus had compassion on a crowd who had nothing to eat, so He called His disciples to discuss the situation. Perhaps we can learn something from their questions and the solution to the problem:

1. Jesus and the disciples looked at the problem.
2. They took stock of what food was available.
3. They gave it all to Jesus.
4. He gave thanks to God.
5. They obeyed what He told them to do.
6. In His hands, what was available became sufficient for all and everyone was satisfied.

That tells me that when I have a problem, I should:

1. Take it to Jesus and look at it with Him.
2. Take stock of the resources I have and give it all to Him.
3. Give thanks to God for what I have.
4. Be obedient to whatever I believe He's telling me to do, even if it seems

as ridiculous as passing out seven loaves and a few small fish to feed four thousand people!

The story of the Transfiguration goes beyond my imagination. Peter, James, and John were given a glimpse of Heaven! Imagine seeing Jesus, Moses, and Elijah talking together. As the disciples watched, they heard the voice of God saying,

This is my Son, whom I love. Listen to him! (Mark 9:7)

The rest of the disciples, even though they had spent so much time with Jesus, lacked the faith to cast out an evil spirit from a young boy. However, Jesus healed the boy when He saw the longing in the boy's father—*"I do believe; help me overcome my unbelief!"* (Mark 9:24)

I can identify with the father. I truly want to believe and have total faith in Jesus, yet so often my faith seems weak; I have an element of unbelief. At church, there's a chorus that still gives me encouragement at times like these:

> The steadfast love of the Lord never ceases
> His mercies never come to an end
> They are new every morning, new every morning
> Great is Thy faithfulness O Lord,
> Great is Thy faithfulness.

I can't always trust my own faithfulness, but I can certainly trust the Lord's! Hallelujah!

READ: Mark 10–11

Jesus didn't have many years to pass on to the world some understanding of the character of God, His plan for us, and how we can participate in that plan. So, as the crowds gathered around Him wherever He went, *"as was his custom, he taught them"* (Mark 10:1).

We feel an urgency today to pass on what we know to our children—and to others as well. When my children were young, it seemed as though the situation of living as a family would go on forever. One day, however, all four of them were gone and my opportunity to pass on to them the love of God was also gone. Well, no, not entirely, because as adults we can still talk and share, but the years of influencing our children's lives pass so very quickly. Now I'm aware how very important each day is. I don't want to waste any time with destructive attitudes, for soon today is over and I can't go back and try again.

The Pharisees did everything they could to find fault with Jesus' teaching—a common political ploy. They touched on an issue so prevalent today that it has almost destroyed our society—divorce. Jesus explained to them God's plan for marriage, quoting from the law of Moses:

"For this reason a man will leave his father and mother and be united to his wife, and the two will become one flesh." So they are no longer two but one. (Mark 10:7)

Because of a "hardness of heart" that destroyed relationships, Moses allowed divorce. But that wasn't God's original plan. Families were meant to be the foundation of communities.

At one time, we lived in a small town which had a Mennonite church. That was not our denomination, but we became friends with many of the people. Everything they did was family-oriented; their services, their social gatherings, and even the cleaning of the church was done by one family each week. No matter what happened in the lives of those children later, I'm sure they carried with them a sense of the importance of the family unit. Strong families build a strong nation!

Following the discussion on divorce, we are given a picture of Jesus spending time with children. With divorce having become so easy in our society, many children have a mixed-up family situation. I often wonder what sort of values they'll take into their adult lives when they influence the next generation.

Jesus loved and valued the children:

And he took the children in his arms, put his hands on them and blessed them. (Mark 10:16)

We must love and value each one as He did.

It is a big temptation to look at monetary wealth as the ultimate aim in life. One rich young ruler wanted to follow Jesus, but the latter told him that in order to do that he would have to give away his wealth, since his love for money would get in the way of loving and serving God. The young man turned and walked the other way. How sad.

Next, the brothers James and John surprise me with their request of Jesus. After three years of being with Him, how could they think they could ask for places of honour in heaven? And yet I realize that my own daily requests to God can be just as self-centred, and not at all in line with His idea of servanthood.

However, when blind Bartimaeus asked for healing, Jesus answered,

Go... your faith has healed you. (Mark 10:52)

READ: Mark 12–13

At the end of Mark 11, a group of religious leaders were questioning Jesus, trying to trip Him up. That conversation continues into Mark 12. The parable He tells could be a challenge to the church today—or even to the individual believer.

God has given us a responsibility to live and share the gospel. He sends various people into our lives, but some we reject, malign, or ignore. This reminds me of Leo Tolstoy's story of the cobbler waiting for a visit from the Christ Child. While waiting, he continued to help people in need. Then he heard a voice saying, *"Inasmuch as ye did it unto one of these my brethren, ye have done it unto me"* (Matthew 25:40, KJV).

In other words, "If you don't love your neighbour, you don't love God."

When asked to name the first and most important commandment, Jesus quotes Deuteronomy 6:4–5.

"The most important one," answered Jesus, "is this: 'Hear, O Israel, the Lord our God, the Lord is one. Love the Lord your God with all your heart and with all your soul and with all your mind and with all your strength.' The second is this: 'Love your neighbor as yourself.' There is no commandment greater than these." (Mark 12:29–30)

He watched the people giving their offerings and called the disciples' attention to the widow who gave a single penny. He said:

They all gave out of their wealth; but she, out of her poverty, put in everything—all she had to live on. (Mark 12:44)

I wonder if the amount of our giving reflects the commitment we're making in our lives. Bob was always very generous. In fact, our kids told us after they grew up that if they wanted money, they would ask their dad. If they asked me, I would say, "What do you want it for?" If they asked Bob, he would say, "How much?"

I was always a penny pincher, which isn't all bad—until it comes to giving. There was a time when God spoke to me about it and said, "Let Bob decide how much you should give—he's more generous than you." So for several years I watched Bob, thinking, *Ten dollars would be a fair donation.* Well, he would pull out a twenty-dollar bill, or even a fifty! Gradually, I learned from him that God always blesses us beyond what we give to others.

My desire today is that all that I am and all that I have should be under God's control.

READ: Mark 14–16

Let's look at particular individuals in this section.

> *…and the chief priests and the teachers of the law were looking for some sly way to arrest Jesus and kill him.* (Mark 14:1)

Imagine! These were religious leaders, planning to kidnap and kill a man because of the threat He posed to their positions. Their minds were so clouded with self-centeredness that they didn't recognize Jesus for who He was. We can easily fall into that same trap and fail to recognize what Jesus would have us see.

> *…a woman came with an alabaster jar of very expensive perfume, made of pure nard. She broke the jar and poured the perfume on his head.* (Mark 14:3)

She was probably like the woman with the penny—giving all she had. Jesus understood and honoured her for it.

> *Then Judas Iscariot, one of the Twelve, went to the chief priests to betray Jesus to them. They were delighted to hear this and promised to give him money.* (Mark 14:10–11)

Just what the priests wanted—an ally who knew everything about Jesus! Every battle has informers who will give information to the enemy; they aren't totally committed to their leader. A half-hearted soldier is a dangerous person, and so is a half-hearted Christian.

Think of Peter. He longed to be a whole-hearted follower of Jesus, but his weakness showed up when he fell asleep. Perhaps if he had prayed with Jesus, he would not have denied Him later.

And what of Pilate? Something about Jesus impressed him, and I'm sure he hoped the crowd would choose to release Him when they were given the chance to request freedom for one prisoner. A crowd can be stirred up and easily swayed, however, so the chief priests soon had them shouting for Barabbas. Pilate succumbed to their wishes, against his better judgment. It can be hard to stand for what is right when the crowd is against you!

Then there was the centurion, who had a sudden spiritual insight and said,

> *Surely this man was the Son of God!* (Mark 15:39)

As for Jesus, what did He do when faced with the most challenging experience anyone ever had?

1. He prayed, committing Himself to God's will.
2. He faced the enemy and continued straight ahead.
3. He didn't defend Himself, instead remaining silent.
4. He watched His friends desert Him, showing no bitterness.
5. He voiced the agony He felt when the load of sin separated Him from God.
6. He rose again, victorious over death.

THE BOOK OF

Deuteronomy

READ: Deuteronomy 1–3

While on the threshold of the Promised Land, Moses delivered a long speech recalling some of the events that had occurred during the journey. He recalled how, as their numbers increased, the responsibility became too much for him so, by God's direction, judges were chosen from the tribes—wise men who could help settle disputes.

Even among believers, differences arise—resentments and self-pity take over and something must be done if unity is to be restored. No team can afford these divisions if they are to move ahead. For example, in my house, daily tidying must be done or the weekly cleaning becomes a major task, too difficult to handle in a few short hours. A build-up of resentment can become a major operation if differences aren't dealt with at the beginning.

Moses also recalled how they reached the border of the Promised Land, but when the report came back about the people who lived there, the people became afraid and didn't want to go ahead. Moses said to them,

> *The Lord your God, who is going before you, will fight for you, as he did for you in Egypt, before your very eyes… In spite of this, you did not trust in the Lord your God.* (Deuteronomy 1:30, 32)

Fear can be a binding force that keeps us from doing what God has prepared for us. He can't use us. In fact, we can't even hear Him if fear is blocking us. Now and then, it's a good thing to stop and ask ourselves, "What's the worst thing that could happen to me? What do I fear most?"

The solution is the same for any mountain that gets in your way. Come into the presence of God through praise and thanksgiving. Then, saturated with the presence of God, look straight into the face of fear. If the Israelites had done that, they would have marched victoriously into the Promised Land.

When threatened with not being allowed to enter, they quickly changed their tune and said, "Let's go!" But it was too late; God was no longer with them. The opportunities placed before us don't always wait for us to change our minds. Their opportunity was taken away from them and given to their children forty years later; the original Israelites ended their lives in the wilderness. Even Moses wasn't allowed to go into the Promised Land. He was only given a mountaintop view of the land to which he had been leading his people for so many years.

Each generation has its own responsibilities and opportunities, but eventually their time comes to leave the earth. The older I get, the more I see the importance of making every moment count.

In Deuteronomy, Moses spoke to the new generation, declaring that God was preparing the way for them:

This very day I will begin to put the terror and fear of you on all the nations under heaven. (Deuteronomy 2:25)

And He chose a new leader for them:

But commission Joshua, and encourage and strengthen him, for he will lead this people across and will cause them to inherit the land you will see. (Deuteronomy 3:28)

READ: Deuteronomy 4–5

In these chapters, Moses reviewed with the people what God had done and what He had taught them.

Hear now, O Israel, the decrees and laws I am about to teach you. Follow them so that you may live and may go in and take possession of the land that the Lord, the God of your fathers, is giving you. (Deuteronomy 4:1)

It's one thing to learn the commandments God has given; it's another thing to follow them. The results of following them should be apparent to all the people around you.

Observe them carefully, for this will show your wisdom and understanding to the nations, who will hear about all these decrees and say, "Surely this great nation is a wise and understanding people." (Deuteronomy 4:6)

It's an exciting thought—and also a sobering one—that we, as Christian believers, can show those qualities to the world around us. The more we live what we believe, the greater will be our influence for good.

I often wonder if people will know by the quality of my life that I'm a Christian. I frequently pray for God's wisdom, love, and understanding of people in order that I may be a channel through which He reaches others. That's really the only purpose worth living for—to be a channel for God's love. Here's a great verse:

> *But if from there you seek the Lord your God, you will find him if you look for him with all your heart and with all your soul.* (Deuteronomy 4:29)

Some years ago, I heard a story, the exact details of which I cannot recall, but it went something like this.

A priest was walking along a river with a young man who had been pestering him about how to find God. The young man was always full of arguments and doubts about the reality of His existence.

Finally, the priest grabbed the young man, walked out into the water, and pushed him under, holding him there until the young man struggled to get out.

"When I was holding your head under the water, what did you want most?" the priest asked.

Gasping, the young man said, "Air."

"Well, when you want God as much as you want air, you will find Him, but not before."

God reveals Himself when our desire to know Him is strong and sincere.

> *So be careful to do what the Lord your God has commanded you; do not turn aside to the right or to the left.* (Deuteronomy 5:32)

The way of the Lord is straight and narrow, and it is easy to turn aside if we aren't constantly asking Him to show us the way. The Bible is our road map and Jesus is our guide. The road isn't always easy, but it is beautiful and full of joyous surprises.

READ: Deuteronomy 6–7

What a sermon Moses delivers to his people! So many of these verses contain important messages, but I'll just pick a few that speak to me. Every time I read this, new gems of truth help me better understand God's character. There's so much to learn about Him and so little time—just one lifetime, and it goes by so quickly!

Hear, O Israel: The Lord our God, the Lord is one. Love the Lord your God with all your heart and with all your soul and with all your strength. (Deuteronomy 6:4–5)

Jesus quoted this in Mark 12:29–30 and then added, *"Love your neighbor as yourself"* (Mark 12:31). Nothing is more important than loving the Lord with our whole being—acknowledging His presence with us, living to please Him.

Here is one of the choruses we used to sing at church:

> I worship You, I worship You
> The reason I live is to worship You.

Unfortunately, God probably finds it hard to believe that, especially when I get irritable and impatient or spend my time wallowing in self-pity. I cannot afford these self-centred attitudes. They're too debilitating! And besides, they cut me off from God.

Moses said we should keep these words in our hearts, teach them diligently to our children, and talk about them at home or when we're out walking, when we lie down, and when we get up. When I'm self-disciplined with my daily quiet times, I'm much more aware of how God is working in my life because I'm looking for evidence of His presence. I'm always astounded by the way He arranges details. Living with Jesus means having an ongoing dialogue with Him.

Deuteronomy 7 begins with a shocking order that when the people entered the Promised Land, they were to utterly destroy the people who lived there. My finite mind cannot understand this, but one thing I do know is that God wanted His chosen people to follow Him and He knew that the strong influence of evil could lead even believers astray. Only He has the whole picture of all people past, present, and future. Only He has the perfect plan for the world. What's more, He never makes mistakes!

Despite the fact that Israel was a small and insignificant nation full of stubborn, rebellious people, Moses reminded them:

For you are a people holy to the Lord your God. The Lord your God has chosen you out of all the peoples on the face of the earth to be his people, his treasured possession. (Deuteronomy 7:6)

That gives me great confidence. That promise also applies to all of us who have given our hearts and lives to Him. We are a people holy in the sight of God, His own possession! What an honour! I can only bow down in thanksgiving, wonder, awe, and praise.

READ: Deuteronomy 8–9

The wilderness years were a time of training as God led the Israelites, often in a roundabout way. He fed them with manna when they were hungry, their clothes didn't wear out, and their feet didn't swell from all the walking in the desert. It was a tough training ground to get them to be obedient to Him. They suffered many hardships and there was no other way but to seek God's help. Of course, they grumbled and complained, but when it came down to the crunch, there was only one answer—obey God or die. And, of course, many of them did die.

Now, however, they were poised to enter the Promised Land where there would be lots of food, material blessings, and opportunities to build fine homes. That's where the real temptation would come!

You may say to yourself, "My power and the strength of my hands have produced this wealth for me." But remember the Lord your God, for it is he who gives you the ability to produce wealth... (Deuteronomy 8:17–18)

Moses then warned them that if they moved away from God, they would perish. If we're going to take for ourselves, as believers, the promises of God, we must also accept His warnings. As Christians, we have a responsibility—a rather awesome one. The world will judge Jesus and Christianity by what they see in us!

Know then in your heart that as a man disciplines his son, so the Lord God disciplines you. (Deuteronomy 8:5)

Just as my child's behaviour reflects on me, my behaviour reflects on my Heavenly Father. I want to be obedient and a credit to Him. The rewards of obedience are great. When we face difficult situations, God goes before us to prepare the way.

It was time now for the Israelites to go in and possess the land, but the enemies awaiting them were big and strong.

But be assured today that the Lord your God is the one who goes across ahead of you like a devouring fire. (Deuteronomy 9:3)

Moses warned them again not to take credit for any of their victories:

Understand, then, that it is not because of your righteousness that the Lord your God is giving you this good land to possess, for you are a stiff-necked people. (Deuteronomy 9:6)

It is a great temptation to:

1. Forget God when things go well.
2. Take credit when we experience success.
3. Think that we deserve the blessings we receive.

Having written that, I must take the time to thank God for all the blessings I am enjoying in my life right now.

READ: Deuteronomy 10–12

Moses reminded the people that God wrote the Ten Commandments for them on stone. These commandments came right from the hand of God and yet, in today's society, we seem to have regarded them as irrelevant. That puts us in a very dangerous position, for God is our final Judge and each one of us must face Him someday. Moses' obedience to God gave the world these laws of life—it was to be a blessing to his nation and to all future generations. Obedience is the one thing God asks of us. When we obey, we bring blessings on ourselves and countless others.

A man once said, "Everything we think or say or do either raises all of humanity or causes it to fall a little lower." I once watched a film where someone said, "The most important thing I can do today is spend an hour alone with God." If we're to be of any use in God's kingdom, that's where we must start. People who pray are the power centre for the world.

One morning in my quiet time, I asked God about obedience. Here was His answer: "I am your Father; you are My children. Just as earthly parents are delighted when their children come to them for love, guidance, and wisdom, so I am delighted when you come to Me to experience My love and receive My directions. Just as it grieves earthly parents when their children ignore them or disregard their wishes, so it grieves Me when My children disregard or disobey Me. I can make your lives so much freer, so much more satisfying, so much more fruitful. Unlike earthly parents, who must take their hands off their children as they approach adulthood, My control of your lives should go on forever, for only in Me can you find perfect fulfillment. Come to Me daily. You have much to learn and I have much to teach you. Through one obedient person, I can bless all mankind."

In Deuteronomy 11:13–17, Moses gives the people God's message: that as they are obedient, their crops will prosper, but if not, the reverse will be true. The words of God are so important that they should be written on the doorposts of the houses.

While visiting Israel, I found in the gift shops small metal "mezuzahs" to be fastened to the entrance of a home. They were to contain the words:

Hear, O Israel: The Lord our God, the Lord is one. Love the Lord your God with all your heart and with all your soul and with all your strength. (Deuteronomy 6:4–5)

If I could keep those words before me every day, life would be a great adventure, with possibilities beyond anything I could ever imagine. It's a picture of heaven to be constantly in the presence of my Heavenly Father. He says that as you live a life of obedience,

…you are to rejoice before the Lord your God in everything you put your hand to. (Deuteronomy 12:18)

That's the way I want to live!

READ: Deuteronomy 13–15

The Lord your God is testing you to find out whether you love him with all your heart and with all your soul. (Deuteronomy 13:3)

Every day is a testing ground for our relationship with God. My reactions to people around me can bring forth a variety of attitudes, and my spiritual life depends on what I do with those reactions.

Some years ago, I taught a first-grade class in Victoria. One morning, I started out with a feeling of gratitude. In my quiet-time book, I wrote:

I'm really grateful for opportunities, for health, for a new day, for the joy of the Lord as a source of strength. I guess if you want to receive God's strength, you have to first accept the joy of His presence. Burdens and concerns sap our strength and do not allow God's strength to flow through. His strength comes only on the wings of joy.

That evening, I wrote:

It sounded so good this morning, but somehow I lost it through the day. Excitement is in the air at school, but there are also tensions and demands. I really blew off at one little boy this afternoon, but thank goodness I had sense enough to straighten things out with him almost immediately. I'm grateful for God's, and the child's, ready forgiveness. Children seem so much quicker to forgive than adults!

Then another day, I wrote:

Why do I feel discouraged at school? It's because I don't want to feel I'm doing a lesser job than the other Grade One teacher. I want the glory of a class doing well!

I have underlined several verses in this section. The following verses contain an important lesson for us:

Be sure to set aside a tenth of all that your fields produce each year. (Deuteronomy 14:22)

Give generously to him [your needy brother] and do so without a grudging heart... There will always be poor people in the land. Therefore I command you to be openhanded toward your brothers and toward the poor and needy in your land. (Deuteronomy 15:10–11)

God expects us to be good stewards of all we possess. First we need to tithe—give one-tenth to the Lord's work. Then, we should freely and willingly give to those in need—without any attempt to control. It's amazing how we can do good things with wrong motives! We need to keep reminding ourselves that God is more interested in our hearts than in our actions. He sees who we are on the inside.

READ: Deuteronomy 16–18

We read in this section of three celebrations that God set out for Israel. The first is Passover, to commemorate their rescue from Egypt, when the angel of death took the firstborn of every Egyptian family but passed over the homes of the Israelites. That was the final episode in the confrontation between Moses and Pharaoh. Passover was to last seven days, the seventh being a day of rest.

Seven weeks later came the Feast of Weeks, the second celebration, when the very first early grain was cut. This was a time for the Israelites to acknowledge God's goodness and remember that they had been slaves but were now free in the Promised Land.

Later, at the time of the full harvest, they were to celebrate the Feast of Tabernacles (or Booths). This, too, would last seven days, and they were told:

Be joyful at your Feast... For the Lord your God will bless you in all your harvest and in all the work of your hands, and your joy will be complete. (Deuteronomy 16:14–15)

I believe God always wanted to reveal Himself to the world and that He chose the Israelites to be the ones through whom He did this. These three feasts tell us something about God's character. We can see His power, faithfulness, and provision for us. He longs for us to be joyous and thankful. By celebrating these every year, the people were reminded who God is.

Jesus participated in these celebrations, and so did the early church. Over the years, as more and more Gentiles became Christians, the Gentiles outnumbered the Jews and began to be hostile to them. All the Jewish festivals were thrown out, and for hundreds of years they have been ignored by the church.

More recently, this has been changing. In Jerusalem especially, Christians are beginning to observe some of them, especially the Feast of Tabernacles. I have attended these Christian celebrations in Jerusalem and they are joyous occasions.

READ: Deuteronomy 19–27

Through Moses, God gave directions for the people to follow as they entered and lived in the Promised Land. They were to go into battle against the people there. Because these people worshipped idols, God didn't want the Israelites to be influenced by them; He said they were all to be destroyed. Then He gave His people a number of rules for living.

Suppose the experience of the Israelites was compared to the Christian walk. When we desire to find a more meaningful way of life, we call out to God for help—just as the Israelites called out to God to rescue them from slavery in Egypt. Miracles were necessary to get them out of the hands of Pharaoh, who had enslaved them. Jesus' death and resurrection is the miracle which allows us to be free of the sinful habits that enslave us. So, when we invite Jesus into our lives, we begin a new life with Him.

We aren't promised an easy time; only by going through wilderness experiences can we learn to trust God. Sometimes we hear His voice clearly and gladly obey. Other times we aren't sure what He wants of us, so we do what seems right. But there are times when we deliberately choose to go our own selfish way and therefore move off from His presence. We may even forget about God for a season, neglecting to spend time seeking His guidance. We end up with a golden calf of materialism, busyness, or some other distraction.

Being a loving Heavenly Father, He draws us back to Himself, and at times this may occur through some very uncomfortable experiences. Maybe even tragic circumstances! God continues to teach us what we need to learn until

He sees we're ready to face the responsibility of some ministry—the Promised Land.

This is when the battle really begins. Our commitment is strong, but the enemy (Satan) wants to render us useless to God's purpose. We become more aware of habits and attitudes that get in the way. Sometimes it's quite a battle to change! However, we aren't alone.

Look at this:

> *When you go to war against your enemies and see horses and chariots and an army greater than yours, do not be afraid of them, because the Lord your God, who brought you up out of Egypt, will be with you... [The Lord says,] "For the Lord your God is the one who goes with you to fight for you against your enemies to give you victory."* (Deuteronomy 20:1, 4)

With God, good always triumphs over evil. But if we deliberately choose to turn our backs on Him, we will suffer the consequences.

READ: Deuteronomy 28–31

Parents at home and teachers at school try to teach a child to be obedient to authority. We know that the only way to have self-discipline as an adult is to practice accepting discipline as a child. In order to train a child to want to be obedient, we try hard to think of constructive punishments.

In our reading, we have been watching God train His people. If He were human, I'm sure He would have felt frustrated and discouraged at times. He set out the rules so clearly, yet they were so often disobeyed. He told the Israelites of the blessings that follow obedience:

> *The Lord will establish you as his holy people, as he promised you on oath, if you keep the commands of the Lord your God and walk in his ways.* (Deuteronomy 28:9)

If one obeys His commandments, He promises prosperity, rain upon the land to make it fruitful, and a leading place among the nations.

As a parent and teacher, I longed for my children to choose what was right, to be obedient, to be responsible in their duties and loving in their relationships with others. I realized I had to model a way of life for them; I couldn't expect them to pick up their belongings if mine were strewn all over the place. I couldn't expect them to be forgiving and caring if they saw me carrying resentments and being critical of others.

God reveals His love for me so that I, in turn, can love others. He blesses me with peace and wants me to share it with others. He accepts and encourages me so that I can accept and encourage others.

However, just as wrongdoing must be punished in a child, so God warns the Israelites that there will be consequences for disobedience.

> *Because you did not serve the Lord your God joyfully and gladly in the time of prosperity, therefore in hunger and thirst, in nakedness and dire poverty, you will serve the enemies the Lord sends against you.* (Deuteronomy 28:47–48)

How can we know what God's will is for us? Well, He says that it isn't so hard. He will make it known to us if we spend quiet time with Him.

> *No, the word is very near to you; it is in your mouth and in your heart so you may obey it.* (Deuteronomy 30:14)

If we attune our hearts with Him, we'll know what He wants of us. The choice is ours:

> *…I have set before you life and death, blessings and curses. Now choose life, so that you and your children may live and that you may love the Lord your God, listen to his voice, and hold fast to him.* (Deuteronomy 30:19–20)

Unfortunately, Israel would turn aside again and again, as Moses well knew.

READ: Deuteronomy 32–34

> *I will proclaim the name of the Lord. Oh, praise the greatness of our God! He is the Rock, his works are perfect, and all his ways are just. A faithful God who does no wrong, upright and just is he.* (Deuteronomy 32:3–4)

Moses' song begins by acknowledging some attributes of God. He is great, immovable, and sure like a rock. His plan is perfect and His ways are just. He can be trusted and He never makes mistakes. He knows what is right for us.

No matter how I feel, the Lord reigns. His plan moves on; the sun rises and sets, there is seed time and harvest, and the days pass. None of this depends on how I feel or what I do. I can choose to be part of His glory or fuss and fume, drag my feet, be bored, and miss the whole thing!

> *The eternal God is your refuge, and underneath are the everlasting arms.* (Deuteronomy 33:27)

Moses prayed a blessing over each tribe of Israel, ending with this verse. It gives me a great sense of peace to picture myself in the protecting arms of God. No matter what's going on around me, I can be assured of His loving presence enfolding me.

This reminds me of a little bird sitting in a deep crevice in the side of a rocky hill. All around the storm rages, cold and blustery, but the bird sits quietly and safely in the shelter of the rock. This is a picture of peace.

Moses had completed the work God appointed for him. He had gone from a baby, hidden in the bulrushes, to living as the son of Pharaoh's daughter. He'd had to flee for his life and live as a shepherd for some years. Then God called him to lead millions of people out of slavery in Egypt through a forty-year training course in the wilderness. Now, standing on the verge of the Promised Land with the most difficult task yet still ahead of them—that of taking the land from the people who lived there—Moses' work was finished. At the age of one hundred and twenty, God took him home. Before he died, he laid his hands on Joshua and passed the spirit of wisdom to the new leader.

God has appointed certain things for each of us to accomplish and then calls us home. I remember a dear friend of mine who was dying of cancer. Many of us prayed for her healing. Her statement to the doctor was, "It's all right. If God has something more for me to do, He will heal me. If not, He will take me home." His work for her must have been finished, because she died shortly after that.

THE BOOK OF

Joshua

READ: Joshua 1–4

In the first chapter, we see the Israelites with their new leader, Joshua, on the threshold of the Promised Land. They had finally arrived. Through Joshua, God delivered a new set of instructions. He told them how much land was to be theirs and assured them they would be able to overcome the present inhabitants.

No one will be able to stand up against you all the days of your life. As I was with Moses, so I will be with you; I will never leave you nor forsake you. (Joshua 1:5)

But there was a condition:

Be strong and very courageous. Be careful to obey all the law my servant Moses gave you; do not turn from it to the right or to the left, that you may be successful wherever you go. (Joshua 1:7)

The walk with God is a straight one—and narrow. It's a fine line from which you can fall away, either to the right or to the left. Even in the matter of sharing my faith! There are times when God wants me to do it, and if I don't, I miss an opportunity to help someone. On the other hand, if I talk about it when it isn't the right time, I turn people off and make them sceptical.

I've often been guilty of the first mistake, realizing later that I missed a chance to tell someone about Jesus. Then, in my extreme enthusiasm, when I first knew I could listen to God and get directions from Him, I certainly turned off a number of people. I mistakenly thought everyone would welcome the idea as readily as I did. My assumption was that I should tell everyone! Through my mistakes, God showed me that I must listen to Him and only speak when He tells me to.

Do not turn from it to the right or to the left, that you may be successful wherever you go. (Joshua 1:7)

There is no road to successful living except the way God leads you.

One evening, I watched a movie. The story was interesting and the actors were very talented, but scattered throughout the movie were expressions of foul language, giving the impression that this was an acceptable and normal way of speaking. No wonder crude language is being heard on the playground! Our society hasn't kept on the straight and narrow course of moral standards God set out for us.

The story of Rahab shows us that God went ahead of the Israelites to prepare the way. Rahab received two scouts in her home and decided to help them. She said:

I know that the Lord has given this land to you and that a great fear has fallen on us, so that all who live in this country are melting in fear because of you. (Joshua 2:9)

He also prepared the hearts of the Israelites to accept Joshua's authority, and His final act in clearing the way for them was to dry up the water of the Jordan River so they could pass over. What a mighty God He is. He's the same today as He was back then!

READ: Joshua 5–8

Circumcision was a sign of dedication to the Lord and an important preparation for the battle ahead of them. Before continuing, the Israelites celebrated the Passover. Another significant happening was that the manna ceased appearing and the land of Canaan began to provide the necessary food.

A heavenly being appeared to Joshua, giving him explicit directions for the taking of Jericho—and what a strange plan it was! With the ark, representing the presence of God, going before the people and the seven priests blowing their trumpets, the men began their march around the city. Imagine being one of those men—or one of the wives watching. Or imagine being one of the inhabitants of the city! What would you be thinking? And then it happened—the city was taken!

We can never reason out a situation and come up with God's plan. His thinking is just not the same as ours. What general would ever have given his men the orders Joshua passed out to his army? We must spend time in His presence if we want to get the mind of God, which is what He calls us to do.

Disaster came when a small contingent tried to take the city of Ai. Joshua and the elders went before the Lord to find out why they had failed. They found out that someone in the camp had been disobedient to God. Our personal disobedience can have a negative impact on the wider group.

> *Israel has sinned; they have violated my covenant, which I commanded them to keep… That is why the Israelites cannot stand against their enemies.* (Joshua 7:11–12)

That is a clear warning for us in the church today. If I'm wilfully disobedient, my family, church, or community may have to suffer for it. I cannot afford to hang on to the tempting resentments and bitterness that satisfy my ego, for they hinder the spiritual growth of those around me. A young woman once said, "But I enjoy my self-pity." There is certainly some satisfaction in wallowing in negatives, but the results can be deadly. Achan, the offending Israelite, had to be removed in order for the people to move on with God.

When they took time to get God's directions, the Israelites were able to conquer Ai. Joshua realized they had better get their minds in line with God's plan:

> *Afterward, Joshua read all the words of the law—the blessings and the curses—just as it is written in the Book of the Law. There was not a word of all that Moses had commanded that Joshua did not read to the whole assembly of Israel, including the women and children, and the aliens who lived among them.* (Joshua 8:34–35)

They all needed to hear the word of God—and so do we.

READ: Joshua 9–12

Joshua 9 tells of some people who feared the power of God as manifested in Joshua and the Israelites, so to save their own lives they tricked the Israelites into promising not to harm them. And here's where Joshua and his leaders made their big mistake:

> *The men of Israel sampled their provisions but did not inquire of the Lord.* (Joshua 9:14)

We cause many of our own problems by doing the same thing—making decisions without seeking God's direction first. Recognizing His leading comes with practice, but it starts with accepting the fact that God can speak to us, and what's more, He wants to do just that. Then we need to take time to be quiet and listen.

However, He has many ways of teaching us. I prefer the direct method, but He knows how easy it would be for me to become spiritually proud, so He often uses other people to teach me. We need to help each other get directions from the Lord through prayer, sharing, and keeping ourselves in tune with God.

Other kings banded together to try to defeat the Israelites, but God's plan couldn't be stopped:

> *The Lord said to Joshua, "Do not be afraid of them; I have given them into your hand. Not one of them will be able to withstand you... The Lord threw them into confusion before Israel, who defeated them in a great victory at Gibeon.* (Joshua 10:8, 10)

In fact, for the only known time in history,

> *...the sun stood still, and the moon stopped, till the nation avenged itself on its enemies... Surely the Lord was fighting for Israel!* (Joshua 10:13–14)

What a great lesson this is for all of us! Once we're committed to God's plan and constantly seek His direction, nothing can stop us. Obstacles will still appear, however. In fact, not only do I believe God allows this to happen, but sometimes He arranges it so we will learn to totally depend on Him. When we do, we catch a glimpse of His power and glory.

I recall a time when Bob and I were travelling by boat from Ireland to Wales. Suddenly, with a horrified look on his face, Bob turned to me and said, "My dental plate just broke. When I got one fixed in Canada, it cost thirty or forty dollars, and the repair took several weeks!" We began to pray, praising God for the answer He was going to provide. That first night in Wales, we were served a lovely soft meal with tender lamb that required minimal chewing. We chuckled our way through it and wondered how God would solve the rest of the problem.

The next morning, we were directed to a building which was at the end of a path found by opening a gate into a lovely garden. There we saw a table covered with teeth! We had two hours before having to make our way to our next appointment. The man at the table examined Bob's plate, checked it for fit, and said, "I'll have it ready in two hours." The charge was a dollar and fifty cents!

Nothing is impossible with God, and He has some unique ways of solving our problems.

READ: Joshua 13–16

Joshua was getting old, but there was still much to be done to get all the tribes of Israel settled into their land. God encouraged him to continue moving and dividing up the land among the tribes. He said that Joshua could count on Him:

> *As for all the inhabitants of the mountain regions… I myself will drive them out before the Israelites. Be sure to allocate this land to Israel for an inheritance, as I have instructed you.* (Joshua 13:6)

If Joshua continued to obey God, he would continue to win the battle. That's the key to any project we undertake—seek God's direction every step of the way and we'll see His plan unfold. It doesn't always happen the way we would plan it, but part of the adventure is being flexible so God can adjust our plans to fit His. Sometimes in my prayers, I try to tell Him how it should be done, but that never works very well and I end up tense and worried, trying to make it happen! There's a great deal more freedom and joy in handing the situation over to Him and saying, "Lord, You know my desires, but here's the situation. Please help me accept Your solution with gratitude." Letting go is hard, but the result is peace of mind, the desire of every human being.

Caleb had been Joshua's partner when Moses first sent a dozen men to spy out the Promised Land. They were the only two who were encouraging, saying, "Let's go! With God in control, we can move into this great land that can produce all the food we need." The people wouldn't listen and God sent them back into the wilderness.

I wonder how often we miss God's greatest plan for us because of fear—particularly a fear of failure. I have always been cautious, especially when it concerns spending money or stepping out into the unknown. However, God partnered me with a husband who was never concerned about spending money or trying something new. Mostly we balanced each other, although sometimes this caused problems as well.

Bob served in the Canadian Army and spent a year in Korea during that war. Twenty-five years later, the South Korean government invited the American and Canadian chaplains who had served there to revisit the country at the government's expense. Bob, bless his heart, said, "I'd like to accept the invitation if it includes my wife." It was agreed that if I paid half my airfare, the government would cover the rest of the expenses. What an opportunity! But the trip came in June, and at the time I was teaching in the public school system.

Our daughter, who had just completed her Bachelor of Education, put her name on the substitute list and my principal allowed her to take over my class. She helped me out for several days. When I left, she carried on with the teaching. In my quiet-time notebook, I wrote:

It was a miracle, an unexpected gift that seemed to come straight from heaven! How else could a school teacher go to Korea for one week in June?

At eighty-five years of age, Caleb was ready to face the enemy, claiming the land in the Lord's name. What an amazing fellow he must have been!

So Hebron has belonged to Caleb... ever since, because he followed the Lord, the God of Israel, wholeheartedly. (Joshua 14:14)

READ: Joshua 17–21

In these chapters, we read of the allotment of land to the twelve tribes. The people of Gad, Reuben, and Manasseh chose land on the east side of the Jordan River, but all the rest were apportioned a section of the conquered territory. Gradually, various tribes were placed until there were seven left. Joshua seemed impatient with them when he said,

How long will you wait before you begin to take possession of the land that the Lord, the God of your fathers, has given you? (Joshua 18:3)

Three men from each tribe were sent to survey the land and divide it into seven portions. When they returned, Joshua cast lots to see where each tribe should settle. So, they finished dividing the land—an amazing feat, considering their large numbers! Certain cities were then designated for the Levites as their inheritance.

So the Lord gave Israel all the land he had sworn to give their forefathers, and they took possession of it and settled there. The Lord gave them rest on every side, just as he had sworn to their forefathers. Not one of their enemies withstood them; the Lord handed all their enemies over to them. Not one of all the Lord's good promises to the house of Israel failed; everyone was fulfilled. (Joshua 21:43–45)

At last, God's promise to Abraham of a land for his people was fulfilled—hundreds of years and many generations later. Maybe it could have happened sooner, if the people had listened to God more closely and obeyed Him. We may let down our side of a promise, but God never fails to carry out His covenant. However, we need to stretch our vision to see the plan of God, a plan which stretches from the creation of the world into Eternity, and appreciate our part in it.

Abraham, Isaac, Jacob, Joseph, Moses, Joshua, and every man and woman born into the Israelite family had a part to play in bringing their nation to the point where it settled in the land God promised to their founder—Abraham. Each person either furthered God's plan or hindered it every day of his or her life.

That's how important my life is in the history of my country. Canada will either be a better country because of my life or a worse one. I ask God daily to help me send forth attitudes of thanksgiving, love, and appreciation so I won't pollute the atmosphere around me with negativity. It takes discipline to switch channels and change thought patterns, but it does get easier with practice.

God planned for me to be born a Canadian. He has a specific plan for my life. The extent to which I follow His plan is the extent to which I help my nation fulfill its destiny in God's plan for the world! It's a mighty goal worth striving for—and we can all take it on together.

READ: Joshua 22–24

A misunderstanding arose between the bulk of the Israelites and those who had helped in the battles and now returned to their homes across the Jordan River. The Reubenites, the Gadites, and the half-tribe of Manasseh built an altar as a witness to future generations that they were a part of Israel and were followers of God. However, the others thought they meant this as a place to worship idols, which upset them so much that they were ready to go to war! Fortunately, a delegation was sent to inquire the meaning of the altar and found it wasn't a rebellion against God at all. Having one group turn from God to idols could have meant disaster for the whole nation.

Seeing humanism, materialism, and even Satan worship creep into our society doesn't bode well for the future of our country. God has created us for Himself. If we stray from Him, we prepare the way for our own destruction.

Joshua was now an old man and knew his days were numbered. His last message to his people was a strong reminder of their responsibility to be God's people and give Him the glory for their victories.

One of you routs a thousand, because the Lord your God fights for you, just as he promised... You know with all your heart and soul that not one of all the good promises the Lord your God gave you has failed. Every promise has been fulfilled; not one has failed. (Joshua 23:10, 14)

But he adds a warning:

But just as every good promise of the Lord your God has come true, so the Lord will bring on you all the evil He has threatened. (Joshua 23:15)

This is the warning of a wise parent to his child: "If you disobey this rule, you will be punished." Most children need this kind of discipline. As parents, we know it is no kindness to let our children get away with bad behaviour when they are small. There are dire consequences if they continue the wrongdoing into adulthood. God, a loving Heavenly Father, longs to lead us in the right way; sometimes it takes a tragedy to draw our attention to the fact that we have strayed from His path.

Joshua's final challenge was this:

...choose for yourselves this day whom you will serve... But as for me and my household, we will serve the Lord... And the people said to Joshua, "We will serve the Lord our God and obey him." (Joshua 24:15, 24)

As long as those particular people lived, they were faithful to the Lord, but their obedience didn't last into the next generation. Each person is responsible for his or her own decisions; we cannot trade on our parents' reputation. As is so often said, "God has no grandchildren." Only I can choose the course of my own life. That is the freedom God has given to each of us.

THE BOOK OF
Luke

READ: Luke 1

Luke, a doctor, an educated man, checked out the stories he had heard about Jesus and then put them down in an orderly account for his friend Theophilus. He is the only one of the Gospel writers who tells of the appearance of the angel to Zechariah.

This wonderful first chapter tells of two miracle births and the divine plan that was to affect the whole world from that point on. As a woman, I thrill to the intervention of God in the lives of these two special ladies.

Elizabeth was beyond the childbearing age, but God chose her to be the mother of John the Baptist, who was to prepare the hearts of the people to receive Jesus.

...and he will be filled with the Holy Spirit even from birth.
Many of the people of Israel will he bring back to the Lord their God... to make ready a people prepared for the Lord. (Luke 1:15–17)

Afterward, Mary, a girl probably in her teens, engaged to be married to Joseph, also had a visitation from an angel. He assured her that she need not be afraid, for she had *"found favor with God"* (Luke 1:30). Can you imagine the emotions she must have felt as the angel told her she was to have a baby boy through the power of the Holy Spirit, and that He would be called holy, the Son of God? To reassure her, the angel told her of the other miracle: Elizabeth, who was related to her, was already six months pregnant.

I never cease to marvel at Mary's quiet acceptance of this astounding announcement that she was to give birth to the Messiah!

> *"I am the Lord's servant,"* Mary answered. *"May it be as you have said."*
> *Then the angel left her.* (Luke 1:38)

It always takes me time to accept a new step I should take—even a small one. For several weeks in our church bulletin, there was a notice that a young couple needed a place to stay for a month. We had a guest room, but right from the start I didn't consider offering it. When Bob mentioned it, my immediate reaction was "No way." I thought no more about it.

A few Sundays later, I saw the notice again and sensed the Lord saying, "You could have them at your house, you know." Even then, it took me another week to tell our pastor I was willing.

But Mary immediately told the Lord she was willing to accept His plan, even though it could have meant disgrace in the eyes of her family. And what would Joseph say? Would he break their engagement? She didn't know how others would react, but she was totally willing to trust God with the results.

> *And Mary said, "My soul glorifies the Lord and my spirit rejoices in God my Savior, for he has been mindful of the humble state of his servant."* (Luke 1:46–48)

No wonder God chose her to be the mother of Jesus!

There was one person who would understand something of how Mary felt—Elizabeth. So Mary hurried across the hills to visit her. The three months these two ladies spent together must have been a wonderful time of sharing and praising God! I would love to have been there with them!

When John was born, the Lord gave Zechariah prophetic words concerning him. God's plan for the redemption of the world was about to begin.

READ: Luke 2

The first part of this chapter is probably the most familiar section of the whole Bible. Everyone knows this story, even those who haven't developed a personal relationship with Jesus. In fact, it's so familiar that we miss the wonder of it all. If there is any event in history that happened exactly as God planned, this is it—the birth of His Son to a totally committed and willing mother. But what an astounding plan it was!

Today, most babies are born in a hospital where everything is clean and sanitary. But Jesus was born in a stable—the lowliest place I can think of. He was born among animals, a smelly place without furniture, and only a manger of hay for a bed! God used Caesar Augustus to get Mary and Joseph to Bethlehem, which is where He wanted Jesus to be born. He also arranged for all the others to arrive first, so there would be no hotel rooms left! Nothing came about accidently; all was as God wanted it to be.

He sent angels from heaven to tell a group of shepherds what had happened and left it to them to spread the word:

...and all who heard it were amazed at what the shepherds said to them. (Luke 2:18)

Matthew tells in his gospel that wise men from the east also received word of a newborn king. What a contrast! Local, lowly shepherds and wealthy, educated Gentiles from a far country. I certainly don't understand God's ways, but I marvel at them and get really excited when I find He can use me in some way to accomplish His plan!

I wish we knew more about Simeon. All the Bible says is this:

Now there was a man in Jerusalem called Simeon, who was righteous and devout. He was waiting for the consolation of Israel, and the Holy Spirit was upon him. It had been revealed to him by the Holy Spirit that he would not die before he had seen the Lord's Christ. (Luke 2:25–26)

As soon as he saw the baby Jesus, Simeon knew who He was. The Holy Spirit had led him to the temple that day. He took the little baby in his arms, felt his own life had been completed, and announced that this child would be:

...a light for revelation to the Gentiles and for glory to your people Israel. (Luke 2:32)

Mary and Joseph marvelled at these words. This prophecy meant Jesus had come for the Gentiles as well as the Jews. That meant the whole world!

They marvelled again when at the age of twelve, Jesus proclaimed God as His Father. Then He went home with them, was an obedient son, and grew mentally, physically, and spiritually. This is our great desire for all children—that they learn obedience, increase in knowledge and wisdom, experience good physical health, and develop a close walk with God.

The trip to Jerusalem with His parents is the last we hear of Jesus until He started His ministry when He was about thirty years of age. He had eighteen years of ordinary family life to prepare Him for His three years of teaching, preaching, and healing.

READ: Luke 3–4

Here we meet John the Baptist as an adult, preaching repentance as a preparation for Jesus' ministry. In answer to questions, he said: "Be honest in all your dealings and have concern for others." And here's a surprising one: "Be content with your wages!" Because he was critical of Herod, John ended up in prison.

In Luke 4, Jesus faced the temptations of the devil. But He answered each temptation with scripture, pointing to God's plan for humanity. The three temptations were:

1. Hunger for things.
2. Desire for position and power.
3. Protection from the result of foolish decisions.

Jesus answered each one with a statement of total trust in God. That's how we need to answer the temptations we face regularly.

Jesus began His ministry in His hometown of Nazareth, where He proclaimed in the synagogue who He was:

The Spirit of the Lord is on me, because he has anointed me to preach good news to the poor. He has sent me to proclaim freedom for the prisoners and recovery of sight for the blind, to release the oppressed, to proclaim the year of the Lord's favor. (Luke 4:18–19)

His neighbours couldn't believe this astounding news. Because He was in danger of their wrath, He left and began healing and preaching elsewhere. It often happens that the farther we get from home, the more important our message becomes.

As Jesus went about the countryside, He received a mixture of reactions. The people of His hometown so resented His message that they would have done away with Him. Evil spirits recognized Him and cried out against Him, but the crowds brought their sick ones and followed Him, even when He tried to escape to a quiet place.

People react the same way today. Many turn their backs on Him, but where His real presence is evident in the lives of those who proclaim Him, many others are attracted and want to receive His freedom.

READ: Luke 5–6

At the beginning of Luke 5, we read an impressive story of Jesus and His fishermen friends. Jesus had been teaching the people from Simon's boat. I can picture everyone gathered on the shore, giving Him some space so He could be heard. The water was probably calm and the day clear and sunny, as it so often is in that part of the country.

Simon had been fishing all night, so he was probably tired. Can you imagine his astonishment when Jesus told him to push out into the deep water and let down his net? No one fished after the sun came up, and besides, he had caught nothing all night in the same area.

Simon answered, "Master, we've worked hard all night and haven't caught anything. But because you say so, I will let down the nets." (Luke 5:5)

The resulting catch was overwhelming and Simon needed help to bring in all the fish! His reaction was unusual:

When Simon Peter saw this, he fell at Jesus' knees and said, "Go away from me, Lord; I am a sinful man!" (Luke 5:8)

Jesus' answer was reassuring and a bit puzzling:

Don't be afraid; from now on you will catch men. (Luke 5:10)

There are several insights we might glean from this incident:
1. If at first you don't succeed, try, try again. I remember my mother telling me this when I got discouraged.
2. Human reasoning isn't enough. In fact, it can get in the way of hearing from God. When we feel a nudging to do something that seems kind of ridiculous, it may be God speaking to us. If so, we need to respond as Simon did and be willing. We may be surprised at the results!
3. In the presence of God, our own unworthiness may make us so ashamed that we wonder how God could ever love us.
4. Jesus' assurance that He is going to use Simon Peter is an indication that we can be part of His kingdom in spite of our unworthiness.

Did you notice in Luke 6:12–13 that Jesus prayed all night before He chose His disciples? How dare we make decisions that will affect others without praying first! If even Jesus needed prayer to be sure of God's plan, it is very presumptuous of us to think our own wisdom is enough!

This chapter ends with the familiar story of a house built on rock or sand. It seems to me that obedience to God is the foundation of rock, and knowing but not obeying is the unstable foundation of shifting sand, which is an invitation to disaster.

READ: Luke 7–8

Even those of us who profess to be followers of Jesus have much to learn about faith. Here is an amazing man, a Roman centurion, who obviously recognized something of God's presence in the Jewish people, for they spoke of him to Jesus:

When they came to Jesus, they pleaded earnestly with him, "This man deserves to have you do this [heal his servant], because he loves our nation and built our synagogue." (Luke 7:4–5)

The centurion was aware of God's power manifested in Jesus, for he sent word to Him that he himself wasn't worthy to have Jesus in his home. But he was convinced that if Jesus spoke a word of healing wherever He was, the beloved slave would recover. Now that's real faith! Jesus even commented on it.

Most of us have some trouble with divine healing. Anyone who asked Jesus was healed. In our day, however, when we pray for others, sometimes they're healed and sometimes they aren't. We know God is love and that He wants the best for us. We also know God never changes, so we find ourselves in a dilemma.

Here are a few observations I have collected over the years:

1. If I say, "God wants everyone healed," I'm saying that I know the will of God. I learned the error of this the hard way. A young pregnant woman asked me to pray for her unborn baby, because she'd had one little boy born with a congenital disease and he had died. In my presumptuous way, I said, "God will surely answer your prayer—a sincere desire for a healthy baby." But He didn't! The little boy was born with the same disease as her first baby and, at four months, he died. I really let that young woman down because she looked at me as older and wiser and I talked as though I had a special "in" with God. Fortunately, she reached out to God and He gave her an assurance of His presence and great love for her.

2. Many people have experienced spiritual growth through physical disabilities. We are all impressed with someone who can speak from a wheelchair and proclaim the love and power of God.

3. I believe that the physical body is just the tent that houses our soul—our real self. It's important to care for that tent and we can ask God for healing when things go wrong. However, where we spend eternity doesn't depend on the health of our bodies; it depends on the health of our souls.

I am interested in Luke 8, where we find out about a few of the women who followed Jesus: Mary Magdalene, whom Jesus had delivered from demons;

Joanna, the wife of Herod's steward (a Christian right in the king's household!); and Susanna (there is no explanation of who she was).

The message of the Kingdom of Heaven is for everyone, but not all respond. It's fascinating to watch how God works and see who He touches—often the one who is least expected to respond. But what a joy it is to watch the transformation He brings about in that life!

These two chapters are rich, indeed, in nuggets of spiritual truths.

READ: Luke 9–10

There's also a lot of truth and wisdom in the next two chapters. I want to point out a few examples:

> *Then he said to them all: "If anyone would come after me, he must deny himself and take up his cross daily and follow me.* (Luke 9:23)

At the time Jesus spoke these words, He hadn't experienced the cross and the disciples found it hard to comprehend His references to His coming death. I, too, have pondered it: what did He mean by taking up one's cross? Was He referring to suffering, to persecution, to death, or was He referring to obedience to God, an acceptance of His plan?

When I commit my life to God's plan, that doesn't guarantee health, prosperity, and success. For Jesus, it meant constant crowds following Him, accusations, and persecution—along with the positive side of love, friends, and the joy of doing God's will. Jesus calls us not to seek physical and material comforts (although these may come), but to seek God's perfect will for our lives. His perfect will for Jesus was to die on the cross for the sins of the world!

I wonder what His will is for my life. All I know is that it includes a daily, intimate walk with Him, which is more valuable than all the treasures of the world. Denying ourselves and taking up our cross daily—giving up all our personal goals to seek the will of God—is simple, but not easy. In Catherine Marshall's books, she calls it a prayer of relinquishment.

Jesus calmed the storm, healed the sick, fed the multitude with one boy's lunch, and then gave Peter, James, and John the amazing experience of the transfiguration. No wonder they didn't know how to react!

He sent the disciples out to try their hand at sharing the gospel with others. He also told them the story of the Samaritan who put himself out to help someone in trouble, then said, *"Go and do likewise"* (Luke 10:37).

Luke 10 ends with a visit to the home of Martha and Mary. Although these sisters loved one another, they were very different. Martha was a good hostess; she prepared the meal but resented Mary, who didn't help. That sounds like a self-pity trip to me—and a very familiar one at that. Jesus didn't deal with whether or not Mary should help her. Instead He dealt with Martha's attitude.

"Martha, Martha," the Lord answered, "you are worried and upset about many things." (Luke 10:41)

In my experience, praise and thanksgiving to God is the best prescription for an attitude problem.

READ: Luke 11

Lord, teach us to pray... (Luke 11:1)

That is probably the most important request we can make of Jesus: "Show us how to have communion with You." If we really want that, we need to ponder His suggestions—then put them into practice in our daily lives. For example:
1. Acknowledge God for who He is—a Holy Father, our Provider.
2. Accept the fact that we can be forgiven for our mistakes to the extent that we forgive others. The responsibility is ours.
3. God can lead us away from temptation.

Lived out daily, these principles can change the course of our lives!

Jesus goes on to tell us to be persistent in praying—keep asking, seeking, knocking, and God will answer through an ongoing dialogue. When our prayers are in line with His will, we will receive, but the condition is there. Only through consistent communication with the Father throughout the day can we receive what God has in store for us.

A few years ago, God sent a new wave of the Holy Spirit through the world. Even though I had read about it in the Bible, I didn't realize this experience was available today. I can remember wishing it was! Then I began to hear of it happening to people around me and I saw changes in their lives. Since it seemed to include praying and speaking in tongues, my initial reaction was, "Oh, I don't think I want that—what would people think?" Gradually that changed to, "Well, if God wants me to have it, I'm willing." Then, when nothing happened, I increasingly thought, "This is obviously of God, so I want it!"

I went to meetings where prayers were offered for the baptism of the Holy Spirit, but nothing seemed to happen. One morning, during my quiet time I read:

If you then, though you are evil, know how to give good gifts to your children, how much more will your Father in heaven give the Holy Spirit to those who ask him! (Luke 11:13)

It suddenly hit me. I had been insulting God by asking and not believing I had received. So I prayed: "Lord, I'm sorry for my unbelief. I will ask once more and then hang on to this verse and believe that I've received." I did that, and though no bells rang or lights flashed, a gentle peace filled my heart. As the days went by, I gradually became aware of more understanding, more boldness in talking about my faith, more love for others, more joy, and more enthusiasm.

One morning, I said, "Lord, I believe speaking in tongues is a gift from You, and since I want to receive all You have for me, please give me that gift now." I began to speak syllables that weren't English as I praised and worshipped Him. Each morning I practiced, and then one morning I realized it was flowing so easily that I knew the Holy Spirit was operating in me. An old chorus says it well:

What a mighty God we serve,
What a mighty God we serve.
Angels bow before Him.
Heaven and earth adore Him.
What a mighty God we serve.

READ: Luke 12

The underlying theme of this chapter seems to be: strengthen your relationship with God so you'll be ready to meet your Maker. While teaching the disciples, Jesus essentially says, "Don't be hypocritical by trying to appear good while you're hanging on to bad thoughts and habits. You will be found out." Some politicians and TV celebrities have experienced just that! You can't just drift along the Christian life and stay on track. Like an athlete, it takes self-discipline and training.

I enjoy watching figure skating on TV. It's easy to see those young people spending hundreds of hours gaining control of their bodies to be able to perform as they do. We, too, must spend many hours training—in our case, our minds—to come under the control of the Holy Spirit, so we can move smoothly and easily on the course set out for us. For each person, the pattern is different. Sometimes a contestant falls; hardly missing a beat, however, she gets back on her feet. In practice, I'm sure she looks honestly at where her mistake was and determines not to do it again. That's how we must operate.

Jesus said it's no use piling up earthly treasure and then saying, "Now I'm ready for the future. I can sit back and enjoy myself, do what I like."

But God said to him, "You fool! This very night your life will be demanded from you. Then who will get what you have prepared for yourself?" (Luke 12:20)

Every one of us is destined to die some time. Suppose it's tonight. Am I ready to meet Jesus face to face? What about all the effort I've put into gaining wealth or trying to be popular? I can't take those things with me.

But seek his kingdom, and these things will be given to you as well... For where your treasure is, there your heart will be also. (Luke 12:31, 34)

With blessing comes responsibility. With more knowledge comes more responsibility. With deeper experiences of God's presence comes more responsibility. Our responsibility is to live in a way that entices others to want Him. It's the most exciting and satisfying way of life, and it's offered to one and all!

READ: Luke 13–14

Repent or perish! The fig tree wasn't bearing fruit and was about to be cut down when the gardener said, "Let me dig around it and fertilize it and maybe it will produce." When I feel that things around me are being shaken, maybe it's the Holy Spirit saying, "Let me dig around her, stir her up, and give her some fresh insights. Then maybe she'll produce fruit."

Now let's look at Luke 14. Jesus is dining in the home of a prominent Pharisee. The Pharisees are still trying to catch Him in some false teaching. However, He takes every opportunity to teach a spiritual truth, such as:

1. The laws are guides, but love must come first.
2. Don't try to get the best for yourself.
3. Don't offer kindness only to those who can repay you.

The banquet story points out the fact that when we know Jesus is calling us, we take a terrible chance by refusing. The invitation may not come again!

READ: Luke 15–16

Somehow, with all their education, the Pharisees missed God's character and His plan for the world, so they missed who Jesus was and His purpose in coming to the earth. Because they hung on to their own way of life, they majored in the negative approach. One of the great joys in life is watching someone become willing to let go of preconceived ideas of life, to repent of wrong attitudes and abandon themselves to finding God's way.

A young man phoned Bob one evening around 9:30 p.m. and wanted to come over right then. We were early risers and usually went to bed early, so Bob suggested perhaps it could wait until the next night. The answer was, "No, this is important and we want to see you now." Well, he and his wife came over, having decided together that they wanted to repent and start a new way of life. There was great joy in our home that night, but more than that:

...there is rejoicing in the presence of the angels of God over one sinner who repents. (Luke 15:10)

It added greatly to our pleasure to picture the angels rejoicing with us over two saved lives!

The parable of the Prodigal Son is so familiar, but it has so much to teach us. The younger son was rebellious and squandered his money, but he admitted his sin and asked for forgiveness, which he received from his loving father. The older son was like so many of us who have been Christians for a long time. When we see the fuss made over someone who has just accepted the Lord, we get jealous and filled with self-pity. Self-centredness, in one of its many forms, seems to be at the root of all our sins!

The rich man and Lazarus remind us that this life doesn't go on forever, but eternity does, and we need to prepare for it here. We cannot assume that a loving God will accept everyone regardless of the choices they make here on earth. He has provided in the Bible all we need to know to walk with Him. He has also provided for the Holy Spirit to be our comforter, guide, and teacher. He is a God of judgment and each of us will be held accountable to Him when our time comes to step out of this life into the next.

This warning is given in Luke 16:13—*"You cannot serve both God and Money."*

Either our goal is living for God or we have a different goal—money, success, popularity, etc. We cannot do both. When I strive for one of these temporal goals, I experience stress and worry, but when I seek God's will, I can relax and leave the outcome to Him while I take the immediate step before me. The stress is replaced by anticipation as I think, *I wonder how God is going to work this one out.* This is a lifelong process.

READ: Luke 17–18

Jesus said to His disciples: "Things that cause people to sin are bound to come, but woe to that person from whom they come. (Luke 17:1)

That's pretty clear! None of us live isolated lives, and everything about us influences the people around us. This shows up most when we are around children, for they learn by imitating adults. We tempt them to become dishonest when they see us not being totally honest. We tempt them to be critical of others when they hear us criticizing someone else. It is a serious matter when we show children a poor example.

It would be better for him to be thrown into the sea with a millstone tied around his neck than for him to cause one of these little ones to sin. (Luke 17:2)

Jesus even says we need to challenge each other when we see sin. Helping each other grow spiritually creates a bond between us.

Then Jesus told his disciples a parable to show them that they should always pray and not give up. (Luke 18:1)

Our sense of time and God's timing may be quite different. Sometimes He answers prayer right away. Other times His answer is "No, that is not My will." Still other times, the answer is "Wait." Not being very patient, we find that hard to accept. There are certain people for whom I have prayed for many years, and this verse helps me keep praying—and believing.

When we start praying for nations and leaders regularly, we see God's hand in events happening around the world. If we aren't in tune with Him, we miss the significance of it all. Right now, there are many major changes happening in the international scene and we hear about them almost immediately through modern technology. It's an exciting time to be alive—if you know you're a child of God!

However, when the Son of Man comes, will he find faith on the earth? (Luke 18:8)

Will He find faith in you? In me? In our churches? In our nations?

Jesus healed the blind man. A friend told me the following story. She was standing at the kitchen sink, feeling really concerned about one eye which had been causing her a great deal of trouble. She had been to the doctor and taken treatments, but she didn't know what the trouble was and was afraid she might go blind in that eye.

As she worked, she was crying out to God, "Please, Lord, show me the problem with my eye." He answered at once, "I'm looking through the eyes of Jesus and I don't see any problem. By His stripes, you are healed." The healing began that day and gradually her eye got better.

When we see through the eyes of Jesus, our negative problems become glorious opportunities for Him to work in our lives.

READ: Luke 19

I have always enjoyed the story of Zaccheus, an unscrupulous tax collector who became rich at the expense of others. Although dishonesty and a love of money was a way of life for Zaccheus, he was curious enough about Jesus to climb into a tree to get a better look at Him. I remember a minister telling this story once and saying, "Jesus looked up into the tree and said, 'Aha, you little rascal, I see you up there. Come on down. I want to stay at your house.'"

Zaccheus was ripe for repentance; he received Jesus joyfully. In His divine presence, Zaccheus saw his own sin and wanted to put things right. This is what happens when we come face to face with Jesus; we see our own sin. When that happens, we have two choices:

1. Confess, change, and follow Jesus.
2. Hold on to our sin and go our own way.

Zaccheus made his choice:

Jesus said to him, "Today salvation has come to this house…"
While they were listening to this, he went on to tell them a parable, because he was near Jerusalem and the people thought that the kingdom of God was going to appear at once. (Luke 19:9, 11)

Apparently, the people expected Jesus to establish the Kingdom of God when He reached Jerusalem. Maybe they expected Him to become an earthly king and free them from the bondage of the Roman Empire. Anyway, He wanted them to learn something from the parable.

Here's one way of looking at it. Suppose the nobleman who was to become king was Jesus and He gave three servants instructions of what they were to do:

1. The first one obeyed Him, so He chose him to take leadership in a responsible position.
2. The second obeyed Him, but only put half as much effort into it as the first one. So he was given a leadership role with less responsibility.
3. The third one did nothing and he was the one who lost everything. Jesus cannot use apathy!

When we accept Him as our Lord and become His servant, He asks for complete obedience and loyalty. Whatever amount we give Him, He blesses, but if we give nothing, we're of no use to Him. Those who rejected the new king lost their lives.

The triumphal entrance into Jerusalem drew the crowds and there was great rejoicing. His followers had such high hopes for the future! But Jesus looked at the city and wept. He knew they would reject Him and a time would soon come when they would be overrun by the enemy. It happened in 70 A.D., when the Romans destroyed the temple. Most of the Jews were banished and they scattered all over the world.

READ: Luke 20–21

In Luke 20, you can see the battle lines being drawn. The chief priests and scribes were out to get Jesus. It's disturbing to realize they were the religious leaders of the day. Is it possible that some of the church leaders of today are missing the mark and being used by Satan to try to foil God's plan?

Jesus told a parable to show them that He knew what they were up to. They became very angry and would have seized Him right there, except they were afraid of the people. If they could only get Him to say something that would condemn Him in the eyes of the Roman government! But no, God's plan was that He die for the sins of the world, not because of a mistake He made.

Jesus went on teaching at every opportunity. He provides a little glimpse of Heaven when He explains at the beginning of Luke 21 why it's so hard for a rich man to experience the Kingdom of Heaven. The reason is that rich people give out of their abundance; it doesn't deprive them of anything.

Someone commented on the beauty of the temple. Jesus reminded this person that buildings don't last forever and that there would be difficulties ahead. There would be false teaching, wars, earthquakes, and famines. There would be persecution for believers, too, but He said they would not have to worry about what to say when they were brought before kings and governors:

For I will give you words and wisdom that none of your adversaries will be able to resist or contradict. (Luke 21:15)

I get uneasy when I hear Christian speakers promise material prosperity to those who accept and follow Jesus. If that's what we're looking for, we cannot be true followers. He doesn't guarantee an easy, comfortable life, but He does guarantee He'll be with us to guide and show us solutions to every situation we face—if we let Him!

Jerusalem is mentioned and Jesus says it will fall to the enemy. It did, and for hundreds of years unbelieving Gentiles ruled the city. Even when Israel became the homeland of the Jews in 1948, Jerusalem was divided and the Old City with the temple mount was under Jordanian rule. During the Six-Day War in 1967, the Jews drove the Arabs back and the whole city became part of Israel. The Israeli government wasted no time moving the capital from Tel Aviv to Jerusalem.

Jerusalem will be trampled on by the Gentiles until the times of the Gentiles are fulfilled. (Luke 21:24)

Did that prophecy come to pass in 1967?

READ: Luke 22–24

Satan is mentioned twice in Luke 22. It was his influence that caused Judas to take the money in return for identifying Jesus. Then again, in Luke 22:31–32, Jesus tells Peter that Satan had demanded a chance to get at him, but Jesus prayed that the experience would strengthen him so he could be an encouragement to others.

It seems that God allows Satan to put temptations in our way. When we come through, by the power of God, He can use us to help others. It is a great comfort to know that whatever we face in life, God has a perfect plan to carry us through the ordeal. He will supply all the necessary wisdom, love, courage, and even material resources—if we fulfill the necessary conditions of praying and trusting Him completely.

Satan's power is evident in the trial and crucifixion of Jesus, especially in the crowd's choice to free a criminal instead of the Son of God, who never sinned. Even Pilate, the Roman governor, saw no sin in Him, but he couldn't sway the opinion of the crowd, who had been stirred up by those who wanted to condemn

Jesus. Satan had his way with Pilate, who, against his better judgment, ordered Jesus to be beaten and finally crucified. Pilate chose his own popularity and a secure position rather than take an unpopular stand for what was right. How human and weak he was! Even as I write that, however, I wonder if I would have done any better.

Even when Jesus was on the cross, we see the contrast between good and evil—Jesus and Satan. While those around Him scoffed,

> *Jesus said, "Father forgive them, for they do not know what they are doing."* (Luke 23:34)

One criminal mocked Him, saying, *"Save yourself and us!"* (Luke 23:39). But the other recognized the truth and said,

> *Jesus, remember me when you come into your kingdom.* (Luke 23:42)

Jesus portrayed a characteristic of God when He answered,

> *I tell you the truth, today you will be with me in paradise.* (Luke 23:43)

When anyone shows he's willing, he is received into the Kingdom of God.

Heaviness must have settled upon the believers when they saw Jesus die and His body was buried in the tomb. Though He had told them what would happen, the reality must have been devastating.

You can imagine the joy, then, when Jesus began to appear to different people and they saw that He had nail scars and that He could eat. But His glorified body wasn't like an earthly body; He could appear and disappear. This they could not understand, but they knew one thing—Jesus was alive!

This is the truth our whole faith depends upon. Jesus took all our sins to the cross. They were left there and we can receive forgiveness. He rose again and is alive forevermore. Hallelujah!

THE BOOK OF
Judges

READ: Judges 1–3

The move into the Promised Land meant war against the inhabitants who worshipped idols. God knew how easy it is for us to be drawn away from our faith in Him, so He told the Israelites to wipe out all the people dwelling in the land. His desire was for His people to be one with Him. That's all He ever desires! They didn't obey His command, however, and through an angel God said,

> *Now therefore I tell you that I will not drive them out before you; they will be thorns in your sides and their gods will be a snare to you.* (Judges 2:3)

Startlingly, the people of Israel again experienced the fact that their neighbours were their adversaries, and there were many dwelling among them who caused problems for their nation. As Christians, we need to constantly pray that God's will be done and that there may be peace in Israel. As He did several thousand years ago, He has drawn His people back to the land He gave them. His plan will be accomplished. Our prayers can be an important part of the drama we're witnessing today.

When Joshua and his elders died, the people forgot what God had done for their ancestors:

> *Then the Israelites did evil in the eyes of the Lord and served the Baals. They forsook the Lord, the God of their fathers, who had brought them out of Egypt… In his anger against Israel the Lord handed them over to raiders who plundered them.* (Judges 2:11–12, 14)

If we turn from God, we must suffer the consequences. When a child knows that he'll be punished if he disobeys his parents, he develops a healthy fear and respect for them. We need to have that same fear and respect for God's judgment upon us. If He's going to train us as His children, He cannot let us get away with wilful disobedience. God raised up a series of judges to guide His people back to Him.

> *Whenever the Lord raised up a judge for them, he was with the judge and saved them out the hands of their enemies as long as the judge lived.* (Judges 2:18)

For eight years, the Israelites served the king of Mesopotamia. Then God sent Othniel. The Spirit of the Lord was upon him, and under his leadership the people of Israel defeated their captors and enjoyed forty years of peace. Then, when they did evil in the sight of the Lord, Moab captured them and they were back in servitude for eighteen years! When they cried out to God, He sent Ehud, another judge, to deliver them—and the land had rest for eighty years.

God is not mocked, and when we look at the wars that were fought in the twentieth century, we can see that people haven't changed much since the time of the judges. We suffer the consequences of disobedience to God in every generation. I wonder, will we ever learn?

READ: Joshua 4–6

The pattern of disobedience, capture, and deliverance continued. For twenty years after Ehud died, the Israelites were oppressed by the Canaanites. Then God sent a woman, the prophetess Deborah, to be their judge and direct them to freedom. The defeat of the enemy and the song of Deborah show how the power of God can bring victory even when the odds are stacked against us.

As human beings, we don't seem to learn the lessons of history! If the Israelites had looked back to see the cost of disobedience, maybe they wouldn't have tried it again, but instead they again did what was evil in the sight of the Lord and were conquered by Midian, under whom they served for seven years. As Judges 6 tells, these years were very frustrating for them.

Here's a lesson for us: as soon as they cried out to God concerning their problem, God sent the Israelites a prophet to remind them of their deliverance out of Egypt and how He had warned them about turning to idols.

Then God, through an angel, selected Gideon. It's a delightful story. With a typical human attitude, Gideon questioned God (maybe a little more politely than we usually do).

> *"But sir," Gideon replied, "if the Lord is with us, why has all this happened to us?"* (Judges 6:13)

Who hasn't asked, "Why me, Lord?" Actually, that was Gideon's response when the angel told him that he should deliver Israel from Midian. He asked for a sign and the angel gave him one. Then the Lord put him to a test, telling him to pull down his father's idols! Gideon and his helpers did it at night, because he was afraid of the consequences. However, God had prepared his father; rather than being angry, he defended his son before the neighbours, who were ready to take Gideon's life.

Gideon had passed the test and God's Holy Spirit came upon him. He still wanted assurances that God would give them the victory, so his "fleece test" was answered twice. It seems that God quite often honours the fleece we put out before Him. He recognizes our weakness and how we need to know for sure that we're embarking on the right course. You'll notice that Gideon's "fleece" was an unnatural phenomenon that could only happen through the power of God.

God wanted Gideon in a position of leadership, so He tested him. But He also assured Gideon of His presence and guidance. We don't always welcome these tests, but if we trust God through difficult times, He finds ways to assure us of His loving presence.

READ: Judges 7–10

Now, here's the real test of Gideon's faith in the Lord. God's plan wasn't just to defeat the enemy, but for everyone to know they were defeated by His power, not by the strength of a powerful army. Gideon obeyed the instructions and his army of thirty-two thousand men was diminished to three hundred!

Gideon passed this test as well. This time, God reassured him by allowing him to hear two of his enemies talking in their tent of a dream one of them had had. His enemies decided that it meant they would be defeated by Gideon and his men. What a great way to build up his courage and cause him to be obedient in every detail to God's plan of battle. It was a very unusual plan, involving trumpets, torches and jars, but it worked!

Things didn't go well after the fighting was over, however. Even Gideon lost his way and wandered from total obedience to God. He died *"in a good old age"* (Judges 8:32).

No sooner had Gideon died than the Israelites again prostituted themselves to the Baals... and did not remember the Lord their God, who had rescued them from the hands of all their enemies on every side. (Judges 8:33–34)

Judges 9 depicts the violence that followed after Gideon's son, Abimelech, killed his seventy brothers and declared himself king.

Thus God repaid the wickedness that Abimelech had done to his father by murdering his seventy brothers. God also made the men of Shechem pay for all their wickedness. (Judges 9:56–57)

The years of the two judges Tola and Jair then passed, a total of forty-five years. Nothing else is told of that time.

Afterward came another period of Israel turning away from God. Serving gods of other nations and doing evil things go hand in hand. This hasn't changed over the years. Today, a very small percentage of people attend church on a regular basis, and probably even fewer have turned their lives over to God and seek His guidance daily. When we read the newspapers and listen to the news on TV or the radio, we can become depressed with what's going on regularly in our country—murder, sexual abuse, crime of every kind, adultery, and the breakup of families.

What will God do to bring this nation to Himself? We need to pray constantly for our leaders. Their lives can influence the direction our country goes. It is our duty, as Christians, to pray that they may be guided by the Holy Spirit.

When the people admitted their sin to God, He heard them:

Then they got rid of the foreign gods among them and served the Lord. (Judges 10:16)

READ: Judges 11–13

For the next thirty years, Israel had a series of judges—Jephthah (who made a rash promise to the Lord), Ibzan, Elon, and Abdon.

Again the Israelites did evil in the eyes of the Lord, so the Lord delivered them into the hands of the Philistines for forty years. (Judges 13:1)

It's all too easy to slip away from obeying God. If my eyes turn away from Him, I begin to respond to my negative reactions and get into all kinds of trouble.

Some years ago, when Bob and I were living with eight other Christians in a building we had rented for our private school, I had just such an experience.

My negative reaction about the amount of housekeeping I had to do reached full bloom in an angry outburst with my daughter and one of the girls—the victims. The following day, I wrote this in my quiet-time book:

> Lord, I need Your forgiveness for my self-righteous, resentful outburst yesterday. Thank You for the two girls, who allowed me to blow off without jumping on me. I don't always allow others to blow off and I need to learn how to do that, too. Anyway, here I am—self-centred, self-righteous, and resentful—a sorry mess! What can I learn from it?

Here is His answer: "Did I not wash the disciples' feet, and did I not say you should do the same? Have I not told you that serving others is a privilege, and when you choose to do it in a positive manner you will be blessed? If you choose not to do it, or do it in a resentful mood, you cut yourself off from the blessing. Here are the facts concerning the serving job: you have the choice—do it or don't do it. If you decide to do it, you can choose to be positive or negative. Only doing it in a positive manner brings about a blessing."

The rest of Judges 13 forms the beginning of the story of God's plan to deliver the people out of the hands of the Philistines. Even before Manaoh's wife became pregnant, an angel appeared and told her she would have a son:

> *...and he will begin the deliverance of Israel from the hands of the Philistines... The woman gave birth to a boy and named him Samson. He grew and the Lord blessed him.* (Judges 13:5, 24)

God never leaves us. We may stray from Him and suffer the consequences, but He always has a plan to get us back on track, a plan which He will reveal to us as soon as we're ready to listen. What a mighty God we serve!

READ: Judges 14–16

The story of Samson has always puzzled me. God chose him before he was conceived to be the one to deliver His people from the Philistines, which meant somehow defeating them in battle. But what unusual methods were used! Although it doesn't speak of him seeking God's guidance, at several points it is evident that God was with him.

When he wanted to marry a Philistine girl, his parents encouraged him to seek a wife from among his own people:

> *But Samson said to his father, "Get her for me. She's the right one for me." (His parents did not know that this was from the Lord, who was seeking an*

occasion to confront the Philistines; for at that time they were ruling over Israel.) (Judges 14:3–4)

And further along in the same chapter:

Then the Spirit of the Lord came upon him in power. He went down to Ashkelon, struck down thirty of their men... (Judges 14:19)

God had given him supernatural strength. He might have given him an army to defeat the enemy, as He did with Gideon, but that was not to be. Samson was to fight the Philistines single-handed. However, there was a condition to his strength. Back in Judges 13:5, when the angel gave his mother instructions concerning the son to be born, he said, *"No razor may be used on his head, because the boy is to be a Nazirite, set apart to God from birth."* A Nazarite was one who separated himself to the Lord for a special purpose. He was not to drink wine, eat grapes, or cut his hair (see Numbers 6:5).

After killing a thousand men, Samson was thirsty and called to God in his need. God opened up a hollow place and water came out of it.

When Samson drank, his strength returned and he revived. (Judges 15:19)

When we drink of the living water God so readily provides, our spirits, too, are revived. In our need, all we have to do is call on Him.

Samson fell into temptation in his relationship with Delilah. When she cut his hair, the power of God departed from him and he had to rely on his own strength. He was in the hands of the enemy; they made him blind and put him in prison. As he worked in the prison, his hair grew again.

Finally, he called upon the Lord once more to give him extra strength to defeat the enemy of his people. God heard his cry, his strength returned, and Samson brought down the roof upon the crowd of people who were gathered together.

Thus he killed many more when he died than while he lived... He had led Israel twenty years. (Judges 16:30–31)

READ: Judges 17–21

The very last verse in this section is repeated several times.

In those days Israel had no king; everyone did as he saw fit. (Judges 21:25)

Within each of us is a desire for a king, a leader, a hero we can look up to. This strong desire may cause us to follow the wrong path in life. When Germany was down and out after World War I, they welcomed the young man from Austria who seemed to offer the leadership they longed for. However, Adolf Hitler didn't seek direction from God and it wasn't many years before he led them into another war to conquer the world for the Aryan race.

In more recent years, we've watched throngs of young people go into a frenzy over rock stars. In the field of sports, a favourite player can cause thousands to rise to their feet in thunderous applause. We all long for a leader, a hero, a king!

As we read on, we'll see that the people of Israel received a series of kings. These kings were given the awesome responsibility of leading the nation. Some of them realized their need of God and sought His direction, but others ruled by their own self-centred desires.

God made provision for that need in us when He sent Jesus to be our King. When we accept Him in the role of our personal leader, we find fulfillment in life. He never makes mistakes, He's always available, and He knows our every thought and desire.

Perhaps the Israelites wouldn't have had a civil war among their own people if they'd had stronger leadership. It's rather amazing to me how they rallied large armies together despite there being no mention of a general in charge.

The fact that they didn't disintegrate as a nation during these years is evidence that God's hand was on them. It's clear that He didn't choose the best, strongest, or wisest to be His chosen ones to reveal Himself to the world. But His plan continued, in spite of His peoples' weakness. He never gave up on them. Even to this day, they are still His people and He has called them back to that little land of Israel.

The more I read the Bible, the more I watch Israel to see what God has in mind for the whole world in this generation.

THE BOOK OF

Ruth

READ: Ruth 1–4

This is the beautiful story of a young woman and her mother-in-law. Ruth was a Moabite, but during her marriage to Naomi's son, she must have been impressed with this Israelite family and their belief in the one true God. After her husband died, Ruth decided she was ready to leave her own home and travel with Naomi to Bethlehem.

Naomi realized the difficulties the girl would face and encouraged Ruth, whom she loved, to go back to her family:

> *Then Naomi said to her two daughters-in-law, "Go back, each of you, to your mother's home. May the Lord show kindness to you, as you have shown to your dead and to me." (Ruth 1:8)*

During her time in Moab, Naomi sustained her faith in God and spoke of Him to these two young women. When Ruth decided to travel with her, she was even ready to accept this faith for herself.

> *But Ruth replied, "Don't urge me to leave you or to turn back from you. Where you go I will go, and where you stay I will stay. Your people will be my people and your God my God." (Ruth 1:16–17)*

Naomi serves as a great example for older people—she lived a quality of life that made the younger woman want to accept her God. For a number of years, I've prayed that God would give me wisdom to help younger women get to know Him better. I must say that I've been greatly blessed by my numerous young friends. Whatever I've taught them has been more than balanced by what I have learned from them!

Ruth's care of her mother-in-law completes the picture of the relationship between the two women—the older one encouraging and making suggestions, the younger caring by doing the physical work as needed.

Boaz recognized this when he said to Ruth:

May the Lord repay you for what you have done. May you be richly rewarded by the Lord, the God of Israel, under whose wings you have come to take refuge. (Ruth 2:12)

God certainly had His hand on this young woman. In fact, He chose her ahead of all Israelite women to be the ancestor of King David, and ultimately Jesus Himself. She became a link in the royal lineage.

Boaz's friends recognized the importance of meeting Ruth, for they offered this blessing over his marriage:

May the Lord make the woman who is coming into your home like Rachel and Leah, who together built up the house of Israel. (Ruth 4:11)

It was the sons Rachel and Leah bore to Jacob who originated the twelve tribes of Israel.

Ruth played her part in the ongoing plan of God for the world. And that's what each of us is called to do.

THE BOOK OF
John

READ: John 1

John begins his gospel with Jesus already an adult. He starts by explaining who Jesus is: The Word.

> *...and the Word was with God, and the Word was God. He was with God in the beginning.* (John 1:2–3)

It's difficult to convey who Jesus is in ordinary language, but somehow He was part of creation. He was the Word—God's communication with us.

> *In him was life, and that life was the light of men.* (John 1:4)

Only in Jesus do we truly see life as it is meant to be lived. He was a light for all of us to follow.

> *Yet to all who received him, to those who believed in his name, he gave the right to become children of God.* (John 1:12)

This concept cannot be explained; it can only be experienced! My identity as a child of God didn't come with my first decision to invite Jesus into my life. As the days and months went by and I had daily quiet times with Him, this truth became a greater reality in my life.

I can lose awareness of my position as a child of God through neglect—when I get too busy and skip my times with Him. That rarely happens anymore; through years of practice, I've come to value that relationship more than anything else. The fact is that prayer is a dialogue between two people who love each other.

I now accept the discipline of having a quiet time every day, whether I feel like it or not. The more quiet times I have, the more I look forward to them and they become a pleasure rather than a duty. My conversations with God are now part of my morning routine.

No one has ever seen God, but God the One and Only, who is at the Father's side, has made him known. (John 1:18)

In Jesus, we can come to know God. As I read through the Bible, that seems to be central in God's plan—that we should come to know Him. He had been revealing Himself in many ways through the ages, but in His only Son we now see His glory shine forth! But not everyone recognized Him.

John the Baptist prepared some to receive Jesus as he preached repentance (which is still the key to receiving Him). In fact, John prepared two of his followers so well that when he pointed out Jesus to them, they followed Him immediately. Andrew was convinced and told his brother that he had found the Messiah. Jesus began to collect a few men around Him to be His disciples, and the criterion seemed to be that they recognized who He was! Nathanael, who was doubtful when he heard about Him—*"Nazareth! Can anything good come from there?"* (John 1:46)—ended up saying,

Rabbi, you are the Son God; you are the King of Israel. (John 1:49)

READ: John 2–3

Jesus, His mother, and His disciples were all invited to a wedding in Cana. While they were there, a terrible thing happened—the host ran out of wine!

I wonder how Mary knew Jesus could solve the problem. Did God tell her, or had her son shown signs of a special power? Was it a mother's intuition that as God's chosen Son, He could do anything? In any case, she was so certain of His capabilities that she told the servants to do anything He asked.

I've always loved this story. Perhaps because it's so encouraging to find that Jesus was interested in the ordinary aspects of life. Perhaps because I can identify with a mother urging her son to help out their friends in a way she knew only He could do. He did as His mother wished, and since everything He did was perfect, the wine was the very best.

This, the first of his miraculous signs, Jesus performed in Cana of Galilee. He thus revealed his glory, and his disciples put their faith in him. (John 2:11)

Jesus increases our faith by giving us glimpses of His glory—for example, His presence and character. After this, He went to Capernaum with His mother, brothers, and disciples, where they all rested for a few days.

Jesus' ministry seems to have been spent preparing people to recognize the significance of His death and resurrection. The encounter with Nicodemus is a wonderful example of His teaching techniques. Like any good teacher, Jesus took Nicodemus from what he understood to a higher level of spiritual understanding. Nicodemus, having seen some of Jesus' miracles, saw Him as a teacher sent from God. Jesus gave him a new idea:

I tell you the truth, no one can see the kingdom of God unless he is born again. (John 3:3)

Nicodemus saw that truth, but only on the human level—the physical birth of a baby. Jesus then used a familiar physical experience (the wind) to explain the moving of the Holy Spirit. Nicodemus still didn't understand and wanted to rationalize—*"How can this be?"* (John 3:9)

In the next few verses, Jesus seems to say, "Don't try to rationalize. Just believe Me. I want to give you a glimpse of heaven, but I can't if you try to put it on a human level."

One summer, our daughter and her friend, both teachers, were asked to lead the children at a family camp. Expecting thirty or forty children, they made careful preparations, collecting all sorts of materials. On the first day of camp, they were presented with seventy children of varying ages! Of course, they prayed—what else could they do? God told them to drop all preconceived ideas and let Him direct them. He gave them creative ideas, beginning with a buddy system so each small child was cared for by an older one. Then they began to think of activities they could all do together. Everyone had a great time!

How often does Jesus say, "Don't rationalize. Just believe Me. I want to give you a glimpse of heaven"?

READ: John 4

Jesus' encounter with the Samaritan woman at the well is a good example of how He wants to lead us from a material way of thinking to a spiritual one.

1. He starts out by doing an unthinkable thing. He asks her for a drink of water. Her response is:

You are a Jew and I am a Samaritan woman. How can you ask me for a drink? (John 4:9)

2. Jesus moves from material water to spiritual, or living, water. She does not understand.

"Sir," the woman said, "you have nothing to draw with and the well is deep. Where can you get this living water?" (John 4:11)

3. Jesus explained a little more about living water: it satisfies to the point that there's no more thirst. The idea of no more thirst appeals to the woman, who is still on the material level. She wouldn't have to come to the well and carry water anymore!

4. Then Jesus reveals His divine nature by letting her see that He knows everything about her. From this, she realizes that He must be a prophet. But she's uncomfortable about her relationship with men, so she changes the subject.

5. He points out that salvation is from the Jews, leading her another step towards recognizing Him as the Messiah.

6. Jesus no longer speaks of Jews or Samaritans but of true worshippers, which could include anyone. This begins to awaken her spirit and she declares her belief in a coming Messiah and her faith in His teaching.

7. Jesus drops the bombshell: *"I who speak to you, am he"* (John 4:26).

8. The woman tells her friends that she thinks she has found the Messiah, and she brings them to Him.

9. They hear Jesus and many believe, not because of her testimony but because of their own encounter with Jesus.

They said to the woman, "We no longer believe just because of what you said; now we have heard for ourselves, and we know that this man is really the Savior of the world." (John 4:42)

We can believe in Him when we hear about others' experiences. But to begin a relationship with Him, we need to come into His presence ourselves.

When Jesus healed the son of the official from Capernaum, *"he and all his household believed"* (John 4:53).

There's nothing like answered prayer to strengthen our faith in Jesus!

READ: John 5–6

John 5–7, referred to as the Sermon on the Mount, is a capsule teaching of all Jesus' instructions for Christian living.

Some among the Jews found Jesus and His message very disturbing. In fact, many of us feel the same way, and immediately we're faced with a choice. Do we believe Him and follow Him, or do we find fault with Him? The church leaders of Jesus' day chose the latter, but they found little wrong about Him they could point to. They had many rules concerning the Sabbath. One of the Ten Commandments says, *"Remember the Sabbath day by keeping it holy"* (Exodus 20:8). They interpreted that to mean, "Don't work, don't carry anything, don't walk more than a certain distance, etc." And here Jesus healed a man on the Sabbath! That would do as one point of accusation. Then Jesus referred to God as His Father—that could be another reason to condemn Him to death!

Today, the same accusations go on. I've been a part of it myself. We become critical of someone's ministry or preaching, and instead of looking at how God might be using that person, we look for ways to accuse him of being wrong. As Christians, in our effort to be aware of the spiritual battle in the world today, we make mistakes when we put ourselves in the position of judges.

Jesus, speaking to those same people, makes two things very clear:

1. He is the Son and God is His Father.

I have come in my Father's name, and you do not accept me; but if someone else comes in his own name, you will accept him. (John 5:43)

2. God has made Him the judge.

For as the Father has life in himself, so he has granted the Son to have life in himself. And he has given him authority to judge because he is the Son of Man. (John 5:26–27)

We tread on dangerous ground when we start judging others!

The familiar story of the feeding of the multitude again shows Jesus using a miracle to bring people closer to God.

1. He asks a material question: "How will we feed them?"
2. Andrew states what is available. Obviously, the need exceeds the supply.
3. Jesus accepted what was there and gave thanks to God.

4. The food was distributed as He ordered. Everyone had enough and there was lots left over. The supply was greater than the need.

What a lesson! When we're in need, if we take what we have to Jesus, give thanks to God, then follow His orders, He will supply our need in abundance. We must be honest and straightforward about the situation, getting rid of all anxiety and panic, bring what we have to Jesus, and let Him take it from there.

So much is packed into these chapters. Jesus' words are the most important ever written. I don't understand them all, but as I read them over and over, new insights come—and often it's just what I need at the time. As long as I keep an open mind, I know I'll keep learning more! Negative questioning closes the mind to spiritual truth.

READ: John 7–8

There are many false teachings going around these days. Wondering how we can know what's really true, we listen to speakers and read books to learn their opinions. However, Jesus gives us one way we can judge for ourselves:

If anyone chooses to do God's will, he will find out whether my teaching comes from God or whether I speak on my own. (John 7:17)

The people who were against Jesus could not be for God.

"You do not know me or my Father," Jesus replied. *"If you knew me, you would know my Father also."* (John 8:19)

This is the safeguard against being drawn into wrong thinking: not only should you give your life to Jesus, but every day seek His will. Then you'll be in tune with His thoughts and be able to evaluate what you hear through Him. The other safeguard is to know what the Bible teaches so thoroughly that you can recognize when the teachings don't line up with the Word of God.

Stop judging by mere appearances, and make a right judgment. (John 7:24)

Right judgment comes from God and from knowing His Word.

Jesus referred to Himself as *"the bread of life"* (John 6:35). Now, in John 7, He speaks of the living water we can receive, and in John 8 He says that He's the light of the world. All these things are vital for life—food, water, and light. The message seems clear that only in Him can we have real life; without Him, we miss out on what life is meant to be. After all, He created us, and only the Creator knows the real purpose of His creation. So if I want to get the most out of life, I need to seek out His specific purpose for me. Only in that place can I find real satisfaction.

However, there is always more to come! No matter how long I live, I still have more to learn. I still enjoy going to workshops, taking courses, and reading books so I can expand my knowledge and experience.

To the Jews who had believed him, Jesus said, "If you hold to my teaching, you are really my disciples. Then you will know the truth and the truth will set you free." (John 8:31–32)

Knowing Jesus' teaching means we can recognize what's right. We will be free. We won't be buffeted about by various philosophies that gain popularity. Jesus goes on to explain this further:

Jesus replied, "I tell you the truth, everyone who sins is a slave to sin… So if the Son sets you free, you will be free indeed." (John 8:34, 36)

Jesus says He will be our bread and water (to meet our needs). He will be our light (to give life and show us the way). He will give us freedom (which we long for). Who can say *no* to such an offer?

READ: John 9–10

Jesus didn't check out the blind man's faith. In fact, He explained the reason for his disability: *"that the work of God might be displayed in his life"* (John 9:3).

1. This man had been blind from birth and everyone knew it.
2. Jesus used a strange method—spittle and mud, and a wash in the Pool of Siloam. The man had to obey in order to complete the healing.
3. Obviously, the people were curious, and their questions led them to observe Jesus more closely.
4. Sometimes it is necessary for us to suffer hardship (not of our own choosing) in order for God to do His work in us, in order for people to turn to Him.

When we say that we're willing to be used by God, do we mean we are willing to be used in this way?

Satan, using the Pharisees, went on the attack against Jesus:

1. The Pharisees said, *"He does not keep the Sabbath"* (John 9:16).

2. Next, the Pharisees put the just-healed blind man on the spot. His answer: *"He is a prophet"* (John 9:17)
3. The Pharisees then put the man's parents on the spot. Their answer: *"Ask him. He is of age."* (John 9:21)
4. They challenged the blind man again. His answer this time: *"I was blind but now I see"* (John 9:25) Then he became bolder and spoke in a challenging manner: *"If this man [Jesus] were not from God, he could do nothing"* (John 9:33). Instead of wearing him down with fear, the Pharisees' questions revealed honesty and strength. Their plan to intimidate him backfired, so they threw him out!

Jesus revealed to the blind man that He was the Son of God. The healed man recognized the truth, declaring, *"Lord, I believe"* (John 9:38). He was ready for a brand new life. But not the Pharisees; they went on questioning.

The sheep, the sheep pen, the gate, the shepherds, the thieves... what does it all mean? Jesus says that He's the gate, or the shepherd. We are the sheep.

As the gate, only through Him do we find safety and salvation. By going through Him, we can find food and shelter.

As the shepherd, He calls us by name. He leads us to the right place, where our needs are met. He protects us from harm. He prepares a safe place for us and brings us home at the end of the day.

Sheep, on their own, would have trouble surviving, but with a shepherd all their needs are met. But only if they answer his call and obey him.

Jesus, the good Shepherd, gives us more than we could supply ourselves—the abundant life. He says that we can know Him as He knows the Father, and they are one. He says there shall be one flock and one shepherd. We're still working towards that oneness, and so is He, two thousand years later!

READ: John 11

Mary, Martha, and Lazarus were close friends of Jesus. When Lazarus falls sick, Jesus suggests an amazing reason for his illness—the glory of God! Because the two sisters sent for Jesus, He was able to turn it into a time of glorifying God. How often do we miss the glory in a seemingly bad situation because we don't ask for Jesus' help? In order to get the most glory, Jesus waited two days, allowing Lazarus to die! Then He broke the news to the disciples:

Lazarus is dead, and for your sake I am glad I was not there, so that you may believe. But let us go to him. (John 11:14–15)

Thomas didn't seem to hear what Jesus said—his mind was on the danger to Jesus' life. Maybe He was weighing in his mind whether or not he was willing to die, too. He decided he would stay with Jesus even if it meant just that.

Then follows the wonderful story of Lazarus being brought back to life. Certain aspects of the story stand out for me. For example, Martha made a strong statement of faith before the miracle happened:

I believe that you are the Christ, the Son of God... (John 11:27)

Jesus wept with His friends. If I had known what He knew, I would have been bubbling over with excitement. I probably would have said, "Don't cry! Wait until you see what God's going to do!" Have you ever belittled other people's feelings when you knew something they didn't know? I'm afraid I have. Jesus entered into their sorrow. He didn't say, "Don't cry." He wept with them!

It took several acts of obedience for the miracle to take place. First, the stone had to be rolled away. Then Lazarus had to come out, be unbound, and let go.

Jesus gave thanks to God, so all would know where the power came from.

Many people believed in Jesus as a result of this miracle, but others reported it to the Pharisees! In the presence of God, we each have to make our own choice—to go with Him or turn away.

The spiritual battle was on. Caiaphas' statement (or was it prophecy?) was the deciding factor. At that point, Caiaphas took on Satan's battle. But it was God's plan that Satan should have victory until Jesus died, at which point God's power took over, showing that there's nothing Satan can do that God can't redeem!

So from that day on they plotted to take his life. (John 11:53)

While the Pharisees made their plans, Jesus withdrew to the village of Ephraim with His disciples until the time God had set.

READ: John 12–13

A dinner was served in Bethany in Jesus' honour. How appropriate! The dinner was held at the home of His dear friends, where one of His most powerful miracles had been performed. Martha served (fulfilling her special gift), Lazarus was His companion at the table, and Mary anointed Him with costly ointment, filling the house with fragrance. Each of the three, loving Jesus, played the role they were created for.

Into this perfect setting, we see Satan at work in Judas, who just couldn't stand the perfection of the occasion. Jesus rebuked Judas and pointed out that what was happening was part of God's perfect plan.

Many years before, God told Jeremiah that the Messiah would ride on a colt. His purpose in telling it probably wasn't so much for Jeremiah as for those who were with Jesus and for those of us who came after.

> *Even after Jesus had done all these miraculous signs in their presence, they still would not believe in him.* (John 12:37)

We find it hard to elevate our thinking above the material, everyday world, above our concerns over what we'll eat, where we'll live, what we should wear, what car we'll drive. So many things occupy our minds that we miss the spirituality Jesus offers us. Even when we see signs and wonders, we soon fall back into our daily routine and neglect setting aside time to be in God's presence. The people of His day had the same problem:

> *...for they loved praise from men more than praise from God.* (John 12:43)

The time was approaching for Jesus *"to leave this world and go to the Father"* (John 13:1). God allowed Satan to use Judas. Jesus, knowing His position, wanted to show how much He loved His friends, so He served them in the lowliest fashion possible, by washing their feet!

Poor old Peter; he always had trouble understanding the spiritual meaning of Jesus' words. Unless we allow Jesus to do things His way, we can have no part in Him. Again, Jesus turns the conversation from the material to the spiritual—physical cleanliness to spiritual purity.

> *Do you understand what I have done for you? ...you also should wash one another's feet. I have set you an example that you should do as I have done for you... Now that you know these things, you will be blessed if you do them... By this all men will know that you are my disciples, if you love one another.* (John 13:12, 14–15, 17, 35)

No wonder the world has trouble accepting Jesus when they look at the divisions among those of us who call ourselves His followers.

READ: John 14–15

Do not let your hearts be troubled. (John 14:1)

We are not to allow ourselves to be anxious or troubled. This is a command. When we get into that state, we should look at the rest of that verse:

Trust in God; trust also in me. (John 14:1)

If I turn my eyes upon Jesus, acknowledge Him as my Saviour and King, accept His forgiveness, and bask in His love, within a very short time I'll no longer be anxious and troubled. The more I practice this, the quicker it happens! It's important that I take this step before making any plans or decisions. Decisions made out of worry and anxiety are highly unlikely to fall in line with God's perfect plan for me!

It's amazing that Jesus is willing to be our vine—our source of life. And God our Father is the gardener! All we need to do is draw life from the vine and allow the gardener to prune, as well as clean off the bugs, dead blossoms, and dry leaves. Nothing is expected of us except to allow the vine and gardener to work through us to produce fruit. What a privilege! Separated from Jesus, we're like dead branches—worth nothing—but completely grounded in Him and saturated with His word, our prayers will be answered. God wants us to bear fruit; it is to His glory.

God loves Jesus as a part of Himself and Jesus says He loves us in the same way. The condition for receiving His love is to be obedient to Him. That's how He remained in God's love—through total obedience. We get an extra bonus of joy as well… Jesus' joy!

The command for us to love one another is the condition for us to be in God's love. If we cut down on love, we automatically move away from God's love. The closer we are to Him, the more we experience His love, just as a child experiences his parents' love when he is near them. I must keep my thoughts positive, loving, and filled with praise and thanksgiving so that my words and actions come from that clear, fresh pool rather than the pollution of negativity—fear, worry, criticism, and resentment.

Nearing the end of His time with His disciples, Jesus prepares them for the difficult times ahead. Thomas and Philip are still in the material realm—*"Lord, we don't know where you are going"* (John 14:5) and *"Lord, show us the Father"* (John 14:8). Jesus repeats some important lessons:

1. Living in Jesus provides us the way (direction), the truth (wisdom), and the life (purpose).
2. Knowing Jesus means knowing God. They are One.
3. When God lives in us, His words and works issue from us. Conversely,

if our words and works aren't in line with His, we aren't allowing Him to live in us.

4. When God lives in us, miracles happen just as they did with Jesus.

READ: John 16–17

In the first of these chapters, Jesus talks to His disciples; in the second, He talks to His Father in heaven. There is a spirit in the world that hates the spirit of God (evil vs. good), so we can expect opposition when we walk closely with the Lord. However, if we hold the Father's hand, He will not let us fall.

While Jesus was in the flesh, He was limited to being with the people near Him, but when He returned to God, He would send the Holy Spirit, the Counsellor who would be able to be with all people everywhere at the same time.

> *But I tell you the truth: It is for your good that I am going away. Unless I go away, the Counselor will not come to you; but if I go, I will send him to you.* (John 16:7)

When the Holy Spirit comes to us:
1. He makes us aware of our sin.
2. He makes God's righteousness (goodness, grace) available to us.
3. We need no longer be in Satan's power, because he has already been judged and condemned. Jesus has broken Satan's hold on the world through His death (making forgiveness possible) and resurrection (giving us eternal life).

The disciples hadn't yet experienced His death. He knew they would feel deep sorrow and grief, but when He rose again they would have great joy! What a lovely metaphor He gives us, by comparing this experience with that of a woman giving birth. She feels pain and extreme discomfort, but when the baby arrives, all is forgotten in the joy of new birth. She's even willing to do it again, enduring the pain so she can receive the joy. Many of our painful experiences bring forth new understanding and great joy.

Jesus talks to His Heavenly Father of all He has done and the followers who have believed in Him. This is an example of how we need to talk to God, sharing everything with Him and praying for those around us.

As Jesus prayed for His disciples, and other followers who would come later, so I pray for my own church family and the leaders in it, that:

1. Jesus may be glorified in them.
2. They may be protected from the evil one.
3. They may be filled with joy and the peace of God.
4. They may have unity with Jesus and with each other.

Jesus doesn't promise His followers an easy road, but He does promise guidance and protection. He says that Heaven (eternal life) is a relationship with God the Father and Jesus the Son. Nothing in this world is as important as building that relationship. It's the only one that lasts for eternity.

READ: John 18–19

Jesus went with His disciples across the Kidron Valley into the garden. Bob and I visited the garden when we were in Israel and saw some olive trees so old that they had probably been there when Jesus frequented the place.

In these chapters, we read John's account of the arrest. Jesus walked directly into the problem and identified Himself to the soldiers. As He spoke, the power of the Holy Spirit was so strong that the soldiers fell to the ground!

Peter, trying to avoid the problem (a very human reaction), resisted the soldiers and cut off the ear of one of the men with a sword. Jesus rebuked him:

Put your sword away! Shall I not drink the cup the Father has given me? (John 18:11)

Jesus knew this was God's plan and it had to be carried out at all costs. He offered no resistance, because He was obeying God and at peace. On the other hand, Peter lied to save himself. I probably would have done the same thing, but this was the exact opposite of Jesus' divine reaction.

Next, Jesus revealed to Pilate who He was and said that anyone really seeking the truth should listen to Him. Here was Pilate's opportunity to receive salvation, but he missed it by asking this question: *"What is truth?"* (John 18:38) How sad! I wonder how many opportunities I have missed through reasoning and questioning.

Pilate hoped the Jews would back off. This was the middle of the night and those present were the ones who wanted Jesus to be found guilty. Jesus watched those He loved—His own people—mock Him, totally missing the point of the message He had come to bring. How His heart must have ached for what they could have been! I wonder if He was thinking, *You foolish little people, buzzing around, trying to get your own way. All the riches of Heaven are available to you, but you refuse to go near and receive them!*

And poor Pilate—torn between Rome, popularity, and his own safety as well as the gnawing awareness that this Man wasn't an ordinary person. There was something strong and free about Him; He had a kingly bearing that was hard to understand. Pilate tried to set Jesus free, but the accusers knew his weak spot—Rome's power over him. Finally, Pilate gave up the struggle between good and evil and succumbed to evil.

This scene paints a vivid picture of how Satan pushes temptation at us. Faced with temptation, each of us must make our own choice. Pilate never rose above human, worldly thinking to the spiritual level. Jesus always wants to raise us there; all we have to do is let go of preconceived ideas and listen to what He says to us. Pressure from the crowd and fear of his own position won out over Pilate's deep awareness that not only was Jesus innocent, but He had the power of God within Him.

Jesus died on the cross with the sign over Him reading, "Jesus of Nazareth, the King of the Jews." The people of the day didn't recognize that Jesus was also King of the Gentiles!

READ: John 20–21

These chapters contain John's version of the appearances of Jesus after His resurrection. In other words, it's an account of some of the last times anyone saw Jesus during His time on earth.

Mary saw Him by the garden tomb, but she didn't immediately recognize Him. I wonder why? Had His appearance changed? It seems He was no longer in His familiar earthly form, an indication that He wasn't going to assume His former way of life. He was there to assure His disciples of His resurrection. His message to His dearest and closest friends was this:

I am returning to my Father and your Father, to my God and your God.
(John 20:17)

In this statement, He acknowledges them as brothers, children of the Heavenly Father. That must have been encouraging, after the discouraging experience of His crucifixion.

Later that evening, Jesus appeared in a room with the disciples, even though the door was closed. His greeting was the familiar Jewish one: *"Peace be with you!"* (John 20:19) In Israel today, the popular greeting remains the same: "Shalom."

Let's take a look at what else Jesus said on this very important occasion:

As the Father has sent me, I am sending you. (John 20:21)

The disciples were to take on the task He had started—namely, to let the world know that in Jesus we can have salvation, forgiveness, and eternal life. That was a pretty big assignment for eleven men!

Then He showed Thomas His nail-scarred hands. Suddenly, Thomas' spiritual eyes were opened and he declared, *"My Lord and my God!"* (John 20:28) Most of us won't physically see Jesus's hands, but we can experience the same spiritual awakening and know in our hearts that Jesus is Lord. Jesus said:

Because you have seen me, you have believed; blessed are those who have not seen and yet have believed. (John 20:29)

John tells in his last chapter the delightful story of the disciples' time with Jesus on the shore of the Sea of Galilee, the same place Jesus met the first fishermen who were invited to become His disciples. I expect there was some bewilderment among them with all the recent traumatic experiences they had gone through, so Peter decided to get back to something familiar and comfortable.

"I'm going out to fish," Simon Peter told them... (John 21:3)

The others, probably glad for something to do, went along with Peter, but that night they caught nothing. However, when they followed Jesus' exact instructions, their net could hardly hold the fish! The key to receiving the blessing is to hear and then follow Jesus' instructions to us.

We can feel Jesus' love for Peter as He challenges him three times concerning his love. His response to Peter's affirmation seems to say, "Love me and care for others." I would love to know more of what Jesus said and did on earth, but I think we have more than enough to whet our appetites for a personal relationship.

THE BOOK OF

1 Samuel

READ: 1 Samuel 1–3

Apparently, it wasn't unusual for a man to have more than one wife. There are a number of examples of this in what we've read so far of the Old Testament. Here we have another case: Elkanah had two wives, Peninnah and Hannah. It was a disgrace in those days for a woman not to have children, and poor Hannah felt it deeply. Peninnah didn't help matters any!

However, Hannah did what we should all do when we're concerned about something. She took her concern to the Lord.

In bitterness of soul Hannah wept much and prayed to the Lord. (1 Samuel 1:10)

When she explained herself to Eli, the priest, she said,

I was pouring out my soul to the Lord. (1 Samuel 1:15)

One of the great comforts about going to God is that I don't have to explain or excuse myself in any way, because He knows everything about me. I usually write down my frustrations, which helps clarify my thinking. It's a great relief to pour out my soul to the Lord. It's like handing the situation over to Him so I no longer have to bear the responsibility for it alone. God will undertake for me. It worked like that for Hannah. Eli encouraged her:

Go in peace, and may the God of Israel grant you what you have asked of him. (1 Samuel 1:17)

So Hannah went her way and *"her face was no longer downcast"* (1 Samuel 1:18). She left the matter in God's hands and He answered her prayer.

It's hard to imagine her giving up her beloved child when he was so young, to serve in the temple with Eli, but God's plan was being worked out for Samuel. Hannah was blessed with five more children!

> *And the boy Samuel continued to grow in stature and in favor with the Lord and with men.* (1 Samuel 2:26)

That reminds me of Jesus' boyhood (Luke 2:52). Samuel heard the voice of God when he was only a boy and was given a message for Eli and his sons.

> *And all Israel from Dan to Beersheba recognized that Samuel was attested as a prophet of the Lord.* (1 Samuel 3:20)

I can think of no greater honour than to be a channel through whom God speaks to others. I expect it could happen to anyone who lives close enough to Him to hear and recognize His voice. Probably the second best would be to know God was speaking through your child. I'm sure Hannah continued to praise God just as she had after Samuel was born.

READ: 1 Samuel 4–6

The Ark of the Covenant was a sign of the presence of God. He had given Moses directions for how to make it and said that He would meet His people within it.

Circumstances weren't going well for the Israelites. They were being defeated by the Philistines and many of their men were killed. The elders began questioning what was happening:

> *Why did the Lord bring defeat upon us today before the Philistines? Let us bring the ark of the Lord's covenant from Shiloh, so that it may go with us and save us from the hand of our enemies.* (1 Samuel 4:3)

As our nation faces economic problems and disunity among the political parties, we, too, need to seek ways to bring God's presence into our midst. We have no ark as a place for Him to meet us, but Jesus said we could each meet Him in our own particular spot.

> *But when you pray, go into your room, close the door and pray to your Father, who is unseen. Then your Father, who sees what is done in secret, will reward you.* (Matthew 6:6)

142

Regardless of our political leaning, each of us has a responsibility to pray for our nation and leaders so their decisions will be in line with God's plan for our country.

The Israelites did bring the ark home, but whether because their hearts weren't right with God or because they weren't ready to give God the glory if they won, the Philistines defeated the Israelites and captured the Ark of the Covenant. This brought great concern! Eli fell to his death and his daughter-in-law, on her deathbed, declared:

> *The glory has departed from Israel, for the ark of the Lord has been captured.*
> (1 Samuel 4:22)

The Philistines soon found out that the God of Israel is mighty and cannot be controlled or defeated by mere man! This can be a lesson for us all. We had better not play around with His plan. At that time in history, the promise of God was for the Israelites, and the ark represented His presence with them. The blessing it embodied couldn't be captured by unbelievers.

And so the ark was sent back on a cart pulled by two milk cows. But even the Israelites weren't immune to the chastisement of God when they broke the rules concerning the ark. When God finally had their attention, they said:

> *Who can stand in the presence of the Lord, this holy God?* (1 Samuel 6:20)

READ: 1 Samuel 7–8

The ark was brought to the home of Abinidab, whose son Eleazar was to be in charge of it. But that didn't solve all the problems. The people's attitude had to be changed. For twenty years, nothing happened. It was as if God had abandoned them.

> *And Samuel said to the whole house of Israel, "If you are returning to the Lord with all your hearts, then rid yourselves of the foreign gods and the Ashtoreths and commit yourselves to the Lord and serve him only, and he will deliver you out of the hands of the Philistines."* (1 Samuel 7:3)

Any barrier in our lives that keeps God out is an obstacle to our prayers being answered. I remember reading of a religious order of sisters who trusted God for all their needs. However, when things didn't go well, their immediate question was, "Which one of us needs to repent?"

Samuel gathered the people together at Mizpah. Before he prayed for them, the people fasted and said, *"We have sinned against the Lord"* (1 Samuel 7:6).

He [Samuel] cried out to the Lord on Israel's behalf, and the Lord answered him. (1 Samuel 7:9)

The Philistines were defeated according to God's plan, in an unusual battle!

To be delivered from their enemies, they fasted for a day, repented, and prayed. If we really mean business in some area of our lives, perhaps we should follow this example.

The dedication of Samuel to the Lord didn't carry over to his sons. Every person has to make the choice whether or not to be committed to God. A parent's faith isn't automatically passed on to his children, but a faithful upbringing certainly makes it easier for children to recognize and understand God's ways.

The elders of Israel began to ask Samuel to appoint a king so they could be like other nations. Here's where they recognized a human need but looked in the wrong direction for the answer. In every one of us is the desire for a king, a hero, someone we can look up to and respect, one who will never let us down.

I once spoke to a young man about our political leaders, discussing how there is no infallible system of government. Too many human weaknesses—such as self-centredness and the desire for power—crop up and undercut the best intentions of the party in power. He said, "The most efficient kind of government would be a dictatorship, but that's too scary, because no person can be trusted with that kind of power." We realized that our innate desire for a trustworthy leader can only be satisfied by Jesus Himself. He's the only King who will never let us down!

The Lord answered, "Listen to them and give them a king." (1 Samuel 8:22)

READ: 1 Samuel 9–12

God chose Saul to be king of Israel. He made it very clear to Samuel.

When Samuel caught sight of Saul, the Lord said to him, "This is the man I spoke to you about; he will govern my people." (1 Samuel 9:17)

This story makes me aware that God watches over everything we do. A group of lost donkeys caused Saul to meet up with Samuel, the prophet. From the time he was a little boy in the temple with Eli, Samuel spent much time in prayer and came to hear and recognize God's voice. While he was judge over Israel, God held back the enemy:

So the Philistines were subdued and did not invade the Israelite territory again. (1 Samuel 7:13)

Now Samuel was getting old. Under God's direction, he anointed Saul with oil and said to him,

Has not the Lord anointed you leader over his inheritance? (1 Samuel 10:1)

God touched Saul that day when he met a band of prophets.

...the Spirit of God came upon him in power... (1 Samuel 10:10)

When God calls us to a task, He also equips us to carry it out. Saul showed his leadership quality when he mustered up a sizeable army (thirty-three thousand men) and rescued the people of Jabesh Gilead from the Ammonites.

So all the people went to Gilgal and confirmed Saul as king in the presence of the Lord. (1 Samuel 11:15)

Samuel spoke again to the people of Israel, reminding them of all God had done for them and how they had wanted an earthly king. Although if they had accepted God as King and been obedient to Him, they wouldn't have needed a man to reign over them. However, He encouraged them:

If you fear the Lord and serve and obey him and do not rebel against his commands, and if both you and the king who reigns over you follow the Lord your God—good! (1 Samuel 12:14)

Samuel said he would continue to pray for them. That message holds true for us today: pray for the nation, turn away from wrong attitudes and habits, and seek God's direction.

But be sure to fear the Lord and serve him faithfully with all your heart; consider what great things he has done for you. (1 Samuel 12:24)

Gratitude to God brings us into His presence, and that's where we get our direction. Samuel warned, however, that there would be dire consequences for those of us who choose to do the wrong thing.

READ: 1 Samuel 13–15

A leader can only be reliable through total obedience. Saul, on several occasions, was *almost* obedient to God but not completely. God's standard is absolute, and it became evident that Saul didn't measure up.

When he became impatient waiting for Samuel, Saul went ahead with the burnt offering to the Lord himself—a task set aside for the priest. His reasons sound rather familiar—"My people are scattering, the enemy will come against us, I can't wait any longer." Fear, imagining the worst, impatience, lack of trust… I've experienced them all. They can be very powerful, to the point of causing wrong decisions. That's what happened to Saul.

> *All the days of Saul there was bitter war with the Philistines…* (1 Samuel 14:52)

Jonathan, Saul's son, fought alongside his father and was highly regarded by the men.

A time came when God spoke through Samuel and told Saul to go out against the Amalekites, who had opposed Israel as they came out of Egypt. This was a fulfillment of His word:

> *I will bless those who bless you, and whoever curses you I will curse.* (Genesis 12:3)

God's order was that all should be slain—men, women, children, and animals! God created man in His own image, to be like Him, and throughout history there have been times when whole nations were wiped out because their idolatry contaminated those around them. This was one example. That God would command this is difficult for us to understand.

However, Saul wasn't totally obedient, giving the excuse that they saved the animals to sacrifice to God! Samuel's reply is a great lesson for us all:

> *Does the Lord delight in burnt offerings and sacrifices as much as in obeying the voice of the Lord? To obey is better than sacrifice, and to heed is better than the fat of rams. For rebellion is like the sin of divination, and arrogance like the evil of idolatry. Because you have rejected the word of the Lord, he has rejected you as king.* (1 Samuel 15:22–23)

The emphasis here is on obeying God. It's important to spend daily time with Him in order to hear and recognize the thoughts He puts into our minds. It isn't enough to assume that if I go to church and offer to help in some activities, I'm obeying His will for me.

At the heart of God's call to each of us is a personal, ongoing relationship with Him.

146

READ: 1 Samuel 16–18

God already had His hand on the man He had chosen to replace Saul. Since Samuel had been faithful in communing with God, and then was obedient to His word, God entrusted him with the anointing of the new king. Had Samuel by himself chosen one of Jesse's sons, he might have chosen Eliab, the eldest, but God said to him:

> *Do not consider his appearance or his height, for I have rejected him. The Lord does not look at the things man looks at. Man looks at the outward appearance, but the Lord looks at the heart.* (1 Samuel 16:7)

What sort of qualities did David have that rendered him fit to be a king?

1. He had learned to serve. While his father and brothers met with Samuel, he was caring for the sheep.
2. He received the Spirit of God when Samuel anointed him.
3. He had an inner peace that flowed through his music and calmed King Saul.
4. He was obedient to his father Jesse.
5. He was trustworthy and courageous in protecting the sheep.
6. He was aware that God had chosen the Israelites for a special purpose.
7. He trusted God's power, not his own.

His words to Goliath, the Philistine champion, demonstrated David's relationship with God:

> *You come against me with sword and spear and javelin, but I come against you in the name of the Lord Almighty, the God of the armies of Israel, whom you have defied.* (1 Samuel 17:45)

He spoke of the reason he knew he would defeat the Philistine:

> *…the whole world will know that there is a God in Israel. All those gathered here will know that it is not by sword or spear that the Lord saves; for the battle is the Lord's, and he will give all of you into our hands.* (1 Samuel 17:46–47)

Our introduction to David shows a young man—a strong and brave young man, a good leader who readily gained in popularity as he became known to the people. He and Jonathan became close friends who understood and enjoyed each other. All this made Saul jealous, a negative attitude which drew the king further from God.

> *Saul was afraid of David, because the Lord was with David but had left Saul.* (1 Samuel 18:12)

Anyone who seeks God's direction in daily life knows the instant and wonderful bond that is felt with others who follow the Lord. Wherever Bob and I have travelled, we've been blessed by warmth and fellowship. Barriers of race, colour, denomination, and even language melt away as the common love for God draws us together, making us feel as though we've known each other for a long time.

On the other hand, if we choose to draw away from God and decide to go our own way, we feel uncomfortable with other believers and automatically draw away from them. This was Saul's position, and he became more uncomfortable and unreasonable as time went on.

READ: 1 Samuel 19–24

Saul's antagonism towards David reached such a height that he urged Jonathan and all his servants to kill David if they had a chance. This was very disturbing to Jonathan, so he warned David to leave. Then he tried to talk some sense into his father. It seemed as though he was successful, for Saul listened to him and said,

> *As surely as the Lord lives, David will not be put to death.* (1 Samuel 19:6)

However, when David won a victory against the Philistines, the intense jealousy returned:

> *But an evil spirit from the Lord came upon Saul...* (1 Samuel 19:9)

I don't understand how an evil spirit could come from the Lord, but that's what the scripture says. God doesn't have to explain Himself to me or to anyone else. I can't help feeling, though, that if Saul had been willing to confess his sin to God in a spirit of repentance, he could have been free from jealousy and experienced real love for David. I believe the course of his life could have been different.

In the meantime, Jonathan and David's friendship remained firm. In trying to help David escape, Jonathan incurred the wrath of his father, who warned him:

> *As long as the son of Jesse lives on this earth, neither you nor your kingdom will be established.* (1 Samuel 20:31)

He tried to get Jonathan to turn against David, since Jonathan couldn't inherit his father's throne as long as David lived. That didn't impress Jonathan at all!

What a deadly thing jealousy is! There was a period of my life when I was jealous of Bob's work among people while I was stuck at home. It was awful. I hated myself for it and struggled greatly to get rid of it. That feeling of "it's not fair" can wreak havoc in our hearts. Over and over again, I asked for the Lord's forgiveness and gradually the jealousy disappeared.

Saul continued to search for David, in order to kill him.

Day after day Saul searched for him, but God did not give David into his hands. (1 Samuel 23:14)

God had other plans for David. Even though David had an opportunity to kill Saul, he refused.

He said to his men, "The Lord forbid that I should do such a thing to my master, the Lord's anointed, or lift my hand against him; for he is the anointed of the Lord." (1 Samuel 24:6)

Saul, in one of his better moments, recognized David's loyalty:

"You are more righteous than I," he said. "You have treated me well, but I have treated you badly." (1 Samuel 24:17)

David promised he would not destroy Saul's descendants and Saul went home.

READ: 1 Samuel 25–31

David was a warrior and fought in many battles, but his desire to take revenge on one of his own countrymen, Nabal—a descendant of Caleb—was stopped by the man's wife. Shortly afterward, the man himself died. David realized that revenge wasn't right, that God was the judge; only He should mete out justice.

When David heard that Nabal was dead, he said, "Praise be to the Lord, who has upheld my cause against Nabal for treating me with contempt. He has kept his servant from doing wrong and has brought Nabal's wrongdoing down on his own head." (1 Samuel 25:39)

David married the widow, and another woman as well. This points out a weakness for women that comes out again later in David's life. Ever since God gave Eve to be a companion to Adam, the relationship between man and woman has been a wonderful gift. Both men and women have misused it throughout history. Destroying this most blessed relationship through infidelity or abuse weakens the very fibre of our nations. Long, strong marriages help both men and women live more abundant lives. There is security in a good marriage, security that allows both partners to give something worthwhile to the world around them.

David again had an opportunity to kill Saul, but he refused. This touched the king so much that he declared that he wouldn't harm David if he returned.

> *"I have sinned. Come back, David my son. Because you considered my life precious today, I will try not to harm you again. Surely I have acted like a fool and have erred greatly."*
> *... Then Saul said to David, "May you be blessed, my son David; you will do great things and surely triumph."* (1 Samuel 26:21, 25)

David still didn't trust Saul, however, so he lived among the Philistines for protection. At that time, the Amalekites burned down the town in which David lived and took all the women, including David's two wives.

> *...and David inquired of the Lord, "Shall I pursue this raiding party? Will I overtake them?"* (1 Samuel 30:8)

God assured him that he should rescue the captives. In our distress, if we turn to God, we, too, can receive guidance, just as David did.

Saul really got off-track when he consulted a medium for advice. When the battle raged again between the Philistines and the Israelites, Saul and his armies were defeated. He and all his sons died, a sad ending to a life that started out with such fine prospects. There's really only one victory, and it comes from staying in God's plan.

THE BOOK OF

2 Samuel

David was greatly saddened by the death of Saul and Jonathan. Even though Saul had pursued and tried to kill him, David saw him as the Lord's anointed king. Saul, as a man, didn't deserve David's respect, but Saul was the one chosen by God to be Israel's first king. David trusted God's choice.

There was something wholesome and good about the friendship between David and Jonathan. The latter had no trace of jealousy that David would be king instead of him, inheriting the position from his father. Each was willing to risk his life for his friend, and circumstances didn't affect that commitment. They trusted and were loyal to each other.

This brings me back to my relationship with Jesus. Though I fail to meet His standards, His love for me is never affected. Though I cannot reach His measure of love, He is pleased with the offering of love I do give. Although David spent several years running for his life, he had two securities he was able to count on—God and his friend Jonathan.

The war between the house of Saul and the house of David lasted a long time. David grew stronger and stronger, while the house of Saul grew weaker and weaker. (2 Samuel 3:1)

Ishbosheth, Saul's son, became king of Israel (the northern province) and David became king of Judah (the south). The war between them raged until Ishbosheth and his general, Abner, were killed. Then the people recalled the words of God to David:

You will shepherd my people Israel, and you will become their ruler. (2 Samuel 5:2)

They gathered at Hebron and anointed David to be king of Israel. It had been a long time coming. He must have wondered how the prophecy given to him by Samuel would ever come about.

One of the first things David did was conquer Jerusalem from the Jebusites.

Nevertheless, David captured the fortress of Zion, the City of David. (2 Samuel 5:7)

That was the beginning of Jerusalem becoming the beloved city of the Israelites. Jerusalem was held by Jordan until 1967, when the Jews drove the Arabs out of the old city and established Jerusalem as the capital of Israel. After regaining the city, the Jews wept as they gathered at the wall to pray and thank God for bringing them back to the city of David.

David continued to seek God's guidance in his dealings with other nations:

And he became more and more powerful, because the Lord God Almighty was with him. (2 Samuel 5:10)

However, he didn't seem to seek God's guidance in his relationships with women! He had a number of wives, and even insisted on Michal being brought back to him, in spite of the fact she had a husband who loved her.

READ: 2 Samuel 6–10

What a picture it must have been as the Israelites carried the ark of God to the city of David! The very presence of God was in the ark, and He is a powerful presence. There was great joy:

David and the whole house of Israel were celebrating with all their might before the Lord, with songs and with harps, lyres, tambourines, sistrums and cymbals. (2 Samuel 6:5)

Can't you just picture it?

For many years, most churches were sombre places. People were expected to be quiet and serious. Once the Charismatic Movement began, however, people sang, clapped, raised their hands, and even danced! More instruments appeared in churches and the music was lively. We began to make a joyful noise before the Lord, just as David and his people did many centuries ago.

Twice Bob and I visited Christ for the Nations Institute in Dallas, Texas when our granddaughter was attending college there. I'll never forget the joyous singing and praise in that auditorium each morning. Hundreds of young people singing, shouting, clapping, and dancing… abandoning themselves to praising God! I think King David would have loved it. We did!

Poor Michal didn't understand what was happening! Maybe she still resented the fact that she'd been dragged away from her other husband, who really loved her. Maybe this caused her to close her heart to God. Instead of recognizing joyous praise to God, she saw only what she thought was her husband making a fool of himself. She missed out on God's blessing.

I'm afraid I've done that. I've allowed criticism and self-centredness to take over my thinking, thereby missed the blessing God had for me. How unfortunate!

Through the Prophet Nathan, God revealed something of His plans and promises for David. When David heard it, he went before the Lord and prayed a beautiful prayer. 2 Samuel 7 helps us catch a glimpse of who God is and how He longs to find someone totally committed to Him, through whom His plan can be worked out.

David reigned over all Israel, doing what was just and right for all his people. (2 Samuel 8:15)

The king showed his love for Saul's family in his care of Mephibosheth. He continued to lead men victoriously in battle against other nations. Although David was a warrior, he had a tender, caring heart as well. Despite the number of wives and children he had, I expect he had real love for them.

It says in 2 Samuel 6:20 that David returned home to bless his family

READ: 2 Samuel 11–15

When God puts His hand on us for a purpose, it doesn't mean we won't have any problems. Nor does it mean we'll be free from all temptation.

David's lust for women led him to having a man killed so he could have the man's wife! Together, they had a baby boy.

But the thing David had done displeased the Lord. (2 Samuel 11:27)

God sent Nathan, the prophet, to confront David. When Nathan told the king a story about the rich man taking the poor man's one and only lamb, David was indignant and said he should be punished. Until Nathan pointed it out, David hadn't seen that his own actions were like the rich man's.

It's so easy to gloss over our own sins and explain them away, especially to ourselves! Failing to recognize and acknowledge our sin is probably one of the main reasons for lack of power in the church today. God knows we'll be tempted and fall, but unless we repent and ask forgiveness, He cannot help us.

That's one point in David's favour. He really wanted to be obedient to God and was ready to ask forgiveness when he failed.

> *Then David said to Nathan, "I have sinned against the Lord."*
> *Nathan replied, "The Lord has taken away your sin. You are not going to die.*
> *But because by doing this you have made the enemies of the Lord show utter*
> *contempt, the son born to you will die." (2 Samuel 12:13–14)*

Two things struck me in this passage:

1. When we sin, it's a sin against the Lord. If I harbour resentment against another person, it's a sin against the Lord. I may hide it from other people, but He'll know and be grieved by it.
2. When I willfully choose to sin, there is a cost to pay, and someone else may suffer for it. In this case, the little boy died because of his father's sin.

In the next few chapters, we read of the very serious problems in David's family, culminating in the attempt of his son Absalom to take over the position of king. Selfish ambition and struggling for power can cause great problems for people around you. In this case, it instigated a civil war, with the northern tribes (Israel) backing Absalom and the southern tribes (Judah) remaining loyal to David.

When the Levites tried to carry the ark into exile with David, he said:

> *Take the ark of God back into the city. If I find favor in the Lord's eyes,*
> *he will bring me back and let me see it and his dwelling place again. But*
> *if he says, "I am not pleased with you," then I am ready; let him do to me*
> *whatever seems good to him. (2 Samuel 15:25–26)*

David was willing to put his full trust in God.

READ: 2 Samuel 16–19

For the second time, David fled for his life from a man he loved. This time it was his son, Absalom. As David and his followers were walking, a relative of Saul began cursing him and throwing stones at him. When his friends suggested they do away with this fellow, Shimei, David said,

Leave him alone… It may be that the Lord will see my distress and repay me with good for the cursing I am receiving today. (2 Samuel 16:11–12)

In the midst of this turmoil, rather than retaliating, David showed humility and compassion. Probably he felt unsure of what God's plan was in all this and wondered what he was meant to do.

This reminds me of a story I heard long ago about Abraham Lincoln. One of Lincoln's opponents publicly called him a fool. A supporter asked him what should be done about it and Lincoln answered something like this: "He is a wise and clever man. If he called me a fool, he is probably right." So the matter was dropped.

When attacked verbally, my human reaction is to be angry, hurt, and defensive. Through the years, I've learned to stop and consider the situation, to see if there's any truth in the attack, and then decide if I should do anything about it. If there's nothing to be done, I must leave it in God's hands without any lingering resentment.

David did that, and further on in the story, Shimei came to ask his forgiveness. David could easily have taken the man's life, but he didn't; he forgave him.

Our Christian walk is made up of two types of relationships. The first is with God and the second is with other people. Really, that's all God asks us to do—to be in right relationship with God and man. Regardless of how others treat us, we are responsible for our own attitudes. The Bible makes that abundantly clear.

Absalom died and David grieved, even though he could now be restored to the position of king. Israel and Judah had been at war and a healing of relationship was needed between the two kingdoms.

READ: 2 Samuel 20–24

David was a warrior—a very successful one—and the fighting raged throughout his lifetime. He was supported by a group of thirty-seven mighty men.

History is repeating itself in Israel today. Since 1948, when Israel was declared a nation, a homeland for the Jews, all her neighbours have tried to destroy her. Israel is such a small area in the midst of large Arab nations. What sort of threat do they feel from the Jews? Why do they suddenly care about that little bit of land they ignored for so many centuries until it was given to the Jews? The only explanation I can come up with is that God has always worked out His purposes through the Jewish people. He chose to be one of them when He lived on earth, so it's a spiritual battle, with Satan using whomever he can to destroy

God's power on earth. Israel is still fighting to be established as a recognized and respected nation.

David knew that only in God could the right sort of victory be won. He was aware that, in spite of the attempts on his life, he lived because God protected him.

> *He said: "The Lord is my rock, my fortress and my deliverer; my God is my rock, in whom I take refuge… I call to the Lord, who is worthy of praise, and I am saved from my enemies."* (2 Samuel 22:2–4)

This is the answer for Israel today—to call upon the Lord and be obedient to Him. That should be our prayer for Israel, that the leaders look to God as their refuge and fortress and seek His guidance in the affairs of their nation. That is the answer, too, for each one of us when we face difficult situations and are fearful of the future.

> *You are my lamp, O Lord; the Lord turns my darkness into light. With Your help I can advance against a troop; with my God I can scale a wall.* (2 Samuel 22:29–30)

The book ends with David buying Araunah's threshing floor, on which he planned to build an altar and make a sacrifice to God. It was offered as a gift to him, but he refused, saying,

> *I will not sacrifice to the Lord my God burnt offerings that cost me nothing.* (2 Samuel 24:24)

The word "sacrifice" means that a price is paid. God doesn't want our leftovers. He wants us to give Him our lives as a living sacrifice.

THE BOOK OF

Acts

READ: Acts 1–2

Luke continues the story written in his gospel to tell what happened after Jesus' ascension. Jesus' last instruction to His disciples was that they should wait in Jerusalem until they were baptized in the Holy Spirit. He gave them this promise:

> *But you will receive power when the Holy Spirit comes upon you; and you will be my witnesses [at home and abroad].* (Acts 1:8)

In order to carry on Jesus' work, the disciples needed extra power from God enabling them to understand more, love more, and proclaim that Jesus was the Messiah, the Son of God. Strangely, for many years this power was missing in the church. In fact, many taught that the Holy Spirit experience was only intended to get the first church started and wasn't meant for today; they were therefore suspicious of anyone who claimed to have received it.

The angels who appeared as Jesus ascended into heaven left the disciples with another promise:

> *This same Jesus, who has been taken from you into heaven, will come back in the same way you have seen him go into heaven.* (Acts 1:11)

The disciples must have been overwhelmed by all this. What did Jesus mean when He talked about baptism in the Holy Spirit? Was He really coming back? If so, when? People today still ask these questions. There was only one thing for them to do to be ready for whatever was in store for them:

> *They all joined together constantly in prayer.* (Acts 1:14)

Some of the women joined them, including Jesus' mother.

Next, we read of the spectacular event when the Holy Spirit came into the room as *"a sound like the blowing of a violent wind"* (Acts 2:2) and the believers began to speak in other languages. Peter stood up and, instead of the uneasy fisherman denying his relationship with Jesus, he was a confident, bold leader proclaiming the good news:

> *Therefore let all Israel be assured of this: God has made this Jesus, whom you crucified, both Lord and Christ.* (Acts 2:36)

As the astounded crowd listened, they asked, *"Brothers, what shall we do?"* (Acts 2:37) Peter replied with the now-familiar words:

> *Repent and be baptized, every one of you, in the name of Jesus Christ for the forgiveness of your sins.* (Acts 2:38)

But he added:

> *And you will receive the gift of the Holy Spirit.* (Acts 2:38)

This gift is available to everyone. We can receive new power daily to become the people God wants us to be.

> *The promise is for you and your children and for all who are far off—for all whom the Lord our God will call.* (Acts 2:39)

READ: Acts 3–5

On the day of Pentecost, we see the results of the outpouring of the Holy Spirit on the group gathered together to worship God. When a crowd witnessed a healed man walking and leaping and praising God, he at once began to proclaim the good news of Jesus Christ. What a stir this created! Everyone had seen this man begging at the gate of the temple, and now he was jumping all over the place and thanking God for his healing. The witnesses were wide open to hear that the very God of Abraham, Isaac, and Jacob, whom they had worshipped through the ages, had sent Jesus into the world, and it was through faith in Him that this man was now in perfect health.

Peter acknowledged that it was through ignorance of the truth that they had put Jesus to death, that this had been foretold by God through the prophets. But he gave them this challenge:

> *Repent, then, and turn to God, so that your sins may be wiped out, that times of refreshing may come from the Lord...* (Acts 3:19)

But many who heard the message believed, and the number of men grew to about five thousand. (Acts 4:4)

When the power of the Holy Spirit is present, many are drawn to the Lord. I pray for that power to be evident in the church today, so that God's word may go forth to the world. We see so much going on in our communities that's wrong, and we feel powerless to change the course of events. On our own strength, we cannot do it. We must heed Peter's word and repent so that God can fill us with the power of the Holy Spirit. Only He can give us the wisdom and boldness Peter had.

Not everyone was excited to hear the good news. The priests and Sadducees were so angered that they arrested Peter and John, but afterwards they didn't know what to do with them. Peter again spoke up and declared that it was in the name of Jesus Christ of Nazareth that the healed man was able to walk. By having Jesus crucified, they thought they had gotten rid of Him. But no, He was still at work in His followers.

They threatened Peter and John, warning them to be quiet. When they were released, however, the two men joined their friends and prayed for the boldness to speak, and for more healings, signs, and wonders to be performed through the name of Jesus.

Again they were arrested, but this time an angel led them out of prison—the very sign and wonder they had prayed for!

Peter and the other apostles replied: "We must obey God rather than men!" (Acts 5:29)

We might heed Gamaliel's warning when we're tempted to criticize someone else's ministry:

...you will only find yourselves fighting against God. (Acts 5:39)

READ: Acts 6–7

The believers lived very near to each other, even sharing their meals. Being human, there began to be some murmuring about unfairness in the daily distribution of food. The apostles showed great wisdom when they suggested seven men be chosen to deal with this problem.

We will turn this responsibility over to them and will give our attention to prayer and the ministry of the word. (Acts 6:3–4)

Unless the work of the church is undergirded with prayer, murmurings and problems will arise. They may arise anyway, but if we're in fellowship with Jesus, He can give us positive, creative answers in every situation. Each man chosen for this new committee was *"to be full of the Spirit and wisdom"* (Acts 6:3).

They presented these men to the apostles, who prayed and laid their hands on them. (Acts 6:6)

The next verse is interesting:

So the word of God spread. The number of disciples in Jerusalem increased rapidly, and a large number of priests became obedient to the faith. (Acts 6:7)

We're inclined to write off all the priests as having been associated with the Pharisees in getting Jesus crucified, but apparently a great many of them became believers. Stephen, for example, was outstanding in his openness to receive grace and power from God. He was a prime target for those who were trying to stamp out this new wave of revival. As he stood before the religious council:

All who were sitting in the Sanhedrin looked intently at Stephen, and they saw that his face was like the face of an angel. (Acts 6:15)

I've never seen anyone whose face shone like this, but I can recall certain people who have had a special peace about them, a gentleness and concerned love for others. You can tell they walk with God because of their quiet wisdom and inner joy. It shows!

When the high priest gave Stephen a chance to answer his accusers, Stephen traced God's plan for Israel all the way from Abraham, culminating in Jesus, God's special gift to mankind. He pointed out that the prophets, God's messengers, had been persecuted and Jesus, the "Righteous One," had been put to death.

As his accusers raged, Stephen had a glimpse of heaven with Jesus standing at the right hand of God! With that assurance, he was able to say, as he was being stoned to death,

Lord, do not hold this sin against them. (Acts 7:60)

The glory of the Lord so filled him that he had the attitude of Jesus. Like Him, Stephen was able to forgive, even at the moment of a physically painful death.

And Saul was there, giving approval to his death. (Acts 8:1)

READ: Acts 8–9

The believers in Jerusalem were persecuted, but many of them escaped. God has a way of using a bad situation for good, and He used this opportunity to spread the gospel.

> *Those who had been scattered preached the word wherever they went.* (Acts 8:4)

A sure sign of the reality of the many Samaritans' experiences, people who listened and accepted Philip's message, is seen in Acts 8:8– *"So there was great joy in that city."* Where the Spirit of the Lord is, people experience great joy.

Simon tried to buy the power of the Holy Spirit from Peter and John! We still try doing this by performing good works and giving, but God revealed to Peter the deeper problem:

> *For I see that you are full of bitterness and captive to sin.* (Acts 8:23)

The Living Bible says "jealousy and sin."

Bitterness, jealousy, and other negative attitudes hold us in bondage. If we give them a place in our minds and hearts, we cut out the Holy Spirit, for He cannot dwell with sin. We cannot have both bitterness and Jesus living in us— the choice is ours.

It sounds as if Simon genuinely wanted to repent and be forgiven. I hope he did; his eternal future depended on it.

Philip's encounter with the Ethiopian eunuch presents an example of God directing us to be in the right place at the right time. Philip used the scripture the man was reading to bring him to a personal relationship with Jesus. Then he baptized the man to confirm his decision.

> *When they came up out of the water, the Spirit of the Lord suddenly took Philip away, and the eunuch did not see him again, but went on his way rejoicing.* (Acts 8:39)

Philip had given him the greatest gift there is.

Saul, who watched Stephen being stoned and *"[breathed] out murderous threats against the Lord's disciples"* (Acts 9:1), was feared greatly by believers, but God had other plans for him. When He sent Ananias to lay hands on Saul, He said:

> *Go! This man is my chosen instrument to carry my name before the Gentiles and their kings and before the people of Israel.* (Acts 9:15)

Saul's change from an opponent of the gospel to a believer makes for a great story. I wonder if people were praying for him? The determination and energy which he'd used in a negative way became a mighty force for good. Eventually, he became an example of total commitment to proclaiming Jesus for all succeeding generations! Only God knows the true potential of each person.

Peter, the bumptious fisherman, also became a powerhouse for God, a channel for healing to reach paralyzed Aeneas and bring Tabitha back to life.

The course of history was changing.

READ: Acts 10–11

I love this story of Peter and Cornelius! It shows God's unique plan for each person. Here was Cornelius, a Roman, who feared God, gave alms, and prayed constantly. What an example that is for us believers! God had something more in store for him, so He sent an angel with a very strange message:

Now send men to Joppa to bring back a man named Simon who is called Peter. He is staying with Simon the tanner, whose house is by the sea. (Acts 10:5–6)

Cornelius must have been filled with curiosity about the purpose of having Peter, a stranger and a Jew, come to his house, but he would have to wait several days before it could be accomplished.

In the meantime, Peter had received an equally strange message from God. A couple of days later, he arrived at Cornelius' house to find a number of people gathered to hear what he had to say. All present must have wondered what was going to happen, but because two men who loved the Lord were willing to obey Him, God was able to fulfill His purpose in the lives of everyone there. More than that, He was able to demonstrate that His anointing was for all people, not just the Israelites.

I don't expect Peter had prepared a sermon. He had no idea why God was sending him to Caesarea, but He opened his mouth and proclaimed the truth.

Then Peter began to speak: "I now realize how true it is that God does not show favoritism but accepts men from every nation who fear him and do what is right." (Acts 10:34–35)

Peter went on to proclaim Jesus and His power to forgive sin. Before he had even finished, the Holy Spirit fell on all who were gathered in that house. They began *"speaking in tongues and praising God"* (Acts 10:46). I would love to have been there! I can only imagine the joy they felt. No wonder they asked Peter to stay a few days!

Back in Jerusalem, the Jewish believers found it hard to accept that the gospel was for Gentiles as well. They had a law which prevented them from associating with any other people. But Peter's story couldn't be disputed.

When they heard this, they had no further objections and praised God, saying, "So then, God has granted even the Gentiles repentance unto life." (Acts 11:18)

We still limit what we think God can do. I heard a young man recently tell of his father being saved. He'd never expected it could happen, for his father was a proud, self-sufficient man. The son really didn't think God could change his father—but He did!

As the believers scattered because of persecution, the gospel was spread to Antioch, where:

...a great number of people believed and turned to the Lord... The disciples were called Christians first at Antioch. (Acts 11:21, 26)

God's plan was unfolding!

READ: Acts 12–13

The first disciple to lose his life because of his belief in Jesus was James, the fisherman. Herod was out to destroy the church.

When [Herod] saw that this pleased the Jews, he proceeded to seize Peter as well. (Acts 12:3)

The first persecution against the church was committed by Jews towards believing Jews. If we read history, however, we find that matters were eventually reversed; when Gentiles (or Christians) came to dominate the church, they persecuted the Jews. How strange that two groups of people who believe in God (who is love) would persecute each other! Following Jesus doesn't allow for animosity.

So Peter was kept in prison, but the church was earnestly praying to God for him. (Acts 12:5)

Then follows the great story of how God answered their prayer and sent an angel to lead Peter out of prison. However, the people who were gathered

at Mary's home couldn't believe God had really answered their prayer, figuring instead that Rhoda must have seen a ghost. Rhoda was so astonished at hearing Peter's voice that she didn't open the gate and Peter had to knock a second time.

I can certainly relate to their reactions. I earnestly pray to God, but I'm usually surprised when He answers.

The story of Herod's death presents an extreme and graphic picture of the danger of selfish pride. There was a time in my life when I developed an uncomfortable—and expensive—gum infection. I had let the problem fester too long and it became rather serious. In my quiet-time book, I wrote a list of what the Lord told me to learn from this:

1. You have prided yourself on your good health and your own wisdom in caring for your body, even to the point of being critical of those you felt were careless in their eating, resting, and exercise habits.
2. You have been proud of going to God for answers rather than asking people for help.
3. You have been proud of how you "suffer in silence" rather than complain about your aches and pains. All these prides have led to the problems you now have.

God uses various methods to get our attention.

If we refuse God's blessing, He may give it to someone else. Many of the Jews refused to accept Jesus, so Paul and Barnabas spoke boldly to them:

> *We had to speak the word of God to you first. Since you reject it and do not consider yourselves worthy of eternal life, we now turn to the Gentiles.* (Acts 13:46)

READ: Acts 14–15

Paul and Barnabas set out on the first ever planned missionary journey. It's interesting to follow their route on a map. It took hardy men to travel in those days, either by walking over land or sailing over water. Neither method was safe. On top of that was the persecution the missionaries faced. It's always easy to stir up a crowd.

> *But the Jews who refused to believe stirred up the Gentiles and poisoned their minds against the brothers.* (Acts 14:2)

When the Holy Spirit comes in power, there can be two extreme reactions. One is that the hearer will hunger to hear and know more, which can lead to total commitment to Jesus; the other is rejection, which can lead to violent opposition.

> *The people of the city were divided; some sided with the Jews, others with the apostles.* (Acts 14:4)

Paul and Barnabas had to flee for their lives, so they went to the area of Lystra and Derbe, cities of Lycaonia. In spite of the miraculous healings which occurred, opposition was stirred up again and Paul was stoned—but he recovered, since God had more for him to do!

Even within the church, there were problems. A disagreement arose concerning circumcision—was it to be required of the Gentiles? Paul and Barnabas went to Jerusalem to settle the matter. After some debate, they sent a letter to the Gentile believers in Antioch, containing this message:

> *It seemed good to the Holy Spirit and to us not to burden you with anything beyond the following requirements: You are to abstain from food sacrificed to idols, from blood, from the meat of strangled animals and from sexual immorality. You will do well to avoid these things.* (Acts 15:28–29)

That left them free to concentrate on the spiritual values emphasized in Jesus' teaching.

Following this, there was a sharp disagreement between Paul and Barnabas, who parted company. There's nothing wrong with parting company with another person, or a church, as long as we don't carry bitterness and resentment along. After all, it's impossible to have bitterness in my life without defiling others. Christians cannot afford the luxury of bitterness!

God can use any situation for His glory. In this case, Paul and Barnabas each took a new partner, so the missionary outreach was doubled!

READ: Acts 16–17

Here we are introduced to Timothy. Paul saw such potential for Christian leadership in the young man that he took Timothy with him as he visited the churches to encourage and strengthen them. Where they went was decided on the basis of God's leading. They must have spent time in quiet with Him, for He was able to stop them from going into an area where the people were probably not ready to hear the gospel.

Paul and his companions traveled throughout the region of Phrygia and Galatia, having been kept by the Holy Spirit from preaching the word in the province of Asia. (Acts 16:6)

They considered going to Bithynia,

but the Spirit of Jesus would not allow them to. (Acts 16:7)

In a vision, God then showed Paul where to go—Macedonia. God has ways of letting us know His will, if we seek it and obey.

It's sometimes dangerous to follow the will of God. He doesn't promise an easy road! When Paul cast a demon out of a slave girl, he and Silas were beaten and cast into prison. Rejection and physical pain can bring on all sorts of negative reactions—self-pity, anger, revenge, discouragement—but if Paul and Silas experienced any of these, they overcame them by prayer and singing hymns!

This should be a great lesson for us all, and certainly me personally. I don't like suffering pain, and I get defensive when I'm rejected in any way at all. I know from my own limited experience that praising God and giving thanks to Him can drive away the negatives and bring me back into His presence.

Paul and Silas knew this and lived out Jesus' injunction:

Blessed are you when people insult you, persecute you and falsely say all kinds of evil against you because of me. Rejoice and be glad... (Matthew 5:11–12)

Their obedience brought great results—prison doors were opened and the guard and all his family were saved. Our obedience opens the way for God to reach others.

In Thessalonica, too, Paul talked to the people in the synagogue first, declaring:

This Jesus I am proclaiming to you is the Christ. (Acts 17:3)

The Jews had looked for the Christ (or Messiah) for hundreds of years after the prophets foretold His coming. Paul tried getting them to see that Jesus was the One they'd been looking for. Some of them believed, but others were jealous and stirred up trouble. Here we see again how easy it is to arouse people against others.

Paul and Silas escaped to Berea, and then to Athens, a city full of idols. While there, Paul found an inscription to an unknown god, and said to the people,

Now what you worship as something unknown I am going to proclaim to you. (Acts 17:23)

He called them to repent and come to know Jesus.

READ: Acts 18–19

In Corinth, Paul met Aquila and Priscilla, who had come from Rome.

…because Claudius had ordered all the Jews to leave Rome. (Acts 18:2)

I cannot help wondering why the Gentiles throughout history singled out the Jews. Were they afraid of them, or perhaps jealous? It could well be that this is a prevailing strategy of the enemy.

In Acts 18, God again uses a bad situation for His own purposes by drawing this couple to Paul. Not only did they share faith in Jesus, but they were able to work together at tent-making, an important trade in those days. Several times, we read concerning Paul:

Every Sabbath he reasoned in the synagogue, trying to persuade Jews and Greeks. (Acts 18:4)

When the Jews opposed Paul and became abusive, he shook out his clothes in protest and said to them,

Your blood be on your own heads! I am clear of my responsibility. From now on I will go to the Gentiles. (Acts 18:6)

If we continually refuse what God offers, eventually the offer will be rescinded. It's extremely dangerous to hang on to self-will and close our ears to God's truth. We may lock the door of our own entrance into heaven!

Acts 19 describes the spiritual battle that's been going on since the time of Adam and Eve—God's plan moving ahead and Satan doing all he can to thwart it. John the Baptist's message, calling people to repentance, had spread as far away as Alexandria and Ephesus. They heard and accepted the challenge, but they didn't know Jesus had come to offer salvation. Nor did they know anything about the power of the Holy Spirit, and so the message of the gospel was completed in these people who were so ready to receive.

Through Paul, God performed many miracles of healing—both in body and in soul. This caught the attention of all:

> *In this way the word of the Lord spread widely and grew in power.* (Acts 19:20)

However, opposition also grew. Satan's method is to cause disruption and confusion, and we see him at work in this passage. He tried tempting exorcists to invoke the name of Jesus, but God stopped that. Demetrius, a craftsmen who fashioned silver idols, then began to riot against Paul and the other believers. I wonder, did that town clerk became a Christian? God certainly used him to speak words of wisdom and bring order out of chaos.

That's the spiritual battle: God bringing healing, love, and order while Satan causes division, hate, and confusion.

READ: Acts 20–23

In Acts 5, we see the pronoun "we" used. This is because Luke, the doctor, joined Paul in his missionary journey.

Paul's talk with the church elders from Ephesus shows his total commitment to obeying God's plan for him. He knew God had called him to preach repentance and faith in our Lord Jesus Christ. He also knew he was being called to go to Jerusalem.

> *I only know that in every city the Holy Spirit warns me that prison and hardships are facing me.* (Acts 20:23)

He had already been imprisoned, beaten, and stoned, so he knew what this torture could mean. He might have been excused for saying, "This is too dangerous and my message is too important to the world to take a chance on losing my life." But no, this is what he said:

> *However, I consider my life worth nothing to me, if only I may finish the race and complete the task the Lord Jesus has given me—the task of testifying to the gospel of God's grace.* (Acts 20:24)

Some years ago, I took a summer university course—two weeks of intensive work. I had some doubts about the prospect and asked myself a few questions:

1. Am I really supposed to do this at my age?
2. Won't I get too tired?
3. Can I read all those books in so short a time?
4. Will I be able to keep up with the other students?

In my quiet time, I read Paul's words about completing the task God had given him. I realized that I didn't need to worry about lack of sleep, or even wisdom. Isaiah said that they who wait upon the Lord will renew their strength, and James said that if we ask for wisdom, God will give it to us. That means I can go with confidence wherever the Lord leads me.

Paul did go on to Jerusalem, not long before a riot started up. He gave his testimony before a crowd, and everyone listened... until he told how God had said to him, *"I will send you far away to the Gentiles"* (Acts 22:21). At the word "Gentiles," the uproar began and Paul was taken into the barracks for his own safety.

To avoid a plot on Paul's life, the authorities took him to Caesarea to appear before Felix, the governor.

READ: Acts 24–26

Paul's accusers said this about him:

We have found this man to be a troublemaker, stirring up riots among the Jews all over the world. (Acts 24:5)

With words, we can paint a positive or negative picture of someone we're talking about. We need to watch the words we use. It's easy to malign another if our thoughts about him are negative—such as if we fear him, are jealous of him, or dislike him for any reason. A tongue can do a lot of damage!

Felix heard Paul, but his trial dragged on for two years. Then a new governor—Festus—came along who agreed to let Paul appear before Caesar in Rome. However, King Agrippa and his wife Bernice came to Caesarea and wanted to hear what Paul had to say. This was another opportunity for Paul to tell of his encounter with Jesus on the Damascus Road. No one can argue with a personal testimony!

Paul reminded them that the prophets had foretold the coming of Jesus; then he told how Jesus spoke to him and gave him a commission—to go to the Jews and the Gentiles:

I will rescue you from your own people and from the Gentiles. I am sending you to them to open their eyes and turn them from darkness to light, and from the power of Satan to God, so that they may receive forgiveness of sins and a place among those who are sanctified by faith in me. (Acts 26:17–18)

In Acts 26:20, Paul summarized his message to all people:

...that they should repent and turn to God and prove their repentance by their deeds.

The church today has lost power in the world because we haven't heeded this advice. Instead of daily coming before God so He can show us where we need to change, we become self-satisfied, even arrogant, looking down on those who don't believe as we do. We ask, "Is he a Christian?" If we think the answer is no, we either dismiss or try to change him. I once heard a speaker say, "I assume that everyone's a Christian. If someone tells me he's not, then the judgment is his, not mine." I have tried to adopt that same attitude, for without it I am in danger of breaking Jesus' commandment: *"Do not judge, or you too will be judged"* (Matthew 7:1).

READ: Acts 27–28

Paul was on his way to Rome, not as a tourist, or even a missionary (although he did perform that role), but as a prisoner. Back in Acts 19:21, when speaking of Jerusalem, he said, *"After I have been there... I must visit Rome also."* I'm sure when he said that, he had no idea he would be taken there as a prisoner!

It's worth following a map to see the places where they stopped. The most harrowing part of the trip was their crossing of the Adriatic Sea's open waters. Paul never lost faith that God was in control; he knew he had been called to Rome, to take the gospel to the people there, so he had to arrive safely. He was obviously praying for all those on board. When everyone else lost hope, Paul assured them no one would die:

Last night an angel of the God whose I am and whom I serve stood beside me and said, "Do not be afraid, Paul. You must stand trial before Caesar; and God has graciously given you the lives of all those who sail with you." So keep up your courage, men, for I have faith in God that it will happen just as he told me. Nevertheless, we must run aground on some island. (Acts 27:23–26)

If a person is in daily communication with God, He'll find a way to get messages to us. The world needs to know that, and we in the church need to practice it. I've never had an angel appear and speak to me. That would be a wonderful and most exciting experience! Perhaps someday it will happen. Many times in my life, however, I've known God has spoken to me, either to point out where I'm wrong or give some clear direction.

While at Trinity Western University, I finished all my assignments two days before the course was over. I spent many hours at the computer and felt rather drained afterward. One hot evening, after dinner, I walked down to a pond to watch some geese. While enjoying the peace and quiet from a shady spot, a very clear thought came into my mind. I recognized at once who had put it there. God said, "You've been willing to give of yourself beyond what was comfortable to complete the assignments for this course. Why are you not willing to put that much effort into the assignment I have given you to write?" I quickly got up, returned to my room, and began typing this book—the very one you hold in your hands.

Paul reached Rome and began spreading the news that Jesus, the Messiah, had come. Some Jews accepted this, but many rejected it, so Paul again realized the message had to go to the Gentiles as well. For two years, he proclaimed the gospel to all who would listen.

THE BOOK OF
1 Kings

READ: 1 Kings 1–3

Family rivalries have always existed, from the time of Cain and Abel. It is sometimes harder to forgive and forget differences between brothers and sisters than with others not so closely tied to us. David's family was no exception.

Adonijah's attempt to take over the throne from his dying father (although it was neither the Lord's plan nor David's) ended in disaster for all concerned. Solomon's mother, Bathsheba, intervened on the advice of Nathan, the prophet, and King David arranged the anointing of Solomon, who was proclaimed king of Israel. It was a great celebration:

And all the people went after him, playing flutes and rejoicing greatly, so that the ground shook with the sound. (1 Kings 1:40)

The next chapter begins with David giving his son Solomon some advice:

"I am about to go the way of all the earth," he said. *"So be strong, show yourself a man, and observe what the Lord your God requires: Walk in his ways, and keep his decrees and commands, his laws and requirements, as written in the Law of Moses, so that you may prosper in all you do and wherever you go."* (1 Kings 2:2–3)

God had promised David that if his sons walked faithfully with God, David's descendants would continue to occupy the throne of Israel. However, it was not to be, because man's part of the covenant was not kept. David's reign over Israel encompassed forty years.

Solomon had a vision from God and was given an opportunity to ask for anything he wished. What an awesome responsibility that would be! But Solomon's answer pleased God. After acknowledging God's goodness to his father, Solomon continued:

So give your servant a discerning heart to govern your people and to distinguish right from wrong. (1 Kings 3:9)

This is a good example for anyone in a leadership position. God said that Solomon's desire would be granted, and though he didn't ask for riches and honour, he would receive those as well.

When all Israel heard the verdict the king had given, they held the king in awe, because they saw that he had wisdom from God to administer justice. (1 Kings 3:28)

READ: 1 Kings 4–6

While David's reign was filled with battles and fighting on all sides, Solomon's reign was a peaceful time.

For he ruled over all the kingdoms west of the River, from Tiphsah to Gaza, and had peace on all sides. During Solomon's lifetime Judah and Israel, from Dan to Beersheba, lived in safety, each man under his own vine and fig tree. (1 Kings 4:24–25)

There was plenty of food for everyone, and Solomon has even been remembered for his huge stables of horses (twelve thousand of them).

God gave Solomon wisdom and very great insight, and a breadth of understanding as measureless as the sand on the seashore… He spoke three thousand proverbs and his songs numbered a thousand and five. (1 Kings 4:29, 32)

We get a few of these in Proverbs and Song of Songs, but the most astounding fact is the generosity of God when He pours out His gifts upon His children. His supplies are never-ending.

The time had come for a temple to be built in which to worship God. The Israelites' wanderings (which had lasted 480 years) had come to an end in the land God had chosen for them. The temple was to be the physical evidence of God's covenant with Abraham, Isaac, and Jacob concerning the land of Israel.

Solomon made an agreement with Hiram, king of Tyre, to receive cedar and cypress from Lebanon and to hire workmen who knew how to cut timber.

The Lord gave Solomon wisdom, just as he had promised him. (1 Kings 5:12)

Probably the greatest wisdom Solomon showed was that initially he obeyed God every step of the way.

The word of the Lord came to Solomon: "As for this temple you are building, if you follow my decrees, carry out my regulations and keep all my commands and obey them, I will fulfill through you the promise I gave to David your father. And I will live among the Israelites and will not abandon my people Israel. (1 Kings 6:11–13)

I haven't counted the number of times God stressed the importance of obeying Him, but that appears to be the theme of the whole Bible—Old Testament and New. God created man and woman in His own image and had a perfect plan for their lives. The world He created for them had everything they would ever need, but they had to discover the treasures for themselves. It boggles my mind to think about what life could be if we did not waste so much time trying to get a fair deal, accumulating as much as we can, seeking comfort for ourselves, and all the other foolish and vain causes we espouse!

God asks only one thing of us—obedience. All striving and stress is removed when I take the time to get God's perspective on a situation before I make a decision. My heavenly Father welcomes me with love and understanding whenever I make time to be with Him.

READ: 1 Kings 7–9

The temple Solomon built must have been a spectacular structure—the stonework, the bronze work, the cedar beams and pillars! The king secured skilled workmen like Huram of Tyre.

Huram was highly skilled and experienced in all kinds of bronze work. (1 Kings 7:14)

...and they brought up the ark of the Lord and the Tent of Meeting and all the sacred furnishings in it. The priests and Levites carried them up... There was nothing in the ark except the two stone tablets that Moses had placed in it at Horeb, where the Lord made a covenant with the Israelites after they

*came out of Egypt. When the priests withdrew from the Holy Place, the cloud
filled the temple of the Lord. And the priests could not perform their service
because of the cloud, for the glory of the Lord filled his temple.* (1 Kings 8:4,
9–11)

Solomon prayed to God with thanksgiving and asked for forgiveness for his
people whenever they sinned— *"for there is no one who does not sin"* (1 Kings 8:46).
It is easy for me to go on day by day, completely unaware of any sin in my life.
Oh, I may get irritable at times, wallow a bit in self-pity, try to manipulate people
to get my own way, or even get in God's way by trying to solve other peoples'
problems. But if I don't stop, acknowledge my sin, and ask God's forgiveness,
those same sins soon deaden my awareness of the presence of the Holy Spirit and
I begin to skip my quiet times. Constant confession and receiving forgiveness
sweeps away the debris and makes room for the Holy Spirit. Solomon knew this
was important.

*...so that all the peoples of the earth may know that the Lord is God and
there is no other.* (1 Kings 8:60)

When the world sees Christians living in freedom and victory, they will
know the Lord is God!

The Lord appeared to Solomon a second time and declared again that if he
would live as David did, with integrity of heart, being obedient, his descendants
would sit on Israel's throne. Then He gives a warning, that if he is disobedient:

*...I will cut off Israel from the land I have given them and will reject this
temple I have consecrated for my Name.* (1 Kings 9:7)

He adds that the temple will be in ruins and the world will know it is because
the Israelites forsook God and turned to other gods. All this did happen to Israel
in later years!

God's chosen people have an awesome responsibility to show the world their
God by demonstrating lives of obedience to Him. If we claim the blessings of
being His children, we must also accept the responsibility.

READ: 1 Kings 10–12

Solomon's fame spread and people were aware that his wisdom was a gift from
God. The Queen of Sheba had heard so much about him that she came to check
him out and ask some probing questions.

Solomon answered all her questions; nothing was too hard for the king to explain to her. (1 Kings 10:3)

She was impressed! She recognized God's hand on Israel, so she said to the king:

Praise be to the Lord your God, who has delighted in you and placed you on the throne of Israel. Because of the Lord's eternal love for Israel, he has made you king, to maintain justice and righteousness... The whole earth sought audience with Solomon to hear the wisdom God had put in his heart. (1 Kings 10:9, 24)

Here was a man who had become king of the people through whom God had chosen to reveal Himself to the world. This man was wiser than anyone who had ever lived because he had asked for and received that gift from God. He had great wealth and riches as well. It looked as if he had achieved success in every sense of the word—but he was not able to handle it!

Throughout history, even in our present day, we see people who have achieved great heights and then fallen. No wonder Jesus said it was easier for a camel to pass through the eye of a needle than for a rich man to enter the Kingdom of God. Riches and power can blind us to God and His plan for us. When our minds are so full of how to make more money, how to achieve success, and how to be more popular, they become so cluttered that we cannot hear the still, small voice of God.

Well, Solomon had his downfall, too. His temptation was women! His lust caused him to completely forget that God had told the Israelites not to marry outside their own nation. It is hard to imagine seven hundred wives and three hundred concubines, but his great wealth caused him to become reckless, and in his disobedience he lost God's gift!

Solomon turned away from God. I expect that deep down he knew he would have to change if he faced God. That is what each of us has to decide—face God and be willing to change or turn our backs on Him.

Solomon's son Rehoboam reaped the consequences of his father's choices and the country became divided—Israel in the north under Jeroboam and Judah in the south under Rehoboam. Neither of these men sought the Lord's guidance, so God was unable to lead His people as He desired. How we grieve the heart of God when we choose not to obey!

READ: 1 Kings 13–15

God had called Jeroboam to be king of Israel and promised a strong rule if he obeyed. However, the king became fearful and turned to other gods. God gave him a chance to change his ways by sending a "man of God" to warn him, but it did no good.

Even after this, Jeroboam did not change his evil ways... (1 Kings 13:33)

The story of the man of God who was persuaded to ignore God's directions points out how easy it is to be drawn away from complete obedience by listening to the wrong people. If he had taken time to investigate the old prophet's invitation, he would have known it was not right to accept. That is an easy trap to fall into. God may speak to us through others, but we need to check it out with what He has told us directly.

I have had to learn this lesson through some rather bad mistakes over the years. At times, I assumed that what someone said must be right because I respected him or her. We each have direct access to God, and it is important to check everything with Him.

Rehoboam did no better as king in Judah, the southern part of the country. He had been given the honour of reigning from Jerusalem—the city God had chosen as His own. However, he did not lead his people to worship and praise God as his grandfather David had. As a result, Judah did what was evil in God's sight.

...the people engaged in all the detestable practices of the nations the Lord had driven out before the Israelites. (1 Kings 14:24)

God keeps giving us opportunities to repent and turn to Him when we get off-track, but if we refuse to listen, we must suffer the consequences. God has given us free will to choose what is right or wrong. No matter our circumstances, the choice is ours. Jeroboam chose the wrong path because he was afraid of losing his position and power. Rehoboam chose the wrong path because he listened to bad advice. These are the temptations we all face at times—what do we choose?

While Jeroboam was still king in Israel, Rehoboam died and his son Abijam became king of Judah.

He committed all the sins his father had done before him; his heart was not fully devoted to the Lord his God... (1 Kings 15:3)

War with Israel continued until Abijam died and his son Asa became king. Here was some light in the darkness of Judah's history.

> *Asa did what was right in the eyes of the Lord, as his father David had done... Asa's heart was fully committed to the Lord all his life.* (1 Kings 15:11, 14)

In the meantime, Jeroboam's son Nadab was king of Israel, and he was overthrown by Baasha, who killed Jeroboam's entire family:

> *He did evil in the eyes of the Lord, walking in the way of Jeroboam and in his sin, which he had caused Israel to commit.* (1 Kings 15:34)

It is important that we pray for our nation's leaders! It is easy to be judgmental and criticize how they lead, but negativity is destructive and prayer brings hope.

READ: 1 Kings 16–18

God never abandons His people entirely. In the midst of sin and destruction, God always finds someone who will listen to Him and obey His words. These are the ones who remind others that He is still the Lord—the God of Israel.

While Asa ruled for forty-one years in Judah, Israel's kings were far off-track. Ahab and his wife Jezebel did all manner of evil things, but God sent Elijah into their midst. Through him, God reached out to the people to catch their attention so they would turn again to Him.

When the widow's supply of food did not run out and her son was restored to life, she said to Elijah:

> *Now I know that you are a man of God and that the word of the Lord from your mouth is the truth.* (1 Kings 17:24)

At that moment, her eyes were opened and she entered into God's eternal kingdom.

All was not lost in Ahab's household, for the man in charge, Obadiah, *"feared [revered] the Lord greatly"* (1 Kings 18:3, KJV). In 1 Kings 18, we see the great test between the power of Baal and the power of God. Ellijah challenged the people for their lack of real commitment to God.

> *How long will you waver between two opinions? If the Lord is God, follow him; but if Baal is God, follow him.* (1 Kings 18:21)

That is a constant daily challenge for each of us. Do I get up early for an hour with God or do I give in to my desire for more sleep? Do I apologize for my wrong attitude or do I continue to blame the other person? Do I speak out for what is right or do I go along with the popular opinion? Just about every day there is a choice to be made, and I have three options:

1. Limp between two opinions.
2. Choose Baal and follow the crowd.
3. Choose God's way.

To make the choice clear, Elijah set up a contest with the prophets of Baal. His prayer to God was:

O Lord, God of Abraham, Isaac and Israel, let it be known today that you are God in Israel and that I am your servant and have done all these things at your command. (1 Kings 18:36)

When the fire fell, the people

fell prostrate and cried, "The Lord—he is God! The Lord—he is God!" (1 Kings 18:39)

May we make this affirmation daily. The choice is ours!

READ: 1 Kings 19–22

Elijah became discouraged and Queen Jezebel threatened to have him killed, so he fled into the wilderness. God sent an angel to minister to him. After fasting forty days, Elijah experienced that memorable earthquake, wind, and fire, but God was not in any of them. Then he heard the still, small voice of God. He speaks in a still, small voice to us today, but we can only hear Him if we spend time in a quiet place and prepare our hearts to receive Him.

Elijah had been on a real self-pity trip, declaring that he had been faithful to God even when all Israel turned away; now he was the only believer left and they were trying to kill him. That sounds familiar! How often I think everyone else is off-track and I am the only one who has it all together!

I once heard a song that went like this: "Isn't it, isn't it terribly sad—that I'm so good and the world's so bad?" I must have gone through a time like that when I wrote this in my quiet-time book:

I have become critical and judgmental and I talk big, as though I am the only one who really knows. I even have a superior attitude towards Bob and his ideas! Lord, I don't want to be like that. I don't want to think too highly of myself and my opinions. I want to be a good listener, to be teachable, to appreciate the wisdom of others, and to build others up.

This is the answer that came to me: "Refuse to harbour critical thoughts; see others as God sees them—with a love that builds."

God assured Elijah that there were seven thousand others who had not bowed to Baal, then sent him on his way to anoint Elisha to be the next great prophet of God.

The kings of Israel and Judah (Ahab and Jehosophat) had trouble distinguishing between false prophets and those who really heard from God. That problem exists today as well. We hear many voices, and if we are not familiar with the word of God as well as being able to distinguish the still, small voice, we can be drawn into false teaching.

Jehosophat, king of Judah, was one of the few kings who did what was right in the sight of the Lord. He had learned to listen to God from his father, King Asa.

THE BOOK OF

2 Kings

READ: 2 Kings 1–4

There is a great danger in seeking direction and advice from those who do not follow the Lord. It cost Ahaziah his life.

Elisha's great desire was to receive a double portion of the Spirit which dwelt in Elijah. In spite of Elijah's humanness, the Spirit of God shone through him and it was evident to those around him. I can identify with Elisha's longing to experience that in his own life. The ultimate success in a Christian's life is for the light of Jesus to shine through so people can see it and be attracted by its radiance!

Elisha did receive the Spirit that was in Elijah, and he also received Elijah's cloak. He purified the waters of Jericho, which showed God's power working through him for good. I find it impossible to understand the incident with the taunting boys; it seems such a terrible way to use that power.

However, 2 Kings 4 tells some lovely stories of how God reached through Elisha to meet the needs of various people. The story of the widow whose supply of oil continued flowing as long as the need existed makes me think of Lighthouse Christian Academy. At times, we wondered how we would be able to pay certain bills. Each time, we received an unexpected gift from someone who might not have even been aware of the need. It is an exciting adventure to work in a business where God is the General Manager and everyone turns to Him for directions before making a decision. His supply of life-giving oil is never-ending and His plan blesses everyone involved.

The wealthy Shunamite woman and her husband prepared a room for Elisha to use whenever he travelled that way. In his desire to give her a special gift, Elisha prayed that she might have a son, even though her husband was well along in years. God granted his prayer. Even more miraculous, through Elisha's prayers, that young boy was restored to life after he had died.

The chapter ends with food being purified and increased to feed a hundred men in a time of famine. It reminds me of Jesus feeding five thousand with five loaves and two fish. Our God is great and nothing is impossible for Him.

READ: 2 Kings 5–7

This well-known story of Naaman points out several truths that are useful to us today:

1. The little Jewish slave girl was used to introduce the captain of the Syrian army to God and His power, reminding us that one believer can make a difference in any situation, whether it be an office, family, or neighbourhood.

2. When Naaman was told to wash seven times in the Jordan, he rebelled—he thought it was too ridiculous, too foolish. However, when he obeyed, he was healed! God often asks us to take a step of faith before He moves in our lives.

3. The consequences of greed and dishonesty usually are not as dramatic as in Gehazi's case, but if someone is caught in a lie, it may take a long time for them to regain a reputation for being trustworthy.

It is really quite amazing how the power of God is shown through Elisha again and again. Nothing is impossible for God. Whether it was to show the people that He was Lord or to alert future generations, I do not know, but certainly I have never seen signs and wonders like those performed by Elisha!

1. He made an axe head float.

2. He told the king of Israel the Syrian king's plans. As one of the servants told the king of Syria:

...but Elisha, the prophet who is in Israel, tells the king of Israel the very words you speak in your bedroom. (2 Kings 6:12)

3. He was able to see the spiritual forces God sent to protect him from the Syrian army. Then he prayed that the entire army be struck blind until he led them away to Samaria. One man with God was able to gain victory over an army.

4. Then he prophesied that there would be food for all at a reasonable price the following day. Sure enough, through a series of strange events, it happened just as Elisha prophesied.

But what are we doing about it? Here it is, written for all to read thousands of years later, and we think "How interesting!" or "I wonder if it really happened?" and go on living as we always have. Maybe we could say, "Lord, if You made an axe head float, You can solve this problem for me" or "If You could open Elisha's servant's eyes, please open my eyes to see this situation as You see it."

If someone said to me, "There will be a famine for seven years," I would be hesitant to believe him. But Elisha had restored the woman's son to life, so she didn't question his advice. It is interesting that when she returned seven years later, her property and all the crops for those years were restored to her. That is a live issue in our country today. The native people are asking for compensation for the land taken from their ancestors two hundred years ago. I wonder who had to give up their home for that woman and her son? Justice is hard to define in human terms.

King Ahab and his wife Jezebel did such evil in their day that other kings were compared to him. Describing Jehoram, king of Judah, it is written:

He walked in the ways of the kings of Israel, as the house of Ahab had done, for he married a daughter of Ahab. He did evil in the eyes of the Lord. (2 Kings 8:18)

However, God had made a promise to David and He never goes back on His word.

Nevertheless, for the sake of His servant David, the Lord was not willing to destroy Judah. He had promised to maintain a lamp for David and his descendants forever. (2 Kings 8:19)

The house of Ahab was doomed! When the young prophet anointed Jehu to be king of Israel, he gave God's word:

The whole house of Ahab will perish... (2 Kings 9:8)

When Jehu became king, he systematically wiped out every descendant and follower of Ahab. Then he devised a plan to get rid of all followers of Baal, and the Lord was pleased.

I find it uncomfortable and disturbing that God would sanction the killing of all those people, but sometimes a portion of the body has to be surgically removed to get rid of a cancer capable of destroying the whole body. Many years later, Paul made this statement:

For the wages of sin is death, but the gift of God is eternal life in Christ Jesus our Lord. (Romans 6:23)

Although Jehu fulfilled a part of God's plan, he didn't carry it through in his daily life.

Yet Jehu was not careful to keep the law of the Lord, the God of Israel, with all his heart. He did not turn away from the sins of Jeroboam, which he had caused Israel to commit. (2 Kings 10:31)

God wants obedience every day, for He knows how quickly we get off-track. When I begin to skip my quiet times, it isn't long before those around me start noticing the change.

READ: 2 Kings 11–13

Joash, while still a baby, was hidden from his grandmother, Queen Athaliah, for six years. This must have been God's plan for Judah, since he was trained by the priest Jehoida and became one of the few kings who *"did what was right in the sight of the Lord all the years Jehoiada the priest instructed him"* (2 Kings 12:2). He was anointed king at the age of seven and reigned for forty years in Jerusalem.

During this time, he repaired the house of God. Money given by the people at the temple was put in large bags and handed to the workmen—the carpenters, builders, masons, and stone cutters. Now, here is an interesting statement:

They did not require an accounting from those to whom they gave the money to pay the workers, because they acted with complete honesty. (2 Kings 12:15)

That kind of trust is rare today!

Israel was not as fortunate as Judah. Their kings neither worshipped God nor sought His guidance.

So the Lord's anger burned against Israel, and for a long time he kept them under the power of Hazael king of Aram and Ben-Hadad his son. (2 Kings 13:3)

The next verse shows that one king remembered God's power:

Then Jehoahaz sought the Lord's favor, and the Lord listened to him, for he saw how severely the king of Aram was oppressing Israel. (2 Kings 13:4)

Unfortunately, Jehoahaz did not really change his ways but continued in the sin of ignoring God. That sounds like many of us today. When things go badly, we call out to God for help. Then, when He answers our call and things begin to get better, we forget all about Him and sometimes even take the glory ourselves for whatever success we have attained. Our tendency towards self-centredness is the same in every generation, in all parts of the world. Only the wisdom and love of God can cure us.

Elisha was dying. He prophesied three victories for Israel over Syria, and sure enough, this happened in the reign of King Joash. The power of God was with Elisha even after he died (2 Kings 13:20–21). God used Elisha mightily to reveal to the people something of His character. Even though it did not seem to change the kings, I imagine many people became believers and followers when they saw the miracles performed through him.

READ: 2 Kings 14–16

After Joash, king of Judah, was put to death by some of his servants (2 Kings 12:20), his son Amaziah became king.

> *He did what was right in the eyes of the Lord, but not as his father David had done. In everything he followed the example of his father Joash.* (2 Kings 14:3)

You may wonder, as I did, about references to "the high places." Back in Deuteronomy, when Moses gave God's commandments to the people of Israel, the Bible says:

> *Destroy completely all the places on the high mountains and on the hills and under every spreading tree where the nations you are dispossessing worship their gods. Break down their altars, smash their sacred stones and burn their Asherah poles in the fire; cut down the idols of their gods and wipe out their names from those places.* (Deuteronomy 12:2–3)

This was the weakness in both Joash and Amaziah:

> *The high places, however, were not removed; the people continued to offer sacrifices and burn incense there.* (2 Kings 14:4)

God had warned them not to leave any vestige of idol worship, for it would weaken their commitment to Him and gradually draw them away from a life of obedience. Many of us call ourselves Christian today but still hang on to things that are not of God, including hurt and self-pity, resentment and bitterness, hatred and fear, inferiority and superiority, prejudice and unforgiveness. There are a host of negatives, which, like the high places, must be cleared away if we are to become true followers. Though King David made some serious mistakes, he desired to be obedient to God and was willing to be cleansed of all his faults.

Although Joash and Amaziah lived good lives and did what was right, because they did not clear out all the negatives, they failed to reach their potential for God. Is this, perhaps, why the organized church is ineffectual in the world today? Are there too many "high places" in the hearts of people for us to clearly hear the voice of God and become a power that turns the world upside down?

Azariah (also called Uzziah), like his father and grandfather, did what was right in the sight of the Lord, but he did not destroy the high places!

> *The Lord afflicted the king with leprosy until the day he died, and he lived in a separate house.* (2 Kings 15:5)

For four generations—Josiah, Amaziah, Uzziah, Jotham—the kings of Judah lived good lives but failed to remove the high places.

READ: 2 Kings 17–19

> *In the ninth year of Hoshea, the king of Assyria captured Samaria and deported the Israelites to Assyria… All this took place because the Israelites had sinned against the Lord their God…* (2 Kings 17:6–7)

This chapter goes on to tell how Israel, even though God had led them out of Egypt into the Promised Land, chose to worship the idols of other nations. They did wicked things, provoking the Lord to anger.

> *The Lord warned Israel and Judah through all his prophets and seers: "Turn from your evil ways…" But they would not listen…* (2 Kings 17:13–14)

And so the people of Israel were exiled to Assyria. Judah was not much better, but then Hezekiah became their king and he did what was right in the sight of the Lord. He even removed the high places and the pillars that had been erected there.

It takes a brave leader to go against the popular trend and make decisions he knows are right but may not be easily accepted. People do not like to change. However, Hezekiah knew where to find the wisdom and strength he needed:

> *Hezekiah trusted in the Lord, the God of Israel… He held fast to the Lord and did not cease to follow him… and the Lord was with him; he was successful in whatever he undertook.* (2 Kings 18:5–7)

That did not mean he had no problems. The king of Assyria had become powerful and sent threatening messages to Hezekiah, mocking the power of his God. Although he was scared, Hezekiah did what had become a habit in his life: he took the letter to the house of the Lord, laid it before God, and prayed for wisdom! He also sent word to Isaiah, a prophet of God, asking him to pray about the situation. You can read the results in 2 Kings 19.

We can learn several things from this short passage about Hezekiah:

1. He chose to do what was right, even if it was not popular.
2. He got rid of the things that hindered his relationship with God.
3. He trusted in God and obeyed the commandments God had given Moses.
4. When faced with a problem, he prayed to God and sought help from a man of faith.

This reminds me to remain in constant communion with God, daily cleaning up places that hinder my relationship with him and choosing to do what I know is right. Then, when faced with any problem, it will be natural to lay it before God, seeking His wisdom and guidance. It is a good thing to ask for prayer support from someone I know to be in a close relationship with God. What was true and right for Hezekiah is also true and right for me, several thousand years later.

READ: 2 Kings 20–25

Hezekiah's life was lengthened by fifteen years in answer to prayer. We will read more about him in Chronicles, which covers much the same period as the books we have just read.

Someone recently asked me, "Do you know how long a revival lasts in an area?"

The answer: "One generation."

God has so arranged it that each of us is totally responsible for our direction in life. I cannot hold my parents, church, or circumstances responsible for where I am. Only I can ask Jesus to be the Lord of my life. It won't happen because I have good parents, a good husband, or because I attend a church that is on fire for the Lord. He will hold me accountable for the path I choose.

Hezekiah was committed to God's plan for his life, but his son Manasseh chose the opposite route. Manasseh turned his back on God and encouraged the worship of Baal and other idols. People are easily swayed by a strong leader, and no doubt many followed Manasseh in his evil course. Judah paid a heavy price for this rebellion.

One more king, Josiah, attempted to save them:

He did what was right in the eyes of the Lord and walked in all the ways of his father David, not turning aside to the right or to the left. (2 Kings 22:2)

That is a great tribute! A book of the law was found in the temple by the high priest, so he took it to the king. It hadn't been read in such a long time that the people had forgotten God's warnings of what would happen if they rebelled against Him.

I wonder if we are approaching a similar time today, in which very few people have really read and know the Bible—even churchgoing people. Throughout the Bible, God warns that disaster will hit if He is not obeyed. We prefer to read about the promises of His blessings, but we must never forget that certain conditions must be met in order to receive those blessings.

Josiah and many of his people made a covenant before the Lord to follow Him, and they attempted to eliminate all idol worship. They even reinstituted the celebration of the Passover.

However, there had been too many years of disobedience in Judah and it would take more than the burning of a few idols to get them in line again. Besides, Josiah's two sons, who followed him on the throne (one was king only three months), did not choose God's ways, so God allowed Nebuchadnezzar, king of Babylon, to take the people into captivity. Only the poorest were left to be vinedressers and ploughmen.

THE BOOK OF
Romans

READ: Romans 1–2

Paul wrote this letter to a group of believers in Rome. By the way he addresses them, it seems there were probably both Jews and Gentiles. He himself longed to see them and we know from what Luke wrote in the book of Acts that he eventually did go—but as a prisoner.

Paul says why he wants to see them:

I long to see you so that I may impart to you some spiritual gift to make you strong—that is, that you and I may be mutually encouraged by each other's faith. (Romans 1:11–12)

I have a host of friends with whom I love to spend time, because as we talk we are encouraged by each other's faith. Some live nearby and some live on other continents. I think especially of a trip my husband and I made to Australia and New Zealand, and how we delighted in the fellowship of people there whose goal was the same as ours—to live a life of obedience to God. They were total strangers until we spoke of our faith and acknowledged that we were all children of the same heavenly Father. Some of them have since visited us in Canada and seeing them is like welcoming family into our home!

The truth that through Jesus we can be restored to a right relationship with God is the good news—the gospel for all mankind—and Paul says he is not ashamed to proclaim it. But at the same time, when we know this truth and yet turn our backs on it, suppressing it, we are in danger of the wrath of God. There is no excuse for this, because we can see God in His creation all around us. When we refuse to honour and give thanks to Him, our minds become clouded and our thinking futile. Though we think we are wise, we are like fools! (Romans 1:18–23)

Paul is startlingly forthright when he lists the evils that will take us over when we choose worldly comforts ahead of our Creator, who is the real source of blessing.

It is almost a paradox as Paul moves from this thought to the next chapter, where he warns against judging others when we have not repented of our own sins. He says:

So when you, a mere man, pass judgment on them and yet do the same things, do you think you will escape God's judgment? (Romans 2:3)

When we draw near to God and see our own unworthiness, our position is secure only if we repent of our wrong attitudes and habits, thus receiving His forgiveness. Then, and only then, are we in a position to help others do the same. If we move from His side and depend on our own wisdom, we become critical and judgmental.

I think of how I exchanged angry, judgmental words with a friend one day. Fortunately, we already had Christian love for each other and were able to apologize and move on. I had stepped away from God's side and become arrogant and proud!

READ: Romans 3–4

Paul, in this section, deals with the place of the Jews in God's plan, and the balance between law and faith. Some of it is hard to follow, but some verses stand out.

…for all have sinned and fall short of the glory of God. (Romans 3:23)

Only God can be totally trusted. When we put our faith in man, we will always be let down. Perhaps that is one reason so many marriages fail. We set up certain expectations of how our spouse should act in order to be a loving, caring, responsible partner, but he or she falls short of that mark. That attitude is doomed to failure, but we all get into it at some time or another. In essence, we set ourselves up as God, with a plan for the other person! The marriage ceremony says "for better or for worse," but when things get worse than our expected plan allows, we want to give up!

We can, and should, believe and encourage the best in those around us but love them unconditionally—no matter what they do! That can be very difficult, but we should remind ourselves, "That is how God loves me."

Blessed are they whose transgressions are forgiven, whose sins are covered. Blessed is the man whose sin the Lord will never count against him. (Romans 4:7–8)

Paul here is quoting King David from Psalm 32:1–2. This is what happens in our relationship with God when we are willing to accept His forgiveness. He not only gives it, but in His eyes we are clean, as though we never sinned at all. That is the ultimate in forgiveness and what I strive for in my own life—that I may never hold a grudge against anyone!

Speaking of Abraham:

Yet he did not waver through unbelief regarding the promise of God, but was strengthened in his faith and gave glory to God, being fully persuaded that God had power to do what he had promised. (Romans 4:20–21)

Abraham was called by God to be the founder of a nation, and for a number of years he had only God's promise of a son to hang onto, since he and his wife were well beyond the child-bearing age. That was a testing time, but his implicit faith that God's word could be trusted made him worthy of God's calling.

This was why *"it was credited to him as righteousness"* (Romans 4:22).

Righteousness can only come from being so close to God that His righteousness spills over onto us. Saying we believe in God while seldom spending time in close communion with Him just doesn't cut it. As I read the Psalms, I get the impression that David spent a great deal of time acknowledging who God is and thanking Him for His blessings. I believe that is what God expects of all His followers.

READ: Romans 5–6

Therefore, since we have been justified through faith, we have peace with God through our Lord Jesus Christ… (Romans 5:1)

I can't imagine now what it would be like to try to cope without the awareness that, because of Jesus, I can be at peace with God, no matter the circumstances around me. When problems pile up and I don't have the answers, it is wonderful to know that by being alone I can experience His presence, draw on His wisdom, and know His peace.

My problems or suffering cannot compare with the accusations, threats, beatings, and imprisonments Paul went through. And yet he says, *"We rejoice in our sufferings"* (Romans 5:3)! He goes on to explain that *"suffering produces perseverance; perseverance, character; and character, hope"* (Romans 3–5). Hope in the worldly sense may end in disappointment, but when it is based on God's love, poured into our heart through the Holy Spirit, it will never disappoint! In other words, if we acknowledge God's presence in our suffering, He can turn it around and make it a blessing to us and to others.

A young man had been in an accident and broke some bones. When I saw him after several weeks in hospital, I said, "That must have been a tough experience."

"Not at all," he answered. "I was able to help my roommate accept Jesus into his life."

His misfortune had become God's opportunity.

For if, when we were God's enemies, we were reconciled to him through the death of his Son, how much more, having been reconciled, shall we be saved through his life! (Romans 5:10)

Jesus' death provided us with forgiveness for our sin, which reconciles us to God. Sin separates us from Him. Now that I am forgiven, I need to look closely at Jesus' life, for in it is the example of how to be safe from sin—in other words, how to keep from sinning.

Therefore do not let sin reign in your mortal body so that you obey its evil desires. (Romans 6:12)

We quickly become slaves to the habits we form. At 10:30 every morning, I become thirsty, so I stop what I am doing and have a hot drink. At noon, I am ready for lunch. These habits are not necessarily bad, but they do control me. We are all slaves to something or someone. Paul says:

But now that you have been set free from sin and have become slaves to God, the benefit you reap leads to holiness, and the result is eternal life. (Romans 6:22)

This is a reward, indeed! By being a slave to God, I can be freed from all guilt in this life and be assured of spending eternity with Him. We are created to desire a just authority in our lives, and no one can provide that except God Himself. We can choose to be guided by God or ruled by self-centred people (ourselves or others).

READ: Romans 7–8

Paul talks about how difficult it is to keep the law and how he does wrong things in spite of his desire to do what is right. I can readily identify with that! My greatest desire is to be like Jesus, and I can really be in tune with Him in my quiet time.

When something happens that I don't like, I immediately react in criticism, self-pity, anger, or fear. If I don't turn immediately to God for direction, I will say and do things that come out of my negative reaction. I am sorry for it later! Each of us has potential for sin, but fortunately God provided a way to freedom.

Therefore, there is now no condemnation for those who are in Christ Jesus... (Romans 8:1)

We may be forgiven and start all over again every time we sin. As I make confession a daily part of my quiet time, it becomes easier to recognize my sin and deal with it before it has done too much damage in the lives of others.

Those who live according to the sinful nature have their minds set on what that nature desires; but those who live in accordance with the Spirit have their minds set on what the Spirit desires. (Romans 8:5)

The emphasis here is on what controls our minds. Where do my thoughts centre? What if all my thoughts were shown on a TV screen? Would they bless the people watching? Would I be happy to have others know how I think? How often would I want to touch the "off" button to censor the negatives on display? God is aware of all my thoughts, just as if they were on a TV screen. Nothing is hidden from Him. How often do I grieve Him because my mind is not set on His path?

The mind of sinful man is death, but the mind controlled by the Spirit is life and peace. (Romans 8:6)

Doctors are now aware that illness and pain can be increased or decreased depending on the thoughts and attitudes of the patient. So, in a very real way, we influence our own health.

Towards the end of Romans 8, we find four wonderful assurances:
1. The Holy Spirit will help us pray when we don't know how.
2. If we love and serve God, He will bring some good out of everything that happens to us.
3. If we are on God's side, we are winners, no matter who is against us.
4. Nothing can separate us from God without our consent.

This life of inner victory and peace is available to all, but we have to make the choice.

READ: Romans 9–10

In these two chapters, Paul expresses the ache in his heart for his people—the Israelites—because so many of them could not see Jesus as the Messiah, God's Son, His ultimate gift to the world. Paul even says that he himself would be willing to be cut off from Christ, if only his kinsmen would believe!

> *...the people of Israel. Theirs is the adoption as sons; theirs the divine glory, the covenants, the receiving of the law, the temple worship and the promises. Theirs are the patriarchs, and from them is traced the human ancestry of Christ, who is God over all, forever praised! Amen.* (Romans 9:4–5)

All God's revelations were given to the Israelites, and even Jesus was born into that nation. As Gentiles, we need to realize how much we have received from the Jewish people. In Romans 9, however, the time had come when they, like us, had to make a choice, and I'm sure God felt the same pain Paul felt as He saw so many of them reject the salvation He provided through Jesus. They were so busy keeping the law that they missed the personal relationship with Jesus.

That misplaced priority is still evident in the church today. We can get so caught up in peace marches, building projects, youth activities, and social programs that we have no time to bask in the love of Jesus and be led by His Holy Spirit. These other pursuits are good, but unless they come out of a personal commitment to follow God's leading, they do not further the kingdom of God.

> *But Israel, who pursued a law of righteousness, has not attained it. Why not? Because they pursued it not by faith but as if it were by works.* (Romans 9:31–32)

> *For I can testify about them that they are zealous for God, but their zeal is not based on knowledge. Since they did not know the righteousness that comes from God and sought to establish their own, they did not submit to God's righteousness.* (Romans 10:2–3)

The kingdom of God can only be established through God's wisdom—not man's. Through quiet times with Him, we may receive a portion of that wisdom—just enough for the matter at hand. That means our times of communion and prayer must be regular and frequent if we are to operate according to His plan.

That if you confess with your mouth, "Jesus is Lord," and believe in your heart that God raised him from the dead, you will be saved. (Romans 10:9)

When I invite Jesus to be the Lord of my life, it is important that I tell someone. I don't quite understand why, but when we put an idea into words, it has power in our lives. By confessing to someone that Jesus is the Lord of your life, it begins to become a reality. If you do not express it, you can begin to doubt and it can soon fade away.

This truth can have a bad effect on our lives if we confess negative statements such as "I'm no good," "Nobody likes me," or "I can't do that." When spoken, they take on power in our lives to become reality. What I think and speak determines the course of my life!

READ: Romans 11–12

In Romans 11, Paul presents the position of the Jews (many of whom were rejecting Jesus) and the Gentiles (many of whom, through Jesus, were experiencing a personal relationship with God). It has occasionally been taught in some churches that all God's promises to Israel are for Christians, and no longer for the Jews, but Paul soundly refutes that belief:

God did not reject his people, whom he foreknew… for God's gifts and his call are irrevocable. (Romans 11:2, 29)

He then issues a challenge to all believers. Still referring to the Jews, he says:

Again I ask: Did they stumble so as to fall beyond recovery? Not at all! Rather, because of their transgression, salvation has come to the Gentiles to make Israel envious. (Romans 11:11)

The challenge is to live a life that will make unbelievers jealous. People want to experience joy and peace. They are attracted to those who have enthusiasm for life and get enjoyment out of the simple things, those who sees the good in others, those who don't complain about their lot in life.

Sad to say, the church has not always portrayed that image to the Jewish people. Throughout history, the latter have suffered persecution and anti-Semitism from those who called themselves Christians. Even today, with Bibles so easily accessible, many ignore Paul's injunction and fail to see God's hand in the establishment of Israel in the Promised Land.

Paul warns that the ingrafted branch of the olive tree (the Gentiles) can be cut off as easily as the natural branch (the Jews). We must remain faithful to God's word.

I do not want you to be ignorant of this mystery, brothers, so that you may not be conceited: Israel has experienced a hardening in part until the full number of Gentiles has come in. And so all Israel will be saved... (Romans 11:25–26)

It has taken a long time, but the time is coming when all Israel will be saved!

Romans 12 is a guide for living and should be read often.

Do not conform any longer to the pattern of this world, but be transformed by the renewing of your mind. Then you will be able to test and approve what God's will is—his good, pleasing and perfect will. (Romans 12:2)

How else can we renew our minds except by coming into God's presence daily for Him to show us which thoughts are good, acceptable, and perfect, and which thoughts should be cast out?

We have different gifts, according to the grace given us. If a man's gift is prophesying, let him use it in proportion to his faith. If it is serving, let him serve; if it is teaching, let him teach; if it is encouraging, let him encourage; if it is contributing to the needs of others, let him give generously; if it is leadership, let him govern diligently; if it is showing mercy, let him do it cheerfully. Love must be sincere... Never be lacking in zeal, but keep your spiritual fervor... Be joyful in hope, patient in affliction, faithful in prayer... Bless those who persecute you... Live in harmony with one another... Do not take revenge, my friends... Do not be overcome with evil, but overcome evil with good. (Romans 12:6–9, 11–12, 14, 16, 19, 21)

These are signposts to keep us on-track in our Christian walk. They all look so appealing! Even though these signs are not easy to attain, they are well worth striving for. Like learning to play the piano, the more we practise, the better we get.

Romans 12 encompasses every expression of relationship in life—with God, (Romans 12:1), with ourselves (Romans 12:2–3), with the Body of Christ (Romans 12:4–8), with His church (Romans 12:9–21), and with every daily relationship.

READ: Romans 13–14

Everyone must submit himself to the governing authorities, for there is no authority except that which God has established. (Romans 13:1)

It is common today to rebel against authority. Children rebel against parents and teachers, workers go on strike, and citizens criticize the government no matter what they do. Paul warns us here to accept authority whether we agree with them or not.

Let no debt remain outstanding, except the continuing debt to love one another, for he who loves his fellowman has fulfilled the law. The commandments… are summed up in this one rule: "Love your neighbor as yourself." (Romans 13:8–9)

There is a new idea for me—I *owe* love to others! Since it is God's commandment that we love one another, I am cheating any person I don't love! I really need God's help for that, because not everyone is lovable!

Therefore let us stop passing judgment on one another. Instead, make up your mind not to put any stumbling block or obstacle in your brother's way. (Romans 14:13)

I don't want to put a stumbling block in another person's path, but do I do just that? I was talking to some students one day about a male teacher.

"He made each of us feel we were important and that what we had to say was valuable to the whole class," one of the students commented.

We have a tendency to belittle others, which can be so devastating! It is important to build self-respect in others, yet when we become impatient our words and actions do just the opposite. I want to strive to live a life that builds the people around me, and I don't want to ever be a hindrance to the spiritual growth of another person! That is another reason to spend time with God every day. It can be a protection against one's own self-centeredness.

For the kingdom of God is not a matter of eating and drinking, but of righteousness, peace and joy in the Holy Spirit. (Romans 14:17)

Indeed, the rewards are great!

READ: Romans 15–16

We who are strong ought to bear with the failings of the weak and not to please ourselves. Each of us should please his neighbor for his good, to build him up. (Romans 15:1–2)

Another way to word these two verses might be, "Make absolute unselfishness one of your goals." We really are very self-centred by nature. We evaluate everything by how it affects us personally.

I remember once sitting at a table full of people and discussing some government policy that had just come out. As I thought about the conversation later, I realized each of us had seen the subject from our own perspective—the farmer, the teacher, the businessman. That is alright as long as we also hear and appreciate other points of view and consider what is best for all. I also realized what a difficult job the government has—to make decisions that benefit the most people.

May the God who gives endurance and encouragement give you a spirit of unity among yourselves as you follow Christ Jesus. (Romans 15:5)

A lot has been said about positive thinking. I have always found the idea very appealing, since the alternative is negative thinking, and who wants that? However, on its own the idea lacks power. In the context of a life centred on God's plan, all our thinking should be positive, based on our faith that He is in control so everything works together for good.

May the God of hope fill you with all joy and peace as you trust in him, so that you may overflow with hope by the power of the Holy Spirit. (Romans 15:13)

In Romans 16, Paul introduces us to some of the church family in Rome. Although not much is said about them, we get a picture of their commitment to Jesus and each other. It was not easy to be a Christian at that time. They were in constant danger of persecution, so only wholehearted commitment would make them take the risk. You can get by with a lukewarm attitude towards Jesus and the church in a free country like Canada, but you miss all the blessings, inner peace, and victory over sin.

Paul encouraged the church with these words:

Everyone has heard about your obedience, so I am full of joy over you; but I want you to be wise about what is good, and innocent about what is evil.

The God of peace will soon crush Satan under your feet. The grace of our Lord Jesus be with you. (Romans 16:19–20)

THE BOOK OF
1 Chronicles

READ: 1 Chronicles 1–10

The genealogy in the first nine chapters of 1 Chronicles is much more extensive than the one found in Matthew. The latter was meant to show Jesus' place, so it only follows one lineage. However, here we are given a broad outline of all of Isaac's sons.

One thing that strikes me is the relentless passage of time. No one really knows how long this earth has been populated except the Creator Himself, but men and women have been born, lived, and died for centuries. No one chooses the circumstances of their birth, but as we grow we make choices which determine our direction in life. God, from the beginning, has offered us guidance, but we can only receive it on His terms.

As I ponder this, I see history as a great river of people. The river keeps changing as individuals enter the flow for a time and then leave it. My own life can be seen this way. I can choose to be in the stream that is moving in God's plan or I can be on my own self-appointed plan with its frustrations and failures. On my own, there can seem to be successes, but without God I have no answer to tension and fear.

Faster than I could have imagined, the years have passed. I am now well along in the last years of my life. According to my own plan, this is scary, because even if I accomplished all I set out to do and achieved my goals, what would lie ahead? In God's plan, the end of life means graduation into heaven where I can be with Him forever. With Him, this life is full of joy and hope, no matter the circumstances. When my life is over, the life to come is even better. My accomplishments are not God's biggest concern for me; it is my relationship with Him.

Of some of the men in the 1 Chronicles genealogy, it was said, "He did what was right in the sight of the Lord." What a great tribute! I would like to have it said of me, "She did what was right in the sight of the Lord"—not in the sight of the world, but in the sight of God! I can only do what is right if my heart, soul, and mind are in tune with Him.

1 Chronicles 10 tells the sad ending of King Saul's story:

Saul died because he was unfaithful to the Lord; he did not keep the word of the Lord and even consulted a medium for guidance, and did not inquire of the Lord. So the Lord put him to death and turned the kingdom over to David son of Jesse. (1 Chronicles 10:13–14)

The worst choice we can make is to not follow God's guidance.

READ: 1 Chronicles 11–13

Much that was written earlier in 1 and 2 Samuel and 1 and 2 Kings is repeated here in 1 and 2 Chronicles. These chapters take us back to King David. While Saul lived, David was constantly on the run to save his own life. Once King Saul died, the elders of Israel gathered with him at Hebron and anointed him king.

David was a warrior who lived at a time when battles were fought constantly. One of his early conquests as king was the taking of Jerusalem from the Jebusites. That was certainly God's plan. From that day to this one, Jerusalem has been known as the city of David. It has always been of prime importance to the Jewish people.

When plans were made through the United Nations for Palestine to become the homeland for the Jews, at least one man gave his whole life to updating the Hebrew language to make it usable as the official language of Israel. Hebrew had been understood by scholars through the centuries, but it lacked everyday modern words like "airplane" and "vacuum cleaner." This man lobbied to have it used in schools and universities, in business and government.

Since Jewish people were coming from all over the world, it was important that they have a unique language, strictly their own. Hebrew had not been used as a common spoken language for many centuries, so it had not changed appreciably over time. Consequently, it is said that if King David returned to his beloved Jerusalem today, he would be able to converse with the people living there.

David knew that Israel could only prosper if God was with them, so he suggested they bring the Ark of the Covenant back into their midst. He gathered leaders together from across the country:

The whole assembly agreed to do this, because it seemed right to all the people. (1 Chronicles 13:4)

Only the Levites were to handle the ark, so they placed it on a cart and the people followed it, dancing and praising the Lord. It was a symbol of their relationship with God, and when that is right, joy naturally follows.

A shocking thing happened when Uzzah reached out to balance the ark. He fell dead!

David was afraid of God that day... (1 Chronicles 13:12)

We can't fool around with our commitment to God—it is a serious business. However, wherever He dwells there is a blessing. When the ark was left at the home of Obed-Edom for three months,

...the Lord blessed his household and everything he had. (1 Chronicles 13:14)

READ: 1 Chronicles 14–16

And David knew that the Lord had established him as king over Israel... (1 Chronicles 14:2)

When we recognize that God has placed us where we are, our attitudes change. Complaining about our position is tantamount to criticizing God. To compare our state with someone else's is another way of saying God is not fair. There are always certain circumstances we can change by ourselves, but there are other circumstances we must learn to accept. Indeed, we should practise thanking God for them. They may help us to see our true nature.

In the midst of my teaching years, I took a year off so Bob and I could go north to the town of New Hazelton, where Bob pastored four small churches. Towards the end of the year, I had an opportunity to travel to Europe with my sister. Bob very generously encouraged me to go, helping with the finances. A few years later, when we were back in Victoria and I was teaching again, he had an opportunity for a few months to serve on a coastal mission boat, the *Thomas Crosby*, but it was during the school year. I struggled with this, because I also longed to go. Here's what I wrote in my quiet-time book:

Am I meant to be an enabler—making it possible for Bob to go on the *Crosby* while I am a full-time worker? He made it possible for me to go to Europe while he was tied to his full-time job. Now I am in the position to do the same for him. I wonder if I can do it as unselfishly as he did? Well, not quite, because I have already longed to go, too. Now I must accept God's plan gratefully and joyously, living each moment to the hilt! A great day is ahead!

There's always a great day ahead when we stay in tune with God's plan.

David sought the Lord's direction and God gave him the victory. When he decided to move the ark again, he did it the right way.

And the Levites carried the ark of God with the poles on their shoulders, as Moses had commanded in accordance with the word of the Lord. (1 Chronicles 15:15)

There was singing and rejoicing with various musical instruments. There follows, in the next chapter, a song of thanksgiving that may have been written by David. The words show us how to approach God:

- *"Give thanks to the Lord, call upon his name"* (1 Chronicles 16:8).
- *"Glory in his holy name"* (1 Chronicles 16:10).
- *"Sing to the Lord, all the earth; proclaim his salvation day after day"* (1 Chronicles 16:23).
- *"Ascribe to the Lord the glory due his name"* (1 Chronicles 16:29).
- *"Worship the Lord in the splendor of his holiness"* (1 Chronicles 16:29).
- *"Let them say among the nations, 'The Lord reigns'"* (1 Chronicles 16:31).

Repeating phrases like these often lifts our spirits, increases our faith, and gives life meaning. We are part of God's creation and should remind ourselves of that constantly.

Then all the people left, each for his own home, and David returned home to bless his family. (1 Chronicles 16:43)

READ: 1 Chronicles 17–22

Even a man of God like Nathan, a prophet, may give good advice that is not representative of God's perfect plan. When David wanted to build a permanent home for the ark rather than house it in a tent, Nathan said:

Whatever you have in mind, do it, for God is with you. (1 Chronicles 17:2)

However, it was not the right time and God spoke to Nathan that night saying that David was not to build the temple, but that his son would do it. King David's prayer shows his complete faith in God. He acknowledges Him to be the God of Israel and far above the gods of the other nations round about.

You made your people Israel your very own forever, and you, O Lord, have become their God. (1 Chronicles 17:22)

We must never forget that it was a covenant "forever," and that it includes the people of modern-day Israel. We must pray that their spiritual eyes be opened to recognize Jesus, their Messiah, in the same way as we pray for friends, neighbours, and members of our own families. How I long to see what a nation like Canada would be like if everyone sought God's plan daily!

David continued to win battles, for God was with him:

The Lord gave David victory wherever he went. (1 Chronicles 18:6)

I don't know why God seemed to allow all the killing. Perhaps the power of idol worship could only be kept out of Israel by defeating the nations who practised it. If we continue to allow the desire for wealth, position, and power to direct our lives, our nation, too, may be in danger of being wiped out or taken captive. Jesus said that you can't serve both God and mammon. I don't understand God's ways, but He created us and we are responsible to Him.

Perhaps Satan had a hand in this, too, for he has always been out to destroy God's people. 1 Chronicles 21 tells how Satan tempted David to go against God's directions by taking a census. In spite of Joab's warning, David insisted on doing it! Looking back, I can remember times when I moved ahead on some plan in spite of warnings either from someone else or from within my own heart. There is always a price to pay. David's people suffered for this mistake until David cried out to the Lord and offered a sacrifice. Then the plague was stopped.

The king did all he could to collect materials and make things ready for his son Solomon to build the temple. As with the first synagogue, it was to be of the finest quality and workmanship. David concluded a talk with Solomon by saying:

Now devote your heart and soul to seeking the Lord your God. (1 Chronicles 22:19)

That is the best advice we can give anyone!

READ: 1 Chronicles 23–29

Many years before, the Levites were appointed to care for the tent tabernacle and all it contained. The men of that tribe now numbered thirty-eight thousand and their duties were to care for the new temple when it was built. Some would be gatekeepers, officers, or judges, but four thousand were designated to offer praise to God with instruments of music.

They were also to stand every morning to thank and praise the Lord. They were to do the same in the evening... (1 Chronicles 23:30)

I wonder how much more power would be evident in our churches if a group of people gathered to praise and thank God every morning and every evening. If even one of us was committed to this, it would make a difference. Perhaps I need to be more disciplined and add an evening time of praise and thanksgiving to my morning quiet times.

All of the people listed in 1 Chronicles 24–27 would have been amazed, I am sure, if they had known that people two or three thousand years later would be reading their names and the responsibilities they were given—but there they are, in the book that has been the world's bestseller for years!

King David was pretty excited about a temple to God being built in Jerusalem, where God said He would dwell forever. No wonder the Jewish people rejoiced to be back in that city in 1967 after the surrounding Arab countries had taken away it from them in 1948! It had been part of the U.N.-designated Israel—a home for the Jews—but neighbouring armies attacked immediately and Jerusalem was divided, with the oldest section going to Jordan. In 1967, Israel took it back and made it the capital of their nation.

David gathered materials and made plans for the temple, but he knew they would only succeed if God's commands were obeyed. He called all the leaders together and shared his vision for a temple with them:

So now I charge you in the sight of all Israel and of the assembly of the Lord, and in the hearing of our God: Be careful to follow all the commands of the Lord your God, that you may possess this good land and pass it on as an inheritance to your descendants forever. (1 Chronicles 28:8)

If we are not obedient to God in our lifetimes, what sort of inheritance will we leave our children? We cannot regulate their lives, but we choose the example we set for them. David's advice to his son was:

And you, my son Solomon, acknowledge the God of your father, and serve him with wholehearted devotion and with a willing mind, for the Lord searches every heart and understands every motive behind the thoughts. If you seek him, he will be found by you; but if you forsake him, he will reject you forever. (1 Chronicles 28:9)

God is available and willing to be part of every plan we make. The exciting part is that He knows everyone else's thoughts, too, and can fit us together. Recently, a friend was given some hamburger buns because she was going to be responsible for feeding a mission group coming to her area. The next day, from an entirely different source, she was given a box of frozen hamburger patties! Even in mundane daily plans, if we ask God's help, He will put things together in a delightfully unique way.

After the offering was taken at David's gathering, he thanked God, praising His glorious name:

Everything comes from you, and we have given you only what comes from your hand… They ate and drank with great joy in the presence of the Lord that day. (1 Chronicles 29:14, 22)

THE BOOK OF

2 Chronicles

READ: 2 Chronicles 1–7

Here, the story of Solomon is very similar to the one in 1 Kings.

> *Solomon son of David established himself firmly over his kingdom, for the Lord his God was with him and made him exceedingly great.* (2 Chronicles 1:1)

His request to God was for wisdom and knowledge. While he obeyed God's commandments and sought His guidance, everything went well. He built the temple according to the directions God gave his father, David. The ark was brought by the Levites and a great congregation performed animal sacrifices before it. When all was in place, the musicians led in praise to God:

> *The trumpeters and singers joined in unison, as with one voice, to give praise and thanks to the Lord.* (2 Chronicles 5:13)

When I read this, I see that beautiful temple and a great crowd gathered inside. Then the singing begins—hundreds of voices—and the air is filled with praise and thanksgiving—a joyous occasion!

And then it happened! The glory of the Lord filled the temple like a cloud. It was so powerful that the priests could not continue the service. King Solomon stood up and spoke:

> *But now I have chosen Jerusalem for my Name to be there, and I have chosen David to rule my people Israel.* (2 Chronicles 6:6)

He went on to say that although David had wanted to build the temple, God chose Solomon to do it. Now it was done and the ark, representing God's covenant with His people, was in place. Solomon prayed to God a prayer of thanksgiving and asked God to be with His people, that they would follow Him.

> *When Solomon finished praying, fire came down from heaven and consumed the burnt offering and the sacrifices, and the glory of the Lord filled the temple.* (2 Chronicles 7:1)

After the celebration was over (seven days), the people went home with joyful hearts.

I have attended a number of retreats and conferences put on by various Christian groups. I have experienced the great spiritual highs of people joining together to reach out to God in praise and thanksgiving. Problems seem to disappear and our souls soar as we worship our heavenly Father. Joy and peace flood over us as the Holy Spirit enters our hearts. It is, indeed, a mountaintop experience and we go away rejoicing.

> *On the twenty-third day of the seventh month he sent the people to their homes, joyful and glad in heart for the good things the Lord had done for David and Solomon and for his people Israel.* (2 Chronicles 7:10)

God again appeared to Solomon in the night and warned that if he and his people turned away from God, they would lose the blessings He had for them. However, He would be ready to receive their repentance at any time.

> *...if my people, who are called by my name, will humble themselves pray and seek my face and turn from their wicked ways, then will I hear from heaven and will forgive their sin and will heal their land.* (2 Chronicles 7:14)

We, too, are God's people, so this promise is for us as well—if we meet the conditions laid down. Be done with arrogance and pride, pray constantly, repent of every wrong attitude and habit—and God will hear our prayers. Then we can praise God as we see His mighty works—and the devil will flee. He cannot stand to hear us praising God. Our country needs people who pray and praise!

READ: 2 Chronicles 8–13

Solomon's wisdom was world-renowned and he was unbelievably wealthy, but it does not seem that he was noted for his consistent obedience to God. It is hard to say whether it was his wealth or numerous wives. In those circumstances, it would be difficult for anyone not to be self-centred.

No wonder Jesus said it would be hard for a rich man to enter the Kingdom of Heaven. Material things can so easily become gods in our lives. Just recently, a man said to me, "When I was earning a really good salary, I always wanted more. But now, we are living on about half the amount and we are happier than we ever were. It is good to have to save up to buy something you want."

I would not wish great wealth on anyone. The responsibility and temptations are just too great for most people to handle and still keep God as the number one priority in their lives.

Rehoboam, Solomon's son, alienated the ten northern tribes and they separated, becoming known as Israel, leaving him king over Judah, the two southern tribes. Rehoboam would have gone to war to get them back, but God told him not to. Under Jeroboam, Israel turned aside from God and the Levites fled south to Judah. Many others who wanted to follow God joined them, and for three years Judah moved in the right direction.

But Rehoboam faced another temptation:

After Rehoboam's position as king was established and he had become strong, he and all Israel with him abandoned the law of the Lord. (2 Chronicles 12:1)

When life is going well, we tend to forget God. Instinctively, we feel we no longer need Him, that we are doing alright on our own. Not only can wealth be a snare used by Satan to distance us from God, but success can do the same thing. Many people ask, "If God is a God of love, why is there so much suffering in the world?" Maybe this is one answer: "Because it takes suffering to make us aware of our need for God."

When Egypt came against Jerusalem, its people did not seek God and were defeated. But God is also forgiving. When the king and the leaders began to pray, God said:

Since they have humbled themselves, I will not destroy them but will soon give them deliverance. (2 Chronicles 12:7)

Rehoboam's son Abijah (the grandson of Solomon) became king of Judah. For a time, he followed God's ways. When Abijah went to battle against Jeroboam of Israel, he warned them that they had gone after false gods:

As for us, the Lord is our God, and we have not forsaken him... Men of Israel, do not fight against the Lord, the God of your fathers, for you will not succeed. (2 Chronicles 13:10, 12)

They fought anyway and Israel was defeated. We can make the same mistake—fighting against and being critical of another ministry and how it is handled—unaware that we are fighting against God. When I begin to think critical thoughts about a fellow Christian or another ministry, I try to remember to switch to prayerful thoughts before that criticism becomes an attitude.

READ: 2 Chronicles 14–16

The stories of the next few kings in Judah point to the danger of becoming complacent in our Christian walk. We need to constantly be on the alert to catch wrong attitudes in ourselves before they begin to direct our lives. It is easy to get off-track and not notice until the damage is done.

Asa did what was good and right in the eyes of the Lord his God. (2 Chronicles 14:2)

A person can become famous in the eyes of the world, but how much better it is to be acceptable in the sight of the Lord!

Asa commanded his people to seek God; he got rid of all the idols, even the high places and incense altars, and he gave God the credit:

"The land is still ours, because we have sought the Lord our God; we sought him and he has given us rest on every side." So they built and prospered. (2 Chronicles 14:7)

God spoke to Asa and all Judea through Azariah:

The Lord is with you when you are with him. If you seek him, he will be found by you, but if you forsake him, he will forsake you. (2 Chronicles 15:2)

Asa and all Judah made a covenant with God that anyone who did not seek God would be put to death! Everything went well for some time. Then Baasha, king of Israel, came against Judah and Asa sought help from Syria. He neglected to check with God first.

Hanani told King Asa that he had made a mistake by relying on man rather than God.

For the eyes of the Lord range throughout the earth to strengthen those whose hearts are fully committed to him. You have done a foolish thing, and from now on you will be at war. (2 Chronicles 16:9)

Instead of repenting, Asa became angry at the criticism, threw Hanani in prison, and inflicted cruelties on his people. He developed a disease in his feet:

Though his disease was severe, even in his illness he did not seek help from the Lord, but only from the physicians. (2 Chronicles 16:12)

It seems that Asa became complacent, maybe even arrogant in his walk with God. Instead of constantly asking God to show him where he needed to change, he reacted violently when told he was wrong! None of us likes to be criticized, but when criticism comes our way, as it surely will, we have two choices:

1. React in anger at the one who gave it, as Asa did.
2. Take it before the Lord to see how He sees it.

If in prayer I feel the accusation is valid, I need to change and put the situation right. If not, I should just ignore it.

When I look back at King David's life, I think he had a very special place in God's heart because he was always ready to repent of his sins. Repentance seems to be the key to the Kingdom of Heaven.

READ: 2 Chronicles 17–20

Asa's son Jehosophat became the next king of Judah. There was still friction with Israel, which was not following God at all.

The Lord was with Jehosophat because in his early years he walked in the ways his father David had followed. He did not consult the Baals but sought the God of his father and followed his commands rather than the practices of Israel. The Lord established the kingdom under his control; and all Judah brought gifts to Jehosophat, so that he had great wealth and honor. His heart was devoted to the ways of the Lord; furthermore, he removed the high places and the Asherah poles from Judah. (2 Chronicles 17:3–6)

He even sent men to all the cities to teach courses on the laws of God. Everything went well until he made a marriage alliance with King Ahab of Israel. The two kingdoms became friendly and decided to join in battle against Ramoth-Gilead, even though a prophet of God warned them against doing so. Ahab was killed.

Though Jehosophat had been a strong believer, he became friendly with an unbeliever and was drawn away from God's plan. Jehu, a prophet, came to him and said:

> *Should you help the wicked and love those who hate the Lord? Because of this, the wrath of the Lord is upon you. There is, however, some good in you, for you have rid the land of the Asherah poles and have set your heart on seeking God.* (2 Chronicles 19:2)

Unlike his father, Jehosophat accepted the criticism and changed. He helped his people get back to following the Lord.

The great story in 2 Chronicles 20 demonstrates that God is all we need, even when we face terrific odds. When faced with a huge army coming against him, the king called everyone to fast and pray. He called out to God, saying,

> *We do not know what to do, but our eyes are upon you.* (2 Chronicles 20:12)

This is the key to facing any adversity—admit your helplessness and fix your eyes upon the Lord. God then spoke through one of their men, assuring them,

> *The battle is not yours, but God's... You will not have to fight this battle. Take up your positions; stand firm and see the deliverance the Lord will give you, O Judah and Jerusalem.* (2 Chronicles 20:15, 17)

The whole company, including the king, bowed down and worshipped God while the Levites praised the Lord with loud voices! Just imagine the next morning when the army lined up to go out to battle and the king appointed a choir to march in front. They began to sing and the whole army followed them. What a sight!

The moment they began to praise God, the enemy troops turned against each other. By the time the Judean army arrived, there was no one left. They returned home with the spoil, rejoicing and praising God. The surrounding nations feared them because God was with them.

That kind of victory is ours if we allow Jesus to be our Lord and Master. There is great power and new spiritual understanding in praising God when we are willing to repent and get back on track.

READ: 2 Chronicles 21–26

Jehosophat's son Jehoram was married to King Ahab's daughter, from Israel, and they did not follow God.

Nevertheless, because of the covenant the Lord had made with David, the Lord was not willing to destroy the house of David. He had promised to maintain a lamp for him and his descendants forever. (2 Chronicles 21:7)

The lamp was not to appear for many years, but when Jesus did come, He provided full redemption for all who accepted Him. When I read of all the misery that results from rejecting the Lord's plan, I wonder why we allow anything else to take priority in our lives. Even today, with all the evidence so easily available, we get too busy to spend time with God, or too preoccupied with entertainment to read the Bible.

Some of the people revolted because Jehoram forsook God, but he continued to lead Judah astray. When he died, it was said, *"He passed away, to no one's regret"* (2 Chronicles 21:20). What a waste of the one life he was given! His son, Ahaziah, was no better, and when he died his mother, the wicked Athaliah, took over.

Jehoiada, the priest, planned her downfall and crowned the young prince, Josiah, who was just seven years old. Under Jehoiada's guidance, Josiah did what was right in the sight of the Lord as long as the priest lived.

This makes me realize that we are greatly influenced by those around us. This is of twofold importance:

1. What kind of person is having an influence on me? Whose counsel do I listen to?
2. What kind of influence do I have on others? Will those around me do what is right in the sight of the Lord because of my example?

After Jehoiada died, his son tried to warn Josiah, but he would not listen. It is a serious matter to consciously reject God. If we do so, where will we spend eternity?

Amaziah, too, followed God for a while, but then resorted to worshipping idols. God sent a prophet to warn him, but he would not listen.

From the time that Amaziah turned away from following the Lord, they conspired against him in Jerusalem... (2 Chronicles 25:27)

He was killed and his son Uzziah became king. He, too, started out well:

As long as he sought the Lord, God gave him success. (2 Chronicles 26:5)

Unfortunately, he was like many of us today:

But after Uzziah became powerful, his pride led to his downfall. (2 Chronicles 26:16)

When we take the glory for ourselves and let self-centredness dominate, we lose touch with God's plan for us and cut ourselves off from His blessings.

Uzziah became angry when the priests tried to steer him back to God's commandments. Leprosy broke out on his forehead. He never recovered from the disease and had to live in isolation for the rest of his life. I wonder, did he repent of his pride and arrogance before he died?

READ: 2 Chronicles 27–30

Here, we read about three kings of Judah—Jotham (Uzziah's son), his son Ahaz, and his grandson Hezekiah.

Jotham did his best to follow God.

The people, however, continued their corrupt practices. (2 Chronicles 27:2)

It must have been disheartening for Jotham to see his people ignore God's plan for them. I wonder if he faced opposition for his beliefs. It takes special courage for a person in a leadership position to live by his convictions when those around him accept the world's material standards.

After his sixteen years as king, he died at forty-one years of age and Ahaz his son became king. Ahaz was a young man, too—just twenty years of age. For the next sixteen years, he undid any good that his forefathers had done in establishing a people of God. He did not seek God's protection, so the surrounding nations—Syria, Israel, and Assyria—gained easy victories over Judah. Many were taken captive. However, some in Israel knew the power of God and persuaded the warriors to release the captives they had brought from Judah.

"You must not bring those prisoners here," they said, "or we will be guilty before the Lord. Do you intend to add to our sin and guilt? For our guilt is already great, and his fierce anger rests on Israel." (2 Chronicles 28:13)

The people of Israel had some fear of the Lord's power, but not enough to change their lifestyle. They recognized their guilt but were not prepared to repent and seek God's leading. That is a dangerous position to be in if you are concerned about where you will spend eternity.

Hezekiah was the next king and things changed under his rule. He immediately started to clean up the temple and put things right with God so Judah would be in right relationship with Him again.

When we, as individuals, stray and get off-track, that is exactly what we need to do—clean out what is wrong in our lives and let God show us the way He wants us to go. It is not an easy step to take, but the rewards are immeasurable, for there is no other place we can find real peace and joy except in right relationship with God.

When the cleansing was complete:

The whole assembly bowed in worship, while the singers sang and the trumpeters played... So they sang praises with gladness and bowed their heads and worshiped. (2 Chronicles 29:28, 30)

When we repent and receive forgiveness, we feel like praising God and worshipping Him. Hezekiah encouraged his people to continue in this, not only for themselves but also for those in captivity:

If you return to the Lord, then your brothers and your children will be shown compassion by their captors and will come back to this land, for the Lord your God is gracious and compassionate. He will not turn his face from you if you return to him. (2 Chronicles 30:9)

The faithfulness of God's people can bring new life to those for whom we pray! That gives me another reason for having daily quiet time with my heavenly Father.

The whole assembly who had gathered in Jerusalem sought the Lord and God blessed them. They had such a great time for the first seven days that they decided to carry on for another seven days. There was great joy in Jerusalem!

READ: 2 Chronicles 31–36

Certain incidents in Hezekiah's life show us something of God's character, as well as that of Hezekiah himself. When Sennacherib, king of Assyria, came against Jerusalem, he taunted them, saying that since the gods of other nations had not been able to protect them against Syria's army, why did they think their God would? However, when Hezekiah and the prophet Isaiah cried out to God, He saved them by sending an angel who disrupted the Assyrian army.

God is greater than any human force. He is the creator of all things and when He intervenes on behalf of His people, no one can stop Him. The most important factor in my life is to be sure that I am on God's side, that I do not slip away because of self-centredness, pride, or neglecting to get my direction from Him.

When Hezekiah became ill, he prayed to God, who healed him:

But Hezekiah's heart was proud and he did not respond to the kindness shown him; therefore the Lord's wrath was on him and on Judah and Jerusalem. (2 Chronicles 32:25)

This points to a human frailty we are probably all guilty of—calling out to God when we are in trouble, but going our own way when things go well. Fortunately for Hezekiah and his country,

Then Hezekiah repented of the pride of his heart, as did the people of Jerusalem; therefore the Lord's wrath did not come upon them during the days of Hezekiah. (2 Chronicles 32:26)

God always hears a penitent heart and is ready to forgive. Only when we hang on to our pride and arrogance can He do nothing for us. Every Christian leader is susceptible to temptation, and through the years many have fallen. Only opening our hearts to Him daily and allowing the Holy Spirit to point out seeds of pride can keep us from falling into this trap.

Manasseh, an evil king, also experienced God's grace:

In his distress he sought the favor of the Lord his God and humbled himself greatly before the God of his fathers. (2 Chronicles 33:12)

God heard him and even rescued him from captivity, bringing him back to Jerusalem:

Then Manasseh knew that the Lord is God. (2 Chronicles 33:13)

Sometime later, his grandson Josiah brought Judah back to the Lord and got rid of all the idols the people worshipped. However, he disregarded a message from the Lord and died in battle.

Bad years followed when Judah again moved away from God's plan.

The Lord, the God of their fathers, sent word to them through his messengers again and again, because he had pity on his people and on his dwelling place. But they mocked God's messengers... (2 Chronicles 36:15–16)

If we mock God, we must face the consequences sometime, somewhere. Only repentance and forgiveness can save us.

216

THE BOOK OF

1 Corinthians

READ: 1 Corinthians 1–3

Here, Paul seems to say that the natural wisdom that had been his since birth was not enough to bring hope to the world. However, the wisdom of God is available to anyone who will receive the Spirit of God and is willing to learn. Even though I have experienced this in small measure, I still find it an awesome thought that the Creator of the Universe can and will impart His wisdom and knowledge to a simple person like me—as much as I am willing and able to accept it.

Some time ago, when I was involved in Lighthouse Christian Academy, I witnessed an example of this. A lovely Christian lady was most anxious for her children to attend our Christian school, but she could not afford the fees. I promised to pray about it. I talked to the people on the board, who agreed to accept whatever decision I made. I didn't sleep too well the following night. My thoughts were a mixture of worry and prayer. Suddenly, as clear as could be, these words came to me:

I tell you the truth, whatever you did for one of the least of these brothers of mine, you did for me. (Matthew 25:40)

At once I could see that some of my concern was for my own reputation. How would I look if it should not work out right? While confessing this, I realized a song was going through my mind. It was:

Faith, faith, faith,
Just a little bit of faith—

You don't need a whole lot—
Just use what you've got.

I chuckled, recognizing my Lord's love for me in giving me an answer, and also His sense of humour. The woman's children did end up attending our school, and as far as I know everything went well.

We have not received the spirit of the world but the Spirit who is from God, that we may understand what God has freely given us. (1 Corinthians 2:12)

Paul points out, too, the importance of putting our complete trust in God and not in some person, even if that person eloquently shares the gospel. Only God can bring the necessary changes in us.

I planted the seed, Apollos watered it, but God made it grow. (1 Corinthians 3:6)

Verses such as the following fill me with excitement at the amazing provision God has made for us.

But we have the mind of Christ. (1 Corinthians 2:16)

Don't you know that you yourselves are God's temple and that God's Spirit lives in you? (1 Corinthians 3:16)

If I do not receive what He offers, it is because I have not set myself up in the right condition. Imagine the privilege of being taught by the Holy Spirit Himself!

READ: 1 Corinthians 4–7

Paul was writing to the church in Corinth, but there may be some truths here that are applicable to our church today.

For the kingdom of God is not a matter of talk but of power. (1 Corinthians 4:20)

Talk is cheap. It is easy to say what we think, but our actions speak louder than words. Any time I speak or teach on some aspect of the Christian life, I am keenly aware that I must put it into practise myself if my words are to have any credibility. What people see in me has much more power than what I say.

Paul urges the members of the Corinthian church to clean out anything in their lives that is not in line with Christ's teaching—immorality, boasting, and taking each other to court. In other words, he calls them to repentance.

Do you not know that your body is a temple of the Holy Spirit, who is in you, whom you have received from God? You are not your own; you were bought at a price. Therefore honor God with your body. (1 Corinthians 6:19–20)

Many diseases today can be caused by people abusing their bodies—for example AIDS, lung cancer, and liver disorders. Doctors are also aware that mental attitudes have a profound effect on physical well-being. Worry, resentment, fear, and hatred can bring on serious trouble in our digestion, circulation, and other systems.

God created our bodies, and they are real masterpieces! All the systems are made to work in harmony. We breathe, our blood circulates, our food digests, and we don't have to plan it at all. But we can certainly mess it up if we do not choose to fit into the rest of God's plan for our lives. When we teach children about good health, we should add love, joy, and faith in God as necessary ingredients.

Keeping God's commands is what counts. (1 Corinthians 7:19)

The acceptance of immorality in our society today is already taking a toll. The Bible teaches chastity outside of marriage and fidelity within marriage. No other way will produce sound character, stable families, and righteous nations.

I would like you to be free from concern. (1 Corinthians 7:32)

I can only be free from concern if I am secure in my relationship with God!

READ: 1 Corinthians 8–10

Yet for us there is but one God, the Father, from whom all things came and for whom we live; and there is but one Lord, Jesus Christ, through whom all things came and through whom we live. (1 Corinthians 8:6)

It must have been very confusing for people to believe in a lot of different gods and feel that they had to please them all. It is equally confusing when we try to please other people around us. In my early married life, I thought it was my primary duty to please my husband. Some of the time it worked, but at other times, try as I might, I couldn't figure out what he wanted me to do. Then I became resentful. It was a no-win situation.

It was a great relief to realize I didn't have to guess what he was thinking, because my number one goal was to please God. In so doing, I was able to love my husband without placing demands on him! This brought both of us great freedom and helped us visualize being the individuals God wanted us to be. It gave us a marriage grounded in God's love.

That is not to say the way was easy. There were many times of misunderstanding when we seemed to be at cross-purposes. However, when we each went to our heavenly Father, confessed our wrong attitude, and got new direction from Him, it was not hard to get back into a right relationship with each other. He was our Counsellor, showing us where we needed to change.

> *Yet when I preach the gospel, I cannot boast, for I am compelled to preach. Woe to me if I do not preach the gospel!* (1 Corinthians 9:16)

Paul knew God had called him to preach the gospel. If he refused, he would be out of God's will—and out of His protection as well. If he obeyed, he would be in God's plan, but that was nothing to boast about. Boasting is being self-centred, the opposite of God-centred.

> *So, if you think you are standing firm, be careful that you don't fall!* (1 Corinthians 10:12)

When things go well, it is easy to become careless about spending time with God. Somehow we are inclined to look at Him as someone to whom we only go when we are in need of help. If my grown children only come to see me when they are in trouble, I would soon doubt their love for me. God must feel the same way.

When things go well, that is the time to go to Him in a spirit of gratitude and praise and acknowledge His presence in all we do. That is the greatest way to prepare ourselves for any trouble we may have to face in the future. That is when we learn to just enjoy being in His presence.

> *So whether you eat or drink or whatever you do, do it all for the glory of God.* (1 Corinthians 10:31)

READ: 1 Corinthians 11–13

Paul tells the Corinthian church of his concern about the division among them. He then describes the Last Supper in the same words so often used in communion services:

Therefore, whoever eats the bread or drinks the cup of the Lord in an unworthy manner will be guilty of sinning against the body and blood of the Lord. (1 Corinthians 11:27)

Paul goes further to say that many have come to the table without first examining themselves to be sure their relationships are right.

That is why many among you are weak and sick, and a number of you have fallen asleep. (1 Corinthians 11:30)

Could it be that some of our illnesses are caused by wrong attitudes?

In the next chapter, Paul talks of the gifts that come when we receive the Holy Spirit. As Christians, we are part of the Body of Christ—the church. We are each unique and different, having a special part to play in the Body. We are given particular gifts so the Holy Spirit can work through us to draw others into the Kingdom.

And in the church God has appointed first of all apostles, second prophets, third teachers, then workers of miracles, also those having gifts of healing, those able to help others, those with gifts of administration, and those speaking in different kinds of tongues. (1 Corinthians 12:28)

Everyone has a part, and then he goes on to say:

But eagerly desire the greater gifts. (1 Corinthians 12:31)

The greater gift is the way of love. No other power, understanding, or knowledge is of any value if we don't have God's love for everyone. That is a tall order. Just to check where I stand in that regard, I find it helpful—and challenging—to substitute my own name for the word "love" in 1 Corinthians 13:4–7. Usually, I don't measure up too well, but it does help me to see where I need to change—whether it is in the matter of arrogance, resentment, impatience, or one of the other areas.

Love can be a feeling, but it is also a decision. It is possible to think only positive thoughts about a person and refuse to entertain negative attitudes. In this exercise, it is important that no critical words are spoken, for our spoken words intensify our attitudes. It has been suggested that we should live as though we love that person who is hard to love. Say nice things about him. Do nice things for him. Go out of your way to create an atmosphere of love around him. As time goes on, you will find that the feeling follows the act. As Paul says, we don't understand it fully, but some day we will.

And now these three remain: faith, hope and love. But the greatest of these is love. (1 Corinthians 13:13)

READ: 1 Corinthians 14–16

Follow the way of love and eagerly desire spiritual gifts... (1 Corinthians 14:1)

If that rule is fundamental in my life, no one will ever hear me speak negative criticism about anyone. That would be wonderful! Negatives tear down, but positive statements bring out the best in others. I have tried to live this way, but every now and then I slip. However, if I follow the way of love, I recognize the slip—I can confess it, receive forgiveness, and move on.

Paul talks about the spiritual gifts. Speaking in tongues is mainly for private prayer, but when it is done in public, it is important to pray for an interpretation.

For this reason anyone who speaks in a tongue should pray that he may interpret what he says. (1 Corinthians 14:13)

Paul encourages the gift of prophecy. This is another reason for engaging in morning quiet times with God. Spending time with Him is an opportunity for God to speak to us, to reveal truth which we can share with others. That is the nature of prophecy; anyone can receive it if we make a practice of opening our minds to the mind of God.

Paul goes on to explain what resurrection from the dead means. I like the idea of a seed being planted in the ground; it disappears and a whole new plant takes its place. The mortal body is often imperfect, and as we grow older our skin becomes looser and more wrinkled, our energy is not what it used to be, and we can't do things we used to do easily. It is comforting to know that when our time comes, we can leave all this behind. We will have a spiritual body that does not grow old or get run down. Only in Jesus can we find this wonderful hope of eternal life with Him.

But thanks be to God! He gives us the victory through our Lord Jesus Christ. (1 Corinthians 15:57)

Without this hope, life would be pretty discouraging. We would have nothing to look forward to but the deterioration of the body and the need for more assistance to survive. On the other hand, with this hope, life never loses its meaning—God has a plan for each of us right to the end.

Therefore, my dear brothers, stand firm. Let nothing move you. Always give yourselves fully to the work of the Lord, because you know that your labor in the Lord is not in vain. (1 Corinthians 15:58)

The next chapter gives us just an inkling of Paul's plans and mentions some of his friends. He gives another bit of timely advice, no matter what age we are:

Be on your guard; stand firm in the faith; be men of courage; be strong. Do everything in love. (1 Corinthians 16:13–14)

I'm sure that goes for women, too.

THE BOOK OF

2 Corinthians

READ: 2 Corinthians 1–3

Praise be to the God and Father of our Lord Jesus Christ, the Father of compassion and the God of all comfort, who comforts us in all our troubles, so that we can comfort those in any trouble with the comfort we ourselves have received from God. (2 Corinthians 1:3–4)

That does not sound as if believers will have trouble-free lives. In fact, it almost guarantees there will be times of affliction. In the midst of trouble, however, we receive comfort from God Himself. His purpose in this is that we be a source of comfort for others. If only I could remember this when I go through difficult times! It would be a great help if I could remember to say, "Lord, I accept your comfort now when I am hurting. Fill me with Your love so that it may flow out from me to others when they are in need."

Paul went through desperate times, but felt there was a purpose in it:

But this happened that we might not rely on ourselves but on God, who raises the dead. (2 Corinthians 1:9)

I guess if life is too easy, we do not see any need of God; our own intelligence seems to be enough.

Not that we are competent in ourselves to claim anything for ourselves, but our competence comes from God. (2 Corinthians 3:5)

When things go well, it is easy to take the credit and glory for ourselves. This can lead to disaster, as we see in the lives of different leaders throughout history. For example, looking back in the Old Testament, King Uzziah became very strong and his fame spread:

> *But after Uzziah became powerful, his pride led to his downfall.* (2 Chronicles 26:16)

In more modern times, Adolf Hitler started out by making improvements in Germany after World War I. He became powerful and proud, but this led to his own destruction and that of thousands of others in World War II.

If we could learn to give God the glory and express thanks to Him, we could avoid a lot of anxiety.

> *Now the Lord is the Spirit, and where the Spirit of the Lord is, there is freedom.* (2 Corinthians 3:17)

This is the kind of freedom that is within us, freedom which is not dictated by our outward circumstances. Even in prison, a person can experience an inner freedom that comes from God, as Paul did.

The chains that remove freedom from us are of our own making—sins of habit, wrong attitudes, and relationships broken through unforgiveness. As we are willing to drop anything that does not glorify God, we make room for the Holy Spirit to come in. We begin to be more like Jesus, changing from glory to glory.

READ: 2 Corinthians 4–6

Sometimes we wonder why others don't get as excited as we do about the gospel. Here is a verse that throws some light on that:

> *The god of this age has blinded the minds of unbelievers, so that they cannot see the light of the gospel of the glory of Christ, who is the image of God.* (2 Corinthians 4:4)

We need to pray for God's guidance as to when and to whom we speak. He can show us those in whom the Holy Spirit has prepared the way so they are ready to receive.

As the years go by (and they seem to go by so quickly), I become more aware of my body running down. I am in really good health, but the wrinkles on my face have deepened and I tire more easily. I can't get in and out of the car as easily as I used to. I am conscious of the daily signs of aging, yet I feel like the same person inside. I can still get excited over plans for some project, but when it comes to carrying out those plans I often don't have the stamina to do it.

My mother must have experienced the same thing. She reached the century mark, but for a number of years she would accept a dinner invitation only to back out when the time came, saying, "You go on without me. I am tired and I think I'll just rest. I'll be thinking of you and I know you will have a good time." Friends and relatives accepted this, knowing the old adage is true: "The spirit is willing but the flesh is weak."

Paul says it this way:

Therefore we do not lose heart. Though outwardly we are wasting away, yet inwardly we are being renewed day by day. (2 Corinthians 4:16)

Because I do not go out in the evenings as much as I used to, I have more time to think, pray, and read. I am very much at peace with God and my position in the world.

Therefore, if anyone is in Christ, he is a new creation; the old has gone, the new has come! (2 Corinthians 5:17)

Nothing compares with the change that comes into our lives when we invite Jesus to be our Lord. One of the greatest blessings is that when I have sinned and am truly sorry, I know Jesus will forgive me. I cannot be sure other people will be that forgiving, but I can be certain Jesus is, which means I never need to carry a load of guilt with me.

God made him who had no sin to be sin for us, so that in him we might become the righteousness of God. (2 Corinthians 5:21)

Not only that, but He promises to live in us—our very thoughts can become His thoughts if we practise acknowledging His presence. Ridding ourselves of anything that is not in line with His will allows us to continue living in freedom.

For we are the temple of the living God. As God has said: "I will live with them and walk among them, and I will be their God, and they will be my people." (2 Corinthians 6:16)

READ: 2 Corinthians 7–9

Since we have these promises, dear friends, let us purify ourselves from everything that contaminates body and spirit, perfecting holiness out of reverence for God. (2 Corinthians 7:1)

Walking with God requires constant change. Just as we wash daily to keep our bodies clean, we need to check daily for the habits and attitudes that need to be cleansed from our lives. Daily confession and cleansing is as refreshing as a shower—and equally as necessary. Looking back at my quiet-time book, here is an entry I made one day:

Today, what is my attitude? Mainly a self-centred desire to rest, self-pity at the thought of a busy day ahead. Lord, I need a cleansing of my attitude. I need a pre-walk through this day with You, to appreciate its possibilities. Two thoughts that must be changed: 1) "How busy I am. Poor me!" 2) "Let's see how little I can do today." These can be changed to: "This is the day the Lord has made. I will rejoice and be glad in it."

Paul talks about giving and sharing with people in other places who are in need.

Remember this: Whoever sows sparingly will also reap sparingly, and whoever sows generously will reap generously. (2 Corinthians 9:6)

This spiritual truth can cause great joy or great despair, depending on what we do. In the case of money, it seems that when we are willing to share what we have, we receive a blessing. I often hear Christians saying, "You can't outgive God." Anyone who has given, even when they are in need themselves, knows this to be true. However, as in every other area of life, the giving needs to be done as God directs. Then He blesses our obedience to Him.

The same principle applies to how we relate to others. As children, we used to enjoy singing a song that went like this: "Love is something if you give it away. You end up having more." If you give love, you receive love. If you give encouragement, you receive encouragement. If you are friendly, you have friends. Conversely, if you give criticism, you receive criticism. If you are rude to others, they will be rude to you. There is no question about the fact that we reap what we sow.

There is an added benefit to the positive attitude: it is the *joy* which is a byproduct of loving, caring, and giving, even before the harvest comes in.

READ: 2 Corinthians 10–13

Paul shows himself to be very human in this part of his letter, as he defends his own position and at the same time shows concern for the spiritual health of his friends in Corinth. A few verses speak to me personally.

> *We demolish arguments and every pretension that sets itself up against the knowledge of God, and we take captive every thought to make it obedient to Christ.* (2 Corinthians 10:5)

This describes the spiritual warfare that often takes place in me. I don't always sleep through the night; sometimes as I lie awake, I feel compelled to get up and write. It is not always easy to get out of a warm bed, gather up my Bible, housecoat, and slippers, and go off into the study for an hour or so. Once I get started, I can lose myself and find the time a real blessing, for it is an hour spent with my heavenly Father. However, to make the decision to get up, I have to destroy all the fleshly arguments in my mind and bring every thought captive to obey what I believe Christ is urging me to do. I can understand what Paul means when he says:

> *But I am afraid that just as Eve was deceived by the serpent's cunning, your minds may somehow be led astray from your sincere and pure devotion to Christ.* (2 Corinthians 11:3)

The more we give in to the thoughts of personal comfort and desire, the further we get from the perfect plan of God, which is centred in a sincere and pure devotion to Christ. The spiritual battle begins in the mind.

The hardships Paul endured are hard to imagine, but there seems to be one particular discomfort which he calls a thorn in the flesh—something that was especially irritating. He prayed to be relieved of it, but God did not remove it. He said:

> *My grace is sufficient for you, for my power is made perfect in weakness.* (2 Corinthians 12:9)

We would like God to make life easy for us, but that is not the way to become strong. He gives us a better way when He promises to go through all life's difficulties with us, allowing us to experience His grace as He supplies all our needs. In our weakness, we are aware of the power of Christ.

The letter ends with a wonderful benediction:

> *May the grace of the Lord Jesus Christ, and the love of God, and the fellowship of the Holy Spirit be with you all.* (2 Corinthians 13:14)

It is well worth the struggle we go through at times to rid ourselves of the thoughts that cloud our minds, in order that we may once again be in total communion with God, our maker, Jesus our redeemer, and the Holy Spirit, our guide and comforter.

This has been a precious hour. Now it is 2:30 a.m. and I am going back to bed.

THE BOOK OF

Ezra

READ: Ezra 1–6

King Nebuchadnezzar took the Israelites captive to Babylon (in Persia), and there they remained for seventy years. Many of those who were adults in Ezra's day had been born there.

God intervened by stirring up Cyrus, who was now king of Persia, telling him to see that the temple of God was rebuilt in Jerusalem. It seems rather amazing that he recognized that this word came from the Lord, the God of heaven, for the Persians were not generally believers. He encouraged the Jewish people to leave Babylon and go to Jerusalem to take on this task. He even urged those who did not feel they should go to assist the others in any way they could.

Almost forty-three thousand people answered this call, including two hundred singers! When they got to Jerusalem, they set up an altar and praised the Lord! For about a year they offered sacrifices to God, celebrating the Feast of Booths (a time of thanksgiving) while collecting enough cedar wood from Lebanon to build the temple.

Finally, the foundation of the temple was laid and everyone gathered to celebrate.

With praise and thanksgiving they sang to the Lord: "He is good; his love to Israel endures forever." And all the people gave a great shout of praise to the Lord, because the foundation of the house of the Lord was laid. (Ezra 3:11)

There were trumpets and cymbals, singing, shouting, and weeping—what a celebration!

Opposition arose when the king of Persia changed. The new king, Artexerxes, issued an order to stop work on the temple. However, God's plan could not be stopped; a third king, Darius, looked back at the decree sent out by Cyrus some years earlier and renewed it, declaring that all the requirements be supplied, even the animals for the sacrificial offerings to the Lord. He even added a warning to any who might consider opposing this construction.

> *So the elders of the Jews continued to build and prosper… Then the people of Israel—the priests, the Levites and the rest of the exiles—celebrated the dedication of the house of God with joy.* (Ezra 6:14, 16)

READ: Ezra 7–10

Ezra, a *"teacher well versed in the Law of Moses"* (Ezra 7:6), was given permission by King Artaxerxes to return to Jerusalem. The king not only allowed others to go with him, but also made it possible for him to collect silver and gold for buying supplies.

Ezra set out with his company:

> *There, by the Ahava Canal, I proclaimed a fast, so that we might humble ourselves before our God and ask him for a safe journey for us and our children, with all our possessions.* (Ezra 8:21)

God's hand was upon them and they arrived safely in Jerusalem. However, they found the people there had seriously disobeyed the Lord. This needed to be put right.

God had commanded the people of Israel not to marry women from the neighbouring countries, but many of them did just that. It must have been a very painful time when they confessed to God and "put away" their foreign wives and children! God wanted a people totally obedient to Him, and He knew the unbelieving wives would draw the men away from their faith.

THE BOOK OF

Nehemiah

READ: Nehemiah 1–7

Through the centuries, the Jewish people have been drawn to the land God promised Abraham. Of all the nations of the world, they are the only people to whom God has designated a particular area. They have a tie to Israel the rest of us cannot understand. After countless generations living in other countries, their hearts are still drawn to Jerusalem and we have seen them flood back to Israel by the thousands in the past century. There is no other explanation than that God's plan is being fulfilled and His people are returning to the land given to their forefathers.

In the first chapter, Nehemiah weeps over the plight of his people back in Israel, although he himself has a good position with King Artexerxes in Babylon. When he hears how the walls of Jerusalem have been broken down and that the Jewish people there are in trouble, he turns to God in prayer. It is interesting to note that first he acknowledges who God is. Then he confesses his own sins and the sins of his people. Perhaps this prayer helped prepare the heart of the king to be sympathetic to Nehemiah's concern for his people, for the king asked, *"What is it you want?"* (Nehemiah 2:4)

The next sentence is significant:

Then I prayed to the God of heaven... (Nehemiah 2:4)

Only then did he make his request to the king that he be allowed to rebuild the walls of Jerusalem. He had already spent time seeking God's direction:

When I heard these things, I sat down and wept. For some days I mourned and fasted and prayed before the God of heaven. (Nehemiah 1:4)

Nehemiah is a good example to follow. Here is what I can learn from his example:

1. When I see a need, I must take it to the Lord in prayer.
2. I then leave it in the Lord's hands and go about my business.
3. When the way begins to open, I pray to God for the right words to say.

The building of the wall is an interesting lesson. Each family took responsibility for one section. The work was divided so everyone had a share.

But when Sanballat, Tobiah, the Arabs, the Ammonites and the men of Ashdod heard that the repairs to Jerusalem's walls had gone ahead and that the gaps were being closed, they were very angry. They all plotted together to come and fight against Jerusalem and stir up trouble against it. But we prayed to our God and posted a guard day and night to meet this threat. (Nehemiah 4:7–9)

History is repeating itself today as the Palestinians seek to cause confusion in Israel. There is only one answer to the division we see in every country, including our own: we must pray to our God and do what we feel He is telling us to do. In this case, God's answer was for them to set up a system of guard duty where some worked while others stood guard.

The wall was finally completed and the nations around them became afraid:

…because they realized that this work had been done with the help of our God. (Nehemiah 6:16)

Nehemiah and his friends made a great witness. I wonder if people see the hand of God in what I am doing? Or what my church is doing?

Nehemiah continued to be obedient to God:

So my God put it into my heart to assemble the nobles, the officials and the common people for registration by families. (Nehemiah 7:5)

That's how I want to live—with a mind so open to God that He can drop thoughts into it!

READ: Nehemiah 8–13

Two great men of God became leaders in Jerusalem—Nehemiah was the governor and Ezra was the leading priest and scribe. They had both been captives in Babylon before Ezra returned to rebuild the temple. A few years later, Nehemiah led the people to build the wall around Jerusalem. Some pretty stiff opposition did not deter him, and the job was finally completed. Israel remained under Persian rule throughout this period.

Now was the time to remind the people of God's laws, which had been given to Moses. Ezra read them aloud in *"the square before the Water Gate"* (Nehemiah 8:3), standing on a wooden pulpit which had been built for this purpose. The people listened from early morning until midday as the laws were read and explained to them. They wept when they heard them—possibly because they had strayed so far. Reading the Bible with a real desire to serve God can make us aware of the areas in which we need to change. Through the word of God, the Holy Spirit convicts us of our sin.

This day is sacred to the Lord your God. Do not mourn or weep… Do not grieve, for the joy of the Lord is your strength. (Nehemiah 8:9–10)

The people did what was necessary to put them in a right relationship with the Lord:

1. They celebrated the Feast of Booths, an eight-day period of thanksgiving.
2. They confessed their sins and the sins of their fathers.
3. They praised God.
4. Ezra led them in a beautiful prayer recalling all that God had done for them over the years.

It is a wonderful experience to come together with a large group of people to worship and praise the Lord, with teaching and sharing, confessing and cleansing. You feel lifted up above the cares of this world and experience the glorious presence of God as you rejoice and praise Him. Hurts are healed, sins are forgiven, and often physical healing takes place. It is like a small foretaste of Heaven!

When it comes time to go home and face your daily routine, the testing begins.

Nehemiah returned to Babylon for a time to report to King Artexerxes. During that time, some of the people got off-track. Tobiah, one of the chief opponents of building the wall, was given an honoured place in the courts of the house of God. Then there were those who abused the Sabbath. Finally, a number of Jews married foreign women. All this meant that rather than being guided by God, the people were drawn away from Him by unbelievers.

If we don't walk closely with Him at all times, we drift off into worldly ways without even being aware that it is happening.

THE BOOK OF
Esther

READ: Esther 1–10

This very moving story concerns the time when the Jews were exiled to Persia, where they had been taken captive. Years had gone by and they had settled into their lives there. Of course, their numbers increased as the young people married and had children.

King Ahasuerus had a lot of power, but he looked to those around him for advice whenever he made decisions. He seemed to be rather easily swayed. This cost Queen Vashti her position—and her marriage. Men were not ready to have their authority in the home weakened in any way. It is disturbing to see that same struggle going on today, where the same problem causes broken marriages. If we could only learn that God has a perfect plan for marriage and families, where every person has their own unique place. There does not need to be a power struggle.

Esther must have been surprised to be chosen as a candidate for queen, since she was a Jew, but apparently no one knew that. Not only was she beautiful, but she was well-liked by all and found special favour with the king.

Mordecai's faith was strong, and he refused to bow to the king. As a believer, he could not bow to another human being. No doubt he was shocked to discover that this was going to mean devastation for all his people. He could do nothing but call on Esther to help. He really didn't give her much choice:

For if you remain silent at this time, relief and deliverance for the Jews will arise from another place, but you and your father's family will perish. And who knows but that you have come to royal position for such a time as this? (Esther 4:14)

Although Mordecai does not mention God, his faith in Him is apparent. He knows that God has chosen the Jews and His hand is on them, so if Esther refuses to help them, God will find someone else. God's perfect plan does not depend on one individual; He can use any person who will listen and obey. If one person refuses, His plan is not thwarted; that person simply misses out on the blessing.

Esther chose to be used by God, and she called the people to fast with her for three days. She doesn't mention prayer, but it can be assumed that is how she spent the time.

Her plan certainly came from God. The king's heart was prepared to hear her request. In fact, he couldn't sleep one night and had someone read to him. They read of memorable deeds that had been done, including how Mordecai had saved the king's life. This prepared the way for Haman's treachery to be known and for Mordecai to be honoured.

This is the story of how the faith and obedience of two people saved the Jewish nation. Who knows how He can use each one of us if we believe, listen, and obey?

THE BOOK OF

Galatians

READ: Galatians 1–3

Paul wrote this letter of encouragement and exhortation to his friends in Galatia. He had helped establish a church there, since a number of the Galatians had accepted Jesus as a result of his evangelical mission. However, they had the same problem as we have today—it is one thing to accept Jesus as Lord and Saviour; the hard part is living out that commitment.

His letter points out some pitfalls:

1. It is easy to be swayed by a good speaker whose message is not the true gospel.

I am astonished that you are so quickly deserting the one who called you by the grace of Christ and are turning to a different gospel. (Galatians 1:6)

2. There is danger in following the crowd or seeking the approval of others.

Am I trying to win the approval of men, or of God? Or am I trying to please men? If I were still trying to please men, I would not be a servant of Christ. (Galatians 1:10)

3. Paul explains how he challenged Cephas, who said one thing and did another.

It is easy to talk the talk, but it is another thing to walk the walk. Yesterday, in my morning quiet time, I realized I had made several critical comments recently about various people, scattered here and there in conversation. As I pondered why this was happening, I realized it was rooted in self-concern about a busy upcoming weekend. I usually try to relax during the weekend, but these plans would offer me little chance of that. Along with things to be done, I wrote, "Could I see this situation as an opportunity, a gift from God to be cherished and enjoyed?"

I know from experience that this attitude does not lead to overtiredness, but worry and self-concern certainly do!

Paul sums up my goal for living in these words:

...and I no longer live, but Christ lives in me. (Galatians 2:20)

Probably even Paul was surprised that his mission was mainly aimed at the Gentiles, since throughout the Old Testament God had revealed Himself only to the Jews. Now, with the sacrifice and resurrection of Jesus, the good news was for the Gentiles as well. Here, Paul makes two important observations:

Understand, then, that those who believe are children of Abraham. The Scripture foresaw that God would justify the Gentiles by faith, and announced the gospel in advance to Abraham: "All nations will be blessed through you." (Galatians 3:7–8)

God never changes. His plan began with Adam and Eve and continues throughout history. Every now and then, He reveals something which He has in mind for the future. We call these prophesies. When they happen, we see the faithfulness of God, which increases our belief and trust in Him. His desire is to draw us more closely to Himself so He can fill us with power and love.

READ: Galatians 4–6

Paul does some great teaching in his letters to the various churches:

Now you, brothers, like Isaac, are children of promise. (Galatians 4:28)

Some Christians have believed that God rejected the Jews because they did not recognize Jesus as the Messiah, but that is not what the Bible says. Here, Paul says again that Gentile believers are descended from Abraham along with Isaac, the natural descendant. God's ways cannot be explained. They can only be accepted—and what a blessing that is!

For in Christ Jesus neither circumcision nor uncircumcision has any value. The only thing that counts is faith expressing itself through love. (Galatians 5:6)

Over and over, I see that the important thing is not the rules we keep but where our thoughts are centred. Having faith in God and love for others should be the foundation upon which all our actions are determined. For the Jews, circumcision was the arguing point. For churches today, it could be how and when to baptize, the authority of scripture in daily life, or marriage issues.

Paul goes on to say that we can have freedom—not to satisfy ourselves, but to serve others! That is not generally how we look at freedom, but there is a great truth expressed here, which we will only recognize if we try it! He then concludes:

The entire law is summed up in a single command; "Love your neighbor as yourself." (Galatians 5:14)

That sounds easy, but when you have to work with a difficult person or someone who cheats you or you are falsely accused, God still expects you to love the other person—without exception!

One of the most challenging parts of the Bible is found here:

But the fruit of the Spirit is love, joy, peace, patience, kindness, goodness, faithfulness, gentleness and self-control. (Galatians 5:22–23)

If Christ lives in me, all these attributes should be evident in my life! That sobering thought can leave me feeling discouraged. To be more practical, I use it as a checklist to identify the areas where I am not letting the Holy Spirit control my thinking.

For example, if I do not experience that bubbly feeling of joy, I am allowing negativity to block its way. If I feel resentment (even a slight one) against someone else, I have shut off the flow of God's love in my heart. If I am confused and churning inside, I have not released everything to God, since that results in the wonderful peace only He can give.

Which fruit of the Holy Spirit is lacking in me? What attitude in me has blocked it? When I can identify it, repentance begins. If I honestly hand over my sin to God, the way is cleared for His love, joy, and peace to flow again! What a blessing! Then I can go on to the next step and be of use to others.

Carry each other's burdens, and in this way you will fulfill the law of Christ. (Galatians 6:2)

The reward is great:

…the one who sows to please the Spirit, from the Spirit will reap eternal life. (Galatians 6:8)

THE BOOK OF

Ephesians

READ: Ephesians 1–3

The more time I spend seeking Jesus to better understand God's plan, the more I want to know. Knowledge creates a thirst for more knowledge. What He has in store for us greatly surpasses what we have experienced so far.

> *And he made known to us the mystery of his will according to his good pleasure, which he purposed in Christ, to be put into effect when the times have reached their fulfillment—to bring all things in heaven and on earth together under one head, even Christ.* (Ephesians 1:9–10)

With so much disunity in the world, it is a wonderful hope that *"when the times have reached their fulfilment,"* whenever that is, there will be total unity in Christ. There is certainly no other hope here on earth. Easy access to each other through modern modes of communication and transportation has not cured the mistrust and lack of understanding between nations and individuals. I'm glad I know that God is in control and that I can trust Him totally.

Here is the great prayer Paul prayed for his friends in Ephesus:

> *I keep asking that the God of our Lord Jesus Christ, the glorious Father, may give you the Spirit of wisdom and revelation, so that you may know him better.* (Ephesians 1:17)

This is my prayer for myself, my family, my church, and for the leaders of our nation. In fact, I think I should memorize it so I can always have it in those odd moments when I feel a need to pray.

Throughout the Old Testament, the Jews were set apart as God's chosen people. God revealed His character to them by speaking through the prophets, giving them the laws by which He wanted them to live. The Gentiles (anyone who was not a Jew) had no part in this, and God warned the Jews not to intermarry but to keep themselves separate from all the neighbouring people so they would not become contaminated by their idol worship. Through Jesus Christ, the floodgates were opened and God's plan was extended to everyone. No wonder we celebrate the coming of Jesus at Christmas! But our celebration has all the wrong emphases and we are inclined to forget the real gift:

> *But now in Christ Jesus you who once were far away have been brought near through the blood of Christ... For through him we both have access to the Father by one Spirit.* (Ephesians 2:13, 18)

Paul was chosen by God to spread the news to the Gentiles. As an educated Jew, he had to drop his preconceived ideas and teachings in order to accept this new revelation from God. Although he wrote this letter from prison (which was an awful place at that time), he prayed with a sense of victory for his friends:

- that they might be strengthened in their spirits.
- that Christ might dwell in their hearts.
- that they might know the love of Christ.
- that they might be filled with the fullness of God.

He ends with this great affirmation of who God is:

> *Now to him who is able to do immeasurably more than all we ask or imagine, according to his power that is at work within us...* (Ephesians 3:20)

His wisdom and power are far beyond what we can even imagine! We serve a mighty God!

READ: Ephesians 4–6

Paul gives his friends (and us) some good advice about day-to-day living.

> *As a prisoner for the Lord, then, I urge you to live a life worthy of the calling you have received.* (Ephesians 4:1)

Paul did not see being in prison as an excuse to sink into self-pity or resentment. Even when he was unjustly confined, he reached out to others, encouraging them to lead lives worthy of the calling of Jesus. No circumstances should draw us away from that life of obedience! What a challenge!

He wrote of the gifts God gives each of us; when they are used together for His glory, His church is built up. Somehow that has not always happened in the church, and today we sometimes see divisions and criticize each other. But I am personally responsible to use the gifts He has given me to build up (not criticize) the Body of Christ.

Paul goes on to encourage the Ephesians to speak truth, deal with anger, do honest work, speak no evil of others, get rid of bitterness, and be kind and forgiving. Then he sums it all up:

> *Be imitators of God, therefore, as dearly loved children and live a life of love, just as Christ loved us and gave himself up for us as a fragrant offering and sacrifice to God.* (Ephesians 5:1–2)

Imitating God and being like Jesus seems like an impossible goal, but if we don't set our sights on the highest possible example, how far down will we set them? These negative thoughts can creep into our thinking, drawing us away from what God has in mind for us:

> *For you were once in darkness, but now you are light in the Lord. Live as children of light (for the fruit of the light consists in all goodness, righteousness and truth) and find out what pleases the Lord.* (Ephesians 5:8–10)

We can only learn what is pleasing to God by spending time with Him and asking what He sees in us. To really dwell in His presence, it helps to have an attitude of gratitude.

> *...always giving thanks to God the Father for everything, in the name of our Lord Jesus Christ.* (Ephesians 5:20)

He speaks, too, of relationships—husbands and wives, parents and children, workers and those in authority. Those relationships form the fabric of everyday life. We need to have respect and love for one another. That is where our Christianity (or lack thereof) really shows.

> *Finally, be strong in the Lord and in his mighty power.* (Ephesians 6:10)

We will face many temptations, and Paul provides a great description of the armour God has provided to protect us from Satan's attacks. As we walk closely with Jesus, we become more aware of the spiritual battle in and around us. Our armour consists of truth, righteousness, peace, faith, and salvation, and our sword is the Bible.

Paul then adds this last word of advice:

And pray in the Spirit on all occasions... (Ephesians 6:18)

There is nothing like an ongoing conversation with God to turn our lives into an exciting adventure!

THE BOOK OF

Job

READ: Job 1–3

If we think that being believers and listening to God guarantees prosperity and freedom from problems, Job's story shows how wrong we are. This is what was said about Job:

This man was blameless and upright; he feared God and shunned evil. (Job 1:1)

Things had gone well for him. He had seven sons, three daughters, and a great number of animals with servants to care for them. God allowed Satan to destroy all this—his children, his oxen, donkeys, sheep, camels, and all the servants as well.

Job's first comments were amazing:

Naked I came from my mother's womb, and naked I will depart. The Lord gave and the Lord has taken away; may the name of the Lord be praised. (Job 1:21)

I went to the hospital one day to see my newborn granddaughter for the first time. She was so tiny and perfect—only four pounds, seven ounces, because she arrived a month early. I was aware of the truth of Job's statement, that she brought nothing with her—just herself. When life is over, we take nothing with us, not even our bodies. Whatever we attain in between is a combination of God's goodness to us and our choices.

Job's first reaction after tragedy struck was to worship God! That is where I want to be—with my relationship with God so much a part of my life that when trouble comes, I naturally turn to Him in the same way a small child runs to his mother.

Satan figured he could shake Job's faith by attacking his good health. Job was smitten with boils. Even his wife suggested he forget about God. Then his friends came to comfort him.

This is not one of my favourite books of the Bible, and I have found it difficult to read. However, some people have found great help in it. Whether or not I agree with Job's friends, in their words are some great truths about God.

As Job wishes he had never been born, he says:

What I feared has come upon me; what I dreaded has happened to me. (Job 3:25)

If we allow ourselves to concentrate on our fears, they are likely to come to pass. I don't understand this, but it seems to be a fact.

I only know one way to defeat fear, and that is to come into God's presence through praise and thanksgiving, looking at fear through His eyes. I remember hearing one time, "Fear knocked at the door; Jesus answered it and there was no one there." God knows no fear. In His presence, we don't have to be overcome by it.

READ: Job 4–7

Should not your piety be your confidence and your blameless ways your hope? (Job 4:6)

There is a kind of fear that is not negative. Rather, it is a positive respect and deep love. For example, I fear being away from God and His love for me. It is the kind of fear that makes a baby cry to be held by its mother, where he feels the warmth and security of her familiar arms.

As I have observed, those who plow evil and those who sow trouble reap it. (Job 4:8)

If I am negative and critical, I can expect others to feel the same way about me. Fortunately, the opposite is true as well. If I portray love and care for others, they will most likely respond in the same way.

When I retired from public school teaching, one of the other teachers, who sent her class to me for music, had my class write a little piece which began, "I like Mrs. Dobson because..." I was touched by the students who wrote, "I like

Mrs. Dobson because she loves me." I have always felt that no child should have to spend five hours a day with someone who does not love them. Consequently, my constant prayer was that God give me His kind of love for each child. Yes, you reap what you sow!

Yet man is born to trouble as surely as sparks fly upward. (Job 5:7)

The Bible gives no promise of an easy life without problems. In fact, we would experience little growth without obstacles to overcome. I once heard a song that went something like this: "If I never had problems, how would I know God can solve them?"

When we are weak, we feel His strength. When we are lonely, we experience His love. When we don't know which way to turn, we can call on His wisdom. He supplies our needs and heals our brokenness.

Blessed is the man whom God corrects; so do not despise the discipline of the Almighty. For he wounds, but he also binds up; he injures but his hands also heal. (Job 5:17–18)

Whatever I go through, God, having allowed it, can bring good out of it. There is often a lesson to be learned in times of trial. I don't always recognize it at the time, but in retrospect I can appreciate what God wants to teach me.

It took a long time for me to recognize my tendency to wallow in self-pity, an insidious sin that makes me feel self-righteous, blaming someone else for my unhappiness or my sense of inferiority. Each time I asked God's forgiveness, I was grateful for the freedom He gave me. He chastens, but He also heals and binds up our wounds.

READ: Job 8–12

Bildad tries to persuade Job to pray to God:

But if you will look to God and plead with the Almighty, if you are pure and upright, even now he will rouse himself on your behalf and restore you to your rightful place. Your beginnings will seem humble, so prosperous will your future be. (Job 8:5–7)

He ends by saying:

He will yet fill your mouth with laughter and your lips with shouts of joy. (Job 8:21)

Then Job answered:

Indeed, I know that this is true. (Job 9:2)

That sounds mighty familiar. When things go badly, it is really hard to get in tune with God. I know He is there. I know He loves me, but it seems impossible to rise above the problem into an attitude of prayer. We have to depend on others to pray for us. Job describes it this way:

When he passes me, I cannot see him; when he goes by, I cannot perceive him. (Job 9:11)

In his despair, Job over and over asks the Lord, "Why?" God seldom answers that question. He, the Creator, is not accountable to us, His creation. Besides, His purpose is not the same as ours. He knows that comfort and ease alone do not make strong people. If He is going to entrust us with responsibilities, He has to test our faith. He had such confidence in Job's steadfastness that He allowed these terrible tragedies to come upon him, believing that Job would not only come through, but his faith would be stronger than it was before.

I'm beginning to appreciate Job's struggle and identify with it. Zophar makes a suggestion:

Yet if you devote your heart to him and stretch out your hands to him, if you put away the sin that is in your hand and allow no evil to dwell in your tent, then you will lift up your face without shame; you will stand firm without fear. You will surely forget your trouble, recalling it only as waters gone by. (Job 11:13–16)

That sounds like good advice. But here is Job's answer:

But I have a mind as well as you; I am not inferior to you. Who does not know all these things? (Job 12:3)

I have been guilty of being on both sides. At times, I have snapped at someone giving me advice with words such as, "I suppose you are always right and I am always wrong!" But I have also given lots of good advice, and sometimes it has been meaningless to the other person, just as Zophar's words were to Job. The latter makes a sobering statement:

Men at ease have contempt for misfortune as the fate of those whose feet are slipping. (Job 12:5)

I have been guilty of that, too. What a lot there is to learn about ourselves!

READ: Job 13–17

But I desire to speak to the Almighty and to argue my case with God. (Job 13:3)

Sometimes we can get help by talking to other people, but the only solution to any problem is to take it to God and work it out with Him. It is important that we place our dependency on Him, because people move or change and we cannot count on them to always be available. They may have problems of their own. Whether we feel His presence or not, God is always near and He hears our prayers.

Job's complaints sound familiar. Who hasn't, in difficult circumstances, asked, "What is the use? Why me? What have I done to deserve this? Maybe I should just get away from it all." At that point, some turn to alcohol or drugs, move out of the family, or even commit suicide. That kind of thinking is a downhill road. If the thinking is not changed, it can lead to disaster.

Eliphaz recognizes this:

But you even undermine piety and hinder devotion to God. (Job 15:4)

Negative thinking, whether it is anger or self-pity or both, draws us away from the presence of God. We draw morbid satisfaction from being in that state. You can blame everyone else and feel like no one understands or cares. Hearing good advice from another can produce an angry response, even when you know deep down that what was said is true. The problem is, in order to accept that truth, you have to change your thinking. How we struggle against that! It is hard to give up feeling sorry for yourself, admit the sin of self-centredness, and ask God for forgiveness. But confession and repentance are the only way out of a negative pit.

In spite of wallowing, Job knows what it means to walk with the Lord:

Nevertheless, the righteous will hold to their ways, and those with clean hands will grow stronger. (Job 17:9)

That is an encouraging truth. Each time I overcome some negative attitude in me, I become stronger and recognize danger more quickly the next time.

A few years ago, I heard a saying that goes like this: "If you don't stand for something, you will fall for anything." If our stand for Jesus is shaky, it is easy to fall into a negative, complaining, destructive attitude when hard times come. Since it can become a habit, we should instead practise praising God and thanking Him when things go wrong. Then we are in a position to hear His positive, creative guidance for us.

And we know that in all things God works for the good of those who love him. (Romans 8:28)

The key is to love the Lord, especially when things go wrong.

READ: Job chapters 18–23

My kinsmen have gone away; my friends have forgotten me. (Job 19:14)

We seem to always have expectations for people around us. When they don't measure up, we feel let down—and sometimes even angry and resentful. That attitude can cause broken relationships, whether in marriages, families, friendships, or even in the church.

I know that my Redeemer lives, and that in the end he will stand upon the earth. (Job 19:25)

In spite of his "woe is me" attitude, Job has a strong underlying faith in the power of God in his life. In the midst of his despair, he utters these words of prophecy. He lived several hundred years before Jesus was born and yet he speaks of a Redeemer who will stand upon the earth! God honours every bit of faith we have in Him, and He shows here how He can reach past our human reactions and understanding and touch the very depths of our souls with His truth. While friends see only what is on the surface, God knows everything about us and can draw out the good even in the midst of trial. He is certainly the One to whom we should go when we need help.

Submit to God and be at peace with him; in this way prosperity will come to you. (Job 22:21)

This is a good verse to memorize or put on a card to stick on your mirror as a daily reminder. I'm not always sure what God wants me to do, but there is no doubt about what attitude He wants me to have. Getting rid of negativity is the first step—no resentments, no fear, no self-centredness. The wonderful part is that God's peace usually comes right away.

...then the Almighty will be your gold, the choicest silver for you. Surely then you will find delight in the Almighty and will lift up your face to God. You will pray to him, and he will hear you... (Job 22:25–27)

I break the first commandment whenever I look at another person, possessions, or position as being more important in my life than God. But when things go wrong, it is hard to be in touch with Him.

If I only knew where to find him. (Job 23:3)

In his despair, Job lost touch with God, but he still hung onto his faith in God's ultimate goodness and wisdom.

But he knows the way that I take; when he has tested me, I will come forth as gold. (Job 23:10)

When we come through fiery times, we are either bitter about it or become stronger, less vulnerable, and more valuable to the building of God's kingdom.

READ: Job 24–31

They drive away the orphan's donkey and take the widow's ox in pledge. (Job 24:3)

The choices we make determine the path we take. I remember a friend once telling me that she had always blamed her parents for the fact that she had never completed her education. Then she realized that the opportunity had been presented to her several times, but each time she refused it. When she admitted her own responsibility, she was free of resentment. When she saw a chance to go to college, she went and received the coveted degree. Circumstances don't defeat us unless we let them.

For a little while they are exalted, and then they are gone. (Job 24:24)

The people who were in positions of power or fame in my youth are now gone—many of them forgotten. Time goes by so quickly. We need to make sure our goals are worth expending time and energy to achieve. That is why we need direction from our eternal Father.

I will maintain my righteousness and never let go of it; my conscience will not reproach me as long as I live. (Job 27:6)

Honesty and integrity are so important in life. Without them, we have nothing. No amount of money can make up for the loss of trust people have in us or the respect we feel for ourselves. This does not mean there is a place for self-righteousness, and of course there is always the danger of falling into that attitude. Job seems to struggle with it in his misery by asking, "Why me? What have I done to deserve this?"

He goes on to talk of the mighty things man has done, and then says:

But where can wisdom be found? …the price of wisdom is beyond rubies. (Job 28:12, 18)

Man may have trouble achieving wisdom, since wisdom is not the same as knowledge. Where do we find it?

God understands the way to it but he alone knows where it dwells… (Job 28:23)

God established the world and all that is in it.

And he said to man, "The fear of the Lord—that is wisdom, and to shun evil is understanding." (Job 28:28)

We gain wisdom by living the way we feel God wants us to—changing evil thoughts and habits into positive ones that fit the teaching in His Holy Word. As we depart from what is wrong, we gain insight about what is right.

At one time, I was with a group of people who were long-time Christians, all of whom were in positions of leadership. When one of them shared about his life, it became clear that he had been holding resentment against another person for several years. We began discussing this because, according to the Bible, we are not allowed to carry resentment if we want the power of the Holy Spirit in our lives.

To depart from evil is understanding; that is where wisdom begins.

READ: Job 32–37

Elihu, a young man, decided to speak:

But Elihu… became very angry with Job for justifying himself rather than God. He was also angry with the three friends, because they had found no way to refute Job, and yet had condemned him. (Job 32:2–3)

That sounds like a problem that might happen today. Self-righteous arrogance can creep in unnoticed when things are going well. Others may be critical of that arrogance, but have no positive answer. Elihu felt that frustration. He realized that, although he was young, he could still have God's wisdom, which is available at any age.

> *But it is the spirit in a man, the breath of the Almighty, that gives him understanding.* (Job 32:8)

When I first realized God will speak to us if we spend time with Him and line up our will with His, I became very excited, because that meant anyone could do it. Neither age nor lack of education is a barrier to hearing the voice of God. Anyone can receive the wisdom of God, and I never need to be intimidated by other people's experience or knowledge. Nor should I ever feel superior to those who have not had the opportunities I have had. The uncluttered mind of a small child may be a better receiving station for God's voice than an adult who has developed prejudices. We need to give young people the opportunity to develop the habit of listening.

Nothing can lift my spirits better than contemplating who God is.

> *His eyes are on the way of men; he sees their every step.* (Job 34:21)

> *God is mighty, but does not despise men; he is mighty, and firm in His purpose.* (Job 36:5)

> *Listen to this, Job; stop and consider God's wonders.* (Job 37:14)

As I ponder (and it is important to take time to ponder) on the wondrous works of God, my mind is lifted above the pettiness, the self-centredness, of my problems. I gain a new perspective by looking at my place in God's eternal plan. The mistakes I make, my concern for what others think of me, my desire to always be right, seem insignificant compared to the spreading of the gospel, the need of God's love to flow through me to others, the second coming of Jesus, and the ways in which I need to prepare to meet Him.

Every day, I must stop and ponder the wondrous works of God.

READ: Job 38–42

At this point, God intervened to show Job his "poor me" attitude and complaints. The questions God put to him are ones we might well ask ourselves when we wallow in self-pity and ask God, "Why me?"

> *Where were you when I laid the earth's foundation? … Who marked off its dimensions? … What is the way to the abode of light? And where does*

darkness reside? …Have you entered the storehouses of the snow or seen the storehouses of the hail…? Can you bind the beautiful Pleiades? Can you loose the cords of Orion? (Job 38:4–5, 19, 22, 30–31)

Do you give the horse his strength or clothe his neck with a flowing mane? … Does the hawk take flight by your wisdom and spread his wings toward the south? (Job 39:19, 26)

The Lord said to Job: Will the one who contends with the Almighty correct him? (Job 40:1–2)

It is a dangerous thing to argue with God. Suddenly, Job recognized his folly. He put his hand to his mouth and said:

I am unworthy—how can I reply to you? (Job 40:4)

Sometimes it takes a real jolt to get us off our high horse of thinking we know it all. In the presence of God, when we really look at who He is, we can see that we are of small account. The Almighty does not have to double-check His actions with us. But it is important for us to check our plans and attitudes with Him. He is the only one with perfect wisdom and knowledge. We are blessed when we get in step with Him.

Job came to a place of repentance as he listened to the voice of God, and then God was able to use him to pray for his friends. If I want God to hear my prayers, I must remove any obstacles of self-centredness. I can then go to Him in a spirit of repentance, aware of His perfection. His love washes away the sins I confess to Him and He reaches out to others through me.

After Job had prayed for his friends, the Lord made him prosperous again and gave him twice as much as he had before. (Job 42:10)

There is a definite link between right relationship with God, answered prayer, and our needs being met. The key to the whole thing is repentance.

The Lord blessed the latter part of Job's life more than the first. (Job 42:12)

Old age can be the most rewarding time of life if we are in tune with the Father. An elderly friend of mine who could neither see nor hear very well, but still loved the Lord, used to say, "Every day is good, but some are better than others."

THE BOOK OF

Psalms

READ: Psalms 1–5

When I look at the Psalms and what they mean to me, I think I could spend the rest of my life talking about them. In my various translations, I have underlined many verses.

Psalm 1 sets a choice before us. We can choose to walk, stand, and then sit with those who are on the wrong path. Through this, we can see the progression of sin. First we walk beside those involved in wrong actions; then we stand and observe; finally, we sit in their midst and become part of it. Our other choice is to regularly read the Bible, as we are doing now. By doing so, we become like trees putting down firm, strong roots. For the one who chooses this path, there is a blessing attached:

Whatever he does prospers. (Psalm 1:3)

Psalm 2 provides a word of caution to our nations' leaders. To conspire against the Lord brings disaster:

Therefore, you kings, be wise; be warned, you rulers of the earth. Serve the Lord with fear and rejoice with trembling... Blessed are all who take refuge in him. (Psalm 2:10–12)

We need to pray for our own country, and other nations as well. We saw the downfall of Communist governments who tried to stamp out all worship of God.

But you are a shield around me, O Lord; you bestow glory on me and lift up my head. (Psalm 3:3)

A notation in my Bible says that David wrote this when he was fleeing from his son Absalom, so he was surrounded by enemies out to kill him.

When life is fearful, it is a great comfort to know that in God I not only am protected, but He is my glory! I can hold my head high because I am His.

In your anger do not sin. (Psalm 4:4)

Anger will come. It even came to Jesus in the temple. But when that anger simmers and settles into resentment, sin enters in. Here is the solution:

...when you are on your beds, search your hearts and be silent. (Psalm 4:4)

To me, that means that when you are angry, you should go into your quiet place and commune with God. He can show you whether you need to change or accept the situation. By communing with Him, the anger dissipates and you become free of self-centredness, receiving wisdom.

But let all who take refuge in you be glad; let them ever sing for joy. (Psalm 5:11)

There is joy in the Lord's presence. If I am not experiencing that joy, I have moved away from Him.

READ: Psalms 6–10
David is at a low ebb. Things are not going well and it is affecting his body.

O Lord, heal me, for my bones are in agony. (Psalm 6:2)

Doctors today realize that a troubled mind (worry and resentment) causes physical problems. David, in his honesty before God, stumbled onto this fact thousands of years ago! After pouring out his troubles to His heavenly Father, David became aware of the power of God, which is greater than any evil.

Away from me, all you who do evil, for the Lord has heard my weeping. (Psalm 6:8)

When I become aware of God in the midst of troubling circumstances, I see victory in Him, no matter how bad the situation seems. One aspect of God is shown in this verse:

O Lord my God, I take refuge in you; save and deliver me from all who pursue me... (Psalm 7:1)

If things go wrong, I can run to Him and tell Him how I feel. But He does not hand out sympathy and pat me on the back to make me feel better. He is also a God of judgment:

God is a righteous judge, a God who expresses his wrath every day. (Psalm 7:11)

My picture of this aspect of God is not quite like King David's. I see Him as saying to me, "All right, Dorothy, this is the situation and this is how you feel about it. Now, what are you going to do about it?"

Rather than sympathy, He gives me understanding and a challenge. If I accept this challenge, repent, and change, I come out stronger and wiser, filled with new joy and purpose. Affirming God and His purpose for me can change my attitude and direction any day, no matter where I am or what I am doing. Verses like the following are most helpful for strengthening that positive attitude:

O Lord, our Lord, how majestic is your name in all the earth! ...When I consider your heavens, the work of your fingers, the moon and the stars, which you have set in place, what is man that you are mindful of him, the son of man that you care for him? (Psalm 8:1, 3–4)

And yet He does! He does care for us! One cannot spend regular quiet time with Him without experiencing wonderful, overwhelming love, which reminds us that each one of us is special and unique.

I will praise you, O Lord, with all my heart; I will tell of all your wonders. (Psalm 9:1)

For now, I'll stop here and give thanks to my loving heavenly Father with my whole heart!

READ: Psalms 11–15

The Lord is in his holy temple; the Lord is on his heavenly throne. He observes the sons of men; his eyes examine them. (Psalm 11;4)

There is something very comforting in knowing that no matter what happens here on earth, God's position never changes. He remains steady, unaffected by the storms and turmoils of life. When I turn my eyes towards Him, I can take refuge in the steadfastness, faithfulness, and sureness of His position—always watching and caring.

This reminds me of when my sister and I used to take our children to the beach—she had five and I had four. We sat on a blanket on the sand and watched all nine of the kids play in the water. Every now and then we would hear a shout of "Look, Mom!" With so many other mothers on the beach, we would look to see if the call had come from one of ours. They felt secure in knowing their moms were watching them. If someone scraped a knee or a toe, he or she could come running.

There is security in knowing that God watches me from His holy temple, always ready to respond with a warning, nod of approval, or word of encouragement.

For the Lord is righteous, he loves justice; upright men will see his face. (Psalm 11:7)

There is an old saying that goes, "It's not about *who* is right, but *what* is right." Even a child is aware of what is right, and that is the only place we find God—when we are willing to do what is right even when it goes against our own personal desires.

And the words of the Lord are flawless... (Psalm 12:6)

Can that be said of me? Can people trust my word? I am made in the image of God, and as such His characteristics can become a part of me.

My dad was a hard-working and trustworthy man. He was highly respected in his work, in our neighbourhood, and in the church we attended. One of the reasons was that people knew they could trust his word. If he promised to do something, you could count on him to carry through. That is a great attribute, and it only becomes a habit through many years of practice.

King David asks the question:

Lord, who may dwell in your sanctuary? Who may live on your holy hill? (Psalm 15:1)

The answer sums up the above thoughts:

He whose walk is blameless and who does what is righteous, who speaks the truth from his heart. (Psalm 15:2)

Our closeness to God is dependent on our obedience to His way of life. Sinful attitudes shut us off from His presence.

READ: Psalm 16–20

I said to the Lord, "You are my Lord; apart from you I have no good thing." (Psalm 16:2)

Giving all the glory to God and not taking credit for myself helps me be free of self-centredness and the desire for approval. Whatever good I say or do is the result of God working through me. My responsibility is to keep the lines of communication with Him clean and free of debris. I must not accumulate negative attitudes!

You have made known to me the path of life; you will fill me with joy in your presence, with eternal pleasures at your right hand. (Psalm 16:11)

This gives us the picture of an ideal life, everything we long for. Right there is the key to living that way—*"in your presence."* The more we are in His presence, the more we experience the joy we long for. There is no other way.

I love You, O Lord, my strength... I call to the Lord, who is worthy of praise... (Psalm 18:1, 3)

Making statements like these can change the course of my life. Constantly acknowledging my loving relationship with God can fill me with self-confidence, gratitude, and love. What more could I possibly want?

When I acknowledged my love for my husband and my appreciation for his fine qualities, I felt increasingly self-confident, grateful, and loving. It helped him to feel the same way, resulting in a more peaceful home. When it was not that way, one (or both of us) was hanging on to some selfishness which cut off the flow of God's love.

You, O Lord, keep my lamp burning; my God turns my darkness into light. (Psalm 18:28)

My limited human mind finds it hard to conceive how a loving God could light the way for all the billions of people on earth! Psalm 19 provides a lovely picture of the heavens declaring the glory of God.

I have always been fascinated with the ever-changing appearance of the sky, the clouds, the sunshine, the moon and stars. While driving, I often draw the attention of my passengers to the cloud formations or the sun shining behind the clouds, forming a silvery outline, or even the colours of the sunset. As the psalmist says:

The heavens declare the glory of God; the skies proclaim the work of his hands. (Psalm 19:1)

As I ponder the awesomeness of God, what I want most is to please Him in all I do.

May the words of my mouth and the meditation of my heart be pleasing in your sight, O Lord, my Rock and my Redeemer. (Psalm 19:14)

When you line up your desires with His desires for you, this prayer may be answered:

May he give you the desire of your heart and make all your plans succeed. (Psalm 20:4)

READ: Psalms 21–25

At times, we feel God has moved away from us. Even Jesus, with the terrible burden of all the sins of the world upon Him, echoed David when He cried out:

My God, my God, why have you forsaken me? (Psalm 22:1)

There is no worse condition than being separated from God. But even in the midst of that feeling, David gives us the key to bridging the gap:

Yet you are enthroned as the Holy One; you are the praise of Israel. (Psalm 22:3)

Today, we can use the word "believers" to describe both Jews and Gentiles. Since Jesus' time, believing Gentiles have been added to the chosen people. Paul says the Jews are the natural branch while believing Gentiles are the branch that has been grafted onto the vine. The way to the throne of God is through praise. That is how we come into His presence.

Next, we come to Psalm 23. What can I say about it? People have memorized this beloved psalm and put it to music down through the ages. It has been a comfort to countless numbers, including me. After picturing God as a loving shepherd, providing all the needs of his sheep—food, water, direction, and protection—David ends with these strong words of faith:

Surely goodness and love will follow me all the days of my life, and I will dwell in the house of the Lord forever. (Psalm 23:6)

Eternity in God's house—that is the ultimate goal! Who shall ascend the holy hill of the Lord and stand in His holy place?

He who has clean hands and a pure heart... (Psalm 24:4)

In other words, it is the person who is honest and trustworthy. Anything less than absolute honesty will not do. Nothing is more important in life than having fellowship with God. King David was so aware of this!

To You, O Lord, I lift up my soul: in you I trust, O my God... Show me your ways, O Lord, teach me your paths. (Psalm 25:1–2, 4)

King David saw God as our instructor, who teaches us the way of truth. He must have spent regular time in quiet communion with God. Maybe these psalms are some of the thoughts he wrote down during those times. In my time with God, I must not just talk to Him, putting my requests before Him; I must listen, seek to learn from Him, and write down the thoughts that come. As a loving Father, He wants His children to come to Him often and learn from Him.

READ: Psalms 26–30

The Lord is my light and my salvation—whom shall I fear? The Lord is the stronghold of my life—of whom shall I be afraid? (Psalm 27:1)

We should memorize this verse to reassure ourselves when fear threatens our peace of mind. If I have a passing acquaintance with God, a "meet you at church on Sunday" relationship, it won't do any good. It is hard to convince myself that He is my stronghold if I only acknowledge Him in the midst of a Sunday congregation. However, if being with Him is part of my daily routine, I can say with confidence, "Yes, He is my light, my salvation, my stronghold. Nothing and no one can take that away. I have nothing to fear."

One thing I ask of the Lord, this is what I seek: that I may dwell in the house of the Lord all the days of my life, to gaze upon the beauty of the Lord and to seek him in his temple. (Psalm 27:4)

If that is not true of me, I am breaking the first one of the Ten Commandments. My number one priority should be to dwell in the presence of the Lord. When that is not so, my selfish desires take top billing. Only by asking His forgiveness can I get right with Him again.

Wait for the Lord; be strong and take heart and wait for the Lord. (Psalm 27:14)

It takes time to hear from the Lord. A five or ten-minute prayer where I do all the talking may make me feel better, but that gives God no chance to speak. What He has to say is more important than what I have to say. We need to learn to wait for the Lord, to spend unhurried time in His presence.

This is one area where I really need to exercise faith! When prayers are not answered the way I think they should be, it is easy to think God has either not heard me or lost interest in me. But I really do know that He hears me. Maybe I have put a stumbling block (a wrong attitude) in the way. Or perhaps God's timing means that there needs to be a waiting period. Some of my loved ones do not acknowledge Jesus as their Saviour and King, and I have prayed and prayed for them. Has God heard me? Of course He has, and the timing of that prayer's fulfillment is His responsibility, not mine. It is hard to be patient and trusting.

I love the last two verses of Psalm 30. They paint a delightful picture of people letting go of their problems and rejoicing in the presence of the Lord.

You turned my wailing into dancing; you removed my sackcloth and clothed me with joy, that my heart may sing to you and not be silent. O Lord my God, I will give you thanks forever. (Psalm 30:11–12)

READ: Psalms 31–35

I will be glad and rejoice in your love, for you saw my affliction and knew the anguish of my soul. (Psalm 31:7)

I need to remind myself often of this truth— that God's love continues, no matter the circumstances. His love never stops or lessens in any way. It is a decision to be glad and rejoice, not a feeling.

In Psalm 31, things are not going well for David:

Be merciful to me, O Lord, for I am in distress. (Psalm 31:9)

However, he decided that he could trust God:

But I trust in You, O Lord; I say, "You are my God." My times are in your hands. (Psalm 31:14–15)

In the midst of trying circumstances, it is easy to forget God or cry out to Him, "Why don't You do something?" When I am upset, I try to remember to go off by myself and spend time in the presence of God, acknowledging His omnipotence and looking at the situation through His eyes. This takes the stress off me and opens my mind to His wisdom. I don't always get an immediate answer, but I do receive His peace and love.

> *Blessed is he whose transgressions are forgiven, whose sins are covered.* (Psalm 32:1)

Repentance is essential to physical and spiritual health. Knowing I am forgiven for my mistakes and blunders grants me freedom to move on.

> *When I kept silent, my bones wasted away...* (Psalm 32:3)

Harbouring resentment, bitterness, or guilt creates a condition in the body that allows diseases to grow and flourish. As we discussed before, negative attitudes can destroy our bodies.

> *Blessed is the nation whose God is the Lord, the people he chose for his inheritance.* (Psalm 33:12)

We need to pray for the nations of the world, that they may turn to God for guidance. We must also seek His direction for all people. We can help bring blessings on our whole nation.

> *I will extol the Lord at all times; his praise will always be on my lips.* (Psalm 34:1)

If I can make this true in my life, there will be no room for self-pity, criticism, or fear. It is the answer to all my attitude problems. I would constantly be in His presence, a channel for His love and wisdom, which would cleanse me and bless others!

READ: Psalms 36–40

The more I read the Psalms, the more I understand the character of God. King David, in spite of his tumultuous life, seems to have experienced various facets of this great Father of all. He used the creative gifts God gave him to put these down in his psalms. Some three thousand years later, we are the benefactors! God is the same as He was then and always will be.

The greatness of God is expressed by comparing it to the mighty things around us—the heavens, the clouds, the mountains, and the deep (ocean).

Your love, O Lord, reaches to the heavens, your faithfulness to the skies. Your righteousness is like the mighty mountains, your justice like the great deep. O Lord, you preserve both man and beast. (Psalm 36:5–6)

In Psalm 37, David may be speaking to himself, or he may have given those words to those around him. No matter his intention, I find them helpful in getting my life on track and in line with God's plan for me. I feel as if He is talking to me personally.

Do not fret because of evil men or be envious of those who do wrong. (Psalm 37:1)

That is really good advice! Don't be upset by the behaviour of other people, a common stumbling block.

Trust in the Lord and do good... Delight yourself in the Lord... Commit your way to the Lord... Be still before the Lord and wait patiently for him... Refrain from anger and turn from wrath; do not fret. (Psalm 37:3–5, 7–8)

If I follow all these directions, I have no room left for selfish goals or self-centred thinking. Rewards are promised as well, beyond the peace of mind and joy that come from being in tune with God:

For evil men will be cut off, but those who hope in the Lord will inherit the land. (Psalm 37:9)

Many, O Lord my God, are the wonders you have done. The things you planned for us no one can recount to you; were I to speak and tell of them, they would be too many to declare. (Psalm 40:5)

It is, indeed, impossible to tell of all the wondrous gifts our Lord has given to us.

READ: Psalms 41–45

Blessed is he who has regard for the weak; the Lord delivers him in times of trouble. (Psalm 41:1)

We must be prepared to give to others that which we want to receive from the Lord. God honours our attitude of caring for others by being available when we are in trouble. Somehow the very act of reaching out to help someone brings us closer to God.

As the deer pants for streams of water, so my soul pants for you, O God.
(Psalm 42:1)

Animals and people alike have a basic need for water. Nothing makes us more desperate than a great thirst. Doctors tell us that the body can go for many days without food, but we cannot survive without water. Satisfying thirst is a matter of survival. The more we experience the presence of God, the more we long for it. This statement shows the psalmist to be a man who has learned to be totally depend on God. To him, satisfying his longing for God is a matter of survival.

Send forth your light and your truth, let them guide me; let them bring me to your holy mountain, to the place where you dwell. Then I will go to the altar of God, to God, my joy and my delight. I will praise you with the harp, O God, my God. (Psalm 43:3–4)

We cannot, through our own knowledge and wisdom, come into God's holy place. We need a personal experience of His presence, which we can receive if we invite Him into our lives. His light then begins to shine and we recognize His truth. However, we must be willing to follow and obey if we are to continue on the journey to His holy place, where we can praise Him forever!

Throughout the ages, the Jewish people have recalled how God led them to the Promised Land. They recognized that the battles were not won by their own swords, but by the hand of God.

It was not by their sword that they won the land, nor did their arm bring them victory; it was your right hand, your arm, and the light of your face, for you loved them. (Psalm 44:3)

Today, Israel is again surrounded by enemies who would gladly wipe them out. Though they spend a lot of money on military forces, they must be aware that should these enemies come against them, only the hand of God could save them. It has saved them in several wars they have fought since becoming a nation.

The Jews have not only suffered persecution when they turned away from God. It has happened over and over throughout history, and anti-Semitism is again on the rise today. It was evident back in the days of King David as well:

If we had forgotten the name of our God or spread out our hands to a foreign god, would not God have discovered it, since he knows the secrets of the heart? Yet for your sake we face death all day long; we are considered as sheep to be slaughtered. (Psalm 44:20–23)

It is a terrible thing to be persecuted not because of the wrongs we have done but because of who we are. Racial prejudice has caused untold misery in the past, and it still happens today. I wonder if our human race will ever learn what it means to be in right relationship with each other. Is that why we long for Jesus to come again?

READ: Psalms 46–50

God is our refuge and strength, an ever-present help in trouble. Therefore we will not fear, though the earth give way and the mountains fall into the heart of the sea, though its waters roar and foam and the mountains quake with their surging. (Psalm 46:1–3)

I remember as a child hearing the term "terra firma," and accepting the fact that the earth was unchangeable and would always remain so. After World War I, known as the "war to end all wars," there seemed to be a false sense of security that things would settle down, that countries would remain as they were. But Hitler came along with distorted ideas of a superior race and a plan to control the world. Suddenly, our complacency was shattered and the nations were at war again. Ever since that time, we seem to be on the brink of another disaster.

Who can we depend on? Where can we turn? Even the "terra firma" is no longer stable and we are aware of the constant danger of earthquakes. We watch floods wash away homes and farmlands and wonder what will happen next. Fear grows in the hearts of people everywhere. The end of Psalm 46 gives us direction:

"Be still, and know that I am God; I will be exalted among the nations, I will be exalted in the earth." The Lord Almighty is with us; the God of Jacob is our fortress. (Psalm 46:10–11)

I can experience His unchangeable presence when I am quiet and still, opening my heart and mind to receive Him. In the midst of turmoil, we can rejoice in His love for us.

Clap your hands, all you nations; shout to God with cries of joy... Sing praises to God, sing praises... God reigns over the nations... (Psalm 47:1, 6, 8)

Great is the Lord, and most worthy of praise… (Psalm 48:1)

The only source of lasting power and security is God. Our days are numbered. Each one of us will come face to face with Him, our final judge. It is important to adopt an attitude of gratitude. Psalm 50 says,

Sacrifice thank offerings to God, fulfill your vows to the Most High, and call upon me in the day of trouble; I will deliver you, and you will honour me. (Psalm 50:14–15)

If we want God to deliver us from our troubles, we need to carry out our part of this covenant—to be thankful and glorify Him in everything we do.

READ: Psalms 51–55

Have mercy on me, O God, according to your unfailing love; according to your great compassion blot out my transgressions. Wash away all my iniquity and cleanse me from my sin. (Psalm 51:1–2)

We all need that cleansing. It has been important for me to recognize that I always have thoughts that need to be cleansed, even if things seem to be going well. If I lose sight of that, I become complacent and self-satisfied, which leads to arrogance and superiority.

Surely you desire truth in the inner parts; you teach me wisdom in the inmost place. (Psalm 51:6)

That is where my struggle to be honest about myself begins—deep inside me. If I convince myself that my anger, self-pity, or resentment is justified, a negative attitude settles in and takes over that area of my life, shutting God out. That is why inner healing is such a necessary process for spiritual growth, and why forgiveness is emphasized in the Bible—*"Forgive us our sins, for we also forgive everyone who sins against us"* (Luke 11:4).

I once watched a very dear Christian lady make a conscious decision never to forgive a particular person who had deeply hurt her. We begged her not to carry resentment and anger, but she chose to harbour it in her inward being. How sad it is to choose chains instead of freedom!

Create in me a pure heart, O God, and renew a steadfast spirit within me. (Psalms 51:10)

It is hard to give up our self-centred attitudes, but when we are willing, God creates a new heart within us. He can fill that spot with positive attitudes of love and joy.

The sacrifices of God are a broken spirit; a broken and contrite heart, O God, you will not despise. (Psalm 51:17)

God knows our inward being, so He is delighted when we face our faults and come to Him in honesty, willing to change. When I taught school, if a child pretended he didn't have a problem in reading or math, it was hard to help him. On the other hand, when he admitted his area of difficulty and faced it honestly, with help it could be overcome. I am sometimes like that—I hate to admit my lack of understanding, but God can't help me if I refuse to face my area of need.

God looks down from heaven on the sons of men to see if there are any who understand, any who seek God. (Psalm 53:2)

A few years ago, I saw a bumper sticker that said, "Wise men still seek Him." We miss out on the greatest opportunity this life offers when we do not seek a relationship with the Living God, the Creator of the universe. He looks for those of us who keep reaching out to Him every day.

Cast your cares on the Lord and he will sustain you. (Psalm 55:22)

READ: Psalms 56–60

These psalms seem to have been written when David felt besieged by enemies, both inside and outside the country. Even as I write this, Israel is surrounded by nations who would gladly see her wiped off the map. We should all be praying for Israel, for its people and land have been designated by God, and that is where Jesus said He would return. It is crucial to His plan.

The answer to David's crises is the same today as it was then:

When I am afraid I will trust in you... Then my enemies will turn back when I call for help. By this I will know that God is for me. (Psalm 56:3, 9)

God is for us. He wants the best for us. He helps us put right what is wrong. No matter how often we fail, He guides us to the right path. He is for us! Other people are for me as well, but they may not always be with me. God is always available, wherever I am, and like David I can say, "This I know, that God is for me."

267

> *Have mercy on me, O God, have mercy on me, for in you my soul takes refuge. I will take refuge in the shadow of your wings until the disaster has passed.* (Psalm 57:1)

I love to imagine taking refuge under God's wings, just as little chicks gather under a mother hen. His presence can protect us from danger. Though something may happen to my body, my soul is in His hands, and no one can change that except me! As long as I am willing to have His hand on me, He will be with me.

Psalm 57 ends with three great verses which have been put to music. They lift my spirits above the pettiness and selfishness of my human nature to an awareness of the greatness of God. They begin with a word of thankfulness:

> *I will praise You, O Lord, among the nations; I will sing of you among the peoples. For great is your love, reaching to the heavens; your faithfulness reaches to the skies. Be exalted, O God, above the heavens; let your glory be over all the earth.* (Psalm 57:9–11)

I feel like adding, "Hallelujah!"

In Psalms 59 and 60, David is in the midst of enemies. Although he keeps reminding himself of God's power, it seems at times that God has deserted him. That sounds familiar! In the last verse, he makes a strong statement that if we are obedient to God, He will give us victory:

> *With God we will gain the victory, and he will trample down our enemies.* (Psalm 60:12)

READ: Psalm 61–65

> *I long to dwell in your tent forever and take refuge in the shelter of your wings.* (Psalm 61:4)

Where we spend eternity depends on the choices we make here on earth. To be in the presence of God forever is heaven, indeed! We can only get an inkling of it here when we experience the joy of His presence and the peace of trusting in Him.

> *My soul finds rest in God alone; my salvation comes from him.* (Psalm 62:1)

When we spend time in silence seeking His presence and listening for His word, we know for a fact that only in Him can we find salvation from our sin and the sin of the world.

Because your love is better than life, my lips will glorify you. I will praise you as long as I live, and in your name I will lift up my hands. (Psalm 63:3–4)

Not long after praising God was emphasized in Christian worship, people were clapping and raising their hands. Personally, I had no trouble clapping—as children, we had often done that as we sang around campfires. But raising my hands? That was new, different, and difficult—strange as it seems now. I would look around and see if anyone else was doing it. If enough people were, I might try it!

It is so natural now to reach out to my Heavenly Father in love and adoration. I watched a little girl recently run up to her daddy and put out her arms to be lifted up. That is what I am doing when I lift my hands to God. I am letting Him know that I love Him, trust Him, and want to be lifted up.

Let the righteous rejoice in the Lord and take refuge in him; let all the upright in heart praise him! (Psalm 64:10)

It is not good enough to sing words of praise if our hearts are not right with God. It is the righteous—those in right relationship with Him—who can really rejoice. At times, I am not in that position. Sometimes God convicts me right in the middle of a praise song; other times it comes later.

In a church I attended, the leadership came to a decision which I did not think was right. For several weeks, I sang the words of the praise songs but felt no joy. In fact, I began to be critical of the praise time! One day, I realized that my resentment was blocking the way. When I went to the Lord and received cleansing, I was able to sing and rejoice, even though the situation had not changed—but my attitude had!

When we were overwhelmed by sins, you forgave our transgressions. (Psalm 65:3)

That is what salvation means—having our sins forgiven.

You care for the land and water it; you enrich it abundantly... The meadows are covered with flocks and the valleys are mantled with grain; they shout for joy and sing. (Psalm 65:9, 13)

Isn't that a wonderful thought? The meadows and valleys sing together for joy!

READ: Psalms 66–70

You let men ride over our heads; we went through fire and water, but you brought us to a place of abundance. (Psalm 66:12)

God does not always remove our obstacles, dangers, and tough times, but He promises to walk through them with us and bring us at last to a "place of abundance." The psalmist suggests that He will try us, testing to see if we are able to come through unscathed. As someone once said, when we come through a trying time, we are either better or bitter. We either do our best, face our weaknesses, trust in God, and come out stronger, or we become critical, bitter, and full of self-pity.

If I had cherished sin in my heart, the Lord would not have listened. (Psalm 66:18)

Repentance is a prerequisite for answered prayer. We cannot consciously hang on to negative attitudes and expect God to listen to us. When we go through the cleansing process of confession and forgiveness, we are ready to pray in the will of God. That is when prayer may be answered.

May the peoples praise you, O God; may all the peoples praise you. (Psalm 67:5)

What a wonderful image this conjures up in my mind—everyone everywhere praising God! It seems to me that God's plan is just that—for everyone to praise Him and seek His direction, as the angels do in heaven. How glorious and exciting!

A father to the fatherless, a defender of widows, is God in his holy dwelling. (Psalm 68:5)

When we lose a loved one, God is ready and willing to fill the gap and bring us peace and fulfillment. Nothing in this life is more precious than the presence of God. If we have that relationship with Him, any loss can be filled with His loving presence. When that happens, we receive a blessing.

You know my folly, O God; my guilt is not hidden from you. (Psalm 69:5)

Nothing is hidden from God. He knows my inner thoughts and motives better than I know them myself. In my quiet time with Him, He shows me what is going on in my heart and where I need to change. No other person can understand what is going on inside me, no matter how well they know me. Even if I try to tell someone, they can only relate to me through their own experiences. Only the One who created me can really recognize and understand my deepest thoughts.

It is a great cleansing to go before God, write down everything that is going on in my mind, and ask Him for His perspective. He sees me as I really am—not as I pretend to be!

READ: Psalms 71–75

In You, O Lord, I have taken refuge. (Psalm 71:1)

This is how I often feel as I start my quiet time in the morning. I can get bogged down, even frustrated when I have financial and personal issues to decide. But when morning comes, it is time to read the Bible and listen to what Jesus has to say. This is my refuge! He knows my situation better than I do. Moreover, He knows the answer to every problem. He may not release those answers to me all at once. In fact, He carefully reveals only as much as I need at the moment, with the promise that if I stay close to Him, He will give me the rest as I can handle it.

Be my rock of refuge, to which I can always go; give the command to save me, for you are my rock and my fortress. (Psalm 71:3)

He is, indeed, a rock, a fortress, a refuge where I can find security no matter what my circumstances are.

My mouth is filled with your praise, declaring your splendor all day long. (Psalm 71:8)

This is the secret to successful living! We may look at wealth, possessions, fame, and popularity as signs of success. But people who were at the pinnacle of achievement in my youth are now dying of old age. I have observed, however, that some had an anchor to help them accept retirement, allowing their lives to be meaningful right to the end. Others fell apart when their careers ended. They did not know the true purpose of life, which is to be filled with the glory of our Creator—not our own glory!

Since my youth, O God, you have taught me, and to this day I declare your marvelous deeds. Even when I am old and grey, do not forsake me, O God, till I declare your power to the next generation, your might to all who are to come. (Psalm 71:17–18)

These words are very meaningful to me in my old age. God has been teaching me step by step ever since my youth, and I long to pass on to others the valuable lessons I have learned and encourage them to seek a personal relationship with the most high God. I wonder why it seems so difficult to get this message across. Why do so many people not seem to want to hear it? The world offers nothing to compare with the joy Jesus offers us.

Our beloved country was called the Dominion of Canada, from this verse:

He will rule [have dominion] from sea to sea and from the River to the ends of the earth. (Psalm 72:8)

How aptly that fits our location from the Atlantic to the Pacific and from the Great Lakes to the Arctic Ocean. I am proud that the fathers of Confederation looked to the Bible for guidance in establishing our country.

READ: Psalms 76–80

In Judah God is known; his name is great in Israel. His tent is in Salem, his dwelling place in Zion. (Psalm 76:1–2)

Israel, Judah, Jerusalem, and Zion—these names have all been designated as the dwelling place of God since the Israelites settled in the land God promised them. The temple was built in Jerusalem, which later became the centre of Jesus' life, teaching, death, and resurrection. Today, after several thousand years of occupation by other nations, God's chosen people—the Jews—are back in that land.

The more I read the Bible, I see how God's relationship with the Israelites, and thus the world, was closely tied to them dwelling in the land He gave them. Now they are settled there again. Thousands of Jews have come from Russia and other lands to live in the land they longed for throughout the generations.

The nations around them have their guns pointed at Israel and talk about wiping them out. I wonder what God's plan is for the future of Israel?

In Psalm 78, the writer reminds the people of God's command to the fathers to teach their children about Him.

Then they would put their trust in God and would not forget his deeds but would keep his commands. (Psalm 78:7)

In each generation, it is the responsibility of the adults to teach the children about God. That is why we started Lighthouse Christian Academy, where we can sing praises to God and ask for His help and guidance. We can recall what He has done in the past and pray for His intervention in the future.

The psalmist goes on to recount how God brought His people out of slavery and provided for all their needs as they travelled to the Promised Land. They were not always true to Him:

> *Yet he was merciful; he forgave their iniquities and did not destroy them...*
> *Again and again they put God to the test; they vexed the Holy One of Israel.*
> (Psalm 78:38, 41)

In Psalm 79, the Israelites have been conquered by their enemies and a cry goes out to God:

> *Help us, O God our Savior, for the glory of your name; deliver us and forgive*
> *our sins for your name's sake.* (Psalm 79:9)

They struggled to be faithful to God and so often failed, having to run to Him for forgiveness. They were aware that their failure reflected on the glory and power of God in the eyes of the world, because they were known to be God's chosen people. Perhaps our churches today need to realize the same truth and be ready to ask God's forgiveness for giving the world a false picture of the love of Jesus. It is a sobering thought to think that the world judges Jesus' character by the way I live.

I long to live with such an attitude of love for everyone that others want to get to know the One who is the source of that love! It is the greatest honour we can receive to be chosen to be representatives of Jesus here on earth, and that is what the church is meant to be! With the Israelites of old, we need to pray the words of Psalm 79:9 again and again.

READ: Psalms 81–85

> *Hear, O my people, and I will warn you—if you would but listen to me, O*
> *Israel!* (Psalm 81:8)

We often say to our children, "Why don't you listen to me?" God's gift of free will allows us to choose to go in the wrong direction. How God must ache, knowing the potential He has put within us and seeing us miss or neglect it!

Many of us pray for Israel today—especially that her people will listen and hear God's direction for them.

If my people would but listen to me, if Israel would follow my ways, how quickly would I subdue their enemies and turn my hand against their foes! (Psalm 81:13–14)

Ever since Israel became a nation in 1948, the surrounding Arab nations have been trying to get rid of her. When you look at a map and see the size of Iraq, Iran, Egypt, Jordan, etc., you might wonder why they care about the little bit of land that has been designated for the Jews. What is it that makes them so vicious in their attitude?

When we read Psalm 83, we realize this is not something new:

O God, do not keep silent; be not quiet, O God, be not still. See how your enemies are astir, how your foes rear their heads. With cunning they conspire against your people; they plot against those you cherish. "Come," they say, "let us destroy them as a nation, that the name of Israel be remembered no more." (Psalm 83:1–4)

The psalm goes on to name various nations, all descendants of Ishmael—in other words, the Arabs. Are they against God? Is this why they want to destroy His chosen people? This must be a spiritual battle.

Psalm 84 brings us back to the wonder of being in God's presence. We are created to be in relationship with Him:

My soul yearns, even faints, for the courts of the Lord: my heart and my flesh cry out for the living God. (Psalm 84:2)

It is important for me to spend regular time with God, because that is what causes my soul to long to be in His presence. Absence does not make the heart grow fonder; it lessens the need and desire for His company!

Our salvation is not just important on a personal level. It is of value to our nation as well:

I will listen to what God the Lord will say; he promises peace to his people, his saints—but let them not return to folly. Surely his salvation is near those who fear him, that his glory may dwell in our land. (Psalm 85:8–9)

May God's Holy Spirit move through my life so that His glory dwells and reigns in our land!

READ: Psalms 86–89

Teach me your way, O Lord, and I will walk in your truth. (Psalm 86:11)

Life is a learning process. A baby learns to walk and talk. A child learns to read, to play with others, and to be creative. An adult continues to read, to listen to others, to expand his or her knowledge. But the most important thing to learn is God's way for us—how to live according to His plan. That is the truth I seek every day and will continue to seek for the rest of my life.

There is one city in the world God has laid His hand on in a special way. That is Jerusalem. The whole world is aware of its importance, and thousands of people everywhere have a strong desire to visit that city.

He has set His foundation on the holy mountain; the Lord loves the gates of Zion more than all the dwellings of Jacob. Glorious things are said of you, O city of God. (Psalm 87:1–3)

At a meeting in Jerusalem during the Feast of Tabernacles, I remember the mayor of the city saying, "This is your city. It is an international city belonging to the whole world." That is where God told the Israelites to build a temple for Him.

Bob and I arrived in our hotel room after dinner and looked out over the city in awe and wonder. A full yellow moon shone down on the cream-coloured stone buildings. We held our breath as we sensed the presence of God in a new and different way.

God designated Jerusalem as a city for His people—the Jews. When they finally had possession of it again in 1967, they wept with joy and gathered at the Western wall to praise God. They are not about to give it up ever again!

There are seasons in our lives when we do not hear the voice of God, when we feel abandoned by Him. The psalmist felt the same way:

Why, O Lord, do you reject me and hide your face from me? (Psalm 88:14)

I do not know why this happens. Perhaps there is something in our lives cutting us off from Him—a sinful attitude or a habit we are clinging to. Or maybe God wants us to practise doing what we know is right and trust Him to speak to us when we need it.

I will declare that your love stands firm forever, that you established your faithfulness in heaven itself. (Psalm 89:2)

One thing I know for sure is that no matter what my condition is, I can count on the faithfulness of God. When I daily reach out in praise and gratitude to Him—whether I feel like it or not, whether my prayers seem to be answered or not—I have an indefinable peace and sense of well-being that can only come from my Lord and Creator, my loving Heavenly Father. He loves me with an everlasting love. I can count on that!

READ: Psalms 90–95

Lord, you have been our dwelling place throughout all generations. (Psalm 90:1)

I like to think of God as being my dwelling place, my home, a place where I am accepted and loved, encouraged, and challenged—a place where I go for comfort, security, teaching, and guidance.

The length of our days is seventy years—or eighty, if we have the strength ... they quickly pass... (Psalm 90:10)

Eighty years is considered a good life. When we reach that age, we realize how fast time has gone by. When I look at history, my life is just a tiny portion of the ongoing saga of the world. This helps me gain a larger perspective and see how futile it is to spend my time in negative attitudes or try to gain wealth or notoriety.

A soldier spends six weeks in basic training in preparation for a career of thirty or so years in the army. Our lives on earth are a bit like basic training for eternity. It is important to do the best we can.

Teach us to number our days aright, that we may gain a heart of wisdom. (Psalm 90:12)

Each day is an opportunity to gain wisdom and experience, if our hearts are free from clutter and open to receive.

He who dwells in the shelter of the Most High will rest in the shadow of the Almighty. I will say of the Lord, "He is my refuge and my fortress, my God, in whom I trust." (Psalm 91:1–2)

To me, the most important words are "dwells" and "rest." It is not enough to drop in now and then and pay our respects to God. To see Him as our refuge and fortress, we must make our dwelling place in His presence. In my life, that means it is important to begin every day in communion with Him and stop often to ask His advice and express my gratitude to Him. The rewards are terrific:

For he will command his angels concerning you to guard you in all your ways. (Psalm 91:11)

Some years ago, I woke up one Saturday morning feeling tired and ready to pack it in for the day. I had been at a conference the day before which had caused me to be mentally alert. I leaned back and pictured myself in God's presence. I consciously thought of His love pouring over me, then His peace, and finally His joy. It was wonderful.

Then I realized that it was not rest, but physical activity I needed. With gratitude in my heart, I got dressed, started the laundry, mixed up some buns, and set them to rise while I baked a batch of cookies. My husband and I then went off to shop for groceries. Shortly after we returned, some of the family dropped in and were delighted to be served coffee, fresh buns, and cookies!

READ: Psalms 96–100

These are wonderful songs of praise to the Lord of the whole universe. It is a most uplifting experience to be part of a group of people who sing and praise God. It lifts me out of my concerns, both large and small, and puts me into a state of knowing God is in control and nothing is too big a problem for Him to solve. I long to pass this idea on to others.

Sing to the Lord a new song… proclaim His salvation day after day… For great is the Lord and most worthy of praise. (Psalm 96:1–2, 4)

It is an awesome privilege to spend time with the Creator—the One who brought the earth into being.

Worship the Lord in the splendor of his holiness; tremble before him, all the earth. Say among the nations, "The Lord reigns." (Psalm 96:9–10)

I wonder what kind of world we would have if everyone—all the earth—worshipped Him. There would still be differences, I am sure, because no two of us are the same. But if our motive was to love and serve each other, so much would be accomplished! There would be no greed or trying to get more for ourselves—no bitterness or envy. Creativity would flow in the absence of negativity or self-centredness to block its way!

He will judge the world in righteousness and the peoples with equity. (Psalm 98:9)

God's standard is righteousness, which is where each of us must face judgment. Jesus is our model of righteousness and He promised His followers that He would send the Holy Spirit to guide them and help them follow His example. Like a good parent, our Heavenly Father encourages and enables us to do what is right, but He also provides judgment if we deliberately choose to be disobedient.

Exalt the Lord our God and worship at his footstool; he is holy. (Psalm 99:5)

When we begin to grasp the holiness of God, His goodness, and His perfect love, what else can we do but worship at His footstool? He wants us to be filled with joy, to be glad, to find fulfillment in this life:

Shout for joy to the Lord, all the earth. Worship the Lord with gladness; come before him with joyful songs. (Psalm 100:1–2)

If my life is not filled with joy and gladness, I am off-track, for a life lived in His presence should make me want to sing for joy! I am learning to search my heart and check my deepest attitudes when life seems less than joyful. The key for getting into His presence again is praise and thanksgiving:

Enter his gates with thanksgiving and his courts with praise; give thanks to him and praise his name. (Psalm 100:4)

The door is open to everyone!

READ: Psalms 101–105

Some years ago, I wrote this in my quiet time book:

I am struggling a little this morning. It is Sunday, and since we make a practice of getting up at 6:30 a.m. every morning for quiet time, Bob did just that. However, I had a restless night, and for an extra half-hour I tried to go back to sleep. It didn't work, so when I roused myself and opened my Bible, I read: *"I will be careful to lead a blameless life... I will walk in my house with blameless heart"* (Psalm 101:2).

It is often quite difficult to get my mind on what the "blameless" way is. It is much easier to think myself into doing what is most comfortable, especially at home where I am inclined to let down. But the psalmist says to keep my thoughts on the perfect way of life, especially in my home! That has challenged me to get my thoughts off my own comfort and turn them to Jesus, whose whole life was blameless. That is what He expects of His followers.

Psalm 103 provides a wonderful description of God. David calls on his soul, his whole being, to bless the Lord. That is where I need to start—by turning my whole attention to praising God's holy name and reflecting on the gifts He has given us. He forgives us, heals our diseases, rescues us from going the wrong way, and pours out His unfailing love and mercy. His goodness is available as long as we live, and He keeps us young at heart. No matter what we have to give up to be His followers, we are winners in the end, for His generosity exceeds our imagination.

God's love for us is higher than the heavens. Though He sees all our failures, He does not punish us as we deserve—He just keeps loving us. As a good earthly father loves and protects his little children, so God loves and protects us—only more so. He knows our lives are short, that our days are numbered, but His love carries right on into eternity.

READ: Psalms 106–110

Praise the Lord. Give thanks to the Lord, for he is good; his love endures forever. (Psalm 106:1)

We should never cease giving thanks to God and praising His wonderful name. Not only is He worthy of all the praise we can give, but that very act puts us in the state of mind to foster creative thinking, wise decisions, and good health! No amount of struggling for success on our own compares with the peace that comes from accepting that God is in control. He will direct our way if we let Him.

We have sinned, even as our fathers did; we have done wrong and acted wickedly. (Psalm 106:6)

The psalmist looks back in history at how his whole nation sinned when they turned away from God, even when they grumbled against Him. Are we each responsible for the sins of our nation? Should we be asking for God's forgiveness for the promiscuity, pornography, abortions, drug addictions, and crimes we hear about on the TV newscasts? Just thinking about it weighs us down with guilt.

Can you imagine what Jesus must have experienced when He took on the sins of all generations and was nailed to the cross? As I ask God to forgive us, as a nation, of all the sins we have committed, I have a small inkling of the intense horror that caused Jesus to cry out, *"My God, my God, why hast thou forsaken me?"* (Matthew 27:46)

The history of Canada is not without periods for which we need God's forgiveness. Why have we waited one hundred fifty years or more to listen to how the Native people feel and think? What about when Canada refused to allow Jewish people from Europe to land on our shores, causing them to return to Europe where many of them died in the holocaust? We need to repent for our nation and pray that God will send His Holy Spirit into the hearts of us all, that we may see a mighty revival in Canada. May it start with me!

Psalm 107 shows how God can do that:

Some sat in darkness and the deepest gloom... Then they cried to the Lord... He brought them out of darkness and the deepest gloom... Let them give thanks to the Lord for his unfailing love and his wonderful deeds for men... (Psalm 107:10, 13–15)

It can be done. God is able to bring us out of darkness into light. He moves in answer to our prayers. Our mandate is clear: repent and pray! Then give thanks and praise to God!

READ: Psalms 111–115

Great are the works of the Lord; they are pondered by all who delight in them. (Psalm 111:2)

If I keep looking at the marvellous works of God, my own problems do not loom as large. I can face anything with His guidance and help.

When we started Lighthouse Christian Academy, we had eight students and two teachers, plus Bob and me to help and encourage in any way we could. Over the years, we have watched God bring in families, remove others, provide finances when we desperately needed it, and help each one involved to grow in awareness and trust of Him. Those of us who were seeking to have a deeper relationship with Jesus have grown.

The fear of the Lord is the beginning of wisdom; all who follow his precepts have good understanding. (Psalm 111:10)

In this case, the word "fear" means love and respect. I remember, as a child, often being kept from doing wrong because of fear of my parents—not fear of their anger, but fear of losing their trust in me. I loved them and did not want to hurt them. Having that kind of respect and love for God, I believe, is the beginning of wisdom. Then I will not want to do anything to hurt Him or make Him lose His trust in me.

Certainly, experience has shown me that if I look at a situation with God's perspective in mind, I gain a better understanding of it. I have more compassion for others when I see them as God's children.

Even in darkness light dawns for the upright... (Psalm 112:4)

Being in tune with God can shed light on any darkness we encounter. Right now, I am trying to see my way through a situation that will entail some difficult decisions. I ask God to shine His light that I might see His plan. I cannot expect to just call on Him now and then. I must spend regular time in His presence if I am to recognize His voice.

From the rising of the sun to the place where it sets, the name of the Lord is to be praised. (Psalm 113:3)

When God created man, He gave him a grave responsibility—to care for the earth and all that is in it.

The highest heavens belong to the Lord, but the earth he has given to man. (Psalm 115:16)

How well have we cared for His creation? We have not always looked ahead, and we are certainly in need of His wisdom and guidance in that area!

READ: Psalms 116–120

I love the Lord, for he heard my voice; he heard my cry for mercy. Because he turned his ear to me, I will call on him as long as I live. (Psalm 116:1–2)

I remember my excitement when I first experienced God very specifically answering my prayers. It happened one evening when Bob was a chaplain in the army. A young couple with two small children had decided to separate and had come to see him. In those days, this was not a common problem and we felt we should do something but did not know what. We called some friends—a couple who made a practice of having quiet times and listening to God. The four of us discussed what we knew of the situation, and then they suggested, "Let's be quiet and see what God has to say about it."

I nearly panicked, since I had never done that before. I even refused paper and pencil, since I really didn't expect God to speak to me. But to my amazement, a clear, detailed plan began to formulate in my mind.

In addition to Bob, there was a senior chaplain on base who also knew this couple. My thought was that he should bring the husband into his office while Bob talked to the wife. Bob would ask where she had been wrong in the relationship but not allow her to talk of her husband's failures. Then she could see where she could begin to change and save the marriage. The same procedure would be followed with the husband in the other office. With each willing to make an attempt to restore their marriage, there was reason to believe it could be saved. They did try, and as far as I know it worked. With army transfers, we soon lost track of them.

My love for God increased as I became aware of His personal interest in my life. Of the four of us that evening, I was the only one who received a clear plan. And I was the one who most needed to know that if we listen, God will speak to us!

Psalm 117, the shortest of them all, is an appropriate prayer at this time when nations are at war:

Praise the Lord, all you nations; extol him, all you peoples. For great is his love toward us, and the faithfulness of the Lord endures forever. Praise the Lord. (Psalm 117:1–2)

Nothing is totally steadfast and enduring except the love of God. How we need Him today as individuals, families, and nations!

It is better to take refuge in the Lord than to trust in man. (Psalm 118:8)

Psalm 119 talks of the importance of knowing and obeying God's word. I have often used it as a basis to pray for someone. I used it first with my grandson when he was having problems, substituting his name wherever it would fit.

When I don't know what words to use to pray for someone, it is helpful to find a Bible passage where I can insert a person's name. If a passage is part of God's word, it must be in harmony with His will.

READ: Psalms 121–125

Bob's favourite psalm was Psalm 121, through which God spoke to him. As a young man, he had an accident while running a thresher-combine on the farm.

He lost his thumb, forefinger, and half the middle finger on his left hand. Since he played a saxophone, that was a devastating experience. However, the following summer at a youth camp, he climbed up a hill during the morning watch. As he opened his Bible, the following verse caught his eye:

The Lord is the shade at your right hand. (Psalm 121:5)

He was right-handed, and he realized that hand was still intact. At that moment, he gave his heart to the Lord and decided to go into the ministry of the United Church. What a great promise that psalm contains:

The Lord will keep you from all harm—he will watch over your life; the Lord will watch over your coming and going both now and forevermore. (Psalm 121:7–8)

God is faithful. I can trust Him to guide me every step of the way—but He can only do that if I spend time listening and seeking His mind.

I once listened to a lady tell her story. She found it very hard to get up early in the morning to have quiet time with God. She then realized that she couldn't say she had given her life to Him if she refused to give Him the first hour of the day. Ever since, she has practiced morning quiet times.

Pray for the peace of Jerusalem. (Psalm 122:6)

God's hand is on Jerusalem today. That is where we expect Jesus to return. Satan does not want that to happen. Where he can, he has stirred up hatred for the Jews. Our mandate, as Christians, is clear—love Israel and pray for the peace of Jerusalem.

Our help is in the name of the Lord, the Maker of heaven and earth. (Psalm 124:8)

There could be no stronger security than to look to the God of all creation, who never changes. He can make us strong, too, if we trust Him.

Those who trust in the Lord are like Mount Zion, which cannot be shaken but endures forever. (Psalm 125:1)

When we look at all the provisions He has made for those who commit their way to Him, it is hard to imagine why anyone would choose to live separated from God.

READ: Psalms 126–130

Blessed are all who fear the Lord, who walk in his ways. (Psalm 128:1)

Special blessings come when I centre my thoughts on God's plan for my life and for everything in which I am involved. We have a tendency to only see a portion of our lives as being God's business (e.g. our church life), whereas other areas are according to what I want (e.g. holiday time). I believe God is just as interested in how I care for my house and spend my free time as He is in how much I give to the church.

In Psalm 128, we see the blessings a man may receive from walking in the way of the Lord: employment that puts food on the table, a wife and children, and finally the opportunity to see his grandchildren. We often take those things for granted, or even see them as rights! It will make a difference in our lives to see them as blessings from God, developing a sense of gratitude for them.

If you, O Lord, kept a record of sins, O Lord, who could stand? (Psalm 130:3)

I am so glad the Lord doesn't keep a little black book in which He keeps track of all my mistakes! He doesn't hold any grudges, as we are so apt to do. He is always ready to forgive.

I wait for the Lord, my soul waits, and in his word I put my hope. My soul waits for the Lord more than watchmen wait for the morning... (Psalm 130:5–6)

Watchmen who are on the graveyard shift long for the morning to come; when the light begins to show, a feeling of joy comes over them. That is how we feel about coming into God's presence. As we get to know Him better, we long to be with Him and take great joy from communing with Him.

O Israel, put your hope in the Lord, for with the Lord is unfailing love... (Psalm 130:7)

That is our greatest security—God's unfailing love!

READ: Psalms 131–136

In Psalm 131, David is not on a spiritual high, but he is at peace: *"But I have stilled and quieted my soul"* (Psalm 131: 2). That is a comfortable place to be. God gives us times of quiet, restful peace.

David longed to build a temple for the Lord, but God promised that his son should do it—and Solomon did. Jerusalem (Zion) was to be the place:

This is my resting place for ever and ever; here I will sit enthroned, for I have desired it. (Psalm 132:14)

In Psalm 133, the writer speaks of the importance of finding unity with other believers.

How good and pleasant it is when brothers live together in unity! (Psalm 133:1)

This is not always found in families or in churches, but it is something we need to strive for.

Psalm 134 ends with a benediction:

May the Lord, the Maker of heaven and earth, bless you from Zion. (Psalm 134:3)

A blessing from Jerusalem! From this city, the capital of Israel, believers from all over the world are experiencing God's blessing. My trips there are definitely highlights in my spiritual growth because of the awareness of God's presence with us.

Psalm 135 is a call to praise God, the Creator of the heavens, the earth, the sky, the sea, and the weather. It outlines how God's plan to establish the Israelites in the Promised Land worked out. Anyone who would not cooperate or got in the way was slain. God gives us a chance (often several chances) to move with His perfect plan, but if we keep refusing, we suffer the consequences. The psalmist warns against making idols that are worthless, and calls on Israel and all believers to bless and praise the Lord. Only He is worthy to be worshipped and praised.

Psalm 136 seems to be a musical version of the ideas in Psalm 135, with a chorus repeated after every line—"His love endures forever."

That is why He is worthy to be praised. There is no other god whose love never fails—a love that gives all, that brings out the best in each person, and that goes on forever.

As I look at the fate of those who opposed the settling of the Israelites in the land God chose for them, I wonder what nations are going to suffer the same fate in this generation for the same reason. Satan would love to destroy Israel to keep Jesus from returning. He will use any people or nation not acquainted with God's overall plan to fulfill his purpose. We need to pray for the leaders of the nations, that they may listen to the voice of God and obey Him!

The Egyptians lost the eldest son in each family, as well as their whole army, when they disobeyed God's call to let His people go. What is in store today for any nation that tries to take the Promised Land away from God's chosen people?

READ: Psalms 137–140

It was hard for the Israelites to sing songs of joy when they were captives in Babylon for seventy years. I wonder if they felt the same way when they were scattered all over the world for two thousand years.

> *How can we sing the songs of the Lord while in a foreign land?* (Psalm 137:4)

They never forgot Jerusalem, however, and when the way was opened for Israel to be established again, they arrived in great numbers. There has been nothing like it since the Exodus. God has put a special tie to the land in every Jewish heart.

> *Though the Lord is on high, he looks upon the lowly, but the proud he knows from afar.* (Psalm 138:6)

That seems to say that arrogance separates us from God. It is very easy to slip into that attitude when everything goes well. In fact, we are more likely to go astray in good times than when things are tough. In good times, we see no need to seek God's direction. The only safeguard I know is constant thanksgiving and praise to acknowledge who God is and to see our position as lowly in respect to Him. Otherwise arrogance, pride, and self-centredness creep in.

In Psalm 139, David demonstrates the intimate relationship we can have with God. He knows everything about us, even before we were born. He fashioned our bodies, and even our thoughts are known to Him. It is hard for us to understand, but it is wonderful to contemplate. No matter how close a child is to his mother, or a wife is to her husband, we can never really understand each other. That is where frustrations begin in relationships.

But God knows everything about me. When I confess my faults, it is such a relief not to have to explain myself to Him. I can feel Him nod, saying, "I am glad you recognize that. Now I can forgive you. Go and sin no more."

I don't always recognize sins in myself, however. If I want to be totally committed, I should say this prayer:

Search me, O God, and know my heart; test me and know my anxious thoughts. See if there is any offensive way in me, and lead me in the way everlasting. (Psalm 139:23–24)

God sees my motives, which I may try to hide, even from myself. It is amazing how we rationalize and excuse ourselves, justifying our thoughts and actions. When we let God's light shine, our selfish attitudes are revealed. Only He can know what is really in my heart.

I have never faced the kind of opposition David speaks of in Psalm 140. His life was constantly in danger, but he knew God was his strength and deliverer. When times are tough, we need to reaffirm our faith and trust in God.

READ: Psalms 141–145

We can learn a lot about effective prayer by reading King David's psalms. Mainly, it involves reaching out to God to have a conversation with Him, but so often we miss the opportunity to listen to what He has to say. In order to hear, we have to be open to make changes in our attitudes—and that is often hard to do.

David is aware of how the words we speak may be damaging and not at all in line with God's thinking:

Set a guard over my mouth, O Lord; keep watch over the door of my lips. (Psalm 141:3)

How I need to pray that prayer! Words slip out that I later wish I hadn't said. The next step should be to examine, with the Lord's help, what negative attitude caused those words to come out of my mouth. I generally find traces of jealousy, self-pity, or pride—none of which have any place in God's plan.

I wonder, was David tempted to go along with men who were involved in wrongdoing? It sounds as if he had those temptations:

Let not my heart be drawn to what is evil, to take part in wicked deeds with men who are evildoers; let me not eat of their delicacies. (Psalm 141:4)

It is hard to stand for what is right when those around you are making wrong, even tempting choices! Throughout Psalms 141–143, David is burdened with his enemies round about him. Perhaps he was fleeing from the wrath of Saul as he wrote these. But interspersed are verses of real trust in God, despite his fear, and a longing for close fellowship with Him.

I remember the days of long ago; I meditate on all your works and consider what your hands have done... my soul thirsts for you like a parched land... for I have put my trust in you. Show me the way I should go, for to you I lift up my soul. (Psalm 143:5–6, 8)

In Psalm 144, he begins to extol God's power:

Praise be to the Lord my Rock... O Lord, what is man that you care for him...? (Psalm 144:1, 3)

Psalm 145 is a song of praise:

I will exalt you, my God the King... Great is the Lord and most worthy of praise... All you have made will praise you, O Lord... Your kingdom is an everlasting kingdom, and your dominion endures through all generations. (Psalm 145:1, 3, 10, 13)

David knew the power that comes from praising God, a power we need to practise if we are to be of any use in His kingdom. That is why I start each morning with a quiet time. I believe that if I start the day by spending time in His presence, I can receive power, love, wisdom—whatever I need to live that day to the fullest.

The Lord is near to all who call upon him, to all who call on him in truth. (Psalm 145:18)

READ: Psalms 146–150

I cannot read these last five psalms without feeling my spirits lift and a sense of wonder and gratitude fill my being. The greatness of our God, our Heavenly Father, extends beyond our wildest imagination. He is everything that is good and loving and powerful. My praise to Him should not happen only when I feel like giving it, when I feel down and need a lift, or when I meet with a group of people in order to worship Him.

I will praise the Lord all my life; I will sing praise to my God as long as I live. (Psalm 146:2)

Everyone, no matter their age, can sing praises to God. I hope I always keep that in mind.

My mother, who lived to be 102, spent her last year in a nursing home. One day when I sat with her, she said, "I never thought I wanted to be in a place like this, but it is lovely. Everyone is so kind. Don't ever fear being in a nursing home when you get old, dear. It is a wonderful place in which to be looked after." Her gratitude made her a joy to be with. She knew the presence of the Lord and appreciated it. Her childhood family had all passed away, and so had her contemporaries.

Do not put your trust in princes, in mortal men, who cannot save. When their spirit departs, they return to the ground; on that very day their plans come to nothing. (Psalm 146:3–4)

Friends and relatives move away or pass on, but God is always near and available. A very young child can accept His presence very easily, and older people can find great comfort in scripture and songs that remind them of His everlasting love. Between those extreme ages, the more we praise and glorify His name, the more meaningful life becomes.

Our God heals the broken-hearted, but He also numbers the stars and names each one. He lifts up the downtrodden, but He also sends the snow and rain. He is the Almighty Creator, but His greatest delight is in those who choose to praise and worship Him.

The Lord delights in those who fear him, who put their hope in his unfailing love. (Psalm 147:11)

I can personally give pleasure to our great and mighty God! In doing so, I can receive all the benefits that come from being in His presence. We cannot praise Him too much! We can sing, dance, and play musical instruments to give praise and glorify His name.

Praise him for his acts of power; praise him for his surpassing greatness… Let everything that has breath praise the Lord. Praise the Lord. (Psalm 150:2, 6)

THE BOOK OF

Philippians

READ: Philippians 1–2

From a prison in Rome, Paul wrote to his friends in Philippi. He never mentions the conditions in which he was living in order to get sympathy (as I probably would have done). He spoke of praying for them with thanksgiving and joy. Here is an example of ignoring the circumstances and letting God lift you above them, into the spiritual realm where you can be filled with the Holy Spirit. Not only was Paul able to selflessly pray for his friends, but he could see that his imprisonment was being used by God.

> *Now I want you to know, brothers, that what has happened to me has really served to advance the gospel.* (Philippians 1:12)

The guards all knew he was there because of his belief in Jesus. As a result, the other believers were emboldened to share their faith. Paul rejoiced that Christ was being proclaimed and he was confident that, through the Holy Spirit and the prayers of his friends, God would be honoured in his life, in spite of him being in prison.

> *For to me, to live is Christ and to die is gain.* (Philippians 1:21)

He could see that there was great joy in living for Christ, but it would be even better to die and be with Christ! He warned his friends that following Christ could bring suffering.

> *For it has been granted to you on behalf of Christ not only to believe on him, but also to suffer for him…* (Philippians 1:29)

He then encouraged them to be like Jesus—totally unselfish. We cannot understand how Jesus, who was one with God, could become a man, choosing the role of a servant among men. In that role, He was totally obedient to God's will.

Therefore God exalted him to the highest place and gave him the name that is above every name, that at the name of Jesus every knee should bow, in heaven and on earth and under the earth, and every tongue confess that Jesus Christ is Lord, to the glory of God the Father. (Philippians 2:9–11)

Those verses always excite me. It seems too good to be true that every person on earth will bow before Jesus and confess that He is Lord. How wonderful that would be! Will that happen when He comes again? I wonder if I will be here to see it.

…work out your salvation with fear and trembling, for it is God who works in you to will and to act according to his good purpose. (Philippians 2:12–13)

God is not finished with me yet. He never will be—that is, until He takes me home. Life is a continuous process of working out our own salvation through constant change to fit into God's plan. Then I read:

Do everything without complaining or arguing… (Philippians 2:14)

It is so easy to slip into a complaining attitude and later wake up to what you are doing. That is when we need to change and move on.

READ: Philippians 3–4

I imagine Paul never thought this letter would be read hundreds of years after his death by people all over the world, but it contains timeless wisdom for us all. For example:

…I consider everything a loss compared to the surpassing greatness of knowing Christ Jesus my Lord… (Philippians 3:8)

Wealth, position, education, fame—these are all taken from us when we die. They are worth nothing compared to a relationship with Jesus. When we accept Him into our lives, He shows us how to use all these things for His glory and honour. Only then are they valuable.

Reflecting on my life, I can see many places where I made mistakes, but that should not hold me back now.

> *But one thing I do: Forgetting what is behind and straining toward what is ahead, I press on toward the goal to win the prize for which God has called me heavenward in Christ Jesus.* (Philippians 3:13–14)

I don't need to carry a burden of guilt. I have received God's forgiveness, so I can leave the past and look forward to the future. I like the idea of God calling me heavenward. He is ever drawing me upward, above the petty thoughts that drag me down.

> *Rejoice in the Lord always. I will say it again: Rejoice!* (Philippians 4:4)

If Paul could rejoice in prison, I should be able to rejoice in my comfortable home! He says "always," not just when things are going well. Although I am sure Paul did not rejoice over his circumstances, I can see how he still had joy in God's love. I believe a life of joy is our right, but we must choose it. Joy comes from getting rid of negative thoughts and replacing them with positive ones. Here is how Paul puts it:

> *Finally, brothers, whatever is true, whatever is noble, whatever is right, whatever is pure, whatever is lovely, whatever is admirable—if anything is excellent or praiseworthy—think about such things... And the God of peace will be with you.* (Philippians 4:8–9)

Paul experienced this truth, and so have I. It is possible to change my thought patterns. One morning, the Lord revealed to me that I had slipped into a pattern of seeing faults in certain people instead of looking at their good points. Every now and then, I would begin to say something and then realize it was a critical remark. I refrained from saying it. I was shocked at how often it happened! I lose God's peace when I become negative.

> *And my God will meet all your needs according to his glorious riches in Christ Jesus.* (Philippians 4:19)

When I consistently put my needs before God and do only what He tells me, I am delighted, and often surprised, to see how He meets those needs.

THE BOOK OF
Proverbs

READ: Proverbs 1–5

When God asked Solomon what he most wanted in life, Solomon said, "Wisdom." God granted this request and Solomon was noted throughout the world for his extra portion of wisdom. In Proverbs, Solomon recorded some of the insights given to him in order to help others live as God intended.

The fear of the Lord is the beginning of knowledge, but fools despise wisdom and discipline. (Proverbs 1:7)

That is where we must start—with an awareness of God and His power. Then we must be willing to learn, to be open to instruction. Life must be very dull for those who have decided in their hearts that they have nothing more to learn.

My son, if sinners entice you, do not give in to them. (Proverbs 1:10)

This is applicable to any age. He is saying, "Do not give in to any temptation—to steal, to gossip, to complain, to criticize, etc." When someone complains about the government, what do we do? Join in? When others complain about the weather, what do we do? My inclination is to agree and start complaining, too!

…and if you call out for insight and cry aloud for understanding… then you will understand the fear of the Lord and find the knowledge of God. For the Lord gives wisdom, and from his mouth come knowledge and understanding. (Proverbs 2:3, 5–6)

We can gain a lot of knowledge through books and college courses, but the wisdom to use that knowledge to make the world a better place can only come from God.

> *Trust in the Lord with all your heart and lean not on your own understanding; in all your ways acknowledge him, and he will make your paths straight. Do not be wise in your own eyes; fear the Lord and shun evil.* (Proverbs 3:5–7)

It is a great relief to know that whatever difficult decision I face, I can look to God for wisdom. I can ask other people, and their ideas may help, but their knowledge and understanding is limited in the same way mine is. On the other hand, God knows everything about the situation. He knows what others are thinking just as He knows my thoughts. He knows the best solution and He has a perfect plan in mind, because He knows the future. If my motives are pure, He can direct my thoughts and words.

Whether it is what to wear, who to see, or what jobs to do, God can direct me in everything!

My health depends on how much trust I put in God. Read again Proverbs 3:5, then look at this:

> *This will bring health to your body and nourishment to your bones.* (Proverbs 3:8)

Solomon reiterates the importance of seeking God's wisdom. Then, in Proverbs 5, he encourages a man to be faithful to his wife. If only the men (and women, too) of our nation would heed that advice! Thousands of our children live with one parent and visit the other on weekends. That was not God's perfect plan for families!

READ: Proverbs 6–10

> *Go to the ant, you sluggard; consider its ways and be wise!* (Proverbs 6:6)

I remember this verse from when I was a child. One of my teachers often quoted it in school to emphasize the importance of work and the sin of laziness. It must have made an impression on me because I have always been intrigued with the busyness of ants as they hurriedly gather food—often pieces bigger than the ants themselves.

Among the seven things that are an abomination to the Lord is *"a man who stirs up dissension among brothers"* (Proverbs 6:19). That can be done by a careless, negative comment from a mind cluttered with critical thoughts. It is so important for me to open myself to God regularly so He can point out any destructive attitudes needing to be cleaned out. Asking His forgiveness gives Him the power to do the cleansing, leaving me free to fill my mind with thanksgiving and accept His love for the person I maligned.

My son, keep your father's commands and do not forsake your mother's teaching. Bind them upon your heart forever. (Proverbs 6:20–21)

My parents were a fine example for me to follow. Their love and respect for each other made me want to have that kind of marriage. Dad's word was law in our house, but as far as I can remember he was fair, and he had a great sense of humour! Mother taught us many things, and both parents were always proud of their four daughters. Because of their example, I wanted to be a good parent. My husband had the same desire. We made lots of mistakes, but I hope we passed on to our children the fine heritage we received from our parents. It is an awesome responsibility to be parents with so much influence on the next generation. We need God's wisdom, for our own is not enough.

To fear the Lord is to hate evil. (Proverbs 8:13)

That begins with the evil in myself. When I hate it enough to admit it, confess it, and ask forgiveness for it, I begin to know what it means to fear, respect, and love the Lord. When I have done that, I am in a position to help others do the same. When I hate sin but love the sinner, I can introduce that person to our loving Saviour, who takes away the sins of the world.

For whoever finds me finds life and receives favor from the Lord. (Proverbs 8:35)

That seems to be a prophetic word about Jesus, who came to earth many years later and gave us an opportunity to "find life" as it was meant to be.

The way of the Lord is a refuge for the righteous, but it is the ruin of those who do evil. (Proverbs 10:29)

Where I fit into that truth is my choice.

READ: Proverbs 11–15

Today, moral standards have little place in our society. The general idea seems to be, "If it feels good, do it." When a nation deems immorality acceptable, it is the beginning of a downfall. This is true of individuals as well. A nation becomes strong as its leaders seek to do what is right for their country, without thought of personal gain.

Bob and I learned a lot from our experience with a movement called Moral Rearmament. We were taught that absolute honesty, absolute unselfishness, absolute purity, and absolute love are the standards by which to measure not only our actions but our thoughts and motives as well. When we face ourselves in this light, we hear the voice of God directing our way.

We can find those standards in Proverbs:

- Honesty: *"The Lord abhors dishonest scales, but accurate weights are his delight"* (Proverbs 11:1).
- Unselfishness: *"When pride comes, then comes disgrace, but with humility comes wisdom"* (Proverbs 11:2).
- Purity: *"The integrity of the upright guides them..."* (Proverbs 11:3).
- Love: *"A kindhearted woman gains respect..."* (Proverbs 11:16)

There are many more examples. Over and over, the word "righteousness" is used to suggest the absolute standard Jesus spoke of when He said, *"Be perfect, therefore, as your heavenly Father is perfect"* (Matthew 5:48). It is easy to dismiss this by saying, "No one is perfect except Jesus Himself." That is true, but if we don't strive for absolute honesty, how much dishonesty are we allowed? Anything less than absolute is no standard at all.

1. This standard speaks of generosity: *"A generous man will prosper"* (Proverbs 11:25).
2. This standard speaks of looking for the good in things: *"He who seeks good finds goodwill..."* (Proverbs 11:27).
3. This standard speaks of the care of animals: *"A righteous man cares for the needs of his animal..."* (Proverbs 12:10).
4. This standard speaks of hard work: *"He who works his land will have abundant food..."* (Proverbs 12:11).
5. This standard speaks of the desire to learn: *"...a wise man listens to advice..."* (Proverbs 12:15).
6. This standard speaks of taking care what we say: *"A gentle answer turns away wrath..."* (Proverbs 15:1).
7. This standard speaks of prayer: *"...the prayer of the upright pleases him"* (Proverbs 15:8).

These are the verses that stand out for me. What a lot to think about and put into practice in my own life!

READ: Proverbs 16–20

All a man's ways seem innocent to him, but motives are weighed by the Lord. Commit to the Lord whatever you do, and your plans will succeed. (Proverbs 16:2–3)

It is common for us to make our plans and then ask God to bless them—but there is a better way. Go before the Lord to make sure your spirit, attitudes, and motives are right with Him. Commit everything to Him and then let the plans formulate.

As I look back over my life, the plans that were most successful are the ones where I put the need before the Lord, then followed the steps that appeared each day. Nothing is more exciting than seeing our plans established by the Lord! The blessings that come are always more than we could have imagined.

When a man's ways are pleasing to the Lord, he makes even his enemies live at peace with him. (Proverbs 16:7)

If we insist on going our own way, the results can be disastrous:

Pride goes before destruction, a haughty spirit before a fall. (Proverbs 16:18)

God created us to be in fellowship with Him. That is the only place we can find peace and security.

Whoever gives heed to instruction prospers, and blessed is he who trusts in the Lord. (Proverbs 16:20)

Therefore, the first and most basic principle in life is to have a strong and consistent relationship with the Lord—in other words, to love Him with all our heart, soul, mind, and strength. That is where we find the wisdom to make right decisions. Jesus added that we must also build right relationships with those around us, and Proverbs provides a few tips on that.

Better a dry crust with peace and quiet than a house full of feasting, with strife. (Proverbs 17:1)

A happy family is a great delight! I have many happy memories of laughter at the dinner table, renting a cottage at the lake in the summer, and all of us being involved in church. After I was married and had children, I remember similar occasions when I was one of the adults. Now I am enjoying the next generations, of my grandchildren and great-grandchildren:

Children's children are a crown to the aged... (Proverbs 17:6)

At any age, it is important to have a positive attitude. Anyone can establish such a habit, which is good for our physical health:

A cheerful heart is a good medicine, but a crushed spirit dries up the bones. (Proverbs 17:22)

READ: Proverbs 21–25

Better to live on a corner of the roof than share a house with a quarrelsome wife. (Proverbs 21:9)

It is so easy to slip into the habit of being quarrelsome without realizing it is happening. Looking back at what I wrote in my quiet-time book, I was doing just that.

> I snapped at Bob last night when he suggested I stay at home today with a cold I did not expect would develop. Why did I react like that? I reacted again when he directed me as I drove the car. What causes these reactions?
> Sometimes I want advice and sometimes I don't. How could Bob possibly know when? I need to learn what I have always said to my kids: "I'll give you advice because my experience may help you. You are free to take it or leave it." Help me, Lord, to hear advice without resenting it. Then give me the wisdom to know whether to follow it or not.

If I don't deal with negative reactions when they first occur, they pile up and become a habit. The result? A quarrelsome woman!

A good name is more desirable than great riches. (Proverbs 22:1)

I was talking to my granddaughter one day about my dad, who was a hard-working man whose word could be trusted. He was a quiet man, which he claimed was a result of having a wife and four daughters! He died some years ago at the age of sixty-seven. Anyone who knew him would comment that he was highly respected in his work, in the church, and in the community. I might add that he was respected in his family as well.

On the other hand, I can think of a man who was respected until he began to accumulate wealth. Soon, dishonesty and greed crept in. It was only a matter of time before he lost his good name—and his riches!

Apply your heart to instruction and your ears to words of knowledge. (Proverbs 23:12)

We are never too old to learn, as long as no disease affects the mind. I took several university courses when I was in my fifties and found them interesting and stimulating. You don't have to go to university to attain knowledge—you can read, discuss, study the Bible, or learn new skills. There are endless ways of maintaining an open and active mind.

If you falter in times of trouble, how small is your strength! (Proverbs 24:10)

We can build our strength in good times, but it is when things are tough that we show what we are like inside. Just as it is good to put money in the bank, so we can draw on it when needed, it is important to build our relationship with God when things are going well. That way, we can draw on His strength in times of adversity.

Here is advice on how to deal with an enemy:

Do not gloat when your enemy falls... Do not fret because of evil men or be envious of the wicked... (Proverbs 24:17, 19)

If your enemy is hungry, give him food to eat; if he is thirsty, give him water to drink. (Proverbs 25:21)

In other words, do not worry about him, but help him where you can! Good advice!

READ: Proverbs 26–31

Without wood a fire goes out; without gossip a quarrel dies down. (Proverbs 26:20)

It has been said that it takes two to make a quarrel, so if one stops answering back the quarrel ceases. I once heard a man put it this way: "On a tennis court, if your opponent keeps hitting balls into your court and you do not return them, he soon runs out of balls." It is hard to keep quiet when someone says insulting things, but if you can, it diffuses the other person's anger. My mother-in-law used to say, "Least said, easiest mended."

As water reflects a face, so a man's heart reflects the man. (Proverbs 27:19)

It is not what we say when we are with other people that reflects our personality; it is what we think when we are alone. What do we daydream about?

I once took a long bus trip. Since I can't read on a moving bus, I had lots of time to just think. That is when I became aware of where my mind is inclined to go. Fortunately, we can control our thoughts. If they go in a negative direction, we can "switch channels" by consciously thinking of something else. If we ask God's forgiveness and ask for His help, the process is easier.

He who conceals his sins does not prosper, but whoever confesses and renounces them finds mercy. (Proverbs 28:13)

An evil man is snared by his own sin, but a righteous one can sing and be glad. (Proverbs 29:6)

I have experienced the joy that comes from confession and forgiveness—even in the middle of changing my thought patterns. In fact, singing praises to God (even inaudibly in your head) can switch the channel of a hurtful thought pattern to one of thanksgiving and praise.

I remember a time when I drove a car along a mountainous gravel road. Real fear sprang up in me. Suddenly, I realized a song was going through my mind—"Put your hand in the hand of the man who stilled the water." As I gave my full attention to the words of that song, my tense muscles relaxed and I could picture Jesus' hands on top of mine on the steering wheel. I sang to myself and rejoiced!

Proverbs 31 poses a challenge to women—sometimes an irritating one! The wife spoken about is just too perfect, too talented, too capable. Perhaps there never was such a woman, but these are attributes we could work towards.

Speaking of her relationship with her husband:

She brings him good, not harm, all the days of her life. (Proverbs 31:12)

I never like to hear a woman belittling her husband, or vice versa—and yet I know I have been guilty of that at times. A wise person once said, "A spouse needs to live to make the other person great." I don't think we would have so many marriage breakups if everyone heeded this proverb—both men and women.

The Proverbs 31 lady works hard. She has strength, dignity, wisdom, and her greatest attribute is her response to God:

> *Charm is deceptive, and beauty is fleeting; but a woman who fears the Lord is to be praised.* (Proverbs 31:30)

THE BOOK OF

Ecclesiastes

READ: Ecclesiastes 1–6

Solomon seems to wonder, what's the use of it all?

What does man gain from all his labor at which he toils under the sun?
(Ecclesiastes 1:3)

I am sure we all wonder about that at times. It was especially strong in me when my toil consisted of cleaning house, doing laundry, getting meals, cleaning up, and grocery shopping. Each day was the same. With a husband and four children to look after, there was no end to it. And that was before we had dishwashers, automatic washing machines, and dryers! If I looked at the jobs to be done, I became easily defeated. However, when I looked at each person in my family, I would not have traded positions with anyone in the world!

Teaching put me in a similar situation. It is a hard job and you are never finished all that could be done, but when you look at each child and the potential you are helping to develop, it becomes a privilege to be a teacher.

When we started a Christian school, I was the principal for the first few years. At times I was tired, wondering why I ever got involved. But when I looked at the children, the parents, the teachers, and the support staff, I realize how blessed I was to have been chosen by God to be in that position!

Generations come and generations go, but the earth remains forever.
(Ecclesiastes 1:4)

With all the earthquakes, floods, and pollution that is so common today, we are beginning to question the permanency of the earth. However, the generations come and go. The older we get, the faster time seems to go by. There are two ways of looking at it:

1. It will all be over soon, so what's the use?
2. Each day is a precious gift that soon passes, so let us not waste a moment being critical or self-centred.

One leads to depression and the other to joyous living!

A man can do nothing better than to eat and drink and find satisfaction in his work... To the man who pleases him, God gives wisdom, knowledge and happiness... (Ecclesiastes 2:24, 26)

What more could we want than wisdom, knowledge, and happiness—except the love of those around us, which God can give us if our lives please Him?

Ecclesiastes 3 contains a lovely passage about there being a time for everything. This passage has helped many people gain a right perspective on things.

Whoever loves money never has money enough; whoever loves wealth is never satisfied with his income. (Ecclesiastes 5:10)

If we could only remember this in our society! Everyone wants their salary to keep going up and up. Canada is having trouble competing in the world markets for that very reason. This could become a serious situation.

READ: Ecclesiastes 7–12

...patience is better than pride. Do not be quickly provoked in your spirit, for anger resides in the lap of fools. (Ecclesiastes 7:8–9)

In most people, patience has to be developed as a habit. Very few of us are born with it. When we face our need for patience and ask God for help, we begin to practise it. God reminds us when our attitudes need to change, but we have to be willing to make the effort to let go of our pride before it becomes a habit. He rewards each success with a sense of accomplishment and inner joy. He wants to change us to be in His image—the One with infinite patience. With our cooperation, He can do wonders!

When times are good, be happy; but when times are bad, consider: God has made one as well the other. (Ecclesiastes 7:14)

No promise in the Bible says life will be easy. Prosperity and adversity are both likely to happen—God has made one as well as the other. If we are rooted and grounded in the love of the Lord, we can face both with a positive attitude, knowing He will see us through and send His blessing into the situation. Our problem is that we can get so bogged down with negativity and fear that we miss the lessons He has prepared for us. We become oblivious to His blessings, which are waiting for us.

However many years a man may live, let him enjoy them all. (Ecclesiastes 11:8)

I took a French class a few years ago at the senior citizens' centre in my area. One day, our instructor gave us a French poem to read. I cannot quote it, but the premise was that the elderly are the favoured ones, for they have been given the gift of a long life. We don't always see it that way and instead consider youth to be the best time. However, age does not really matter. It is the quality of our lives that counts. Do I spread joy or gloom around me?

Some time ago, my little granddaughter came into my house. She was all smiles and had a sparkle in her eye.

"You look as if you are going to have fun today," I said.

"I am," she replied. And off she went.

I'm sure she did, too. She was rejoicing inside!

Remember your Creator in the days of your youth… (Ecclesiastes 12:1)

My family started a Christian school so that we could help children be aware of God's presence every day. While it was small, we started each morning by singing His praises in the chapel. Hopefully, praise became a habit for them. We gave those children a very precious gift—to begin each day acknowledging their Creator.

Fear God and keep his commandments, for this is the whole duty of man. (Ecclesiastes 12:13)

THE BOOK OF

Colossians

READ: Colossians 1–2

Here, Paul writes to his fellow believers in Colossae. In Colossians 1, he explains how he is praying for them:

1. He gives thanks for them and their faith. (Colossians 1:3–4)
2. He prays that they may be filled with the knowledge of God's will. (Colossians 1:9)
3. He prays that they lead a life worthy of the Lord, a life that is pleasing to Him. (Colossians 1:10)
4. He asks that their work may bear fruit and that they may increase in the knowledge of God. (Colossians 1:10)
5. He prays that they may be strengthened in power, developing endurance and patience with joy. (Colossians 1:11)

I would do well to learn that model of how to pray, not only for my Christian friends but for myself as well. It describes the life I long to live.

Then Paul writes a beautiful description of Jesus:

1. The firstborn of all creation. (Colossians 1:15)
2. By Him, all things were created. (Colossians 1:16)
3. In Him, all things hold together. (Colossians 1:17)
4. He is the head of the church. (Colossians 1:18)
5. God was pleased to have all His fullness dwell in Him. (Colossians 1:19)
6. He has reconciled all things to Himself by the cross. (Colossians 1:20)

Paul says that Jesus went to the cross so He could present us holy in His sight, free from accusation, but there is a condition:

If you continue in your faith, established and firm, not moved from the hope held out in the gospel. (Colossians 1:23)

In Colossians 2, Paul warns about being drawn away from our central focus on Jesus:

So then, just as you received Christ Jesus as Lord, continue to live in him, rooted and built up in him, strengthened in the faith as you were taught, and overflowing with thankfulness. (Colossians 2:6–7)

God has offered us total forgiveness through Jesus:

...having cancelled the written code, with its regulations, that was against us and that stood opposed to us; he took it away, nailing it to the cross. (Colossians 2:14)

Paul warns that we could be drawn into rules and regulations set up by people who appear to have wisdom. But the rules have no value.

READ: Colossians 3–4

Set your minds on things above, not on earthly things. (Colossians 3:2)

It is hard to know just what Paul meant by this, yet it seems like sound advice. How does one do it? One way I can make it practical in my own life is to start each day with a time of thanksgiving and praise. That helps me get God's perspective on what is going on in my life.

Paul goes on to say that we must get rid of all our negative attitudes like immorality, covetousness, anger, and foul talk, replacing them with positive attitudes of compassion, kindness, and patience. But most important for me are these:

1. I must forgive others as God has forgiven me. (Colossians 3:13)
2. I must love, since love binds all things together. (Colossians 3:14)
3. I must let the peace of Christ rule in my heart. (Colossians 3:15)

Next to that last verse, I wrote: "The inheritance of every Christian." It seems that if I don't have peace, it is because I haven't created the right condition to receive it.

Finally, Paul writes, *"giving thanks to God the Father"* (Colossians 3:17). This gives us a good place to start. Sometimes it is hard to be forgiving and loving, but as soon as I focus on being thankful, ideas flood into my mind. As long as I don't stop the flow, I soon feel my spirit lifting and I can face the need for love, forgiveness, and patience.

My relationships with those around me are where my real character shows. As Paul points out each type of earthly relationship, he identifies how it affects the way we relate to God—*"as is fitting in the Lord"* (Colossians 3:18), *"for this pleases the Lord"* (Colossians 3:20), and *"with sincerity and reverence for the Lord"* (Colossians 3:22). We cannot say we love the Lord if we have negative attitudes towards those around us.

Whatever you do, work at it with all your heart, as working for the Lord, not for men... (Colossians 3:23)

I should clean my house for Jesus, prepare an attractive meal to please Him, and dress in a way that honours Him. When we remind ourselves that we are doing it to please God—not other people—the effort becomes worthwhile.

Devote yourselves to prayer, being watchful and thankful. (Colossians 4:2)

THE SONG OF
Songs

READ: Song of Songs 1–8

There are two characters in this romantic song—the man and the maid—though it is not always clear which is speaking. I remember hearing a speaker say that although King Solomon had many wives and many concubines, that was not God's perfect plan for him. There was one girl the king loved in a very special way—and that was the girl God created for him. Perhaps he was thinking of her when he wrote this song.

I believe God can lead us to the right person, the one with whom we are to spend the rest of our lives, if we seek His guidance. But life won't all be romance, no matter how strong our love is when we marry. Perhaps that is our problem today. When a couple finds that the romance is gone, they decide to get a divorce. God's plan for marriage is that it is a relationship through which we can grow closer to Him, which can only happen if both people are willing to change and adjust.

I believe we must decide to nurture lasting love with our spouse, no matter what happens. As I looked into some of my old quiet-time notebooks, I read about my struggle to adjust to some of Bob's ways, to face selfish attitudes in myself and be willing to let go of my preconceived ideas about marriage. I know he had some of the same struggles. Looking back, it was well worth it, and of course there were lots of good times along the way.

But back to the romantic love expressed in this song. It has been likened to God's relationship with His people—the Jews. It has also been suggested that since the church has been referred to as the bride of Christ, this is the kind of love Christ shares with the church.

A few verses have special meaning to me, including this one, which we used to sing in church:

He has taken me to the banquet hall, and his banner over me is love. (Song of Songs 2:4)

As we sang, we were reminded that Jesus' banner of love protects us and guides us.

Then there is Solomon's lovely description of spring:

See! The winter is past; the rains are over and gone. Flowers appear on the earth; the season of singing has come, the cooing of doves is heard in our land. The fig tree forms its early fruit; the blossoming vines spread their fragrance. (Song of Songs 2:11–13)

Spring is, indeed, a lovely time of year. I love the daffodils, fruit trees in blossom, and birds singing in the trees. The whole world seems to come alive.

THE BOOK OF
Isaiah

READ: Isaiah 1

The first verse of Isaiah gives us an idea of when Isaiah lived. It was a time when Israel was divided into two countries—Israel and Judah. Isaiah lived in the south country of Judah. In the first chapter, God's word shows that the people had turned away from Him.

> *The ox knows his master, the donkey his owner's manger, but Israel does not know, my people do not understand... They have forsaken the Lord.* (Isaiah 1:3–4)

As a parent grieves over a child who has gone astray, so God grieves over His people who do not listen to Him. At this point in history, everything had gone wrong with them, but they continued to rebel and go their own way.

> *Why should you be beaten anymore? Why do you persist in rebellion?* (Isaiah 1:5)

This can happen in individuals, churches, and nations. The only way we can receive the blessings provided for us is to align our lives with Him—change our attitudes to be like those of our loving Heavenly Father.

One day, I listened to a conversation between a bus driver and a passenger as he drove along the highway. According to the passenger, everything was wrong with the government and the company he worked for. He had a few good ideas of changes that could be made. He half-jokingly said, "I could run the company better myself." Later I wished I had said, "Young man, with that negative attitude you will never be the head of a successful company." He was going to resign and could hardly wait for the day he stopped work. Unfortunately, unless he changed his thinking, he would end up taking all the problems with him!

In spite of Israel's waywardness and the resulting catastrophes, they were never completely wiped out. There were always a few survivors.

Unless the Lord Almighty had left us some survivors, we would have become like Sodom, we would have been like Gomorrah. (Isaiah 1:9)

God calls us to be totally committed to Him. He does not want us to merely look good on the outside while having negative thoughts and intentions inside. He said:

Stop bringing meaningless offerings! ...I cannot bear your evil assemblies. (Isaiah 1:13)

For many years, I dutifully went to church and became familiar with much of the Bible, but I had no idea how to make that relevant in my daily life. How many churchgoers are like that? Now that my greatest desire is to live totally committed to Him, He often points out where I need to change. Iniquity in me negates my praise and worship of Him.

He will help us find the solution to this problem:

Stop doing wrong, learn to do right! "Come now, let us reason together," says the Lord. "Though your sins are like scarlet, they shall be as white as snow... If you are willing and obedient, you will eat the best from the land. (Isaiah 1:16–19)

I believe the Jewish people have shown obedience to God in returning to the land of Israel in the last hundred years. Instead of the barren, unproductive place it was for centuries, it now produces all kinds of fruit, vegetables, and grain for the people to eat. God's promises are true for both individuals and nations.

READ: Isaiah 2–5

In the last days the mountain of the Lord's temple will be established as chief among the mountains. (Isaiah 2:2)

Here is a glimpse of what Isaiah prophesied would happen at the end of the world as we know it. The house of God will be established on Mount Zion (Jerusalem) and people from all over the world will go there:

He will teach us his ways, so that we may walk in his paths... (Isaiah 2:3)

When Bob and I arrived in a beautiful auditorium in Jerusalem for the Feast of Tabernacles, we wondered if that was the beginning of the fulfillment of this prophecy. Our group represented many nations from all over the world. This feast now happens every year, so perhaps it is a preparation for when Jesus comes again to Jerusalem.

> *He will judge between the nations and will settle disputes for many peoples. They will beat their swords into plowshares and their spears into pruning hooks. Nation will not take up sword against nation, nor will they train for war any more.* (Isaiah 2:4)

If Jesus should come today and judge the nations, I wonder what He would have to say. There is no real sign of peace anywhere. Even in Canada, we see conflicts between English and French, labour and management, Natives and non-Natives, broken families—how can we ever get to a place where there is no more fighting?

> *Come, O house of Jacob, let us walk in the light of the Lord.* (Isaiah 2:5)

Only the Lord's light can shine into the depths of our hearts and make us aware of the evil that needs to be washed away and replaced with the light and love of God. Nations cannot change until individual hearts within that nation change.

> *The arrogance of man will be brought low and the pride of men humbled; the Lord alone will be exalted in that day, and the idols will totally disappear.* (Isaiah 2:17–18)

All our striving for more money and power seems petty when we look at the world from God's perspective. A person's life is a short span in the ongoing history of mankind; wealth and power have little significance. It is our quality of life that counts. Each of us influences those around us for good or evil, which we do, not with money but by our attitudes. A judgment day is coming, and none of us can escape.

In Isaiah 5, the prophet tells of a vineyard which does not produce good grapes. It is therefore trampled down and destroyed.

> *The vineyard of the Lord Almighty is the house of Israel, and the men of Judah are the garden of his delight.* (Isaiah 5:7)

If we (the church) are going to accept God's promises to Israel, having been ingrafted onto the vine, we must also accept that His warnings apply to us as well!

READ: Isaiah 6–9

Isaiah gives us a beautiful picture of God appearing to him. Uzziah had been king for over fifty years. Once Uzziah died, Isaiah saw God sitting on His throne. What an awesome sight! Angels were calling:

Holy, holy, holy is the Lord Almighty; the whole earth is full of his glory. (Isaiah 6:3)

That is a great affirmation! If I started each day repeating those two lines over and over again, I could have a more positive attitude towards life and recognize miracles of God as they happen. I'm sure His hand directs circumstances more than we realize, because we are not always tuned into His wavelength.

"The whole earth is full of His glory" is meant to refer to the place where I am, and all the places I pray for daily.

In God's holy presence, Isaiah became aware of his own sin. It is significant that as soon as he confessed it, he was forgiven. Then he was open to God's calling to a special task and was ready to respond.

Here am I. Send me! (Isaiah 6:8)

If we want God to show us exactly where He wants us to be and what He wants us to do, we must draw close to Him, through praise and thanksgiving, allowing His light to shine into our very souls and help us recognize our *"unclean lips"* (Isaiah 6:5). Only after we confess and receive forgiveness can we hear Him call us to a particular task. We might not like what He asks of us—it may be something we do not want to do, or it may be to stay where we are and carry on with what we are already doing. If we want to continue receiving His blessing, we must answer, "Here I am. Send me."

Twice in this passage God tells Isaiah that He is going to send a Saviour. This was five hundred years before Jesus was born!

The virgin will be with child and will give birth to a son, and will call him Immanuel. (Isaiah 7:14)

Generation after generation held on to this promise, waiting for it to happen. I wonder if it would have happened sooner if the people of Israel had been more consistent in following God's plan. What blessings from God do we delay or miss altogether because we ignore His presence in our lives?

Isaiah 9 is often quoted at Christmas, when we celebrate Jesus' birth:

The people walking in darkness have seen a great light... For to us a child is born, to us a son is given, and the government will be on his shoulders. And he will be called Wonderful Counselor, Mighty God, Everlasting Father, Prince of Peace. Of the increase of his government and peace there will be no end. (Isaiah 9:2, 6–7)

He is our only hope of lasting peace in the world—and in our own hearts.

READ: Isaiah 10–13

God holds each of us responsible for our own choices and decisions. Although He chose the Israelites as His own people and Jerusalem as His city, they could not escape punishment for wrongdoing.

Shall I not deal with Jerusalem and her images as I dealt with Samaria and her idols? (Isaiah 10:11)

However, God has never allowed the Jewish people to be wiped out—not even by Hitler, who attempted to do just that during World War II. There has always been a remnant left.

When the Lord finished all his work against Mount Zion and Jerusalem, he will say, "I will punish the king of Assyria for the willful pride of his heart and the haughty look in his eyes... In that day the remnant of Israel, the survivors of the house of Jacob, will no longer rely on him who struck them down but will truly rely on the Lord, the Holy One of Israel. (Isaiah 10:12, 20)

God is all-powerful. When people or nations stray too far from Him, He has a way of bringing them down and removing their power. Arrogance and self-centred pride have no place in His kingdom.

A shoot will come up from the stump of Jesse; from his roots a Branch will bear fruit. The Spirit of the Lord will rest on him—the Spirit of wisdom and understanding, the Spirit of counsel and of power, the Spirit of knowledge and the fear of the Lord—and he will delight in the fear of the Lord. (Isaiah 11:1–2)

I am sure Isaiah had difficulty understanding the message of a coming Redeemer, for it certainly did not happen in his lifetime. We can be very grateful that the message was written down so we could read it today. It helps us to realize the ongoing plan of God. Men may come and go, but His plan continues forever.

There follows a delightful picture of righteous judgment in the world, and even peace among the animals. Everyone shall come to know the Lord:

> *...for the earth will be full of the knowledge of the Lord as the waters cover the sea... He will raise a banner for the nations and gather the exiles of Israel; he will assemble the scattered people of Judah from the four quarters of the earth.* (Isaiah 11:9, 12)

Could it be that this prophecy is being fulfilled in our generation? If there ever was a time when the world needed a Saviour, it is today. In the midst of war, famine, lawlessness, and immorality, here is our hope:

> *Surely God is my salvation; I will trust and not be afraid. The Lord, the Lord, is my strength and my song; he has become my salvation.* (Isaiah 12:2)

READ: Isaiah 14–17

God has never rejected Israel, although it has been taught in some churches that when so many refused to accept Jesus, God did reject them. It seemed that way, when they were scattered around the world and Israel (Palestine) was ruled for centuries by others. However, there is nothing in the Bible to support this view.

> *The Lord will have compassion on Jacob; once again he will choose Israel and will settle them in their own land.* (Isaiah 14:1)

Because this seemed impossible, the church ignored statements like these for a long time. Perhaps they thought the happenings related in the New Testament nullified God's word in the Old Testament. Then, in the twentieth century, thousands of Jewish people from all over the world moved to Israel. Christians began to take an interest in how often the prophets in the Old Testament foretold this.

> *The Lord has established Zion, and in her his afflicted people will find refuge.* (Isaiah 14:32)

Following the holocaust, thousands of survivors—some in very bad physical condition—headed for Israel, in spite of opposition. How they must have rejoiced when they finally reached their destination—the Promised Land!

Starting at Isaiah 14:12, we learn of how Satan came to be. He was called *"morning star, son of the dawn."* He must have been in God's company until he became too ambitious:

> *You said in your heart, "I will ascend to heaven; I will raise my throne above the stars of God; I will sit enthroned on the mount of assembly, on the utmost heights of the sacred mountain. I will ascend above the tops of the clouds; I will make myself like the Most High." (Isaiah 14:13–14)*

God does not allow anyone to take His place. Those who try will have a mighty fall. This is a warning to us as well. It seems that Satan was close to God, but when he tried to take power unto himself, he fell to the depths. In my lifetime, I have watched various leaders, both political and religious, rise to a high position in the eyes of the world before falling for having taken glory unto themselves rather than experiencing the glory of God. Satan was told:

> *But you are cast out of your tomb like a rejected branch... Surely, as I have planned, so it will be... (Isaiah 14:19, 24)*

God's plan carries on in spite of what we do. We can choose whether or not to fit into it. If I decide to let Him be the Lord of my life in a practical, day-to-day way, He can use me wherever I am.

When I was in my seventies and was still principal of Lighthouse Christian Academy, I began to feel uneasy about whether or not I was supposed to continue. One morning, the Lord put a clear thought into my mind: "If Lighthouse is My school, I need a principal who will listen to Me and follow My direction. Age has nothing to do with it."

I realized my calling was to spend time in quiet with Him every morning to get directions for the day ahead. I was to leave the principal's position when He told me to. So I did just that!

Even crops will not do well if the people planting them turn from God. He is the Lord of the harvest:

> *You have forgotten God your Savior... Therefore, though you set out the finest plants... yet the harvest will be as nothing... (Isaiah 17:10–11)*

READ: Isaiah 18–22

> *This is what the Lord says to me: "I will remain quiet and will look on from my dwelling place..." (Isaiah 18:4)*

This truth can be a great help to us if we accept and refer to it in our lives. Knowing that God is always watching me is a comfort when things do not go well. Knowing that I can draw on His love for me (no matter how I am treated) or His wisdom (He knows all the circumstances while I know only a portion) gives me security and refuge. On the other hand, if I am tempted to do wrong, it can be a mighty deterrent knowing that God is watching me, longing to steer me in the right direction.

> *The idols of Egypt tremble before him, and the hearts of the Egyptians melt within them.* (Isaiah 19:1)

The power of God is greater than any other power in the universe. He is able to overcome any evil spirit, no matter where it manifests. This is a wonderful truth for us to hold on to. When our habits control us and we seem powerless against them, here is the answer. Countless people have been delivered from alcohol, tobacco, drugs, anger, fear, and self-centredness. This deliverance is available if we line up our lives to fit His perfect plan. We need to take time with Him daily to be aware of the areas where we need to let go, so that He can heal and deliver us from "the idols of Egypt."

In the midst of the conflicts going on in the Middle East, the mistrust between the Arabs and the Jews, and even between one Arab nation and another, the following verses seem highly improbable:

> *In that day there will be a highway from Egypt to Assyria. The Assyrians will go to Egypt and the Egyptians to Assyria. The Egyptians and Assyrians will worship together. In that day Israel will be the third, along with Egypt and Assyria, a blessing on the earth. The Lord Almighty will bless them, saying, "Blessed be Egypt my people, Assyria my handiwork, and Israel my inheritance."* (Isaiah 19:23–25)

There has been a division between Jews and Arabs ever since the time of Isaac and Ishmael. Is it possible these three nations might worship God together and be a blessing to the world? What a miracle that would be!

Isaiah 21–22 presents a different picture—one of great destruction brought about because the people did not seek the Lord:

> *You built a reservoir between the two walls for the water of the Old Pool, but you did not look to the One who made it, or have regard for the One who planned it long ago.* (Isaiah 22:11)

READ: Isaiah 23–26

The Lord Almighty planned it, to bring low the pride of all glory and to humble all who are renowned on the earth. (Isaiah 23:9)

It is dangerous to seek honour and glory for oneself. This produces pride and self-centredness, opening the way for other sins to creep in. I can think of a man who reached the top position in his field only to come crashing down when his dishonesty became known. It may be greed that creeps in when pride takes over—or lust or covetousness. Pride opens the door to a host of other sins.

When God created the earth, He gave man dominion over everything. In other words, He gave us a responsibility to care for His world. In the last hundred years, we have failed to look at the long-term effects of our progress. Cars were hailed as a wonderful invention, and they are now a necessity, but the exhaust from these vehicles may ruin the air for future generations. God gave a warning in Isaiah:

The earth is defiled by its people; they have disobeyed the laws, violated the statutes and broken the everlasting covenant. Therefore a curse consumes the earth; its people must bear their guilt. (Isaiah 24:5–6)

It has not happened yet, but we expect the following to come to pass:

…for the Lord Almighty will reign on Mount Zion and in Jerusalem, and before its elders, gloriously. (Isaiah 24:23)

Imagine Isaiah getting that message 2,500 years ago! He knew, as we do, that the way to rise above our difficulties is to praise God and acknowledge Him for who He is:

O Lord, you are my God; I will exalt you and praise your name… The Sovereign Lord will wipe away the tears from all faces… let us rejoice and be glad in his salvation. (Isaiah 25:1, 8–9)

He is the mighty God who loves each one of us and longs to comfort us, to remove our tears and give us joy. We can experience His peace, no matter what is happening around us, if we keep trusting Him.

You will keep in perfect peace him whose mind is steadfast, because he trusts in you. (Isaiah 26:3)

READ: Isaiah 27–30

In days to come Jacob will take root, Israel will bud and blossom and fill all the world with fruit. (Isaiah 27:6)

The Lord spoke these words through Isaiah. As far as I know, Israel today is closer to fulfilling that prophecy than she has ever been. I think of the fruit and vegetable stalls we saw in various markets in Israel and know they have been making shipments abroad to other countries. Certainly, Israel has been blossoming as it never has before.

And in that day a great trumpet will sound. Those who were perishing in Assyria and those who were exiled in Egypt will come and worship the Lord on the holy mountain in Jerusalem. (Isaiah 27:13)

On our first trip to Israel, our tour guide was from Baghdad, Iraq (Assyria). I don't know how many others had come from that country, but I do know that the Jews had very little freedom in the Arab countries. When they settled in Israel, they were able to vote for the first time.

In that day the Lord Almighty will be a glorious crown, a beautiful wreath for the remnant of his people. (Isaiah 28:5)

Without a doubt, Israel has made lots of mistakes. What country hasn't? But certainly they have always been able to turn back the battles that have come against them. It is my belief that God has intervened on their behalf a number of times.

For all of us who believe, God has promised to teach us His way. It is a lifelong process:

So then, the word of the Lord to them will become: Do and do, do and do, rule on rule, rule on rule; a little here, a little there... (Isaiah 28:13)

This is the way we learn—little by little. However, He warns us against being rebellious or disobedient:

"Woe to the obstinate children," declares the Lord, "to those who carry out plans that are not mine, forming an alliance, but not by my Spirit, heaping sin upon sin." (Isaiah 30:1)

We have a choice every day—every moment, really—to follow either His way or our own, to have His attitude or a self-centred one, to seek to please Him or make life comfortable for ourselves.

He promises that although there will be adversity, He will always be with us.

Whether you turn to the right or to the left, your ears will hear a voice behind you, saying, "This is the way; walk in it." (Isaiah 30:21)

He seems to find ways of letting us know His will. Sometimes it is clearer than others, almost an audible voice. Other times He speaks to us through a verse in the Bible, or someone will say something that provides just the answer we have been looking for. There are times, too, when the way is not clear and we have to make our decision by what seems best at the moment. He is a God of variety and He speaks to us in many ways. Our job is to listen and obey.

READ: Isaiah 31–35

Woe to those who go down to Egypt for help... but do not look to the Holy One of Israel, or seek help from the Lord. (Isaiah 31:1)

When we depend on others for help and not go to the Lord, we run into trouble. God wants us to depend on Him. He may use others to reach us. Sometimes by sharing our problem with another, it is easier to find the solution. However, only God can be trusted to be pure and righteous in His judgment.

There can never be true justice and righteousness without the Spirit of the Lord. Our own thinking is always motivated by some degree of self-centredness, unless we invite the Holy Spirit to cleanse and guide our thoughts.

The fruit of righteousness will be peace; the effect of righteousness will be quietness and confidence forever. (Isaiah 32:17)

My only chance of attaining righteousness is to consistently spend time alone with God and receive it from Him. The result is peace, quietness, and trust—gifts of inestimable value that are available to all. How badly the world needs people who have that kind of relationship with God!

A young woman once told me of the town where she lived. She had known the people there for a long time, but her heart ached for the messed-up lives she knew were there. Many people do not give God a chance to show them the way to righteousness, peace, quietness, and trust.

O Lord, be gracious to us; we long for you. Be our strength every morning, our salvation in time of distress. (Isaiah 33:2)

It is easy to say that the Lord is our ruler or our King, but do we act as if that is true? Is He ruler in my life? Does He direct all my decisions? I long to be able to answer yes to those questions. If I believe He is Lord, I need to act as though He is.

...and the ransomed of the Lord will return. They will enter Zion with singing; everlasting joy will crown their heads. Gladness and joy will overtake them, and sorrow and sighing will flee away. (Isaiah 35:10)

Once, when we drove into Jerusalem, our guide said, "We are entering Zion, so we will stop the bus in the parking lot. You may want to sing." So we did! All thirty-seven of us joined hands in a circle and sang praises to God! Our hearts were filled with joy, just as the Bible says.

READ: Isaiah 36–40

The King of Assyria had already taken some of the cities of Judah. This time, he sent some of his leaders to threaten Jerusalem, where King Hezekiah lived. They scoffed at the king's faith in God.

When King Hezekiah heard this, he tore his clothes and put on sackcloth and went into the temple of the Lord. (Isaiah 37:1)

He sent word to Isaiah, asking him to pray for him. The message came back that he did not need to be afraid, because God would intervene. However, the delegation came again from Assyria with a letter of mockery and threats.

Hezekiah received the letter from the messengers and read it. Then he went up to the temple of the Lord and spread it out before the Lord. (Isaiah 37:14)

What a great way to deal with a difficult letter—or any problem or decision! Go into the Lord's presence and spread it out before Him. Hezekiah's prayer is worth looking at. He acknowledges who God is and then states that other nations have fallen before Assyria because they worshipped idols.

Now, O Lord our God, deliver us from his hand, so that all kingdoms on earth may know that you alone, O Lord, are God. (Isaiah 37:20)

Isaiah brought God's answer to the king—that He would protect Jerusalem from the king of Assyria and his army.

God's purpose is that the world should know that He alone is the Lord, and He uses people like Hezekiah to spread the word. That prayer has been read for centuries to let people of every generation see what God can do for a nation through one man's prayer. I don't expect my words will be read several thousand years from now, but maybe a few people will read my testimony of God's power and love. My faith grows as I read of how other people's prayers are answered.

Hezekiah was not always as wise as he was in this incident. He demonstrated indiscretion when messengers came from the King of Babylon and he showed them his treasures. He also demonstrated self-centredness when Isaiah shared a prophecy with him (Isaiah 39:5–8).

Isaiah 40 contains some lovely, familiar passages:

Comfort, comfort my people, says your God. Speak tenderly to Jerusalem… (Isaiah 40:1–2)

Many Christians feel this is a message for the church today to have compassion and love for Israel.

Before Christmas, we often hear the passage starting in Isaiah 40:3 as we prepare to celebrate the birth of Jesus.

And the glory of the Lord will be revealed… (Isaiah 40:5)

There is a sense of expectancy and hope. There is also a sense of security in the following words:

The grass withers and the flowers fall, but the word of our God stands forever. (Isaiah 40:8)

And for very practical help when you are tired and still have duties to be done, try repeating these words as I have done many times:

But those who hope in the Lord will renew their strength. They will soar on wings like eagles; they will run and not grow weary, they will walk and not be faint. (Isaiah 40:31)

READ: Isaiah 41–43

So do not fear, for I am with you; do not be dismayed, for I am your God. I will strengthen you and help you; I will uphold you with my righteous right hand. (Isaiah 41:10)

These words were given to Israel, but as believers we know they are for all who ask God to reign in their lives. Many times in life, I need to make an important decision that may affect others. The above verse is an assurance that, at the right moment, God will give me the wisdom I need.

Here, Isaiah's prophecy seems to refer to the coming of Jesus:

Here is my servant, whom I uphold, my chosen one in whom I delight; I will put my Spirit on him and he will bring justice to the nations. (Isaiah 42:1)

Then He speaks of how God put His hand on the Israelite nation in order that the world could become more aware of Him.

I, the Lord, have called you in righteousness; I will take hold of your hand. I will keep you and make you to be a covenant for the people and a light for the Gentiles... (Isaiah 42:6)

As believers, that is our position—to hold God's hand and show the light of His love to all people. No wonder we are called to sing praises to Him!

Over and over, we see the words "Fear not." In Isaiah 43, God declares that He will be with His people through deep waters and through fire. Whatever the circumstances, His promise remains. That is probably why the Jewish people have survived through the centuries in spite of discrimination and abuse.

Isaiah tells of their return to the Promised Land from all over the world:

Do not be afraid, for I am with you; I will bring your children from the east and gather you from the west. I will say to the north, "Give them up!" and to the south, "Do not hold them back." Bring my sons from afar and my daughters from the ends of the earth. (Isaiah 43:5–6)

In the past century, thousands of Jewish people have moved from many different countries to live in Israel. They arrived by the plane load day after day, week after week—a most amazing thing. The thousands who settled there had to clear land and plant trees and crops. Under the Turks, this land had become a wilderness where nothing grew. The Jews also needed to learn Hebrew, which had been adopted as the official language. How they must have worked to make Israel a land that people from all over the world now want to visit! It is also one of the countries leading the world in technology of all kinds.

Here is one more wonderful promise God made to His people:

I, even I, am he who blots out your transgressions, for my own sake, and remember your sins no more. (Isaiah 43:25)

READ: Isaiah 44–47

Occasionally, I have had experiences in which God uses words originally spoken to Israel to speak to me personally. When He uses this particular verse while I'm in prayer for my grown children, I feel wonderfully assured:

> *I will pour out my Spirit on your offspring, and my blessing on your descendants.* (Isaiah 44:3)

I like the word "descendants," because it includes grandchildren and great-grandchildren as well.

Throughout Isaiah, God calls His people to do away with idols and turn to Him:

> *I am the first and I am the last; apart from me there is no God.* (Isaiah 44:6)

It seems so foolish to take a piece of wood, use some of it to make a fire, then fashion the rest into an idol to worship. It seems just as foolish today to build up a bank account and try to make more and more money, so that it becomes your aim in life—the god you worship. Yet I see people doing that. There is no real lasting happiness in accumulating money or material possessions. You become a slave to them.

> *I am the Lord, and there is no other; apart from me there is no God... Woe to him who quarrels with his Maker...* (Isaiah 45:5, 9)

This reminds me of a puppy learning to walk on a leash. He runs and pulls and struggles against it, but his master talks quietly and firmly holds the leash until at last the dog realizes he can enjoy a good walk while also obeying the rules. He becomes happy, and so does his master, who rewards him with love and affection. We can struggle against God's laws of life, but He gently calls us back. When we listen to His voice and obey, we find great joy and receive all the blessings He has ready to pour out upon His obedient children.

As He promised Abraham, He will use Israel to reveal Himself to the world.

> *But in the Lord all the descendants of Israel will be found righteous and will exult.* (Isaiah 45:25)

My constant prayer for Israel is that her people will truly and completely open their hearts to hear the voice of God. Now that they are together in the land

God chose for them, they are in a position to fulfill the purpose of God—and we will all receive the blessing! That is, if our hearts are right. Still speaking of Israel, He warns Babylon:

I gave them into your hand, and you showed them no mercy. (Isaiah 47:6)

As I want others to love my children, so God wants us to love His people, whom He has chosen—both Jews and Christians. But most of all, He wants us to love His Son.

READ: Isaiah 48–51

From now on I will tell you of new things, of hidden things unknown to you. (Isaiah 48:6)

The exciting thing about the Christian life is that there is always something new to learn. It may be a new insight into my own personality or a new awareness of how God is at work in someone else's life. I've been going through old quiet-time notebooks and discarding them. The lessons of the past are very useful, and I've used many of them as I write, but I don't want to close my mind to what God wants to teach me today and in the days to come. There is always something new.

See, I have refined you, though not as silver; I have tested you in the furnace of affliction. (Isaiah 48:10)

We grumble and complain when things go wrong and the going gets tough, but just as silver has to be heated to get rid of its impurities, in times of affliction we face our own impurities and seek the perfection of God.

I spoke to a young woman recently whose family was going through some difficult times. There were hard decisions to be made. Through it, she found that she had to let go of material securities and depend on God. She had been tried in the furnace of affliction and come through with a stronger faith. God revealed new things to her.

This is what the Lord says—your Redeemer, the Holy One of Israel: "I am the Lord your God, who teaches you what is best for you, who directs you in the way you should go. If only you had paid attention to my commands, your peace would have been like a river, your righteousness like the waves of the sea. (Isaiah 48:17–18)

That is a pretty clear promise. If I am not at peace, I need to discover where I have strayed from God's commandments. He assures us that He will lead us. If we obey, His peace and righteousness can be ours. When I get off-track, it is so easy to blame those around me for what I consider to be their mistakes rather than asking God where I need to change. The Bible calls it repentance. When I practise it, I experience peace! It is worth the discomfort of admitting my failures to receive the gift of inner peace.

...I will not forget you! (Isaiah 49:15)

Each one of us feels lonely at times, such as when a certain responsibility falls on me or when I realize that no one else can really enter the space I am in and understand how I feel. That is when I appreciate the presence of the Holy Spirit, who knows everything about me and will never leave me. He will even go with me when I die and leave this earthly life. I have nothing to fear.

I, even I, am he who comforts you. (Isaiah 51:12)

This reminds me of a chorus we used to sing at church: "He is all I need. Jesus is all I need."

READ: Isaiah 52–56

God's love is for the whole world:

...and all the ends of the earth will see the salvation of our God. (Isaiah 52:10)

Within Isaiah 53 is an amazing passage describing what Jesus' life meant to the world—but it was written several hundred years before He was born! It tells how He would take upon Himself our griefs, sorrows, transgressions, and iniquities, and because of the beatings He would suffer, we are healed! Yet it sounded as if it had already happened. Somehow, this sacrificial giving of Jesus was for all time—past, present, and future. Even in the time of Isaiah, some believers were aware of it.

We all, like sheep, have gone astray, each of us has turned to his own way; and the Lord has laid on him the iniquity of us all. (Isaiah 53:6)

That is God's plan for mankind. Through Jesus, He has offered us a means of redemption from the sin that is in all of us, the sin to which we so often succumb.

Seek the Lord while he may be found; call on him while he is near. (Isaiah 55:6)

God has supreme respect for our personhood and will never violate our free will. This truth has been borne out in the vast pool of Christian experiences down through the ages. He will only come into our lives as far as we invite Him. He will fill us only to the degree that we are willing to be filled. He will only be a welcome guest in our hearts—never an intruder!

"For my thoughts are not your thoughts, neither are your ways my ways," declares the Lord. (Isaiah 55:8)

There we have it! If we refuse to invite God into our lives, we shut off the possibility of tapping into His wisdom and plans, leaving ourselves stuck with only our own intelligence and experience to guide us. With the Holy Spirit as our constant, acknowledged companion, we open ourselves to receiving what He chooses to give us from God's storehouse. It is my belief that He is willing to share with us much more than we are willing to receive!

In Isaiah 55:10–11, we are given a delightful comparison. The rain and snow from heaven doesn't just go back up again; it fulfills its purpose of watering the earth so grain can sprout and grow, producing more seed to be planted. In the same way, God's word does not return to Him without accomplishing its purpose of touching peoples' lives and bringing forth spiritual growth, which is passed on to future generations.

You will go out in joy and be led forth in peace. (Isaiah 55:12)

Joy and peace will be ours when we allow the Holy Spirit to operate in our lives. They are everyone's desire. We can choose to have them by letting go of all the self-righteousness that gets in the way.

READ: Isaiah 57–60

For this is what the high and lofty One says—he who lives forever, whose name is holy: "I live in a high and holy place, but also with him who is contrite and lowly in spirit... (Isaiah 57:15)

It has always been an awesome thought to me that the great Creator, who lives forever, should also dwell in my heart, but here He says just that! However, there is a condition. To qualify as *"contrite and lowly in spirit,"* I must face my own weakness and negative attitudes and desire to be changed.

Going through the motions of being religious isn't enough. Even fasting, without a change in attitude, is useless.

> *Yet on the day of your fasting, you do as you please… You cannot fast as you do today and expect your voice to be heard on high… Is not this the kind of fasting I have chosen: to loose the chains of injustice and… set the oppressed free…? Is it not to share your food with the hungry and to provide the poor wanderer with shelter…?* (Isaiah 58:3–4, 6–7)

When we let go of all our wrong habits, no longer oppress others with our resentment and bitterness, and reach out to help others, He assures us:

> *Then your light will break forth like the dawn, and your healing will quickly appear… The Lord will guide you always; he will satisfy your needs in a sun-scorched land and will strengthen your frame. You will be like a well-watered garden, like a spring whose waters never fail.* (Isaiah 58:8, 11)

The next chapter seems to contain a prophecy concerning the Israelites:

> *But your iniquities have separated you from our God.* (Isaiah 59:2)

That would bring disaster. The Israelites would be mistreated by others, but in spite of all that, they would remember the covenant God made with them. Then, in Isaiah 60, He promises new hope:

> *Arise, shine, for your light has come, and the glory of the Lord rises upon you.* (Isaiah 60:1)

As God's plan for His people unfolds, nations who oppose it will be in danger of God's wrath. How I wish all governments would pay attention to this proclamation. There is pressure today on Israel to accept a Palestinian state in their land, but how can they allow this when the Palestinians will not recognize Israel as a Jewish state? Many people do not realize that the former country of Palestine was divided into two parts—twenty-three percent of it became Israel, a home for the Jews, and seventy-seven percent became Jordan, a home for the Arabs. What God originally designated as the Promised Land included all that territory. We had better be sure we are not opposing God's plan!

> *For the nation or kingdom that will not serve you will perish; it will be utterly ruined.* (Isaiah 60:12)

328

READ: Isaiah 61–66

The Spirit of the Sovereign Lord is upon me, because the Lord has anointed me to preach good news to the poor. (Isaiah 61:1)

Here is the verse Jesus quoted in Luke 4:18–19. He knew that Isaiah's prophecy was about Him. Isaiah goes on to tell more of what the coming of Jesus would mean to those who accepted Him—beauty for ashes, gladness for mourning, praise instead of a faint spirit—and that through these God might be glorified!

Isaiah is talking specifically to the people of Israel. As He speaks of building up ruins, the devastation of many generations, it sounds like modern-day Israel with Jewish people streaming in from many countries to make their homes in the Promised Land. Where the land was desolate, the Jews produced all kinds of food for their own use and for export.

Could it be that after hundreds of years, this prophecy is now being fulfilled?

Instead of their shame my people will receive a double portion, and instead of disgrace they will rejoice in their inheritance; and so they will inherit a double portion in their land, and everlasting joy will be theirs... Their descendants will be known among the nations and their offspring among the peoples. All who see them will acknowledge that they are a people the Lord has blessed. (Isaiah 61:7, 9)

It is my prayer that the thousands of Jews who have made their home in the land God gave them will become aware that Jesus is the Messiah they have looked for. My prayer is that they will seek His guidance. Many are doing just that, though this fact does not appear in the news releases!

For as the soil makes the sprout come up and a garden causes seeds to grow, so the Sovereign Lord will make righteousness and praise spring up before all nations. (Isaiah 61:11)

Wouldn't it be wonderful if Israel, while all the eyes of the world are on it, could experience a mighty and powerful move of the Holy Spirit, that even the news reports would tell about it?

There is great hope for Israel in these last chapters.

Can a country be born in a day or a nation be brought forth in a moment? (Isaiah 66:8)

Yes, it can. Israel became a recognized nation on May 14, 1948!

THE BOOK OF

1 Thessalonians

READ: 1 Thessalonians 1–3

Paul must have had a special experience in Thessalonica when the presence of the Holy Spirit became plainly evident.

> *...because our gospel came to you not simply with words, but also with power, with the Holy Spirit and with deep conviction.* (1 Thessalonians 1:5)

At times, a person has a physical experience of the Holy Spirit. I remember going forward at a Full Gospel Businessmen's meeting, praying that God would use me to reach my children, who were young adults by then. The speaker said, "God will surely answer that prayer," and as he laid hands on me I began to shake from head to foot. It only lasted a few seconds, but it was a beautiful experience of knowing God's presence in a physical way. I went back to my seat with a big smile on my face and a warm feeling in my heart.

> *...we speak as men approved by God to be entrusted with the gospel. We are not trying to please men but God, who tests our hearts.* (1 Thessalonians 2:4)

Paul knew that it was an honour for him to be chosen by God to spread the gospel, so it was done to please Him. That meant Paul's thoughts and motives had to be right, as well as his words. Men hear our words, but God sees our hearts.

In 1 Thessalonians 3, Paul refers to the afflictions the people of Thessalonica suffered for their belief in Jesus. Paul himself had been sent away from there at night (Acts 17) because of the uproar his preaching caused. He was afraid that persecution would cause them to drop their faith in Jesus, so he sent Timothy to see how they were doing.

Paul, too, was suffering persecution, but he was delighted to hear they were strong in their belief.

...we were encouraged about you because of your faith. (1 Thessalonians 3:7)

Being constant in my relationship with God not only helps me personally, but it encourages others.

At one time, Bob and I travelled from Vancouver Island to the mainland in order to attend the memorial service of a dear Christian brother at whose home we had often gathered to share fellowship and a good meal together. At the reception, we spoke with two other couples who had been a part of that group. We exchanged stories of what God was doing in our lives since we had last met. It was a great encouragement to find that all of us had continued to seek His will, trusting in Him no matter the circumstances. I can understand Paul's feelings.

Love for everyone is the key to a strong bond with the God of love:

May the Lord make your love increase and overflow for each other and for everyone else, just as ours does for you. (1 Thessalonians 3:12)

As the time of Jesus' return draws nearer, we dare not harbour any grudges, resentments, or unforgiveness.

READ: 1 Thessalonians 4–5

Finally, brothers, we instructed you how to live in order to please God, as in fact you are living. (1 Thessalonians 4:1)

Living in order to please God is a tall order. Taking the first step is reasonably easy, but carrying on day by day for a lifetime is something else! Daily morning quiet times is one practice that takes strong self-discipline. It is easy to think, *This is Saturday, so I'll sleep in.* That is the beginning of the end. We think we are saying, *I need the rest,* but what we are really saying is, *My rest is more important than spending time with God.* Our bodies do need rest, but there are other times of day for that—going to bed early, for example, or perhaps taking an afternoon nap. It has taken years of discipline for me to establish a habit of spending the first part of my day reading the Bible, praying, and listening to God.

Paul goes on to say that God has called us to live holy lives:

Therefore, he who rejects this instruction does not reject man but God, who gives you his Holy Spirit. (1 Thessalonians 4:8)

Our goal can be nothing less than perfection if we are to receive the Holy Spirit. We will fail now and then, but we must never lower our goal.

Brothers, we do not want you to be ignorant about those who fall asleep, or to grieve like the rest of men, who have no hope. (1 Thessalonians 4:13)

Here is a word of encouragement for when a loved one dies. We believe that Jesus died and rose again to assure us of everlasting life with Him, so rather than grieving we can rejoice in the graduation from this life to a better one. I find it hard to picture how it will happen, but Jesus promised in John 3:16 that if we believe in Him, we shall have everlasting life. We can trust in Him, who is the source of all knowledge and truth.

...for you know very well that the day of the Lord will come like a thief in the night. (1 Thessalonians 5:2)

In other words, no one knows when Jesus will come again. When I know guests are coming, I get the house ready and prepare food for the occasion, but sometimes people drop in unexpectedly. If I have been remiss in tidying my house, it can be embarrassing.

I can be prepared for Jesus' return by keeping my relationship with Him a daily, ongoing experience. I'm sure the very sight of Him will remind me of things I have not done. His purity will show up my impurity, just as unexpected guests make me aware of the untidiness of my living room. But if I have been communing with Him daily, I can welcome Him in person—or even in the unexpected guest who appears at my door.

Here is how we can be prepared:

Be joyful always; pray continually; give thanks in all circumstances, for this is God's will for you in Christ Jesus. (1 Thessalonians 5:16–18)

Living this way brings great joy, but it requires consistency and discipline. I know I am at my best when I am praising and thanking God—praying for His guidance and waiting with joyous anticipation for what He is going to do next.

THE BOOK OF

2 Thessalonians

READ: 2 Thessalonians 1–3

In spite of suffering and persecution (2 Thessalonians 1:5), the church in Thessalonica grew in faith and love. Paul assured them that God would judge those who were against Him. Paul's prayer for them was threefold:

1. God makes you worthy of His call. (2 Thessalonians 1:11)
2. He may fulfill every good purpose and every act prompted by your faith. (2 Thessalonians 1:11)
3. The name of the Lord Jesus may be glorified in you. (2 Thessalonians 1:12)

These are the very things I would pray for myself.

In the next chapter, it sounds as if Paul expected Jesus to come again soon— even in his lifetime. However, he says:

...for that day will not come until the rebellion occurs and the man of lawlessness is revealed, the man doomed to destruction. (2 Thessalonians 2:3)

He will exalt himself and *"[set] himself up in God's temple"* (2 Thessalonians 2:4). Our only safeguard against being drawn into this false teaching is the *"sanctifying work of the Spirit and through belief in the truth"* (2 Thessalonians 2:13). We need to exercise this daily if we want to be strong in our faith.

Paul has words of encouragement for his friends:

May our Lord Jesus Christ himself and God our Father, who loved us and by his grace gave us eternal encouragement and good hope, encourage your hearts and strengthen you in every good deed and word. (2 Thessalonians 2:16–17)

In other words, we are to do what we say.

But the Lord is faithful, and he will strengthen and protect you from the evil one... And as for you, brothers, never tire of doing what is right... Now may the Lord of peace himself give you peace at all times and in every way. (2 Thessalonians 3:3, 13, 16)

Encouragement, hope, and strength—all these we can receive from God our Father. The reward is peace at all times. That is worth striving for!

THE BOOK OF

Jeremiah

READ: Jeremiah 1–3

God called Jeremiah to be His spokesman to the people of Israel. He said:

Before I formed you in the womb I knew you, before you were born I set you apart; I appointed you as a prophet to the nations. (Jeremiah 1:5)

It is rather awesome to think that God has a plan in mind for a person before he is born. I wonder how many of us have refused to hear His call or have been so involved in other interests that we weren't even aware of His call. How many of us have fallen short of the mark God prepared for us?

Although Jeremiah heard God's call, like Moses and the rest of us he found an excuse:

I do not know how to speak; I am only a child. (Jeremiah 1:6)

God is not deterred by our excuses, but He assured Jeremiah that He would give him the words to say. His message was the same as it is to each of us today—"Obey Me and trust Me, and I will provide all your needs."

As I read God's words to Jeremiah concerning Israel, I see a warning to each of us as Christians, and to our nation of Canada.

I remember the devotion of your youth… But my people have exchanged their Glory for worthless idols. (Jeremiah 2:2, 11)

It is easy to be enthusiastic when we first experience the salvation of Jesus. New Christians just cannot keep quiet about the wonderful change in their lives. But as the years go by, we easily become complacent, self-satisfied, and ill-disciplined in seeking God's guidance.

Our country, too, used to be based on Judeo-Christian principles. The Bible was respected and prayer was an accepted way to open a school day or public meeting. Today, immorality and lawlessness are prevalent and Bible reading and prayers are forbidden in schools. We may be in danger of the dreadful conditions prophesied for Israel:

> *Have you not brought this on yourselves by forsaking the Lord your God when he led you in the way?* (Jeremiah 2:17)

Our loving Heavenly Father is always ready to receive us when we are ready to repent of our sins, which separate us from Him:

> *"Return, faithless Israel," declares the Lord, "I will frown on you no longer, for I am merciful, "declares the Lord, "I will not be angry forever."* (Jeremiah 3:12)

That is not easy to read for those of us who have been Christians for a long time. We may be so used to our own attitudes that we don't recognize the sin in them—resentment, criticism, and self-centredness.

One morning, in a half-awake state, God recalled to my mind some of the stubborn, self-righteous stands I took at various times in my life. It was painful because I could see that they had been costly to others. When I began my quiet time, I asked God what I was meant to learn from this experience. This is what He impressed on my mind: "You are in danger of slipping into an arrogant position. I have blessed the work you have been doing, but if you take the credit for yourself rather than keeping your eyes fixed on Me (the source), you could ruin everything."

At that point, I asked His forgiveness and again thanked Him for His bountiful mercy.

READ: Jeremiah 4–7

We have a choice, just as Israel had, according to God's word, given through Jeremiah:

> *"If you will return, O Israel, return to me," declares the Lord… "Then the nations will be blessed by him and in him they will glory."* (Jeremiah 4:1–2)

Returning to the Lord in repentance opens the way for others to be blessed. It works for individuals, churches, other organizations, and even for nations. That is a sobering thought if one is grappling with a wrong habit, but if our greatest desire is to serve the Lord, it is exciting to think that we can be a blessing to others even when we don't see the results.

The other side of the coin is that disobedience brings disastrous results to those around us, as well as to ourselves:

Your own conduct and actions have brought this upon you. This is your punishment. How bitter it is! How it pierces to the heart! (Jeremiah 4:18)

There is no place for half-hearted commitment. Trying to give the appearance of being a Christian while refusing to deal with the sin inside does not please our Heavenly Father.

Although they say, "As surely as the Lord lives," still they are swearing falsely... They made their faces harder than stone and refused to repent. (Jeremiah 5:2–3)

Rich or poor, of a high or lowly position, it does not matter—only the repentant person who is willing to change can be trusted to do God's will.

Although Israel and Judah had experienced God's hand on them in the past, at the time Jeremiah was alive, they no longer trusted Him, nor did they fear the consequences.

"The house of Israel and the house of Judah have been utterly unfaithful to me," declares the Lord. "They have lied about the Lord; they said, 'He will do nothing! No harm will come to us.'" (Jeremiah 5:11–12)

That is a dangerous attitude to take, but it is common in the world today. In our western nations, greed, the accepted immorality in our society, and the increase in crime and violence are all flagrant sins that must be grievous to the heart of God.

"Should you not fear me?" declares the Lord. "Should you not tremble in my presence?" (Jeremiah 5:22)

He constantly offers the way out, but we don't always accept it.

This is what the Lord says: "Stand at the crossroads and look; ask for the ancient paths, ask where the good way is, and walk in it, and you will find rest for your souls. But you said, 'We will not walk in it.'" (Jeremiah 6:16)

How sad! Considering that Jesus offers us abundant life filled with love, joy, and peace, how can we be so foolish as to refuse it because we don't want to let go of our self-centredness, pride, security, or any of the false idols we hang on to so fiercely? These people lived before Jesus came to earth and yet God's anger was roused by their disobedience. How must He feel towards us who know Jesus died, so that our sins might be forgiven, yet refuse to confess them and accept His healing?

Perhaps He will say of Canada,

> *This is the nation that has not obeyed the Lord its God or responded to correction.* (Jeremiah 7:28)

READ: Jeremiah 8–11

When we pray, we are inclined to talk a lot, telling God how to solve our problems and then closing off with a definite "Amen," not giving God a chance to speak to us. He tells Jeremiah:

> *I have listened attentively, but they do not say what is right. No one repents of his wickedness, saying, "What have I done?" Each pursues his own course like a horse charging into battle.* (Jeremiah 8:6)

We cannot hear God's voice unless we let Him show us where we need to change. Unless we listen to words like fear, pride, self-pity, and greed—which He drops into our mind—we won't hear any positive direction from Him. He can only use us after He cleans us up, after we confess and repent of any negativity clogging our spiritual progress.

> *From the least to the greatest, all are greedy for gain.* (Jeremiah 8:10)

That sounds like our society today—a constant demand for increases in salary and the acceptance of shady business deals.

> *They dress the wound of my people as though it were not serious. "Peace, peace," they say, when there is no peace.* (Jeremiah 8:11)

We think of peace as being the absence of war, but it is so much more than that. It is a positive force within us that comes from God. It is the power of the Holy Spirit filling our being and giving us confidence and wisdom. We cannot legislate or force peace on anyone; we can only accept it from God and live it!

But the Lord is the true God; he is the living God, the eternal King. When he is angry, the earth trembles; the nations cannot endure his wrath. (Jeremiah 10:10)

When I was a child, my father was a loving, caring man—a hard worker and good provider. I loved and respected him. I was a reasonably well-behaved child and was kept from being tempted to do wrong because of a wholesome fear of him. It was not so much a fear of his punishment, which was seldom evident, but a fear of disappointing him or losing his trust in me. That love, respect, and wholesome fear carried over into my relationship with God. It gives me courage to stand for what is right and reject the temptation to be less than He would have me be. I slip, of course, but I have the assurance that God's love is constant and He will receive me again when I am ready to confess and say that I am sorry.

The Lord said to Jeremiah,

Obey me and do everything I command you, and you will be my people, and I will be your God. (Jeremiah 11:4)

I know in my heart that I want more than anything to please Him, to be one of His people. No other goal can bring well-being, for we are created in His image and He intended us to be His people. What a wonderful privilege that is!

READ: Jeremiah 12–16

Yet you know me, O Lord; you see me and test my thoughts about you. (Jeremiah 12:3)

This is a comforting thought—most of the time. I can come into God's presence and not have to explain anything. No one else ever quite understands what my position is or what I am thinking, but God knows it all. The flip side is that I may be able to hide some of my feelings, attitudes, and even habits from others, but I can't hide them from my Heavenly Father. That really is a blessing, because the weight of hidden dishonesty can be an intolerable burden!

The story of the waistcloth points out the importance of being faithful to God and the danger of turning our backs on Him. When our self-centred pride creeps in and takes over our lives, we are heading for a fall.

This is what the Lord says: "In the same way I will ruin the pride of Judah and the great pride of Jerusalem." (Jeremiah 13:9)

There is no other way to recover except to confess our sin, and even take responsibility for the sins of our nation. It is then that we acknowledge we have no righteousness apart from God. We also recognize that He is the only One who can supply our needs.

> *O Lord, we acknowledge our wickedness and the guilt of our fathers; we have indeed sinned against you.* (Jeremiah 14:20)

Jeremiah then received word from God of events that would occur hundreds of years after he died. In fact, some of it has been happening very recently. Because of the Israelites' faithlessness to Him, God says:

> *So I will throw you out of this land into a land neither you nor your fathers have known...* (Jeremiah 16:13)

The Jews were scattered all over the world for centuries while their land was ruled by other people. It became known as Palestine. Since World War II, the following prophecy is being fulfilled:

> *"However, the days are coming," declares the Lord, "when men will no longer say, 'As surely as the Lord lives, who brought the Israelites up out of Egypt,' but they will say, 'As surely as the Lord lives, who brought the Israelites up out of the land of the north and out of all the countries where he had banished them.' For I will restore them to the land I gave their forefathers."* (Jeremiah 16:14–15)

In recent years, we have heard of thousands of Jews moving back to Israel. It is truly amazing how they heard the call of God to return to their Promised Land.

> *"But now I will send for many fishermen," declares the Lord, "and they will catch them. After that I will send for many hunters..."* (Jeremiah 16:16)

The Zionists (the fishermen), before World War I, urged the Jews to go to Israel, but many were comfortable and did not want to leave their homes. Then came anti-Semitism (the hunters) in all its fury, ending with the holocaust, when millions were killed. God is not mocked! If we disobey Him, we must suffer the consequences!

READ: Jeremiah 17–21

> *But blessed is the man who trusts in the Lord, whose confidence is in him. He will be like a tree planted by the water that sends out its roots by the*

stream. It does not fear when heat comes; its leaves are always green. It has no worries in a year of drought and never fails to bear fruit. (Jeremiah 17:7–8)

What a great picture! I can see that tree sending its roots to where the stream can always provide the moisture it needs. It doesn't wait until the heat comes to find the water—by that time, its roots are already in place. I want to be like that tree, making sure I spend daily time with God to establish my roots and receive living water from the throne of God. I do not need to fear the tough decisions that have to be made and difficult times that are inevitable in this earthly life. Even in the midst of a drought, that tree was able to have green leaves and bear fruit. If my roots are firmly established in the stream of living water, no circumstances can stop me from being filled with the Holy Spirit.

Another wonderful promise follows:

The heart is deceitful above all things and beyond cure. Who can understand it? "I the Lord search the heart and examine the mind, to reward a man according to his conduct, according to what his deeds deserve." (Jeremiah 17:9–10)

Watching a baby, you can see the natural self-centredness in all of us. When the baby is comfortable, he smiles easily and is happy, but when that same baby is tired or hungry, what a fuss it makes! That self-centredness is with us from the beginning, but God has provided a way out. He gives that little baby loving parents to guide him as he grows up. He knows everything about us and still loves us more than our earthly parents do.

Does the snow of Lebanon ever vanish from its rocky slopes? Do its cool waters from distant sources ever cease to flow? Yet my people have forgotten me. (Jeremiah 18:14–15)

Nature is obedient to God's plan, but people ignore and turn away from Him:

This is what the Lord says: See I am setting before you the way of life and the way of death. (Jeremiah 21:8)

The choice is ours. God's warning to Jeremiah has been handed down to us so we might know that we can choose life in all its fullness if we commit our lives to the King of kings.

READ: Jeremiah 22–25

This is what the Lord says: "Go down to the palace of the king of Judah and proclaim this message there: 'Hear the word of the Lord, O king of Judah, you who sit on David's throne.'" (Jeremiah 22:1–2)

There is no better advice to give anyone than "Hear the word of the Lord"! It was God Himself who gave that advice and I believe it was not just for the king, but for all people. If I practise listening to the word of the Lord—whether it comes to me directly, through the Bible, or from some other person—I can experience the full and abundant life Jesus promised.

At one time, I prayed about our need for another classroom at Lighthouse Christian Academy. While reading from Isaiah in the Living Bible at the time, these words popped out at me:

Enlarge your house; build an addition. Spread out your home, and spare no expense! For you will soon be bursting at the seams. (Isaiah 54:2–3, NLT)

I don't have a very good imagination for picturing how buildings can be changed and additions be put on, so I thought, *Where, Lord? How can that be done?* Then I looked across the page and saw these words, which seemed to stand out from the rest:

This plan of mine is not what you would work out, neither are My thoughts the same as yours! (Isaiah 55:8, TLB)

God has a wonderful sense of humour, so I felt Him chuckling along with me. I shared the verse at our school board meeting, and suddenly all sorts of creative ideas poured forth. Before too long, we were able to add on to our building and make room for more children.

There are conditions to receiving God's guidance, and we see them repeated over and over again in the Bible.

Do what is just and right... For if you are careful to carry out these commands... But if you do not obey these commands... (Jeremiah 22:3–5)

We dare not let up on praying, repenting, and seeking God's guidance in our daily lives. Self-centred sin can creep in so stealthily, getting us off-track. That happens every now and then, forcing me to backtrack, confess, and start over.

Through Jeremiah, God refers again, as He did in Isaiah, to the coming of the Messiah:

"The days are coming," declares the Lord, "when I will raise up to David a righteous Branch, a King who will reign wisely and do what is just and right in the land." (Jeremiah 23:5)

Jesus reigns as King in any person's life, if He is invited into their heart. He doesn't rule by force, but He does deal with us wisely to free us from sin and fill us with His righteousness.

Generations come and go, but God's love for the Jews, His chosen people, has never faltered, even though it appeared at times that He had forgotten them:

My eyes will watch over them for their good, and I will bring them back to this land... I will give them a heart to know me, that I am the Lord. (Jeremiah 24:6–7)

READ: Jeremiah 26–29

The entire book of Jeremiah shows God wooing the people of Judah. He longs to draw them to Himself, but Jeremiah seems to be the only one listening. All He asks is for them to give up evil practices and be obedient to Him. He tells Jeremiah to call them together and pass on a message:

Perhaps they will listen and each will turn from his evil way. Then I will relent and not bring on them the disaster I was planning because of the evil they have done. (Jeremiah 26:3)

Again Jeremiah warns them of the consequences of continuing to do wrong when they know what is right. You would think this would scare them into repentance, but no, the prophets' and the priests' answer was "You shall die." Jeremiah again urges a change of heart:

Now reform your ways and your actions and obey the Lord your God. Then the Lord will relent and not bring the disaster he has pronounced against you. (Jeremiah 26:13)

Joshua showed the true commitment of a believer in his willingness to give up his life while refusing to disobey God's call to issue that warning. However, it was not God's plan for Jeremiah to die at that time, and some of the people came to his rescue. Perhaps there were those who recognized the voice of God speaking through him.

It seems to me that God uses various ways to speak against the evils in our society today. Why hasn't lung cancer scared people away from smoking? Why hasn't AIDS awakened people to the danger of promiscuous sexual relations? And what will God's punishment be for the violence, crime, and abortions that take place daily?

> *With my great power and outstretched arm I made the earth and its people and the animals that are on it, and I give it to anyone I please.* (Jeremiah 27:5)

So, God decided to give His people into the hands of King Nebuchadnezzar of Babylon, forcing them to serve him. There were false prophets who spoke out against this, one being Hananiah. That did not stop God's plan, for He sent Jeremiah to rebuke Hananiah and tell him he would die for trying to make the people trust in a lie. God is supreme in His creation. We cannot turn our backs on Him without facing the consequences!

The good news is that He never gives up on us and is always ready to receive us when we are ready to change. It would take seventy years for that to happen while the Jews were in exile in Babylon.

> *"For I know the plans I have for you," declares the Lord, "plans to prosper you and not to harm you, plans to give you hope and a future. Then you will call upon me and come and pray to me, and I will listen to you. You will seek me and find me when you seek me with all your heart. I will be found by you," declares the Lord, "and will bring you back from captivity."* (Jeremiah 29:11–14)

Seventy years! That was a whole generation whose children refused to listen to Jeremiah. What conditions are we preparing for our children?

READ: Jeremiah 30–33

> *This is what the Lord, the God of Israel, says: "Write in a book all the words I have spoken to you."* (Jeremiah 30:2)

What a blessing that message has been to us. Imagine me sitting in my home reading what God said to Jeremiah some 2,500 years ago! The timelessness of God is evident in that His words are still pertinent to the world today. The warnings He gave Israel are equally valid for us. In these chapters, He says a lot about bringing the Israelites back to their own land from all parts of the world, an event which has been happening during the last hundred years. Wouldn't Jeremiah have been surprised to know that?

There are other details, too, like:

This is what the Lord says: "Cries of fear are heard—terror, not peace." (Jeremiah 30:5)

Although there were other times in history when this was so, it sounds like the holocaust during World War II.

"But I will restore you to health and heal your wounds," declares the Lord... "I will restore the fortunes of Jacob's tents... the city will be rebuilt... From them will come songs of thanksgiving..." (Jeremiah 30:17–19)

In recent years, we have seen Jewish people from Russia, Ethiopia, and other countries weep with joy as they stepped off the plane onto Israeli soil. For centuries, they dreamed of returning to the land God gave their forefathers.

"At that time," says the Lord, "I will be the God of all the clans of Israel, and they will be my people." ... The Lord appeared to us in the past, saying: "I have loved you with an everlasting love; I have drawn you with loving kindness." (Jeremiah 31:1, 3)

That is a wonderful truth to hang on to—God loves me, and that will never change. In our human relationships, even the closest ones, we often think to ourselves, "He just doesn't understand me" or "I can't understand her attitude." But in my relationship with God, I can count on the fact that He does understand everything about me—how I feel, how I think, and how I react. I certainly don't understand everything about Him, but I trust Him totally—His love, His wisdom, and His power. It is the most complete and satisfying relationship there is.

Ah, Sovereign Lord, you have made the heavens and the earth by your great power and outstretched arm. Nothing is too hard for you. (Jeremiah 32:17)

He can do anything He chooses to do—create a world, heal an illness, cure an alcoholic, or change the direction of a person's life. All we need to do is be in step with His plan to experience His blessings.

At one time, Bob prayed for an adventure playground at Lighthouse Christian Academy, because the playing area was small. Without knowing of his prayer, a father of one of our boys began to build one during the winter, with the help of one of the other dads. One day in May, it was assembled by half a dozen men as an answer to Bob's prayer. What a wonderful time the children had. They swarmed over it like flies on a honey pot, laughing and shouting to each other. God can take one person's prayer and inspire someone else to bring it about!

READ: Jeremiah 34–38

It is an awesome responsibility to be chosen by God to be His spokesman—but it can be downright dangerous, especially if the words are warnings. That is the position Jeremiah found himself in when God told him what would happen to Judah. The warnings must have come over a period of time, because several kings were involved. None of these kings worshipped God or obeyed His commandments.

No one likes to hear about bad times, though. When Jeremiah proclaimed that Israel and Judah would be defeated by the king of Babylon and the people would be taken into captivity, he was not very popular. In fact, in order not to hear such disturbing words, the people tried to get rid of him.

God's words also show His faithfulness to His people, even though they were not faithful to Him.

> *But I have spoken to you again and again, yet you have not obeyed me. Again and again I sent all my servants the prophets to you. They said, "Each of you must turn from your wicked ways and reform your actions; do not follow other gods to serve them. Then you will live in the land I have given to you and your fathers." (Jeremiah 35:14–15)*

God keeps telling us to repent when we get off-track, but the choice to change is ours. He told Jeremiah to write the warnings on a scroll so it could be read to the king. Maybe that would make him turn to God and encourage his people to do the same. Had this happened, the course of history would have changed for the Jewish people. But no, he tore up the scroll and burned it! God told Jeremiah to write it again. A new king came on the throne, but he wouldn't listen either!

There was no hope of saving the city from destruction. Disobedience to God inevitably leads to destruction. God does not guarantee an easy life when we follow Him, and certainly Jeremiah did not have an easy time of it. People who hang on to evil also hate those who are on God's side. Unwavering in his faith, Jeremiah continued to hear the voice of God.

In every generation, some people are willing to spend time listening to Him. However, there is a tendency to prophesy good news and revival. That may not be what God is saying, but it is what people want to hear. Jeremiah was not seeking to be popular; he chose rather to be faithful. That was not an easy choice to make, since it led to persecution.

READ: Jeremiah 39–45

All the destruction God threatened through Jeremiah came to pass and most of the people were taken into exile to Babylon. You cannot play around with disobedience to God without paying a price.

It is surprising to read what the captain of the guard in Babylon said to Jeremiah concerning Judah:

The Lord your God decreed this disaster for this place... All this happened because you people sinned against the Lord and did not obey him. (Jeremiah 40:2–3)

I wonder how he knew. In any case, he had real respect for Jeremiah, for he went on to say:

Look, the whole country lies before you; go wherever you please. (Jeremiah 40:4)

There is no suggestion that anyone else was given that choice. Jeremiah stayed in Judah *"among the people who were left behind in the land"* (Jeremiah 40:6).

That is really the only encouraging part of this story. The rest deals with the disobedience of the people who were left in Judah. They came to Jeremiah, asking him to pray for guidance for them because they wanted to go to Egypt where they thought they would be safe from the Babylonians. The word from God was "No, stay where you are."

Do not be afraid of the king of Babylon, whom you now fear. Do not be afraid of him, declares the Lord, for I am with you and will save you and will deliver you from his hands... O remnant of Judah, the Lord has told you, "Do not go to Egypt." (Jeremiah 42:11, 19)

But they went! It is so devastating to give advice that you know for certain is the right thing to do and then watch it be ignored. You know there will be a price to pay, but you cannot stop it from happening. Parents of rebellious teenagers or young adults know how it feels. Throughout the ages, God must have had that heart-breaking experience over and over as He watched His people deliberately choose to go the wrong direction.

In many areas of our lives we, too, deliberately choose to do what we know is not right. Perhaps we refuse to forgive someone, or we may hang on to self-pity. We may destroy our health by using drugs, alcohol, or tobacco, or even by eating the wrong foods. We may choose sleep instead of spending regular time with God every day. Disobedience can take many forms, and all of them are serious.

One form of disobedience can lead to another. After the people went to Egypt, they began to burn incense to other gods. Conversely, one step of obedience makes the next step easier. When we ask, "Lord, what would You have me do now?" He will be there to help us get in step with Him again.

READ: Jeremiah 46–52

Although God allowed the Israelites to be taken into captivity, He still promised never to leave them:

> *"Do not fear, O Jacob my servant, for I am with you," declares the Lord...*
> *"I will discipline you but only with justice; I will not let you go entirely unpunished."* (Jeremiah 46:28)

God's punishment was not just for Israel. Any nation that turned its back on Him could be destroyed—such as Moab, which had become proud and arrogant:

> *Moab will be destroyed as a nation because she defied the Lord.* (Jeremiah 48:42)

This can happen today, too. For seventy years, the U.S.S.R. persecuted those who worshipped God—Christians and Jews alike. Then we saw the breakup of that union and the appalling state of their economy became known throughout the world. A nation cannot stand forever if it opposes God.

Jeremiah foretells the downfall of Babylon:

> *For I will stir up and bring against Babylon an alliance of great nations from the land of the north.* (Jeremiah 50:9)

I don't know enough about history to identify the fulfillment of this prophecy—whether it took place in the past, whether it refers to the recent Gulf War, or whether it is still to come. The truth that stands out in this book is that no nation or individual can escape the punishment that comes from refusing to acknowledge God.

He made the earth by his power; he founded the world by his wisdom and stretched out the heavens by his understanding. (Jeremiah 51:15)

When we look at the world around us—mountains, oceans, prairies, trees, and flowers—the wonder, the beauty, the variety, the grandeur, and the delicacy—we are aware of the Creator. Then we look at the blue sky, the passing clouds, and the moon and stars at night, we realize that He created them, too! How can we consider images a worthy alternative to Him?

They are worthless, the objects of mockery. (Jeremiah 51:18)

Jeremiah 52 tells again how the king of Babylon attacked Jerusalem and carried the people away into captivity. Zedekiah, Judah's king, had not followed God's commandments:

He did evil in the eyes of the Lord... (Jeremiah 52:2)

Those in leadership have the awesome responsibility of guiding the ship, of leading others along a particular course. When he chooses to follow God's lead, he brings blessing upon his people, but when he chooses evil, he brings disaster and ruin. It is a choice: he can be diligent in seeking God's direction daily, or rely on his own knowledge and experience. The one brings blessing, but who knows where the other may lead?

THE BOOK OF
Lamentations

READ: Lamentations 1–5

The Hebrew alphabet has twenty-two letters, and I note that Lamentations 1–2 and 4–5 each have twenty-two verses, apparently written in an alphabetical acrostic. Lamentations 3 has sixty-six verses and there are three verses beginning with each letter of the alphabet. This seems to be a form of Hebrew poetry.

In one translation of the Bible, this book is called "Lamentations of Jeremiah." In it, he laments over the condition of the people, exiled to other countries.

How deserted lies the city, once so full of people! (Lamentations 1:1)

Jerusalem, the city of David, dearly beloved by the people of Israel and so central to their worship of God, was at that time deserted. God had warned them, but they didn't listen.

The Lord has brought her grief because of her many sins... Jerusalem has sinned greatly and so has become unclean. (Lamentations 1:5, 8)

Is this the city that was called the perfection of beauty, the joy of the whole earth? (Lamentations 2:15)

Jeremiah grieves for what has happened, although he knows the people brought it on themselves. He also knows that God's purpose is not vengeance, but rather to bring them back to Him. Any good parent punishes a child when he does wrong in order to help him choose what is right. The parents do not love the child less, and neither does God.

Because of the Lord's great love, we are not consumed, for his compassions never fail. They are new every morning; great is your faithfulness. (Lamentations 3:22–23)

In the midst of his mourning, Jeremiah recalls to mind that God's love never fails and each day brings new blessings. No matter our circumstances, we need to remind ourselves to look at the evidences of God's love, which are all around us.

One day, Bob and I prayed for a friend who had lost sight in one eye. The doctors said a blood vessel had been clogged. As we prayed, we realized what a blessing it was that it had only affected one eye and she had good sight in the other.

For men are not cast off by the Lord forever. (Lamentations 3:31)

Whatever problems we face, they won't last forever. Jeremiah has the answer for us:

Let us examine our ways and test them, and let us return to the Lord. (Lamentations 3:40)

Here, we read again that same message: repent of anything that separates us from God. To knowingly continue in sin brings trouble, not only to ourselves but to those who come after us:

Our fathers sinned and are no more, and we bear their punishment. (Lamentations 5:7)

When we make our confession to God, we should include the sins of our ancestors as well, in order to be totally healed.

You, O Lord, reign forever; your throne endures from generation to generation. (Lamentations 5:19)

THE BOOK OF

1 Timothy

READ: 1 Timothy 1–3

Paul warns Timothy to be concerned about people who teach a different doctrine or occupy themselves with myths and endless genealogies. *"These promote controversies..."* (1 Timothy 1:4). These intellectual pursuits can draw us away from *"love, which comes from a pure heart and a good conscience and a sincere faith"* (1 Timothy 1:5). When we get away from daily repentance and cleansing, allowing our focus to shift away from God's plan for us, we drift into *"meaningless talk"* (1 Timothy 1:6)—useless, even harmful conversation with others.

In 1 Timothy 1:12–16, Paul says that he is thankful to God, who saw beyond his blasphemy and persecution and judged him to be one who could be faithful in service to Him. By changing the old Saul into the wise and courageous Paul, Jesus showed the world what He could do in a person's life.

This chapter ends with a warning to those who reject conscience, which can ruin our faith. If I am uneasy in my heart, I need to quickly examine why, so I can get rid of whatever is causing it. Somewhere I have gone off-track. Unless I deal with it, I am likely to drift further away.

In 1 Timothy 2, Paul calls Timothy (and us) to intercessory prayer for everyone, especially leaders:

...that we may live peaceful and quiet lives in all godliness and holiness. (1 Timothy 2:2)

No matter who I pray for, God will be pleased because:

[He] wants all men to be saved and to come to a knowledge of the truth... I want men everywhere to lift up holy hands in prayer, without anger or disputing. (1 Timothy 2:4, 8)

Prayer, then, should include repentance, but also intercession for others. There is no place for negative attitudes towards anyone.

Paul goes on to explain to Timothy which qualities are needed for leadership positions in the church. It is not enough to be able to carry out the responsibilities of those positions. Each person must be highly respected in every area of life—at home as well as in public.

If anyone does not know how to manage his own family, how can he take care of God's church? (1 Timothy 3:5)

The real test of our character is what we are like at home. We can put on a good front and do a fine job in public, but then be irritable and hard to get along with at home. For some reason, having harmony in the family seems to be the hardest thing to achieve. We are willing to give our best at the office, but we tend to become self-centred and demanding with those we love most. Yes, the real test of our walk with Jesus is what we are like at home, whether we are in a leadership position or not.

READ: 1 Timothy 4–6

The Spirit clearly says that in later times some will abandon the faith and follow deceiving spirits and things taught by demons. (1 Timothy 4:1)

I expect that this has been true at other times in history, but we certainly see a lot of evidence of it today. If we do not stand strong in our faith, we are apt to fall for any idea that appeals to us.

...train yourself to be godly. (1 Timothy 4:7)

It takes self-discipline to train ourselves in godliness, just as it takes self-discipline to train our bodies. Both are important, but the former has to do with where we spend eternity as well as how we fare in this life. The world places physical fitness high on the list of priorities but pays little attention to the need for godliness.

This is a trustworthy saying that deserves full acceptance (and for this we labor and strive), that we put our hope in the living God, who is the Savior of all men, and especially of those who believe. (1 Timothy 4:9–10)

It is easy to let up every now and then in seeking God's direction, especially if we are on holidays or out of the regular routine. We take a chance when we do that, for wrong thinking can creep in and take root.

> *Don't let anyone look down on you because you are young, but set an example for the believers in speech, in life, in love, in faith and purity.* (1 Timothy 4:12)

A person's age does not matter, but their quality of life does—whether it be a child, a teenager, an adult, or a pensioner! In fact, each person's life has an influence on those around him, so we need to show a good example in what we say, what we do, and even in what we think.

The next chapter deals with relationships within the family and in the church, with an emphasis on caring for each other. Paul sums up his advice to Timothy like this: *"Keep yourself pure"* (1 Timothy 5:22). That sounds like Jesus' words: *"Be perfect, therefore, as your heavenly Father is perfect"* (Matthew 5:48). There is no excuse, it seems, to aim for anything less than a life that is pure and perfect.

> *But godliness with contentment is great gain.* (1 Timothy 6:6)

In life, we begin with no material possessions, and we end the same way. I wonder why we develop such a hunger for accumulating wealth in between? There is always a lineup at the lottery ticket counter—people hoping to be the big winner of a million dollars! The desire for more can lead us into all kinds of temptations.

> *For the love of money is a root of all kinds of evil. Some people, eager for money, have wandered from the faith and pierced themselves with many griefs.* (1 Timothy 6:10)

We see this desire for more everywhere in society. People go on strike to force the issue of more pay and companies ignore the pollution they cause in order to make more money. Canada is in danger of pricing herself right out of the world market because everyone wants to receive higher pay. This could cause the downfall of the nation. It is a serious problem.

Paul's final words to Timothy are a challenge to all believers:

> *But you, man of God, flee from all this, and pursue righteousness, godliness, faith, love, endurance and gentleness. Fight the good fight of the faith. Take hold of the eternal life to which you were called... keep this command without spot or blame until the appearing of our Lord Jesus Christ...* (1 Timothy 6:11–12, 14)

THE BOOK OF
2 Timothy

READ: 2 Timothy 1–4

Paul has some good advice for Timothy. Fortunately, it has been preserved so we can all benefit from it.

For this reason I remind you to fan into flame the gift of God, which is in you through the laying on of my hands. (2 Timothy 1:6)

In moments of spiritual high, we are convinced that we can do anything because God's presence is so real. But later, while in our daily routine, we let our earlier enthusiasm fade, allowing fear to set in. This may have happened with Timothy, so Paul encourages him, and us:

For God did not give us a spirit of timidity, but a spirit of power, of love and self-discipline. (2 Timothy 1:7)

I have found this verse to be a helpful reminder when fear overcomes me. I can repeat it to myself, acknowledging God's power and love within me until the fear dissipates. I know many people who have experienced scarier experiences than I have, but I believe the same principle can work for anyone. Fear is not of God, and He is the most powerful force there is.

In order to teach others, Timothy had to be willing to:

1. Endure hardship. (2 Timothy 2:3)
2. Be single-minded. (2 Timothy 2:4)
3. Compete according to the rules. (2 Timothy 2:5)
4. Work hard. (2 Timothy 2:6)

If every Christian lived this way, society would see profound change. The easier way is to seek out one's own comfort, get side-tracked by other activities, and let up when the going gets tough.

But God's word is not chained. (2 Timothy 2:9)

Despite the centuries that have passed since the Bible was written and the often lukewarm obedience of Christians, this amazing book is still the bestseller! It is unique. Those who value it most see it as the inspired Word of God. In Russia, where it was banned for seventy years, it is now being shipped by the case. People are hungry to read it. The Word of God cannot be bound!

...and the time has come for my departure. I have fought the good fight, I have finished the race, I have kept the faith. (2 Timothy 4:6–7)

Paul sees his life coming to an end. As he looks back, he is confident that once he recognized who Jesus was, he was faithful in his commitment to Him, despite severe hardships. He is secure in his faith that God has prepared a place for him, that a crown of righteousness awaits him.

What a wonderful hope we Christians have—not only for strength and wisdom in this life, but a place in heaven when we complete the course. With my hand in God's hand, I am a winner!

THE BOOK OF

Ezekiel

READ: Ezekiel 1–4

Ezekiel was called by God while he and a great number of other Israelites were in exile in Babylon. Jeremiah was still active in his prophetic ministry.

Ezekiel had a most unusual vision, which ended with the awareness of the presence of God on His throne, His glory shining forth like a rainbow. It was such an awesome sight that Ezekiel fell on his face. He was overwhelmed by the experience and knew that the voice he'd heard came from God Himself.

The mission He gave Ezekiel was not an easy one:

He said: "Son of man, I am sending you to the Israelites, to a rebellious nation that has rebelled against me." (Ezekiel 2:3)

There was no assurance that they would listen to him, even though they knew he was a prophet.

And whether they listen or fail to listen—for they are a rebellious house— they will know that a prophet has been among them. (Ezekiel 2:5)

God knew it would not be easy for Ezekiel to speak the truth to his own people. In fact, it would have been much easier to go to a foreign country, even with a language barrier. God gave Ezekiel a definite assignment. If he neglected to warn his people, the consequences would come upon him.

Son of man, I have made you a watchman for the house of Israel; so hear the word I speak and give them warning from me... [if] you do not warn him... I will hold you accountable for his blood... But if you do warn the wicked man and he does not turn from his wickedness... you will have saved yourself. (Ezekiel 3:17–19)

That is pretty strong stuff. Ezekiel must have had some misgivings about whether or not he could measure up to this challenge. There was more to come: Ezekiel was to take on the punishment for both Israel and Judah. Being God's chosen does not necessarily mean we will have an easy life!

You are not being sent to a people of obscure speech and difficult language... Surely if I had sent you to them, they would have listened to you. But the house of Israel is not willing to listen to you because they are not willing to listen to me... (Ezekiel 3:5–7)

Sometimes it is easier for missionaries to go to foreign countries, and through sharing their faith see the results in the lives of people, than it is for Christians here in Canada to talk about their faith with their neighbours. Often in countries where churches are a common sight, people are less willing to hear the voice of God than those in countries where there are very few Christians. Obviously the same was true in Ezekiel's day.

And he said to me, "Son of man, listen carefully and take to heart all the words I speak to you." (Ezekiel 3:10)

I believe He is speaking to me as well as to Ezekiel. I always want to listen to what God says to me personally.

READ: Ezekiel 5–9

It is rather frightening to read what happens when people who have been given a special place in God's plan turn away from Him. God had chosen Jerusalem to be the place where His presence would be evident to all the world. The temple was built to His specifications—a place where people could praise and worship and feel His holy presence.

This is what the Sovereign Lord says: This is Jerusalem, which I have set in the center of the nations, with countries all around her. (Ezekiel 5:5)

The location was right for these people to reveal to the world that God, the Creator, has a perfect plan for all. Rather than be an example to others, however, the people of Jerusalem followed the practices of the nations around her:

Yet in her wickedness she has rebelled against my laws and decrees more than the nations and countries around her... You have been more unruly than the nations around you and have not followed my decrees or kept my laws. (Ezekiel 5:6–7)

This could be taken as a warning for nations like Canada today. We are comfortably well-off, we have a good deal of freedom, and we are blessed in many ways. We have the opportunity to demonstrate to the world what it means to be under the Lordship of Jesus. But are we doing that?

A strange thing is happening. Some nations of the former U.S.S.R. which did not allow worship of God for many years, such as Kazakhstan, have asked for people to show their teachers how to bring Christianity back into the schools. I was part of a group that went from B.C.—a province that does not allow the Bible to be read in the schools! Are we in danger of experiencing what God said would happen to Jerusalem?

And when I have spent my wrath upon them, they will know that I the Lord have spoken in my zeal. I will make you a ruin and a reproach among the nations around you, in the sight of all who pass by. (Ezekiel 5:13–14)

We might wonder why a God of love would threaten His chosen people with death, destruction, and exile, but He gives this reason:

I will repay you in accordance with your conduct and the detestable practices among you. Then you will know that it is I the Lord who strikes the blow. (Ezekiel 7:9)

If a parent ignores disobedience and misbehaviour in a child, he will continue to do what is wrong and become a bad influence on those around him. In order to teach him to do what is right, his parents must punish him in some way, otherwise he will never respect their authority. In order for the Israelites to acknowledge God and change their ways, they had to be punished. Over and over, God proved Himself willing to forgive when they were ready to repent, but now they would not.

Ezekiel had another vision in which the Spirit of God showed him the utter wickedness that was going on in the city. Then he saw the destruction of all. But there was an exception.

Go throughout the city of Jerusalem and put a mark on the foreheads of those who grieve and lament over all the detestable things that are done in it. (Ezekiel 9:4)

It is a dangerous thing to choose what is evil in the sight of the Lord.

READ: Ezekiel 10–15

God gave some very clear visions to Ezekiel. I don't pretend to understand their full meaning, but one idea that seems pretty clear is that some terrible things would come upon the Israelites because of their disobedience. God showed Ezekiel the depth of some of their sins:

Therefore prophesy against them; prophesy, son of man... You will fall by the sword, and I will execute judgment on you at the borders of Israel. Then you will know that I am the Lord. (Ezekiel 11:4, 10)

Whether we obey or disobey Him, God's constant purpose is that we may know that He is the Lord. He longs to reveal Himself to us. If we are open to Him, He reveals Himself with blessings and revelations, and we experience His love, peace, and wisdom. If we turn our backs on Him, we may experience His power in a negative way.

God's word to Ezekiel was that the people of Israel would be scattered and those who inhabited Jerusalem would say:

They are far away from the Lord; this land was given to us as our possession. (Ezekiel 11:15)

But God's promise to Abraham was that this Promised Land was to be the possession of his descendants forever. So the prophecy goes on:

This is what the Sovereign Lord says: I will gather you from the nations and bring you back from the countries where you have been scattered, and I will give you the land of Israel. (Ezekiel 11:17)

That sounds like a repetition of the prophecies in Isaiah and Jeremiah, that God would bring the Jewish people back to Israel from many countries around the world. And here is the hope for the future of that little country:

I will give them an undivided heart and put a new spirit in them... Then they will follow my decrees and be careful to keep my laws. They will be my people, and I will be their God. (Ezekiel 11:19–20)

We had better be careful that we do not oppose this plan of God. In Ezekiel 12, God tells Ezekiel to act out the idea of exile for the people to see, that it might be a sign for them:

360

They will know that I am the Lord, when I disperse them among the nations and scatter them through the countries. (Ezekiel 12:15)

Have you ever wondered, as I have, why there are Jews in so many countries? There is the answer: God ordained it!

I will make the land desolate because they have been unfaithful, declares the Sovereign Lord. (Ezekiel 15:8)

That has been the way the land of Israel was for hundreds of years—a wilderness—until it became the home of the Jews in 1948. Now it blossoms like a rose.

READ: Ezekiel 16–20

I gave you my solemn oath and entered into a covenant with you, declares the Sovereign Lord, and you became mine. (Ezekiel 16:8)

The covenant between God and Israel was like a marriage commitment—an intimate relationship with direct communication between the two. Just as in marriage, when both parties work to bring out the best in each other, this covenant relationship with God can strengthen our inner beauty for all to see.

And your fame spread among the nations on account of your beauty, because the splendor I had given you made your beauty perfect, declares the Sovereign Lord. (Ezekiel 16:14)

A nation guided by God will catch the attention of the whole world. Unfortunately, at that time, Israel listened more to those around her than she did to God. However, He has kept His side of the covenant and is always ready to forgive.

So I will establish my covenant with you, and you will know that I am the Lord. Then, when I make atonement for you for all you have done, you will remember and be ashamed... (Ezekiel 16:62–63)

The big picture is very simple. It boils down to this:

For every living soul belongs to me... Suppose there is a righteous man who does what is just and right... He follows my decrees and faithfully keeps my laws... he will surely live, declares the Sovereign Lord. (Ezekiel 18:4–5, 9)

God's desire is that all men, women, and children everywhere should obey His commandments and do what is right. Anyone willing to repent of evil and change the direction of his life will readily be accepted. God holds no grudges or resentments against anyone.

> *But if a wicked man turns away from all the sins he has committed and keeps all my decrees and does what is just and right, he will surely live... Therefore, O house of Israel, I will judge you, each one according to his ways, declares the Sovereign Lord. Repent! Turn away from all your offenses; then sin will not be your downfall.* (Ezekiel 18:21, 30)

That is a wonderful promise, that God's forgiveness is available for anyone who repents. It is such a vital truth that Jesus was willing to go to the cross so that you and I would not have to carry a burden of guilt! As we seek God's direction and obey it, we come to know Him. This information does not come from reasoning or intellectual knowledge; it only comes from experience—by taking a step of faith.

I remember hearing a man share his testimony. As he listened to an evangelist, his heart was touched and he invited Jesus into his life. There was no spectacular experience, but the foul language he had been accustomed to using totally disappeared. God showed him His healing power.

> *I am the Lord your God; follow my decrees and be careful to keep my laws.* (Ezekiel 20:19)

For the nation of Israel, He promised that when He gathered them together again in their own land:

> *I will accept you as fragrant incense when I bring you out from the nations and gather you from the countries where you have been scattered, and I will show myself holy among you in the sight of the nations. Then you will know that I am the Lord, when I bring you into the land of Israel, the land I had sworn with uplifted hand to give to your fathers.* (Ezekiel 20:41–42)

This promise has now been fulfilled and the Jews are back in their own land. We must watch and pray for them, that God's will may be done.

READ: Ezekiel 21–25

In Ezekiel 22, a number of sins are listed that were evident in the lives of the Israelites—parents were treated with contempt, there was extortion, the fatherless and widows were treated badly, God's Sabbath was profaned, sexually immoral acts were committed, there was dishonest gain, and most important of all:

And you have forgotten me, declares the Sovereign Lord. (Ezekiel 22:12)

For these sins, the Israelites were punished, making us aware of our own society and what we hear on the daily news. I don't want to grieve the Lord in my own life, and I don't want our nation to grieve Him either! The Book of Ezekiel shows the aching heart of God when His people go astray.

I looked for a man among them who would build up a wall and stand before me in the gap on behalf of the land so I would not have to destroy it, but I found none. (Ezekiel 22:30)

Perhaps that is how we should pray—that leaders who are strong in the Lord will rise up to be an example for others to follow. My own circle of influence is rather small, but the way I live affects those around me—for God or against Him. My constant prayer is that He will help me create an atmosphere where others find Him and want to follow Him.

I watched a young woman on TV who had many strikes against her—abuse, a history of foster homes, and cancer—serious problems that could have left her bitter and self-centred. But no, she was radiant, happy, and beautiful. When asked how she could be so positive, she answered, "Because Jesus is my best friend."

It is not circumstances that make or break us; it is our attitude towards them and what we do with them. We can choose to be bitter and demanding or we can look for a way to use those circumstances as stepping stones to arrive at a more abundant life.

Ezekiel 25 is a warning to nations who are against Israel. The Ammonites, the Philistines, and the men of Moab and Edom suffered destruction for being enemies of God's chosen people, even though the chosen ones were also to be punished. His purpose is again stated clearly:

Then they will know that I am the Lord. (Ezekiel 25:11)

The countries of the world today should take heed. Israel may not make all the right decisions, but God will not look with pleasure on nations who are against her and want to destroy her. Our loving Heavenly Father is also a God of judgment. We will all have a day of accounting with Him.

READ: Ezekiel 26–33

Tyre was a thriving city at one time, but she, too, faced destruction for not supporting Jerusalem. King Nebuchadnezzar of Babylon was used against Tyre. God's word to the city was:

You will never be rebuilt, for I the Lord have spoken... (Ezekiel 26:14)

As a centre of commercial trade, Tyre had been an important seaport and become very wealthy. In worldly terms, it was a very successful city.

By your wisdom and understanding you have gained wealth for yourself...
By your great skill in trading you have increased your wealth, and because of
your wealth your heart has grown proud. (Ezekiel 28:4–5)

There is the danger! When we achieve success, pride is likely to set in and we shut God out. No wonder Jesus said it was easier for a camel to go through the eye of a needle than for a rich man to enter the kingdom of God. It is not that wealth is bad in itself; rather, our attitudes cause the problem. We take all the credit upon ourselves, thinking we don't need help and we don't need God.

While Tyre would be destroyed and never rebuilt, God's promise to Abraham, Isaac, and Jacob remained. Someday they would return to the Promised Land.

This is what the Sovereign Lord says: When I gather the people of Israel from
the nations where they have been scattered, I will show myself holy among
them in the sight of the nations. Then they will live in their own land, which
I gave to my servant Jacob. They will live there in safety and will build
houses and plant vineyards; they will live in safety when I inflict punishment
on all their neighbors who maligned them. Then they will know that I am
the Lord their God. (Ezekiel 28:25–26)

Egypt, too, would fall from a position of power and wealth:

Son of man, take up a lament concerning Pharaoh king of Egypt and say to
him: "You are like a lion among the nations." (Ezekiel 32:2)

Worldly wealth and power seem so indestructible, but they are not. Not very long ago, it was said that the sun never set on the British Empire. They had seemed such a mighty force!

Then we come to God's call upon us to turn from wickedness and seek the way of righteousness:

*Say to them, "As surely as I live, declares the Sovereign Lord, I take no
pleasure in the death of the wicked, but rather they turn from their ways and
live." (Ezekiel 33:11)*

He created us in His own image that we might be like Him. We each have
the potential within us to be obedient children of God, if we care to make that
our daily choice.

READ: Ezekiel 34–36

Many years ago, God designated the land of Israel as the Promised Land for His
chosen people—the Jews. Countries that have interfered with that plan have put
themselves in a dangerous position:

*This is what the Sovereign Lord says: In my burning zeal I have spoken
against the rest of the nations, and against all Edom, for with glee and with
malice in their hearts they made my land their own possession so that they
might plunder its pastureland. (Ezekiel 36:5)*

The land of Israel has God's special mark on it for all the world to see. It is
where Jesus was born and lived. It is where He will come again when He returns
to the earth. It is not just a piece of land to be traded among the nations. It is
unique and significant because God chose it for His own special purpose.

*But you, O mountains of Israel, will produce branches and fruit for my
people Israel, for they will soon come home. (Ezekiel 36:8)*

It is not that the Jewish people are better than other people—they have
sinned like everyone else.

*Son of man, when the people of Israel were living in their own land, they
defiled it by their conduct and their actions... I dispersed them among the
nations, and they were scattered through the countries. (Ezekiel 36:17, 19)*

Here is what God then promised these people:

*For I will take you out of the nations; I will gather you from all the countries
and bring you back into your own land. I will sprinkle clean water on you,
and you will be clean... I will give you a new heart and put a new spirit in
you... You will live in the land I gave your forefathers; you will be my people,
and I will be your God... I want you to know that I am not doing this for
your sake, declares the Sovereign Lord. Be ashamed and disgraced for your*

A Journey Through the Bible

conduct, O house of Israel! ... The desolate land will be cultivated instead of lying desolate in the sight of all who pass through it... Then the nations around you that remain will know that I the Lord have rebuilt what was destroyed and have replanted what was desolate. I the Lord have spoken, and I will do it. (Ezekiel 36:24–26, 28, 32, 34, 36)

Those prophecies have been fulfilled as of the beginning of the twentieth century. The Israelites are back in the Promised Land and are growing all kinds of crops where there was desolation for centuries. Woe to any nation who tries to drive them out! God has His own reasons and purposes, which are not dependant on man. We can choose to cooperate with Him or not.

READ: Ezekiel 37–39

When the Israelites were scattered, they lost hope. It seemed as if God had forgotten His covenant with them. He showed Ezekiel the valley of dry bones and said:

Son of man, these bones are the whole house of Israel. They say, "Our bones are dried up and our hope is gone; we are cut off." (Ezekiel 37:11)

But God's plan was to restore them to life again:

I will bring you back to the land of Israel... I will put my Spirit in you and you will live, and I will settle you in your own land. Then you will know that I the Lord have spoken, and I have done it, declares the Lord. (Ezekiel 37:12, 14)

The Jewish people hung on to that promise for hundreds of years. But the story of the dry bones is a hope for us, too. No matter how bad life is or how dead it seems, God can breathe new life into us and into our situations. It is important to get our eyes on Him.

I found this passage in one of my quiet-time books:

I had lost the joy of living and everything seemed a burden—situations around me, society in general, world conditions, etc. In the middle of the night, this thought came to me: "You are neglecting your thanksgiving to God, so your thinking has become problem-centred." Starting today, I must give thanks to God in everything.

Here is a prophecy again concerning Israel as a nation:

366

This is what the Sovereign Lord says: I will take the Israelites out of the nations where they have gone. I will gather them from all around and bring them back into their own land. I will make them one nation in the land, on the mountains of Israel. (Ezekiel 37:21–22)

It goes on for the rest of the chapter:

Then the nations will know that I the Lord make Israel holy, when my sanctuary is among them forever. (Ezekiel 37:28)

Well, the nations don't seem to know that yet, but since God said it, it will happen! However, in Ezekiel 38 it sounds like there will be some bitter fighting before that time. A mighty host will come from the north (Gog) and:

...at that time there shall be a great earthquake in the land of Israel. (Ezekiel 38:19)

But God is all-powerful and will intervene:

I will summon a sword against Gog on all my mountains, declares the Sovereign Lord. (Ezekiel 38:21)

A terrible price must be paid for disobeying God's plan for the world! When we stray too far from Him to hear His call, a catastrophe is needed for Him to get our attention.

From Ezekiel 38:21 to the end of Ezekiel 39, God tells the prophet to pass along the news that Israel will come to know Him. All the world will know that it was Israel's sin of disobedience that caused them to be exiled—but God will restore them to their own land.

I will no longer hide my face from them, for I will pour out my Spirit on the house of Israel, declares the Sovereign Lord. (Ezekiel 39:29)

READ: Ezekiel 40–48

I wonder if Ezekiel's vision of the city and the magnificent temple is a prophecy of things yet to come? What an experience it must have been for Ezekiel!

...and I saw the glory of the God of Israel coming from the east. His voice was like the roaring of rushing waters, and the land was radiant with his glory... Then the Spirit lifted me up and brought me into the inner court, and the glory of the Lord filled the temple. (Ezekiel 43:2, 5)

I have felt the glory of the Lord, but I have never seen it. I remember a couple once telling me about a time when they were sitting in church and the wife said to her husband, "Do you hear that beautiful singing?" He answered, "Yes, where is it coming from?" They realized it must have been angels, because no one else heard it. I have never heard the angels sing. Wouldn't it be glorious to experience God's very presence through our senses, as Ezekiel did?

When we become aware of the perfection of God, we see our own sin:

> *Say to the rebellious house of Israel, "This is what the Sovereign Lord says, Enough of your detestable practices, O house of Israel!"* (Ezekiel 44:6)

We always have a choice—to repent and come closer to God or hang onto our old nature and move further away from Him.

God reminded the Israelites of the place and duties of the Levites, who were the priests, and of the offerings to be made for the atonement of sin. We are most fortunate to be living after Jesus made the final and complete atonement; now, genuine repentance is all we need to receive forgiveness.

He reminded them, too, to celebrate the Feast of Passover, and later in the year, the Feast of Tabernacles.

In Ezekiel 47, the prophet saw a river flowing from the temple:

> *Swarms of living creatures will live wherever the river flows... so where the river flows everything will live... Fruit trees of all kinds will grow on both banks of the river... Their fruit will serve for food and their leaves for healing.* (Ezekiel 47:9, 12)

John had a similar vision in Revelations 22. I wonder if there is any significance to the fact that Canada is the only country with a leaf on its flag? Could we become those trees growing beside the water of life that comes from God's holy temple? Could we provide food and healing for the world? If more and more of us listen to God daily and carry out His plan in our lives, He can use us to be part of His perfect plan for our country! Now, that is an exciting thought!

> *And the name of the city from that time on will be: THE LORD IS THERE.* (Ezekiel 48:35)

Will people someday say that of our city or our country? Only if you and I and many more people are faithful in our commitment to Him!

THE BOOK OF

Daniel

READ: Daniel 1–5

The story of Daniel is a very familiar one. I can remember as a child singing in Sunday School: "Dare to be a Daniel, dare to stand alone. Dare to have a purpose firm, and dare to make it known."

As I read the story again, I feel that same admiration for the four young men who dared to stand against all odds for what they believed was right. They are an example to those of us who have trouble saying no to rich and tasty foods. They chose vegetables and water! I expect they thanked God for giving them a sympathetic steward who agreed to let them try this, although it could have meant his life if their physical condition deteriorated. Their attitude of gratitude, along with the vegetable and water diet, put them in a healthy state. This is key for us, too—what we eat and what we think can affect our physical well-being.

Daniel also trusted God to give him special wisdom to be able to tell Nebuchadnezzar his dream and interpret it. Then he gave credit to God, not taking it for himself.

> *…but there is a God in heaven who reveals mysteries… As for me, this mystery has been revealed to me, not because I have greater wisdom than other living men, but so that you, O king, may know the interpretation and that you may understand what went through your mind.* (Daniel 2:28, 30)

The other three young men also showed amazing faith. Faced with being thrown into a fire, they demonstrated fearless belief in God's wisdom and power.

If we are thrown into the blazing furnace, the God we serve is able to save us from it, and he will rescue us from your hand, O king. But even if he does not, we want you to know, O king, that we will not serve your gods or worship the image of gold you have set up. (Daniel 3:17–18)

When faced with a life-threatening challenge, how strong is our faith?

God rewarded them. Their witness had a profound effect on the king, although it did not immediately remove his cruel and vicious nature. He decreed that anyone who spoke against this God who had saved the lives of these young men

…be cut into pieces and their houses be turned into piles of rubble, for no other god can save in this way. (Daniel 3:29)

He did not commit his life to God at that time. Despite a dream warning that he could be brought down from his high position, his arrogant nature was his downfall. For seven years he lived like an animal until he learned:

…that the Most High is sovereign over the kingdoms of men and gives them to anyone he wishes. (Daniel 4:32)

When Nebuchadnezzar came to himself again, he worshipped and praised God:

Now I, Nebuchadnezzar, praise and exalt and glorify the King of heaven, because everything he does is right and all his ways are just. (Daniel 4:37)

His son, Belshazzar, did not follow his father in this. God let him know that He was not pleased through the writing that appeared on the wall. Again, Daniel was able to interpret God's message.

God can use those who put their total trust in Him, and I believe that is where He longs for us to be. Some of the assignments may not be easy, but there is no greater reward than knowing that God has trusted me to be a channel for His love or wisdom to touch someone else. I am sure Daniel and his friends had a real love relationship with God.

READ: Daniel 6–12

A few highlights in Daniel's life are told to us, but there are many days and years in between. What was he doing then? All we can assume is that he spent time every day seeking the Lord.

Now when Daniel learned that the decree had been published, he went home to his upstairs room where the windows opened toward Jerusalem. Three times a day he got down on his knees and prayed, giving thanks to his God, just as he had done before. (Daniel 6:10)

At that time, he was about to face death in a lions' den, but he went on doing what he had always done—praying to God three times a day. That is the only sure way of facing any crisis. Through continuous daily prayer, we become aware of God's nature, more certain of His power, and we gain an assurance of His love. Then we know that we do not face our problems alone.

The visions described in this book are rather terrifying—even Daniel was greatly alarmed. People have speculated for years as to what nations are referred to and if we have arrived at that period in history. No one knows for sure.

Daniel knew the importance of prayer before God, both for his nation as well as for himself.

I prayed to the Lord my God and confessed: "O Lord, the great and awesome God, who keeps his covenant of love with all who love him and obey his commands, we have sinned and done wrong... We do not make requests of you because we are righteous, but because of your great mercy." (Daniel 9:4–5, 18)

When we approach God in prayer, it is important to focus on His greatness, awesome power, and faithfulness. Then we can see where we need to confess our own unworthiness and self-centredness. When we get into the right perspective in our relationship with God, He communicates with us. He sent Gabriel to Daniel:

He instructed me and said to me, "Daniel, I have now come to give you insight and understanding." (Daniel 9:22)

Very few people have had the privilege of an angel appearing before them, but anyone who spends regular daily time with God, seeking His will, soon begins to recognize the thoughts that come from Him.

Do not be afraid, Daniel. Since the first day that you set your mind to gain understanding and to humble yourself before your God, your words were heard, and I have come in response to them. (Daniel 10:12)

God is most interested in our thoughts and attitudes. He sees right into our hearts and wants to help us keep them clean and pure. It is the people who are in right relationship with Him who are strong. Speaking of the enemy:

> *With flattery he will corrupt those who have violated the covenant, but the people who know their God will firmly resist him.* (Daniel 11:32)

After telling Daniel of the disasters to come, God gave him an assurance of peace for his faithfulness:

> *As for you, go your way till the end. You will rest, and then at the end of the days you will rise to receive your allotted inheritance.* (Daniel 12:13)

THE BOOKS OF
Titus & Philemon

READ: Titus 1–3 and Philemon

There seems to have been some problems in the church at Crete, so Paul left Titus there:

> *...that you might straighten out what was left unfinished...* (Titus 1:5)

It sounds like a tall order! He was to appoint elders and a bishop. Paul then lists the specific qualities these leaders must have. The problem was that some leaders felt they could carry out their duties even though they were dishonest, impure, and self-centred in their private lives. We have that same problem today. We cannot trust people who say one thing in public but have different standards in private.

> *They claim to know God, but by their actions they deny him.* (Titus 1:16)

We all have this tendency—to show our best side when we are out with others, but be selfish and demanding when we are at home.

When I taught Grade One in the public school system, I loved my work and the people I worked with. One Saturday, I wrote this in my quiet-time book:

> A beautiful day! A gift from God! I have been willing to work hard for others Monday to Friday, but I have wanted to keep Saturday and Sunday for my own plans! Maybe that is why I have been having headaches nearly every weekend—not from overwork, just over-selfishness! Praise God and be thankful the phone wakened me to this glorious day! I must be ready to spend myself for others—that is where joy comes in!

Here is a description of what followers of Jesus should be like:

Remind the people to be subject to rulers and authorities, to be obedient, to be ready to do whatever is good, to slander no one, to be peaceable and considerate, and to show true humility toward all men. (Titus 3:1–2)

This is only possible through the redemption of Jesus and renewal in the Holy Spirit. But it is possible, and that is the good news!

I wish we knew Philemon's answer to this letter Paul wrote him. Philemon had become a Christian. After that, his slave Onesimus ran away, but God had a special plan for this slave. Onesimus met up with Paul and became a Christian! This changed Onesimus' whole attitude, and he was now prepared to go back to his master and put things right.

What a testing ground this must have been for both Philemon and Onesimus. The latter had probably stolen from his master in order to be able to run away, but Paul offered to pay that back. There had apparently been a real change in this man who had been a slave.

Formerly he was useless to you, but now he has become useful both to you and to me. (Philemon 1:11)

Philemon, on the other hand, as a believer, was an inspiration to others. Paul says to him:

Your love has given me great joy and encouragement, because you, brother, have refreshed the hearts of the saints. (Philemon 1:7)

With the love of Jesus drawing these two men together as brothers—not as master and slave—they must have made a great witness to their friends and neighbours. Jesus can melt away all barriers and draw us together in one bond of fellowship. I believe He did that for Philemon and Onesimus.

THE BOOK OF

Hosea

READ: Hosea 1–5

Hosea lived before Jeremiah, Daniel, and Ezekiel. According to the kings mentioned in Hosea 1:1, he lived during the time of Isaiah. I am not a historian by any stretch of the imagination, but I believe that was about 750 years before Jesus was born.

This book contains the oft-repeated message that God longs for His chosen people to obey Him and experience life as He intended it to be for us here on earth. He likens His relationship with Israel to one's marriage to an unfaithful harlot.

God told Hosea to take a prostitute to be his wife, so Hosea chose Gomer. They had children, but Gomer was not faithful, so there was little hope for her offspring. This was parallel to Israel's unfaithfulness to God. Yet God said:

> *I will betroth you to me forever; I will betroth you in righteousness and justice, in love and compassion. I will betroth you in faithfulness, and you will acknowledge the Lord.* (Hosea 2:19–20)

God's love was constant and true, no matter what Israel did. He urged Hosea to love his wife in the same way.

> *The Lord said to me, "Go, show your love to your wife again, though she is loved by another and is an adulteress. Love her as the Lord loves the Israelites, though they turn to other gods and love the sacred raisin cakes."* (Hosea 3:1)

We probably wouldn't have as many broken marriages if more men took the advice God gave Hosea—love your wife as God loves the Israelites. Hosea obeyed and even bought her back from whatever slavery she was in.

Jesus paid the price for Israel's sins—and for ours, too—so that we might come into an intimate relationship with Him. He promises a time will come when Israel is ready.

Afterward the Israelites will return and seek the Lord their God and David their king. They will come trembling to the Lord and to his blessings in the last days. (Hosea 3:5)

In the meantime, God wasn't happy with what He saw going on—swearing, lying, killing, stealing, and committing adultery. It sounds like our society today, and I am sure God is not happy with us, either! His words through Hosea show that we cannot follow the wrong path and escape the consequences.

…because you have ignored the law of your God, I also will ignore your children. (Hosea 4:6)

It is an awesome responsibility to have children, since the quality of the parents' lives will affect the lives of their family. As parents, we set the stage for our children's relationship with God.

READ: Hosea 6–14

Your love is like the morning mist, like the early dew that disappears. (Hosea 6:4)

What a terrible kind of love it is that comes and goes like a cloud and disappears like the dew! Yet that is often the kind of love we have for each other. If our spouse, child, or friend behaves the way we think they should, we love them, but if they don't measure up to our expectations, we reject them and withdraw our love.

That is often the kind of love we exhibit towards God. We praise Him when everything is going well but complain or even blame Him when things go wrong. But He says that He does not want certain behaviours from us, but rather love and a deeper knowledge of Him.

For I desire mercy, not sacrifice, and acknowledgement of God rather than burnt offerings. (Hosea 6:6)

The more time I spend reading the Bible and meditating on it, the more the knowledge of God and His purpose increases in my life. The more I take every situation in my life into prayer to see His perspective, the more I appreciate His wisdom and never-ending love for me. He is my best friend, and my love for Him continues to grow as I get to know Him better.

How He longed to reach the hearts of the Israelites!

I long to redeem them but they speak lies against me. (Hosea 7:13)

They would not listen to Him or seek His guidance, instead going their own way, seeking their own leaders.

They set up kings without my consent; they choose princes without my approval. (Hosea 8:4)

If we say we are Christians, it is important for us to get our directions from the Lord. However, when we do make wrong decisions, God is ready to forgive when we confess and are ready to repent:

Return, O Israel, to the Lord your God. Your sins have been your downfall! *...I will heal their waywardness and love them freely...* (Hosea 14:1, 4)

There is a simplicity about God's message to all people: get to know Him, do what you know is right, and be what He wants you to be.

Who is wise? He will realize these things. Who is discerning? He will understand them. The ways of the Lord are right; the righteous walk in them, but the rebellious stumble in them. (Hosea 14:9)

THE BOOK OF

Joel

READ: Joel 1–3

The Bible does not tell us anything about Joel except that his father's name was Pethuel. However, God told him of some experiences Israel would have in the future.

First, he tells of a plague of locusts that would come in waves and destroy the crops. How well I remember the plague of grasshoppers that hit Saskatchewan in the late thirties! They would sweep through a field or garden—thousands of them—and destroy it completely within hours. The experience was devastating for farmers!

The destruction caused by the locusts, however, would be nothing compared to God's judgment:

Alas for that day! For the day of the Lord is near: it will come like destruction from the Almighty. (Joel 1:15)

The day of the Lord is great; it is dreadful. Who can endure it? (Joel 2:11)

A nation who turns away from God cannot escape His judgment. If we look through history, we find that it has happened before. God created man in His own image that we might have fellowship with Him.

The next picture Joel gives us is one of hope:

"Even now," declares the Lord, *"return to me with all your heart, with fasting and weeping and mourning." Return to the Lord your God, for he is gracious and compassionate...* (Joel 2:12–13)

When the people turned again to God and sought His forgiveness, their circumstances changed. God had pity on them and said:

I am sending you grain, new wine and oil, enough to satisfy you fully; never again will I make you an object of scorn to the nations. (Joel 2:19)

Be glad and rejoice! This is what happens when our relationship with God is restored. He replaces what we have lost and blesses us beyond what we would expect.

You will have plenty to eat, until you are full, and you will praise the name of the Lord your God, who has worked wonders for you. (Joel 2:26)

God then promises that there will come a time when He will pour out His Holy Spirit upon all flesh. This happened during the Charismatic Movement in the 70s when thousands of people all over the world received a special infilling and empowering of the Holy Spirit. I personally believe there is more to come!

Joel 3 tells that after Judah and Jerusalem are restored, the nations will gather in the valley of Jehoshaphat and the Lord Himself will judge them *"because of violence done to the people of Judah"* (Joel 3:19)

Then you will know that I, the Lord your God, dwell in Zion, my holy hill. (Joel 3:17)

THE BOOK OF

Hebrews

READ: Hebrews 1–4

The first three chapters deal with who Jesus is. Anyone who has read the Old Testament is aware of how God spoke through the prophets, but then He sent His Son to speak to us for Him.

> *The Son is the radiance of God's glory and the exact representation of his being, sustaining all things by his powerful word.* (Hebrews 1:3)

There is a tendency in people to reject the divine nature of Jesus until they come into a personal relationship with Him. But God has made Him superior to the angels:

> *Let all God's angels worship him [Jesus]...* (Hebrews 1:6)

He was with God from the beginning of time, at the creation of the earth and the heavens, and God's word says that Jesus remains forever.

Here are a few statements about Jesus:

1. He will remain forever: *"But you remain the same, and your years will never end."* (Hebrews 1:12)
2. He has control over everything: *"You crowned him with glory and honor and put everything under his feet."* (Hebrews 2:7–8)
3. He died for all people: *"...so that by the grace of God he might taste death for everyone."* (Hebrews 2:9)
4. He is our High Priest: *"For this reason he had to be made like his brothers in every way, in order that he might become a merciful and faithful high priest in service to God, and that he might make atonement for the sins of the people."* (Hebrews 2:17)

Moses was God's faithful servant, but Jesus is above him since He is the very Son of God. The people of Israel were disobedient to God's word, given through Moses, and the writer of Hebrews warns against that hardening of the heart:

See to it, brothers, that none of you has a sinful, unbelieving heart that turns away from the living God. (Hebrews 3:12)

God's word is available to all of us through the Bible, and through our quiet times when He speaks to us directly. If we are to enter His heavenly kingdom, it is imperative that we listen and obey.

Today, if you hear his voice, do not harden your hearts. (Hebrews 4:7)

His word not only shows us the way to go; it also corrects us when we are wrong.

For the word of God is living and active. Sharper than any double-edged sword, it penetrates even to dividing soul and spirit, joints and marrow; it judges the thoughts and attitudes of the heart. (Hebrews 4:12)

When I started reading the Bible one morning, I grew uncomfortable about a recent conversation with a friend. I had been telling her that I was praying for another lady but was concerned about some unforgiveness she was carrying. As I came into God's presence, I knew I had said too much. My words had become gossip. The word of God is, indeed, like a double-edged sword, discerning our very thoughts and intentions.

Nothing in all creation is hidden from God's sight. (Hebrews 4:13)

Because Jesus was tempted just as we are, He understands us. We can confidently come to Him for forgiveness and love. What a blessing!

READ: Hebrews 5–7

A high priest is someone appointed to act on behalf of the people in relation to God. It needs to be recognized that he, too, has weaknesses.

This is why he has to offer sacrifices for his own sins, as well as for the sins of his people. (Hebrews 5:3)

Jesus, on the other hand, though He was the Son of God, went through temptations and suffering. However, He was totally obedient in everything.

...and, once made perfect, he became the source of eternal salvation for all who obey him... (Hebrews 5:9)

There is a word of exhortation to these priests, who are still at the milk stage rather than being able to teach others.

But solid food is for the mature, who by constant use have trained themselves to distinguish good from evil. (Hebrews 5:14)

It seems to me that we can never help others set their lives straight if we have not learned to set right the wrongs in our own lives. Pastors who do not make a daily practice of allowing God to point out where their attitudes are wrong will not progress to solid food—the more mature wisdom—that allows them to teach and lead others. In fact, this advice holds true for all Christians who want to grow and mature in their faith.

The writer of Hebrews warns that if we receive God's blessings but do not bring forth results, we are like a field that receives God's rain but produces only thistles even though the seeds of vegetation are present. However, he also gives encouragement:

God is not unjust; he will not forget your work and the love you have shown him as you have helped his people and continue to help them. (Hebrews 6:10)

God appreciates what we do but encourages us to be all that He would have us be and not be content with a lesser standard. Jesus said, "Be perfect." That is the standard we must set for ourselves. Anything less is no standard at all!

Jesus is not a high priest, as the Levites were, to carry out the law. He is a priest *"in the order of Melchizedek"* (Hebrews 7:11, 17). We do not know much about the latter, but:

...Abraham gave him a tenth of everything. First, his name means "king of righteousness"; then also, "king of Salem" means "king of peace." (Hebrews 7:2)

That rightly describes Jesus as well—King of righteousness and King of peace. Death finished the Levites' time in office, but Jesus goes on forever. As we draw near to God, He makes intercession for us. What a comforting thought! Even as I pray to God and seek His guidance, Jesus prays with me, making intercession to the Father. As He is one with the Father, I, too, can enter into that relationship as a beloved child of God. That makes me worthwhile, a child with abundant potential, immersed in a love that seeks the very best for me!

If God is for us, who can be against us? (Romans 8:31)

READ: Hebrews 8–13

God never changes. He told Jeremiah He would make a new covenant with Israel. In Hebrews 8:10–11, He made the astounding promise that everyone will know the Lord, from the least to the greatest. This same promise appears in Romans 11, that when the full number of Gentiles comes into belief *"all Israel will be saved"* (Romans 11:26). Are we Gentiles holding up their salvation? Any rejection of God's plan on my part is a hindrance to others, so who knows how far that hindering effect might reach?

Our only hope is in Jesus:

But now he has appeared once for all at the end of the ages to do away with sin by the sacrifice of himself. (Hebrews 9:26)

Because of Him, we can come into God's presence:

...having our hearts sprinkled to cleanse us from a guilty conscience and having our bodies washed with pure water. (Hebrews 10:22)

The writer suggests that we encourage each other and meet together regularly. Some years ago, a few of my friends met together to consider disbanding our Women's Aglow Fellowship. One of the ladies had been directed to Hebrews 10:25, and almost single-handedly resurrected the fellowship meetings as she became willing to take on the leadership and encourage others to join. God honoured her obedience and the group flourished.

It is a dangerous thing to sin deliberately after receiving the knowledge of truth.

The Lord will judge his people. (Hebrews 10:30)

Hebrews 11–12 contain great teaching on faith. Without faith in who God is, we cannot please Him. When we make our desire to please Him our top priority, we have Jesus, *"the author and perfecter of our faith"* (Hebrews 12:2), to help us.

There follows a lot of good advice, such as:

1. Endure hardship as discipline.

2. Make every effort to live in peace with all men.

3. Be thankful.

4. Marriage should be honoured by all.

5. Keep your lives free from the love of money.

6. Offer to God a sacrifice of praise.

7. Obey your leaders and submit to their authority.

The letter ends with a great benediction often used in church services. These few words are the core of it:

May the God of peace... equip you with everything good for doing his will, and may he work in us what is pleasing to him, through Jesus Christ, to whom be glory for ever and ever. Amen. (Hebrews 13:20–21)

What a wonderful way to close a letter to a friend!

THE BOOK OF

Amos

READ: Amos 1–9

Amos answered Amaziah, "I was neither a prophet nor a prophet's son, but I was a shepherd, and I also took care of sycamore-fig trees. But the Lord took me from tending the flock and said to me, "Go, prophesy to my people Israel." (Amos 7:14–15)

It is important to listen to God on a regular basis, because He may have something in store for us that we would never expect. I am sure Amos had no intention of training in theology. As a herdsman, he must have spent many quiet hours caring for his animals; maybe that was when he heard the voice of God. Or maybe he spent time with the Lord before his day's work began. In any case, he did hear God's call and was obedient, even though the message was not all good news.

He lived at the time of King Uzziah in Judah and King Jeroboam in Israel. His words are full of warnings to all the nations who strayed from God's desire for them, mistreated each other, and did not remember the covenant of the brotherhood. God's judgment is sure and we cannot escape it, either as an individual or as a nation.

Because the people of Israel had been chosen by God, they had a special responsibility to be faithful to Him—but they, too, had failed in this.

You only have I chosen of all the families of the earth; therefore I will punish you for all your sins. (Amos 3:2)

If your own child is in the class you are teaching, he knows your expectations better than the other children do, making it harder to deal with his misbehaviour. As we commit our lives to God and begin to receive His blessings, our responsibility to be obedient increases. Privileges and blessings go hand in hand with responsibilities. We are all accountable for our own actions.

...prepare to meet your God, O Israel. (Amos 4:12)

As a teacher, I knew that it was important that I help a child and reward him in any way I could when he was doing his best. I believe God does the same thing. He gives us difficult tasks so we can grow in wisdom and knowledge, but He encourages and helps us along the way.

Seek good, not evil, that you may live. Then the Lord God Almighty will be with you... (Amos 5:14)

God told Amos, just as He told other prophets, that one day His people would prosper in the land He had given them. It appears that we are living in that promised day! What a privilege!

"I will bring back my exiled people Israel; they will rebuild the ruined cities and live in them. They will plant vineyards and drink their wine; they will make gardens and eat their fruit. I will plant Israel in their own land, never again to be uprooted from the land I have given them," says the Lord your God. (Amos 9:14–15)

THE BOOKS OF
Obadiah & Jonah

READ: Obadiah and Jonah 1–4

Obadiah had a vision concerning the Edomites, who were Esau's descendants, just as the Israelites were descendants of Jacob. Because Edom conspired against Israel, God said their nation would come to an end. If we go our own way, there is a price to pay.

> *The day of the Lord is near for all nations. As you have done, it will be done to you; your deeds will return upon your own head... There will be no survivors from the house of Esau.* (Obadiah 1:15, 18)

However, He says the Jewish exiles will possess their land again *"and the kingdom will be the Lord's"* (Obadiah 1:21).

Jonah's story is often told, and even people who never read the Bible could tell you what happened when he tried to run away from God's plan for him. He had a close enough relationship with God to be able to hear and recognize His voice. His reaction to God, unfortunately, was not always positive. Instead of obeying Him and going to Ninevah, he went to Joppa and got on a ship bound for Tarshish, intending *"to flee from the Lord"* (Jonah 1:2).

However, when the storm came, Jonah was honest with the crew, and this honesty nearly cost him his life. After being thrown overboard, God sent a whale to rescue him and eventually spit him up on the shore.

> *Salvation comes from the Lord.* (Jonah 2:9)

This very dramatic lesson made Jonah change his mind, so he travelled to Ninevah and warned the people that their wickedness would bring on their destruction. He still was not totally in tune with God, however, and became angry when the people repented and turned from evil, thus escaping destruction. God showed Jonah, through a plant, that his anger did not line up with God's compassion for people.

Several things occur to me through this story. The first is that God can reach people through us, even when we are not ourselves on-track.

After Jonah was thrown overboard:

> *At this the men greatly feared the Lord, and they offered a sacrifice to the Lord and made vows to him.* (Jonah 1:16)

The people of Ninevah listened to Jonah's warning and the king called them all to fasting and repentance. God heard and forgave.

The second thing I notice is that God did not give up on Jonah, but instead constantly watched him, protecting him and teaching him. At some time, Jonah must have committed his life to the Lord, for talking to Him became a natural part of his life. This made him worth something in God's eyes. This is comforting to know. I have committed my life to the Lord, too, and can count on the fact that He will never give up on me.

He will always watch over me, protecting me and teaching me, even when I become rebellious or petulant, as Jonah did. I am worth something in God's sight!

THE BOOK OF

James

READ: James 1–3

It seems that James is writing to the *"twelve tribes scattered among the nations"* (James 1:1), encouraging them to live what they believe. It could be taken as a letter to a modern-day church, for we all need to constantly remind ourselves, as well as each other, that knowing God's word intellectually is not enough. That is why so many church leaders have fallen. They "talk the talk" but do not "walk the walk." His first piece of advice is a tough one!

> *Consider it pure joy, my brothers, whenever you face trials of many kinds, because you know that the testing of your faith develops perseverance.* (James 1:2–3)

That is not our natural reaction, and only deep trust and faith in God can produce it. We can experience no joy through our trials unless we believe God has the answer. We can have a sense of anticipation as we watch it unfold. If our faith is strong, we can both believe He has the answer and ask Him for wisdom to do our part.

> *If any of you lacks wisdom, he should ask God, who gives generously to all without finding fault, and it will be given to him.* (James 1:5)

I often prayed this for Lighthouse Christian Academy when we were faced with tough decisions. Many times, an idea came to one of us that we knew must have come from our Heavenly Father. At one board meeting, one of our members came up with a long-term vision which made us realize we had been focusing on solving only our immediate problems; when we looked at the big picture, we found new and different solutions. We all had a sense of excitement, knowing this had come from God. Within minutes we knew what our first step should be. There is no greater adventure than being a part of God's plan for the world!

Do not merely listen to the word, and so deceive yourselves. Do what it says. (James 1:22)

This is a tough one! We know the word tells us to *"love one another"* (John 13:34–35) but we find it hard not to be critical or resentful. The word goes even further, telling us, *"Love your enemies and pray for those who persecute you"* (Matthew 5:44). It also says, *"Do not judge, or you too will be judged"* (Matthew 7:1). It is not enough to read the Bible, or even memorize parts of it. When we begin to adopt right attitudes, we really begin to see God in action!

The tongue also is a fire… Out of the same mouth come praise and cursing. (James 3:6, 10)

What comes out of our mouths shows what we are on the inside! At times, the words I speak startle me, for I was unaware of some hidden resentment or jealousy. My own unkind words have revealed the state of my heart. We need to watch our tongues. Once spoken, words cannot be recalled!

READ: James 4–5

You do not have, because you do not ask God. When you ask, you do not receive, because you ask with wrong motives… (James 4:2–3)

It sounds as if God wants us to bring all our needs to Him. If our requests are to be granted, however, they should be in line with His will. When a child comes to his parent and asks for something the parent knows would be harmful to the child, of course the answer will be no. When we ask God for something that comes from selfish desire and would be harmful to our spiritual growth, we can be sure the answer will be no. The only way I know how to pray in His will is to read and obey His word, then practise praying. As James says:

Come near to God and he will come near to you… Humble yourselves before the Lord, and he will lift you up… Brothers, do not slander one another. (James 4:8, 10–11)

As we practise these things, they become a way of life. Quiet times become part of everyday living. We don't become perfect, but we recognize our mistakes more readily. We ask God's forgiveness, we confess our sins to others, and when appropriate we apologize to the one we wronged. Only then are we ready to move on.

> *Therefore confess your sins to each other and pray for each other so that you may be healed. The prayer of a righteous man is powerful and effective.* (James 5:16)

Confession of sin and prayer are connected with healing. That is a truth worth putting into practice. Perhaps there would be less illness if we confessed our sins to God and to one another, praying for each other regularly.

THE BOOK OF

Micah

READ: Micah 1–7

God spoke to Micah during the same period when He spoke to Isaiah and Hosea. To all of them, He warned of the dire results if Judah and Israel continued on their paths of disobedience. Parents warn their children once or twice when they misbehave, after which punishment must follow if the children do not choose to change their behaviour pattern. God's children have to learn the same way.

> *All this is because of Jacob's transgression, because of the sins of the house of Israel.* (Micah 1:5)

A strong word is given to the leaders, the prophets who led the people astray, and the rulers *"who despise justice and distort all that is right"* (Micah 3:9).

However, in the latter days the house of God was to be established on the mountain:

> *Many nations will come and say, "Come, let us go up to the mountain of the Lord, to the house of the God of Jacob. He will teach us his ways, so that we may walk in his paths." The law will go out from Zion, the word of the Lord from Jerusalem.* (Micah 4:2)

Christians from all over the world travel to Israel, especially during the Feast of Tabernacles. Is this the beginning of the fulfillment of Micah's prophecy?

Micah goes on to say that there will be no more wars. Obviously, we have not yet come to that time! There is no real peace today, and fighting continues in many parts of the world.

Only one leader can bring everlasting peace:

But you, Bethlehem Ephrathah, though you are small among the clans of Judah, out of you will come for me one who will be ruler over Israel, whose origins are from of old, from ancient times. (Micah 5:2)

When Jesus comes back to Israel and is accepted by the people, a new day will dawn!

He will stand and shepherd his flock in the strength of the Lord, in the majesty of the name of the Lord his God. And they will live securely, for then his greatness will reach to the end of the earth. (Micah 5:4)

It sounds too good to be true—a leader we can totally trust to be wise, honest, and loving, someone who will serve God and serve the people with integrity and justice. How we long for such a leader! The wonderful news is that, as individuals, we can have that leader now. Jesus is ready and willing to receive us into His kingdom when we are ready to turn to Him. What then is our part?

He has showed you, O man, what is good. And what does the Lord require of you? To act justly and to love mercy and to walk humbly with your God. (Micah 6:8)

Walk humbly with your God: that is the key, a daily seeking of His will and then doing it. It is so simple, but not always easy!

Though I sit in darkness, the Lord will be my light. (Micah 7:8)

Micah ends with an assurance of God's forgiveness and compassion, and that God never changes. He is the same today.

THE BOOKS OF

Nahum &

Habakkuk

READ: Nahum 1–3 and Habakkuk 1–3

Nahum contains a prophecy concerning the destruction of Ninevah, the capital of Assyria. As prophesied, what was once a great city passed into history. God is shown here as *"slow to anger and great in power,"* but He is also a God of righteousness and judgment, and *"the Lord will not leave the guilty unpunished"* (Nahum 1:3).

> *The Lord is good, a refuge in times of trouble. He cares for those who trust in him, but with an overwhelming flood he will make an end of Ninevah; he will pursue his foes into darkness.* (Nahum 1:7–8)

This brings to mind the spiritual battle at which God's enemies are Satan and his evil spirits, which are so destructive when they get a foothold in people's lives. But God's power is greater than Satan's and He can bring an end to the powers of darkness. When we take refuge in Him and secure our position as a child of God on a daily basis, we are protected by His power.

I don't know how to date the destruction described here. Perhaps it refers to a battle yet to come. All I know for sure is that God is my Father, a refuge in time of trouble, but He is a disciplinarian as well. He wants His children to do their best in order that they may experience a full and abundant life here which prepares them to spend eternity with Him.

Habakkuk complains to God that the Chaldeans, a *"ruthless and impetuous people"* (Habakkuk 1:6), are victorious against Israel; they are being used as a judgment on Israel. Though there will be difficult times, God gives him some great assurance and encouragement.

...but the righteous will live by his faith... (Habakkuk 2:4)

Nations that turn against God cannot stand forever. Sometimes there seems little reason for the collapse.

For the earth will be filled with the knowledge of the glory of the Lord, as the waters cover the sea. (Habakkuk 2:14)

That will be a great day! How we long for people everywhere to be aware of the glory of God. There is no limit to how well our conditions could improve if everyone acknowledged Him and sought His wisdom.

But the Lord is in his holy temple; let all the earth be silent before him. (Habakkuk 2:20)

That is when we will know peace on earth—when we come in silence before Him and receive His Holy Spirit in our hearts and lives.

Habakkuk ends with a great commitment, saying that though crops fail and there is no food:

...yet will I rejoice in the Lord, I will be joyful in God my Savior. (Habakkuk 3:18)

No matter what happens, I can always rejoice in who God is.

THE BOOK OF

1 Peter

READ: 1 Peter 1–5

Peter wrote this letter to the believers who were exiled from their homeland and scattered all over the place. Although the message was sent to them, it could have been written to believers today. I can find many messages in it that are appropriate for me:

> *But just as he who called you is holy, so be holy in all you do; for it is written: "Be holy, because I am holy." (1 Peter 1:15–16)*

It took me many years to accept my own capabilities. Fortunately, I had a husband who encouraged me and often said, "Of course you can do it—go ahead." Not all wives are that lucky. But then, how often have we encouraged our husbands?

This letter tells me that I have been ransomed:

> *…with the precious blood of Christ, a lamb without blemish or defect. (1 Peter 1:19)*

That means I am holy because He is holy! I am capable and worthwhile, and I have a place in God's perfect plan for the world—and so have you!

Not everyone sees the wonderful gift God has given us in Christ. Many rejected Him when He was here on earth, and many reject Him now.

> *Now to you who believe, this stone is precious. (1 Peter 2:7)*

Peter has lots of sound advice. He cautions women about paying too much attention to our outward appearance, when our real value is what is on the inside.

Your beauty should not come from outward adornment... Instead, it should be that of your inner self, the unfading beauty of a gentle and quiet spirit, which is of great worth in God's sight. (1 Peter 3:3–4)

He has advice for husbands as well, to *"be considerate as you live with your wives, and treat them with respect..."* (1 Peter 3:7). I know some Christian men who are strong on the idea of their wives' submission but weak on the position of husbands to love and cherish their wives.

Above all, love each other deeply, because love covers over a multitude of sins. (1 Peter 4:8)

There is that call to love again. If our love is strong, our mistakes do not have such a bad effect. This is most clearly demonstrated in our relationships with children. They recognize when they are loved and quickly forgive our impatience because they are secure in that love. As adults, we need to learn from them and not let our level of love be dictated by our expectations of their behaviour.

We can be sure suffering will come our way, but here is the answer to that:

Cast all your anxiety on him because he cares for you... And the God of grace, who called you to his eternal glory in Christ, after you have suffered a little while, will himself restore you and make you strong, firm and steadfast. (1 Peter 5:7, 10)

This is a great promise to hang on to when times are tough!

THE BOOK OF

2 Peter

READ: 2 Peter 1–3

[Jesus'] divine power has given us everything we need for life and godliness through our knowledge of him who called us by his own glory and goodness. (2 Peter 1:3)

Jesus can provide everything we need for a full, abundant, and godly life. Unfortunately, we have a strong tendency to find satisfaction from other sources—material wealth, the approval of others, success, and power. When we do this, we miss what life is meant to be. God created us in His image; only by lining up our lives with His plan can we attain our potential.

Peter, who knew Jesus as an intimate friend, assures us that we can have this close relationship, too. However, he strongly warns of the devastating effect of turning away from Him, especially after we have once been walking with Him.

If they have escaped the corruption of the world by knowing our Lord and Savior Jesus Christ and again are entangled in it and overcome, they are worse off at the end than they were at the beginning. (2 Peter 2:20)

Peter writes of a time when this earth will be no more, though no one knows when that will be. He also speaks of the timelessness of God:

But do not forget this one thing, dear friends: With the Lord a day is like a thousand years, and a thousand years are like a day. (2 Peter 3:8)

My lifetime only represents a small part of history. When I make long-term plans, I consider ten to thirty years. God's plan spans thousands of years, offering us a unique perspective on time. This makes me want to tap into His omnipotent wisdom and not depend on my own extremely limited knowledge! God's desire is for everyone to experience all He has in store for us:

> *...not wanting anyone to perish, but everyone to come to repentance.* (2 Peter 3:9)

He has given us free will, which can get us into trouble or bring us into wonderful fellowship with Him. He does not violate the gift of choice He has created within us. Sometimes I wish He would, but then we would be puppets or robots, unable to reach the level of intimacy He wants to have with us.

> *But in keeping with his promise we are looking forward to a new heaven and a new earth, the home of righteousness. So then, dear friends, since you are looking forward to this, make every effort to be found spotless, blameless and at peace with him.* (2 Peter 3:13–14)

That would be utterly impossible if Jesus had not made provision for us to receive total forgiveness when we repent. That means that when I honestly ask God to show me my sin, forgive me, and help me to never sin again, I am without sin or blemish. I am at peace!

THE BOOK OF

Zephaniah

READ: Zephaniah 1–3

Zephaniah delivers a message to his people that still resonates with us today: a warning that nations which do not acknowledge God will face destruction.

> *Be silent before the Sovereign Lord, for the day of the Lord is near.* (Zephaniah 1:7)

We need to heed that advice before it is too late to save our nation.

> *Seek the Lord, all you humble of the land, you who do what he commands. Seek righteousness, seek humility.* (Zephaniah 2:3)

We need to clear our relationships with other people, especially those closest to us. This reminds me of a problem a woman once shared with me. She told me that when her husband was in a down mood, she felt guilty and tried to think what she had done to cause him to be so unhappy. Then she realized that his darkness was his problem, not hers, and that all she needed to do was keep close to God and wait for her husband to work out his own solution. I could definitely relate to this, since I had done the same thing. Not only did this give her freedom, it also meant that when she got out of the way, God had a chance to help her husband let go of the negativity and find his own freedom.

Yes, Zephaniah's message is for today—we need to seek righteousness and humility! He encourages the people of Israel, telling them that God will bless them in a situation that sounds like what seems to be happening today:

> *Sing, O Daughter of Zion; shout aloud, O Israel! … The Lord has taken away your punishment, he has turned back your enemy. The Lord, the King*

of Israel, is with you... The Lord your God is with you, he is mighty to save... "At that time I will gather you; at that time I will bring you home. I will give you honor and praise among all the peoples of the earth when I restore your fortunes before your very eyes," says the Lord. (Zephaniah 3:14–15, 17, 20)

Since God is for Israel, woe to any nation who is against her!

I will make you into a great nation and I will bless you; I will make your name great, and you will be a blessing. I will bless those who bless you, and whoever curses you I will curse; and all people on earth will be blessed through you. (Genesis 12:2–3)

THE BOOK OF

Haggai

READ: Haggai 1–2

Is it a time for you yourselves to be living in your paneled houses, while this house remains a ruin? (Haggai 1:4)

God spoke to Haggai about how the people improved their own homes but neglected to rebuild the temple. Because they did not put God first, nothing went right for them.

You have planted much, but have harvested little. You eat, but never have enough. You drink, but never have your fill. You put on clothes, but are not warm. You earn wages, only to put them in a purse with holes in it… Because of my house, which remains a ruin, while each of you is busy with his own house. (Haggai 1:6, 9)

As I read this, I begin to wonder, am I neglecting God's house? I didn't see how that connected with my life until I realized that the temple was where the people went to meet with God. My home is "my temple," the place where I meet with the Lord.

There is another way of looking at this message. We should ask, are we neglecting His perfect plan for our lives by choosing to make our own plans instead? What are the tasks I know I should do but keep putting off? There is a cupboard that needs clearing out, a phone call I have been avoiding, and numerous others tasks I keep delaying. God is just as interested in how I do my daily tasks as He is in my personal time spent with Him. Worship and work are really one.

"Be strong, all you people of the land," declares the Lord, "and work. For I am with you," declares the Lord Almighty... "And my Spirit remains among you. Do not fear... The glory of this present house will be greater than the glory of the former house," says the Lord Almighty. "And in this place I will grant peace," declares the Lord Almighty. (Haggai 2:4–5, 9)

Like the father in the story of the Prodigal Son, God is ready to welcome us back when we are ready to fit into His household. What a joyous homecoming it is when we drop our own self-centred plans and do what we know He wants us to do!

THE BOOKS OF

1 John, 2 John, 3 John & Jude

READ: 1 John 1–5, 2 John, 3 John, and Jude

John writes to convince those in doubt that Jesus did live in the flesh. Through Him, we can be forgiven from sin and have the promise of eternal life. John reminds his readers of several basic truths:

If we confess our sins, he is faithful and just and will forgive us our sins and purify us from all unrighteousness. (1 John 1:9)

1. God is light, and when we walk with Him we are in that light.
2. We have all sinned, but if we confess it, we can be forgiven.

Anyone who claims to be in the light but hates his brother is still in the darkness. (1 John 2:9)

3. If we willfully disobey God's commandments, we separate ourselves from Him.
4. If we hate (or resent) anyone, we are not in God's light.
5. If we put God first (ahead of the pleasures and securities of this world), we can have eternal life.

…but the man who does the will of God lives forever. (1 John 2:17)

6. We cannot know God if we deny Jesus.

No one who denies the Son has the Father; whoever acknowledges the Son has the Father also. (1 John 2:23)

How great is the love the Father has lavished on us, that we should be called children of God! And that is what we are! (1 John 3:1)

It is such a wonderful gift to know that when things go wrong, when people are critical or don't understand, we can always run to our Heavenly Father, who understands and forgives each of us.

Love is probably the most powerful force in the world. If we cut out love, we cut out God. Love changes the one who gives it and also the one who receives it. We can decide to love anyone, even the unlovable person, because ultimately it doesn't have anything to do with behaviour or looks.

And this is love: that we walk in obedience to his commands. (2 John 1:6)

We can pray silent love messages for people we see on the street, or the driver in the car next to us, etc. I can picture God's love flowing through me to that person. The Holy Spirit takes hold of my willingness to love and changes it into the real thing.

Dear friend… (3 John 1:5)

If we are serious about being followers of Jesus, there is no other option; we are commissioned to love with God's kind of love—unconditional, total, absolute. The love of Jesus is available to everyone. We can choose to accept it or reject it. My love should be the same—available to all, for them to accept or reject as they choose!

Jude calls for us to persevere, pray in the Holy Spirit, and be merciful.

He finishes with a beautiful benediction often sung at the end of church services. It is a great inspiration!

To him who is able to keep you from falling and to present you before his glorious presence without fault and with great joy—to the only God our Savior be glory, majesty, power and authority, through Jesus Christ our Lord, before all ages, now and forevermore! Amen. (Jude 24)

THE BOOK OF
Zechariah

READ: Zechariah 1–7

"Return to me," declares the Lord Almighty, "and I will return to you..."
(Zechariah 1:3)

That is such a great promise! Whether I stray a little or a lot, as soon as I turn around, I know He is waiting to receive me. Sometimes I am not even aware that I have strayed until I realize my thoughts are disturbing, confusing, or self-centred. He can even show me where I have gone wrong. It is a real joy to get back into His presence again.

Zechariah had a number of visions. They may have been meant to encourage the people to rebuild the temple. God's message reassured them of His love.

...for whoever touches you touches the apple of His eye... "Shout and be glad, O Daughter of Zion. For I am coming, and I will live among you," *declares the Lord.* (Zechariah 2:8, 10)

I once read that Israeli soldiers take an oath at the Western wall, where thousands go to pray. The prayer includes this line:

"Not by might nor by power, but by my Spirit," says the Lord Almighty. (Zechariah 4:6)

If all the armies of the world moved by the wisdom and power of God rather than by their own strength of numbers and weapons, world conditions would change dramatically. If every Christian moved by the wisdom and power of God, I believe there would be a profound change in the course of history. It is too easy to slip into our own rationalizations and decision-making rather than spend regular time daily seeking God's direction.

Some Christians are not conversant enough with the prophetic utterances in the Bible to see that God's hand has always been on Israel, and still is. Many of these prophecies are coming true today. My oft-repeated prayer is: "Lord, let me see this situation through Your eyes." His perspective is not the same as mine.

Israel did not listen to Zechariah's word from the Lord, and we know from history that God did as He warned:

"When I called, they did not listen; so when they called, I would not listen," says the Lord Almighty. *"I scattered them with a whirlwind among all the nations, where they were strangers. The land was left so desolate behind them that no one could come or go. This is how they made the pleasant land desolate."* (Zechariah 7:13–14)

The Jews were scattered all over the world, and that's where they lived for more than eighteen centuries. In the meantime, the land of Israel (known as Palestine) was, indeed, desolate and very unproductive.

We should heed that warning. Failing to listen to what God calls us to be may be why our prayers do not seem to be answered.

READ: Zechariah 8–14

There seem to be three historical events prophesied in this passage which were to take place in the distant future. I wonder what Zechariah was thinking as he wrote them down, and whether God gave him any understanding of these events to come.

Chronologically, the first is Jesus' life on earth, which occurred about five hundred years after Zechariah:

Rejoice greatly, O Daughter of Zion! Shout, Daughter of Jerusalem! See, your king comes to you, righteous and having salvation, gentle and riding on a donkey, on a colt, the foal of a donkey. (Zechariah 9:9)

Here is a description of Palm Sunday, when the crowds waved branches and welcomed Jesus into Jerusalem. Zechariah even includes the detail of it being a colt, not an older donkey, which Jesus rides (Luke 19:33–34).

I told them, "If you think it best, give me my pay, but if not, keep it." So they paid me thirty pieces of silver. And the Lord said to me, "Throw it to the potter"—the handsome price at which they priced me! So I took the thirty pieces of silver and threw them into the house of the Lord to the potter. (Zechariah 11:12–13)

Judas was paid by the chief priests thirty shekels of silver for delivering Jesus to them (Matthew 26:15).

"Awake, O sword, against my shepherd, against the man who is close to me!" declares the Lord Almighty. "Strike the shepherd, and the sheep will be scattered..." (Zechariah 13:7)

The chief priests hoped that by killing Jesus, His followers would scatter, bringing an end to this group which seemed to affect so many people. Jesus proclaimed Himself to be a Shepherd, ready to lay down His life for the sheep (John 10:11).

The second prophecy is of God bringing His people back to Israel. That has been happening for the last one hundred years, and it continues today. They have been coming from just about every country in the world, even from Africa.

This is what the Lord Almighty says: "I will save my people from the countries of the east and the west. I will bring them back to live in Jerusalem; they will be my people, and I will be faithful and righteous to them as their God." (Zechariah 8:7–8)

I will signal for them and gather them in. Surely I will redeem them; they will be as numerous as before... I will bring them back from Egypt and gather them from Assyria. (Zechariah 10:8, 10)

In the third prophecy, Zechariah speaks of the end times, when God will stand with Israel against other nations and the Messiah will come again to Jerusalem. That event is still to come.

On that day, when all the nations of the earth are gathered against her, I will make Jerusalem an immovable rock for all the nations... Then the leaders of Judah will say in their hearts, "The people of Jerusalem are strong, because the Lord Almighty is their God." (Zechariah 12:3, 5)

On that day his feet will stand on the Mount of Olives, east of Jerusalem... The Lord will be king over the whole earth. (Zachariah 14:4, 9)

The annual celebration of the Feast of Tabernacles held in Jerusalem may be a preparation for this prophecy:

Then the survivors from all the nations that have attacked Jerusalem will go up year after year to worship the King, the Lord Almighty, and to celebrate the Feasts of Tabernacles. (Zechariah 14:16)

We are blessed to live in a time of fulfillment of God's prophecy, given so long ago to one of His faithful followers!

THE BOOK OF

Malachi

READ: Malachi 1–4

"I have loved you," says the Lord. "But you ask,"'How have you loved us?'"
(Malachi 1:2)

We have all, now and then, wondered if God really loves us when things go wrong and problems weigh us down. Has your child ever said, "You don't love me anymore," just because you refused his immediate desire?

Jesus never said He would take away our problems, but He said He would walk through them with us and that He would never forsake us. If I remember to face my problem, knowing His loving presence is with me, I have a far different attitude from the one I have when I start questioning His love, allowing fear and anxiety to creep in!

When an eagle flies and a storm strikes, it doesn't give up and crash to the ground; it sets its wings in such a way to use the wind to rise above the storm! By holding onto our faith in God's love, we use our trouble and pain as an opportunity to rise above the storm.

A son honors his father, and a servant his master. If I am a father, where is the honor due me? (Malachi 1:6)

God uses Malachi to show the Israelites the areas of their lives that need to change. Here, he points out that the sacrifices they offer to God are less than perfect—an animal that is blind or lame or sick.

With such offerings from your hands, will he accept you? (Malachi 1:9)

If we wonder why our prayers do not seem to be answered, perhaps we should ask God where we need to repent and change. If we are not experiencing God's blessings, it may be because we have blocked the channel by giving Him less than our best. Maybe we go to church but refuse to forgive someone, or perhaps we give to missions but are critical of others who don't act as we think they should.

Speaking of giving, God points out the importance of tithing. Early in His teaching of His chosen people, He said that one-tenth of all they had should be given to the Lord's work, but they became careless about this law. Here is the reminder:

"Bring the whole tithe into the storehouse, that there may be food in my house. Test me in this," says the Lord Almighty, "and see if I will not throw open the floodgates of heaven and pour out so much blessing that you will not have room enough for it." (Malachi 3:10)

I do not know anyone who has consistently given the tithe to the Lord's work and has not been blessed by doing so. You cannot outgive God. There is no human explanation for it, but when you give, you receive—whether it is money, time, help, or friendship. If what you give is negative, the principle still holds, for that will be what you receive.

After the writing of Malachi, there was a four-hundred-year stretch of silence before the greatest event in history—the birth of Jesus, and the start of the New Testament!

THE BOOK OF

Revelation

READ: Revelation 1–3

The disciple John, in his later years, was imprisoned on the island of Patmos. While there, he had a clear vision of Jesus and was taken up into heaven itself. Since there is a lot of imagery used in this book, and possibly even a code, we cannot be sure what it all means. However, the parts we do understand help us see more clearly God's plan for His children. In fact, John says we will be blessed even as we read it.

> *Blessed is the one who reads the words of this prophecy, and blessed are those who hear it and take to heart what is written in it, because the time is near.* (Revelation 1:3)

The timing of God's plan has always been a puzzle to us. I have often had to remind myself to be patient and wait for His perfect time. Here is a reference to Jesus coming again:

> *Look, he is coming with the clouds, and every eye will see him, even those who pierced him.* (Revelation 1:7)

John describes his vision of Jesus with a long robe and shining eyes. It was so overwhelming that John fell down under the power of His presence! Jesus then gave a message to each of the seven churches.

When He speaks to a group (like a church or a nation), He is really speaking to each of us as individuals. In order to change a church, you have to change the people in it. Therefore, I need to look at where I fit into these messages given to John. Here is what they seem to say to me:

1. Ephesus—When you first gave your life to Jesus, you were excited and eager to reach out to others to share this new experience. You were willing to take on responsibilities in this outreach because you wanted to please Jesus. You are still doing those same things, but they are no longer an extension of your daily fellowship with Jesus (which seems to have faded away) and your activities are done to build up your own ego. The answer to that is, "Repent!"

2. Smyrna—I know the troubles you have had, and you are going to have more. It is a testing of your faith in God. Hold on to My hand and don't be afraid. Trust in God brings the only real reward life offers.

3. Pergamum—You claim faith in Me, but you have allowed some wrong thinking to creep in which does not line up with My word. Spend time with Me to clean it up.

4. Thyatira—You have been doing well, but there is a temptation there, because you have allowed evil to continue in your midst. Hold on to what you know is right, for the judgment day is coming.

5. Sardis—Your life looks good on the outside, but you are dead inside.

6. Philadelphia—*"I know you have little strength, yet you have kept my word and have not denied my name"* (Revelation 3:8). Hang on to what you have; don't be drawn away by others and you will have a place in heaven.

7. Laodicea—You are lukewarm, which is useless. Repent! Jesus is at your door, waiting to be invited into your life.

It is amazing how relevant these warnings are to us today, both as churches and as individuals. Looking back on our lives, we can probably identify with each of the messages to the seven churches. The message is the same for all: repent, allow Jesus to be the Lord of your life, and get your daily directions from Him.

READ: Revelation 4–7

John was taken up into heaven, where he saw the Almighty God upon the throne and those around Him singing praises.

Holy, holy, holy is the Lord God Almighty, who was, and is, and is to come. (Revelation 4:8)

I once heard a man say that when we praise God, we are practising for heaven. The Bible does not say that we will be teaching and preaching there, but it does say we will praise God, so perhaps we should begin practising now!

I find it helpful to pause often and acknowledge who God is.

You are worthy, our Lord and God, to receive glory and honor and power, for you created all things, and by your will they were created and have their being. (Revelation 4:11)

My thoughts and attitudes are directed as I remind myself that God created all things, that He is in control, and that He loves me, no matter what is going on around me. My feelings of annoyance or frustration seem rather petty. He helps me see where I need to change. He, indeed, is worthy of all our honour and praise!

In Revelation 5, the Lamb appears and the elders fall down before Him. But look what they are carrying:

Each one had a harp and they were holding golden bowls full of incense, which are the prayers of the saints. (Revelation 5:8)

In other words, your prayers and mine! Sometimes we wonder if our prayers ever reach heaven, but here they are, brought before Jesus in a golden bowl!

All of God's creation in heaven and on earth praise:

To him who sits on the throne and to the Lamb be praise and honor and glory and power, for ever and ever! (Revelation 5:13)

That, I expect, is God's purpose for all creation. We are meant to join together in praise to our Creator and His Son, whose death and resurrection was for us. Through Him, we have access to the very throne of God! It would be wonderful if we could all drop our differences and join together in praising and honouring God.

I don't understand all the imagery in these chapters, but there seems to be a great contrast between the suffering and turmoil on earth and the multitudes in heaven calling out together:

Salvation belongs to our God, who sits on the throne, and to the Lamb. (Revelation 7:10)

The suffering on earth will be gone.

And God will wipe away every tear from their eyes. (Revelation 7:17)

Acknowledging God and praising Him together may be the one uniting force that can draw people together and bring an end to war and strife. I wonder if that will ever come to pass? We have so many divisions, and the prevailing attitude seems to be, "We are right and they are wrong." And yet we pray, "Thy will be done on earth as it is in heaven." According to John's vision, it seems to be God's will that all should come before His throne and bow in adoration—as it is done in heaven!

READ: Revelation 8–11

I couldn't begin to interpret the imagery in these chapters. I'm not sure anyone can. However, a few things stand out for me. The first is that the prayers of the saints are mentioned as being mingled with incense on the golden altar, rising as smoke before the Lord. I believe God really values our prayers, and I don't think He minds how we word them or how intellectual they are. Sometimes we are fearful about praying in front of other people because we want to impress them. God must often wish we would just talk to Him easily and naturally, telling Him our joys and concerns as a child would tell a loving parent.

Another thing I notice is that the star that fell from heaven to earth (Revelation 9:1) was given the key to the bottomless pit. This makes it seem like Satan opened the pit and allowed the smoke and locusts to torture *"those people who did not have the seal of God on their foreheads"* (Revelation 9:4).

There was a time when God destroyed all the people on earth except Noah and his family, because they had become so separated from Him and His plan for them. Although the rainbow assures us He will not send that kind of flood again, this passage is a warning that He may use other methods.

After reading about all those disasters to come upon the earth, a word of hope appears:

> *The seventh angel sounded his trumpet, and there were loud voices in heaven, which said: "The kingdom of the world has become the kingdom of our Lord and of his Christ, and he will reign for ever and ever."* (Revelation 11:15)

The great musician Handel put this to music in the Hallelujah Chorus. Even as I write these words, I can recall the sound of a mighty choir triumphantly singing it. I wonder if that is how the heavenly choir sounded to John in his vision?

We all long for the day when the kingdom of the world becomes the kingdom of the Lord. I once heard a man on television speak of a time when Jesus will return to the earth and reign for a thousand years. This verse says He will reign forever and ever! That just boggles my imagination. Could it really happen? Could everyone on earth really know Him and hear Him?

I long for the people around me to experience His love in a personal way, yet my words seem totally ineffective in creating that desire within them. Will it take the coming of Jesus Himself to open their ears and hearts?

I know my experience is very limited, since I am just one human being, but the taste I have had of His inexpressible joy makes me want to know more and more of Him!

READ: Revelation 12–18

For the accuser of our brothers, who accuses them before our God day and night, has been hurled down. They overcame him by the blood of the Lamb and by the word of their testimony; they did not love their lives so much as to shrink from death. (Revelation 12:10–11)

The accuser, Satan, has been at work among believers in many parts of the world. Countless numbers have lost their lives, but we know he has been ultimately defeated at the cross of Jesus.

Here we read of a great tribulation when Satan is banished from heaven and thrown down to earth, where he takes out his vengeance:

Then the dragon was enraged at the woman and went off to make war against the rest of her offspring—those who obey God's commandments and hold to the testimony of Jesus. (Revelation 12:17)

Then a beast appears who blasphemes God:

He was given power to make war against the saints and to conquer them. (Revelation 13:7)

It sounds terrible. I don't know how to interpret this in terms of life here on earth today. Many people have tried, and some may be right. Only God Himself knows what His divine plan entails. We can be sure of just one thing: He is not going to tolerate evil in the hearts of men indefinitely. His judgment will come.

However, when things look bad around us, there is always hope:

Then I looked, and there before me was the Lamb, standing on Mount Zion... (Revelation 14:1)

That is where we need to look—to Jesus. When I focus on Him, my perception changes. I can experience hope in the midst of trouble, joy in the midst of suffering, and overwhelming love in the midst of hatred and strife.

416

The angel with *"the eternal gospel to proclaim to those who live on the earth"* (Revelation 14:6) puts it this way:

Fear God and give him glory, because the hour of his judgment has come. Worship him who made the heavens, the earth, the sea and the springs of water. (Revelation 14:7)

If we stay in touch with God through regular quiet times, keeping our lines of communication open with Him, we do not need to fear His judgment. We already recognize His voice and endeavour to obey His guidance.

Meanwhile, the judgment continues with the beast that represents evil gaining power in the world. The angels pour out plagues that represent the wrath of God. Here is a sad commentary to man's attitude:

They were seared by the intense heat and they cursed the name of God, who had control over these plagues, but they refused to repent and glorify him. (Revelation 16:9)

Babylon, known as a city of great wealth, the centre of world trade dealing in everything from jewellery and wood to spices and slaves, was to experience a mighty downfall. It was the centre of sin and evil, which God will no longer tolerate.

Evil can never win in the end. A godless society may endure for a time, but it will fall.

They will make war against the Lamb, but the Lamb will overcome them because he is Lord of lords and King of kings—and with him will be his called, chosen and faithful followers. (Revelation 17:14)

God is supreme. He is in control. Hallelujah!

READ: Revelation 19–20

Here is the proclamation of the power of God:

"Hallelujah! Salvation and glory and power belong to our God, for true and just are his judgments..." Then a voice came from the throne, saying: "Praise our God, all you his servants, you who fear him, both small and great!" (Revelation 19:1–2, 5)

When we picture God, we must see Him in all His power and glory. If not, our vision is too small and we miss the possibilities. Even as I write that, I know that our finite minds are incapable of comprehending who God really is. At this point, I find it best to just relax and admit my own weakness and smallness, allowing myself to consider God's presence—all the love, all the wisdom, all the goodness, and all the power of the universe flowing into me and through me. When I do that, my problems seem to diminish and a wonderful peace assures me that there is a way through them to victory.

"Hallelujah! For our Lord God Almighty reigns. Let us rejoice and be glad and give him glory! For the wedding of the Lamb has come, and his bride has made herself ready. Fine linen, bright and clean, was given her to wear." (Fine linen stands for the righteous acts of the saints.) (Revelation 19:6–7)

The bride of Jesus is the church, and it seems that He has been waiting for many centuries for her to be ready for the marriage feast. If the fine linen she wears represents the righteous deeds of church members, that makes each one of us responsible. What kind of linen is my life producing for the church? That is a sobering thought. Each time I let myself sink into self-pity, resentment, or pride, I soil the wedding garment! The good news is that in Christ I can be forgiven and the stains removed when I confess, repent, and change.

God is all-powerful. Even Satan, the beast, and his followers cannot stand against Him. When the right time comes, they will be defeated and thrown into the pit for a thousand years, when Christ shall rule on earth!

In my day-to-day life of being involved in my home, in the church, and with my family and friends, I cannot conceive how this can be done. But I know without a doubt that Jesus loves me and there is nothing in this life He and I cannot face together, if I keep holding His hand and never let go.

READ: Revelation 21–22

Then I saw a new heaven and a new earth, for the first heaven and the first earth had passed away, and there was no longer any sea. (Revelation 21:1)

God is in control. He is the Creator of the earth and all that is in it. In His word, He says that the world as we know it will pass away. What an astounding thought! However, He is not about to abandon us:

And I heard a loud voice from the throne saying, "Now the dwelling of God is with men, and he will live with them." (Revelation 21:3)

Even though there will be mighty changes, God is everlasting—*"the Alpha and the Omega, the Beginning and the End"* (Revelation 21:6). If we trust Him, obey Him, and keep in close touch with Him, we have nothing to fear. On the other hand, if we do our own thing, satisfy our own desires, and ignore His plan for us, we have everything to lose!

We read of a new Jerusalem *"coming down out of heaven from God"* (Revelation 21:10) and wonder how that could be. The water of life is to flow like a river through the leaves of the tree of life *"for the healing of the nations"* (Revelation 22:2). We certainly need that healing in the nations today. There is so much turmoil everywhere! No sun or artificial light will be needed, for the glory of the Lord shall be the light and Jesus the Lamb will be a lamp to guide the way for the nations to walk. There will be no more tears, pain, mourning, or death. It sounds like heaven coming down to earth!

This must have been an awesome experience for John—so much so that he fell down to worship at the angel's feet. But the angel stopped him and pointed out that we must not worship anyone but God Himself! We have a tendency to emulate great leaders, those who bring us the gospel in a way we can respond to. If that leader looms larger in our thinking than God does, we are in great danger of breaking the first of the Ten Commandments. God must be our number one priority or we will get off-track!

Jesus spoke directly to John:

Behold, I am coming soon! My reward is with me, and I will give to everyone according to what he has done. (Revelation 22:12)

We cannot escape judgment. A day will come for each of us to stand face to face with Jesus, when we will see ourselves as He sees us. I believe He will look deep into our hearts and expose our thinking about Him and others.

Blessed are those who wash their robes, that they may have the right to the tree of life and may go through the gates into the city. (Revelation 22:14)

Repentance through the blood of Jesus is the washing machine that cleanses our souls, allowing us to wear the robe of righteousness which He provides.

He who testifies to these things says, "Yes, I am coming soon." (Revelation 22:20)

I want to be ready to meet Him. Don't you?

CONCLUSION

Now we have come to the end of this particular journey through the Bible. I hope, if you have gone all the way with me, that it has whetted your appetite to keep reading this wonderful book and to write down the lessons you learn from it.

No doubt, there will be some passages that appeal to you more than others, as there are with me. However, to get an overall picture of God's plan for the world, and for each one of us, it does help to read through the Bible more than once.

There are times when I feel the need of a special touch from the Lord, and in such a case I often just look through the Bible, reading the verses I have underlined because they have special meaning for me.

As a textbook for living, there is nothing finer than the Holy Bible. I hope it will be your daily companion and a guide for the rest of your life. God bless you as you continue to read His word.

POEMS

I attended a number of CFO (Camps Farthest Out) camps over the years, and part of their daily program is to have an hour of "Creatives." It could be music, writing, art, or dance. I have enjoyed all of those at various times.

Here are a few poems I wrote during the creative writing times.

I'm filled with gratitude sitting here
With my Heavenly Father very near
The wonder of His creation through the window I see
But perhaps the most wonderful creation is ME.

My body is His temple the Bible will tell
Where His Holy Spirit longs to dwell;
He made it with love and with infinite care
So in His plan I could have a share.

He gave me eyes so that I could see
His world and His people all about me;
He gave me ears to hear the sound
Of thunder, of children, and life all around.

While deep down inside, my body contains
A heart pumping life blood through my veins;
And even though I never give it a thought
My lungs take in oxygen and never stop.

My Father made it possible for me to walk,
To communicate with others, He allowed me to talk.
He gave me a mind to imagine and ponder
He gave me experiences that fill me with wonder.

He placed in my spirit a spark that is Divine
He said, "If you're willing, I'll make you Mine –
My love is never ending and My Son has made you free;
My Holy Spirit will guide you into eternity."

While reading the familiar story in Luke of Jesus' birth, I was overwhelmed with the wonder of it all and wrote this poem:

I wonder how Mary felt that day
When Joseph said, "We'd better get on our way,
It's a long journey to Bethlehem, you know
And our little donkey is pretty slow."

I think Mary must have deeply sighed
And wondered how she could make that long ride
"Help me, Joseph," she might have cried,
"I feel heavy and weary and anxious inside."

But God had a perfect and wonderful plan
It would happen His way, in spite of man!
He kept His hand on them as they went,
When they arrived in Bethlehem, the day was far spent.

There was no room, for God had planned it that way!
His Son was to be born in a stable that day;
Mary and Joseph looked at their new Baby Boy
They were filled with wonder and awe and joy!

It brings tears to my eyes when I think of how God
Chose to be born in a stable of sod!
Why do I long for possessions and gold
When I can find in His stable those riches untold!

This next poem came from reading the story of Jesus walking on the water (Matthew 14:22–33).

The disciples went out in a boat one day
They started out in the regular way,
They took their places from bow to stern
One skipper took charge, for it was his turn.

And then the wind began to blow—
The boat seemed so frail, tossing to and fro;
When suddenly—could it really be?
Someone was walking on the sea!

Peter called out, "Lord, if it's really You
Please let me walk on the water too!"
Jesus said, "All right, Peter, step out, come along
You can do as I do, if your faith is strong."

So Peter stepped over the side—
He began to walk—then fear and pride
Rose up and his faith didn't last—
"Help me," he called, "I am sinking fast!"

I'm like Peter—I love Jesus too,
I know whatever He says is true,
I can start out with faith, but it doesn't always last
And I cry out with fear that I'm sinking fast!

But Jesus smiles—with His wonderful love
He reaches out with a hand from above
And says, "You can even walk on the sea
If you take My hand and walk with Me."

One morning at camp, when I was trying to think of something to write about, I came across this experience in my Quiet Time notebook and put it into a poem.

One day, I was lonely, dissatisfied
I wanted to run away and hide
I didn't want to dust and clean the floor
I wanted to be used for something more!
I was tired of being a mother and wife
Being a backup person for the rest of my life
Didn't sound glamorous, exciting or fun
But my watch said, "Lunch time" so I had to run!
Later that day I had time to spare
So I went to my room for a quiet prayer:
I said, "Lord, I know that selfishness is a sin
Can You help be content with the position I am in?"
He said, "My dear, I've given you the most satisfying work of all,
The same as Mine was – serving others – hold your head up and stand up tall!
Don't try to reach for a distant star,
Let Me give you a vision for the place where you are,
Let love be your aim in all you do
And abundant satisfaction will come to you!"